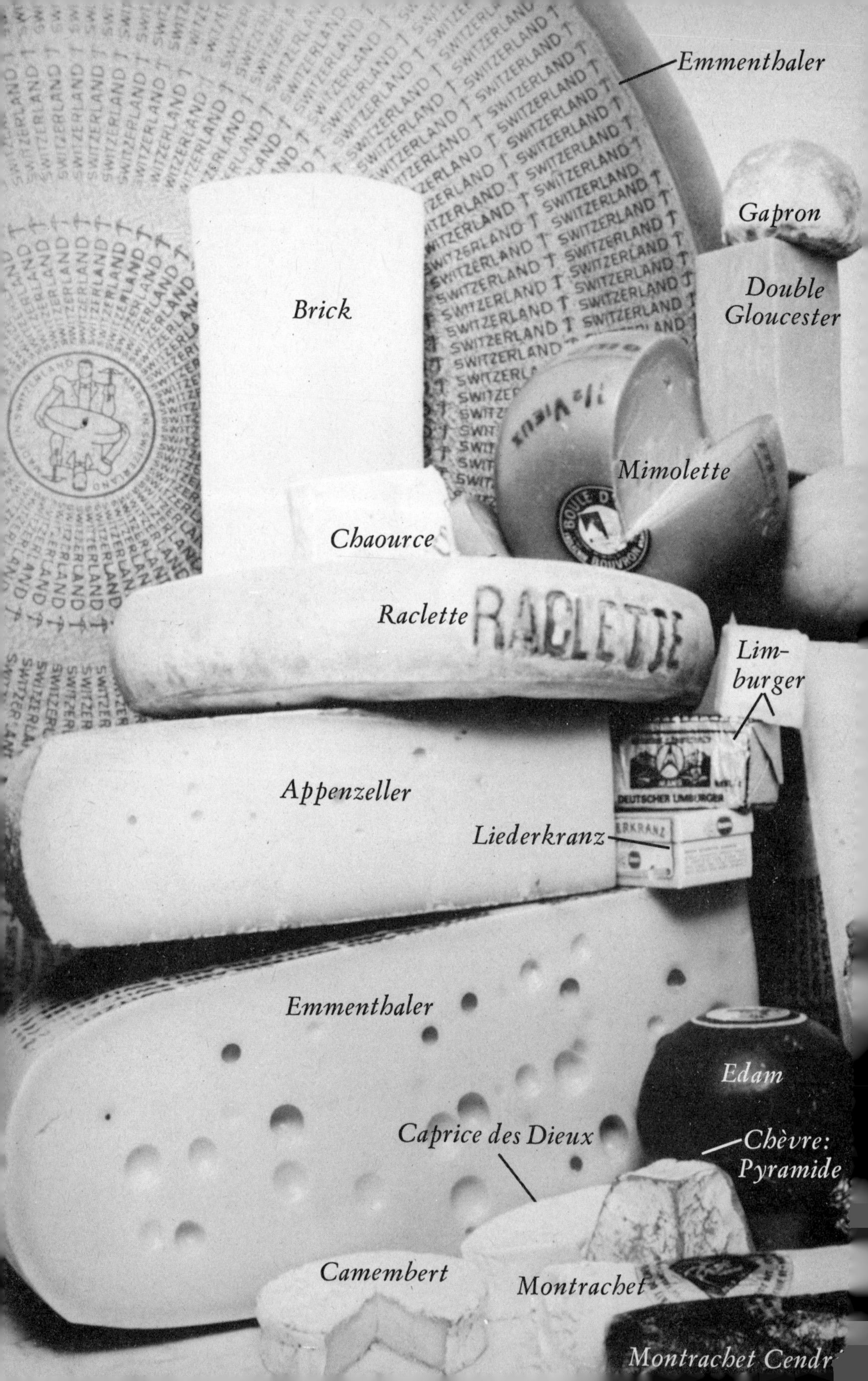

Emmenthaler

Gapron

Double
Gloucester

Brick

Mimolette

Chaource

Raclette RACLETTE

Lim-
burger

Appenzeller

Liederkranz

DEUTSCHER LIMBURGER

ERKRANZ

Emmenthaler

Edam

Caprice des Dieux

Chèvre:
Pyramide

Camembert

Montrachet

Montrachet Cendr'

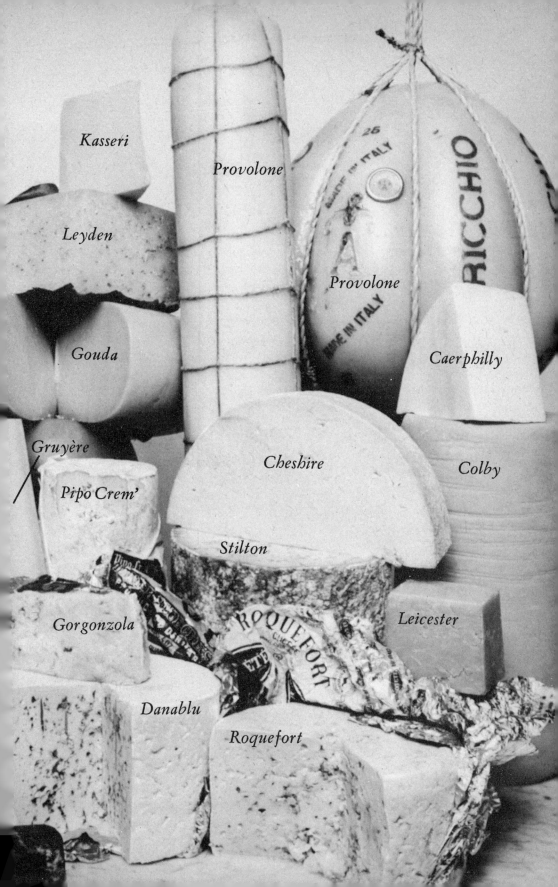

Kasseri

Provolone

RICCHIO

Leyden

Provolone

Caerphilly

Gouda

Gruyère

Cheshire

Colby

Pipo Crem'

Stilton

Gorgonzola

Leicester

ROQUEFORT

Danablu

Roquefort

BOOKS BY EVAN JONES

Hidden America
   (with Roland Wells Robbins)

The Father: Letters to Sons and Daughters

Trappers and Mountain Men

The Minnesota: Forgotten River

Citadel in the Wilderness

American Food: The Gastronomic Story

The World of Cheese

The World of Cheese

Evan Jones

The World
of Cheese

Alfred A. Knopf
New York   1979

THIS IS A BORZOI BOOK
PUBLISHED BY ALFRED A. KNOPF, INC.

The front-cover photograph, and those of the cheeses
at the beginning and end of the book, by Dan Wynn;
mezzotint illustrations of cheeses from photographs
by Bronwyn Dunne.

Cover design by Karolina Harris

Library of Congress Cataloging in Publication Data

Jones, Evan, [date]   The world of cheese.

Bibliography: p.
Includes index.
1. Cheese.   2. Cheese—Varieties—Dictionaries.
I. Title.
SF271.J66   1976   637'.3   76–13697
ISBN 0–394–49755–4
ISBN 0–394–73622–2 (paperback)

Manufactured in the United States of America
Published October 12, 1976
Reprinted Once
Third paperback printing, May 1979

To Mary Frances

Contents

In Appreciation ix

PART ONE *THE WORLD OF CHEESE*

To Begin—The Mastery of Cheese 3
1 Mastering the Mystery 6
2 British, American, and Continental Firm Cheeses 16
3 Thin Skins and Creamy Centers 28
4 The Blues 38
5 Holey Cheeses 47
6 Telling the Goats from the Sheep 54
7 Assertive in Flavor and Aroma 60
8 Monastery Products, and Related Types 66
9 Parmesan and Other Hard Cheeses 75
10 Fresh and Creamy 79
11 Spiced and Spirited 85

PART TWO *SOME PRACTICAL MATTERS*

12 How to Make Cheese 95
13 Tips on Buying and Serving 103
14 Good Drinking Companions 115

PART THREE   RECIPES

APPETIZERS FOR DRINKS, OR FOR MEALS   123

SOUPS   130

MEAT AND FISH DISHES   132

BREAKFASTS, BRUNCHES, LUNCHES, ONE-DISH MEALS   141

VEGETABLES   159

SALADS   169

SAUCES   170

BREADS   174

DESSERTS   176

SAVOURIES   181

PART FOUR   AN INTERNATIONAL CHEESE LEXICON   183

For Further Reading   295

Mail Order Sources   296

Index   follows page 298

In Appreciation

I want to thank the following persons who were helpful guides in the long search for much of the material in this book:

Nobuaki Abe, Bronxville, N.Y.; E. D. Adamson, London; Pierre Androuët, Paris; Carl Anger, Van Wert, Ohio; Judy V. Antcliff, New York; Jack Ayres, Woodstock, Vt.; Peter G. Basloe, Herkimer, N.Y.; Simone Beck, Châteauneuf-de-Grasse, France; George Bélanger, St.-Hyacinthe, Quebec; M. E. Beneke, Faribault, Minn.; H. John Bessunger, New York; John H. Bidwell, London; Anthony Biesada, New York; N. C. Blacklaw, Edinburgh; A. P. Breseman, Madison, Wis.; Lillian Brittain, New York; Jean-Claude Bruneau, Le Sueur, Minn.; Willi Bühlmann, Berne, Switzerland; M. M. Campbell, Newton, Iowa; Daniel Carter, Mayville, Wis.; Fred Chesman, New York; Mr. and Mrs. Paul Child, Cambridge, Mass.; Daniel Considine, Portage, Wis.; John Coolidge, Plymouth, Vt.; H. R. Cornwell, London; Daniel Courtonne, St.-Germain-de-Montgommery, France; Dorothy Demeter, Lena, Ill.; Laura Denman, New York; Richard A. Dennler, Des Moines, Iowa; H. S. Dixon, Tillamook, Ore.; Signora Domenica Donadio, Castelmagno, Italy; Bronwyn Jones Dunne, Old Greenwich, Conn.; Erskine Early, Spring Hill, Tenn.; T. A. Evans, Lincoln, Neb.; Henri René Fresson, Paris; Dr. Robert H. Frey, Chapel Hill, N.C.; David A. Frigo, Torrington, Conn.; Pete Frigo, Lena, Wis.; Margaret Gale, New York; Margaret Gleason, Madison, Wis.; Victor Golay, Les Charbonnières, Switzerland; N. S. Golding, Victoria, B.C.; Jane Grigson, Broadtown, Wilts, U.K.; Hedy Guisti-Lanham, New York; Oskar H. Gunnarsson, Reykjavik, Iceland; Arline Harris, New York; James P. Harrison, Salem, Ore.; T. H. Hassall, Whitchurch, Wilts, U.K.; Ernest Henegar, Jr., Lewisburg, Tenn.; Arno A. Hertzog, New York; Jean Hewitt, New York; Dr. Heinz P. Hofer, New York; Patricia Hummel, Minneapolis, Minn.; Alex A. Hunt, Ottawa, Ont.; K. Jaeckle,

New York; Jacques Jaffry, New York; H. W. E. Johnson, London; Mr. and Mrs. Russell Jones, Moscow, U.S.S.R.; J. Jordens, Brussels; Father M. Justin, Oka, Quebec; Christoph Kappeler, Berne, Switzerland; Mr. and Mrs. Bradford Kelleher, New York; Gunilla Krantz, Stockholm; A. J. Ladrach, Columbus, Ohio; Gerald Lawlor, Dublin; Ron Lawton, Rease-heath, Cheshire, U.K.; T. A. Layton, London; Paul Leyton, Priddy, Somer-set, U.K.; Mary Lyons, New York; Paul Machia, Richmond, Vt.; Michel Marnette, Liège, Belgium; Terrence McCabe, Washington, D.C.; Neil McPherson, Sacramento, Calif.; Jean Mittaine, Roquefort-sur-Soulzon, France; Ruth Morrison, New York; Herbert Mossholder, Appleton, Wis.; Mary E. Murphy, Columbus, Ohio; Richard V. Myott, Nantwich, U.K.; Lennart Olsson, Bronxville, N.Y.; Vrest Orton, Weston, Vt.; Wallace Par-rish, Cache Valley, Utah; Henri Picot, Paris; David N. Rademacher, St. Paul, Minn.; Ester Rasmussen, Concord, Calif.; Alfred Ratzlaff, Rochester, Minn.; J. Reerslev, Aarhus, Denmark; Dr. George Reinbold, Ames, Iowa; Claudia Roden, London; Helen C. Rohrbaugh, Washington, D.C.; Robert Rouzaire, Tournan-en-Brie, France; W. C. Scully, Nauvoo, Ill.; Randolph Smith, Healdville, Vt.; Gwenyth Jones Spitz, St. Paul, Minn.; Susannah H. G. Stone, Blarliath, Tain, Scotland; Pierce Thompson, Petaluma, Calif.; T. A. Thompson, Chewton Mendip, Somerset, U.K.; Norman A. Toft, Chicago; Buhnne Tramutola, Clinton, N.J.; Justine Valenti, London; Dave Viviani, Sonoma, Calif.; Julian J. de Vries, Amsterdam; Sutherland Wat-son, Kirkwall, Orkney, U.K.; Edward Weiss, New York.

I am grateful to Jane Montant of *Gourmet* for her early interest. I want also to thank Gerald Halpern of San Francisco and Mr. and Mrs. Wayne Owen of Northfield, Vt., for valuable comments on the manuscript. In gathering illustrative material, Helga Gruenstrass of New York was exceedingly helpful, and the cooperation of Cornelius Hearn IV and the Cheese Shop International, Inc., Greenwich, Conn., was indispensable in the production of *The World of Cheese*.

My gratitude to Judith Bailey Jones is beyond my ability to express adequately; and to Robert Lescher, friend and mentor, I owe much that cannot be repaid. Had I two perfect cheeses to offer, I would send one to each of them.

Part One

The World of Cheese

To Begin—
The Mastery of Cheese

Cheese has been described as everything from food for the gods to "a surly elf, digesting all things but itself." Mere mortals thrive on it, but not many have probed its mystery.

When my brothers and sister and I were young, our mother's unchanging Sunday night supper was based on cheese, and week after week, year after year, we thrived on the menu. The cheddary golden-orange *pièce de résistance* was called Old English and was served simply, with graham crackers, accompanied by mugs of hot chocolate. Not only was it a sensible meal to end a day that had been "parted in the middle," as our mother would say, by the traditional abundance of Sunday dinner just after noon; it was a family ritual. It was also character-building, I can hear our parents saying. The difference between honest cheese and that which was ersatz was important to know.

But we didn't learn much else about cheese at home. We had the usual version of macaroni and cheese, and Welsh Rabbit, but never cheese as an end-of-dinner course—nor did anyone else we knew. The function of cheese in those days, and in that part of America, was as a meat substitute, in casseroles, sauces, a sandwich here and there. It gained status only when served with pie, as in the old British saying: "Apple pie without cheese is like a kiss without a squeeze."

It took the airplane and a sort of gastronomic revolution to change things. There was plenty of cheese being made in the United States, but very little variety. If you wanted to add to your knowledge you almost had to go to Europe, where there were (and are) cheeses in so many variations as to seem astounding. You learned that the English made others besides Cheddar and Cheshire, that the Italians weren't limited by Parmesan so hard it had to be grated, and that the Danes were making copies of Europe's best. But you had to go to France to find more mysterious wonders of the cheese world—cheeses made in almost every shape imaginable, cheeses produced only in certain seasons of the year, others that oozed mellifluously when their white skins were broken, some even that smelled rank but tasted ineffably of sweet cream and savor.

It is hard to remember the first *fromager* to whom we went regularly when we lived in Paris but easy to realize that the kind of store he proudly operated did not begin to proliferate in America until the beginning of the 1970's. In France the windows of such stores are often filled with cheeses so decoratively arranged they mislead you into thinking the place a pastry shop. Maybe it is the floury-white rinds that fool you—or the crusty look of others reminiscent of country bread. Inside, the counters are *sérieuse,* cheese piled upon cheese because the storekeeper knows his stock moves quickly enough to prevent the weight of one from squashing another. The shapes are myriad: starlike cheeses, balls, cubes, cones, squares, pyramids, millstones, chariot wheels, cucumbers, bricks, parallelepipeds, rhomboids, ingots, hearts, melons, crescents, ostrich eggs, and pears. My wife or I would bring home newly discovered forms as cheerfully as newly discovered flavors—as if we had found a new toy.

In this country, few retailers need be masters of the finishing process, as is the *fromager affineur,* who sells so many shapes in France. Here the challenge is eliminated because all imported dairy products have to be pasteurized. But a traditional French retailer has been as apt as not to get his stock directly from farmers and small creameries. He keeps the cheeses in a cool, humid cellar where some are ripened on wooden shelves, some on straw, some on metal racks, depending upon their type. He turns them over almost daily so they will ripen evenly, washing the rinds in beer, wine, or spirits to aid their maturation. They are living cheeses because pasteurization has not arrested their development, and they need tender loving care.

Pasteurized products do not require so much attention, and a variety of cheeses deemed suitable for the swift migrations of the jet age is increasingly available in America. Certain French manufacturers are reducing the time factor further by producing facsimiles of Normandy, or Burgundy, cheeses in stateside plants. American dairymen also are turning out better copies of European originals than ever before. So cheeselovers, like those in my family, are no longer reduced to nostalgia for the tempting shops we discovered abroad; even my mother's version of a cheese and cracker snack has been so metamorphosed it may now be called a buffet or, with certain extensions, a "wine and cheese party."

For thousands, cheese has become a preoccupation. Like wine and other good things of life, it is an engrossing subject, to be mastered in easy stages, and to be read about with pleasure. It was with such pursuits in mind that I began to veer off on side excursions when my wife and I made various trips abroad. We went together to Cheddar country in the Mendip Hills of Somerset, to Pecorino farms in rugged parts of Tuscany, and to the venerable caves of Combalou at Roquefort-sur-Soulzon, where rude sheep's-milk cheeses once were aged by early Celts. Though we traveled for recreation, the accumulating information was serious. Asked by the editors of *Gourmet* to write several articles, I made more trips on my own. Even now it seems to me that the pursuit of the world's cheeses is a never-ending one—and one more than usually touched by quirks of nature and the idiosyncrasies of mankind.

So this book, in a way, is a work in progress, an effort to probe more deeply into a world that is full of surprises.

Caseum uerus.

1

Mastering
the Mystery

Cheese can be stodgy, or it can be full of grace. Like many gastronomic pleasures it is older than recorded history and has been a staple in the diet of mankind since animals first were domesticated. It may, in a way, have been the earliest of the "convenience foods," for the basic process of turning milk into dry curds transformed a highly perishable liquid into a comestible that could be stored successfully for use in another season; and the curds traveled so well when matured that they constituted a ready source of energy on any sort of peregrination. As it is for you and me, the cheese sandwich—or bread and cheese in some simple form—has always been as likely a choice as any food that might be taken on a trip.

Cheese is really little more than a form of artificially coagulated milk, yet the craftsmanship that has developed over the ages has modified a rustic recipe to the point that there now are eighteen distinct categories recognized, and the variations number easily over a thousand. No single person knows every delicate cheese for which individuality is claimed. Were I to cite those of France alone, the total from all the localities claiming their products to be unique might be considerably more than those of all other European countries combined. Yet dairymen throughout Europe are today busier inventing new ways of presenting old formulas than ever before—in the world of cheese there are always discoveries to be made.

Sometimes cheese shows value beyond its intrinsic worth. A biographer has it that Charlemagne, while the guest of a French bishop, was bowled over by a new cheese set before him by his host. When the great man discarded the cheese's edible mold and ate only the rich, creamy paste, the distressed bishop asked, "Why do you do that, my lord emperor? You are throwing away the best part!" Dubiously, Charlemagne ate every bit, but he remained noncommittal. He said, without further comment, "Be sure to send me every year at Aachen two cartloads of cheeses exactly like this." Only after the bishop had kept the bargain for three years did the king admit the degree of pleasure the cheeses had given him, and he rewarded his benefactor by settling on him a fortune in land and power.

There is more than one moral in this tale. Indeed, as kings came and kings went in the Middle Ages, it was the men of the church who did more than any others to keep alive and improve the craftsmanship that has resulted in many of the world's great epicurean moments. "Helped by a hundred fast-days, whose strict observance would have reduced every priest in Europe to a stringy skeleton," M. F. K. Fisher has observed, "the plump brothers spent much time and thought in making delicious dishes appear frugal." And she added that those "fast-days in the Middle Ages forced the Church's greatest minds to invent ways to make eggs and cheese taste like roast veal." What is equally true is that on even more days of the year many monks were at work making their own cheeses that improved upon formulas evolved on farms.

Long before there were monks, there were sophistications developing among cheesemakers. Dairymen of the Lake Constance Stone Age community contrived at least four thousand years ago a pottery collander for draining off whey—that is, the residue of liquid when milk forms curds—the first step in making cheese. But the discovery itself must have come even long before that. In the Iraq Museum in Baghdad a frieze showing Sumerians milking cows six thousand years ago can be seen. The Old Testament, also, has references to cheese. Eventually the Greeks came up with a word —*tyrophile,* one who loves cheese. It is a subject that engenders much affection. Yet a tyrophile today must speculate still about how and when his favorite morsel was conceived.

An ancient, if dubious, yarn illustrates as well as anything one of the ways in which cheese first may have been recognized—its origin an accident. A traveler named Kanana, crossing the desert, had one morning put milk in his primitive canteen made from the stomach of one of his tribe's domesticated animals. It might have been from a slaughtered calf, the source of today's rennet (see Lexicon), or it might have been the dried intestines of another convenient beast. At nightfall, when he turned to his canteen to restore himself, it seemed that the contents had been transformed in the desert heat; as he lifted the bag to his lips he discovered that only a thin sourish liquid came—the milk had coagulated. Sunstruck and famished, the traveler assayed the risk, and Kanana ripped open the soggy, leathery container. Perhaps the combination of heat and the movement of his mount had produced the separation of curds and whey. He knew that milk carried in pottery jars could be agitated without so curious a change in consistency. Nevertheless he tasted the solidified milk and found it

SUMERIAN FRIEZE

good. It was primitive cheese, of course. The beneficial effects of intestinal acids on milk had at last been recognized.

EARLY CHEESE AND ITS FLAVORS The discovery of this form of dairy chemistry was only one step toward the proliferation of cheese in great variety. Enzymes like those in animal rennet, which brings about the coagulation of milk, were found also in certain plants. Accident again, perhaps, led farmers to recognize that certain thistles, and herbs known as butterwort and lady's bedstraw, could be used to start milk on its way toward cheese. Greek dairymen had used the green branch of a fig tree to coagulate milk from goats and sheep, and in Athens, where great quantities were sold, Antiphanes, that witty author of Greek comedies, in the fourth century B.C. spoke of "green [fresh] cheese, dry cheese, crushed cheese, grated cheese, sliced cheese, and cream cheese." In the Roman heyday safflower seeds were substituted for rennet, and the idea of cheese enhanced by herbs and spices seemed to be gaining ground.

Among gourmands of the empire there were tastes for cheeses flavored with thyme, green pine nuts, garlic, or pepper; there was a Roman recipe, one that has come down to us, that called for marjoram, mint, coriander, as well as seasoning with onion, then dusting the cheese with chives and salt. A grating of cheese was thought to be one of the condiments necessary to improve the taste of an onion, according to Athenaeus—such pungent morsels being ingratiating fillips in Greek meals. Some Athenians who considered themselves enlightened preferred the products of Sardinia, while Romans were connoisseurs of cheese that had been basted with wines, or had been smoked over coals of apple boughs and sold in the market at Velabrum, on the city's outskirts.

ON BEING NATURAL   None of these ideas has been outmoded, nor were their effects on dairy products much different from those techniques or additives used today. Natural cheese in the twentieth century (as opposed to "processed cheese" and "cheese food"—see the Lexicon) is no more or less than milk that has been encouraged to solidify by means of curdling and draining before a period of aging. As in ancient times, differences in flavor and character are obtained by curing various lengths of time, as well as through the influence of soil factors, the kinds of vegetation upon which the animals feed, and the distinctions in the milk of various beasts from which cheese in the Western world is produced.

For centuries cheesemaking was considered a mysterious craft, a family secret to be passed from father to son or, more often, from mother to daughter. One of the most famous women of Normandy folklore is Marie Harel, remembered for a kiss supposedly bestowed on her cheek by Napoleon and honored by a statue near her home farm that describes her as the "inventor" of Camembert. Three British women have been given credit for being in on Stilton's beginning, and in Denmark a farmer's wife named Hanne Nielsen traveled through Europe, taking down notes on cheesemaking and helping eventually to perfect a Danish product called Havarti, the name of her home place.

Still, nobody really invents a cheese. The secrets passed from generation to generation were the knacks a craftsman learned in dealing with conditions over which he had little control: the kind of milk produced by his animals, whether they were asses, buffaloes, camels, cows, goats, mares, reindeer, sheep, yaks, or zebras; the kind of rennet, or rennet substitute, available in a given region; the type of bacteriological influence introduced naturally; and the atmospheric conditions present in caves, cellars, or other spaces occupied by cheeses during the period of maturation, whatever the length of time.

THE BASIC KINDS OF CHEESE The four basic classifications under which to consider the numerous variations of cheeses are: soft, semisoft, firm, and hard. The soft category includes, first of all, the unripened or fresh types that most people know as Cottage Cheese, Cream Cheese, Pot, or Ricotta, as well as such others as Mysost and Neufchâtel. More sophisticated soft types ripen naturally in a matter of days and include Brie, Camembert, and the so-called double creams and triple creams—cylinder shapes that develop thin downy-white crusts and tender, almost fluent interiors. Among those technically described as semisoft is the group ripened with bacteria and yeasts that includes Brick and Munster, and the group, including Liederkranz, Limburger, and Port Salut, which requires surface microorganisms as well. A third semisoft subdivision takes in the blue-veined cheeses like Roquefort and Gorgonzola. Firm cheeses include the Cheddars and their English cousins, such as Cheshire and Lancashire, and the various members of the Caciocavallo family; and they also include those having noticeable holes, like the Swiss products called Emmenthal and Gruyère, as well as such new Scandinavian creations as Jarlsberg. Hard cheeses are made in much the same way but develop a smooth, grainy texture that is characteristic of grating types called Asiago, Parmesan, Romano, Sapsago, and Spalen.

Femmes faisant des fromages.

The simplest unripened, fresh cheese requires nothing but a starter, such as buttermilk, and with minimum attention to temperature is produced in a matter of hours. The milk separates and forms the curds, which are drained thoroughly and salted to taste. In a dozen lands—and for thousands of years—the basic process has remained unaltered, just as the result has continued to be one of the most satisfying and healthful of simple foods. All cheesemaking is the same in essence—just as breaking eggs and cooking them in a pan varies only in technique. Making Cottage Cheese can be compared to scrambling eggs, while perfecting the art of making an omelet is not unlike the attention which must be exercised in turning out sophisticated cheeses like those of Normandy and other parts of France. They vary more because of method than because of content. Except for additives, items such as herbs, spices, wine, or liqueurs, the prime ingredients for making one cheese are no different from those needed for another.

CAMEMBERT BY HAND As one of the most storied dairylands of the world, Normandy is a realm of grass where the native breed of cows can be traced to those brought a thousand years ago in Viking ships: it is a land where, more pertinently, grass becomes a commodity (as a cheesemaker once told me) when it is transformed by cows. Normandy's 4 million acres of grass are converted regularly into milk, into butter, and—because of a knack evolved in the distant past—into half of the soft fermented cheeses made in France.

Of them all, none is more famous than the small white disk that takes its name from the tiny hamlet of Camembert, and no other seemed more likely to offer a way to understand the mystery of cheese. But it was luck that gave me the chance to watch the last Norman producing handmade Camemberts go about his chores. In the early 1970's he was still pursuing this vanishing craft in the small community called St.-Germain-de-Montgommery, not far from Camembert itself, and one misty December day I visited Daniel Courtonne and his wife, Simone. Their production each day was limited to the size of their farm and the number of cows its meadows can support—for neither silage nor any feed other than fresh grass is considered good enough. Because of their commitment to quality, the Courtonnes were turning out only 300 or so cheeses a day, as compared to 40,000 to 50,000 produced daily by nearby automated factories. And, unlike those of the modern plants, the Courtonnes' small wheels of delicate flavor achieved their character because they were made of unpasteurized milk, a practice this *maître fromager* refused to abandon.

"A pasteurized cheese," he said, "is all right, of course." His tone belied his words, as if he had added, "just barely." He shrugged slightly. "It's not disagreeable. It's neutral."

I followed M. Courtonne down to his barn that day. Just outside, he showed the wood-burning fire that heated milk fresh from his fifty or so cows in a sort of large double boiler he had rigged. He used a thermometer to show that the milk must register 32 degrees Centigrade (89 degrees Fahrenheit) before passing through a rubber hose to a series of vats in the cellar below. His forty years of experience, plus highly developed intuition, guided his assessment of acidity in the milk, and he added a little rennet to help the curds form. "The more acid in the milk, the less rennet is needed," he said.

After the milk was thoroughly clotted, Mme. Courtonne began to dip into the mass of curds, ladling the thick white stuff into perforated, circular, open-ended molds that had been set out on handmade reed mats, covering the large table. She repeated this operation—carefully adding one ladleful to a mold each time—over a three-hour period, thus permitting the whey still clinging to the curds to drain slowly away. The mats, her husband said, were made by a neighbor who collected the reeds from a nearby marsh. The Courtonnes would use no substitute materials and insisted on maintaining their wooden table instead of accepting modern metal equipment.

"Industrialization and gastronomy don't mix," Daniel Courtonne said, repeating a favorite sentiment. "One does not upset nature."

His method required about twenty-four hours for the contents of the molds to solidify sufficiently for turning, and to be salted by Mme. Courtonne first on one side and later on the other. In a concession to the new times, the infant cheeses were sprayed with the culture called *Penicillium camemberti,* whose name derives from the pencil-like fungi that help to make Camembert different from other mold-ripened cakes.

The developing Camemberts next were moved to a room with a temperature of about 70 degrees Fahrenheit for about forty-eight hours. When a white hairy mold appeared, the developing Camembert went to a drying room with cooler temperature. There the white hairs effloresced so that very fine, long, feathery fluff surrounded the cheeses to form what the French call *poil de chat,* cat fur. Mme. Courtonne brushed off each cheese by hand when it was ready to be boxed, and the shipment was divided among several French cheesemongers who were trusted to continue the maturation process before selling the Camemberts at six weeks of age.

It is hard for some to believe that a delicate Camembert—four and a half inches in diameter, an inch or so high, and creamily pliant within—is directly related to the dry and nutty, firm and hole-ridden, giant cheese wheels for which Switzerland is most famous. A finished, uncut Camembert weighs about 8 or 9 ounces; an Emmenthaler weighs in at about 200 pounds and appears to be so sturdily made that it could be put to good use on the axle of any traditional wooden cart.

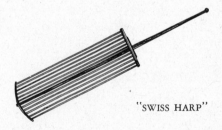

"SWISS HARP"

WHAT MAKES SWISS DIFFERENT? To see for myself what differences there were between the ancient Norman craft and that of producing Swiss cheese, I drove south one day from Berne, the Alpine capital city, to visit a government cheesemakers' school with Willi Bühlmann of the Swiss Cheese Union. Coming down past Lake Morat, we arrived soon after dawn at Moudon, in the hilly canton of Vaud, where the École Cantonale de Fromagerie, beside the town church of St. Étienne, looks on the outside a good deal like any stone school building erected early in the century.

There was no comparison between Daniel Courtonne's farm dairy and the large white-tiled room in which we found a dozen strong young men from Switzerland and various other parts of the world learning to make the cheese, so often badly imitated, that is named for the valley of the Emme River. The proper term for the original "cheese with the holes" is Em-menthal, or Emmenthaler, but at cheese counters around the world it is more commonly labeled "Switzerland Swiss," to keep it from being confused with other products labeled "Swissconsin," or "Austrian Swiss," for example.

The only true Swiss cheese is made by man, not by machines. Like the independent dairymen on Alpine farms who take pride in turning out Em-menthalers, the fledgling cheesemakers we met that day began by mixing fresh, unprocessed morning milk with milk that had been left overnight; it was stirred in 220-gallon copper vats and gently heated. "A micro-organism known as proprionic acid-former is added along with the rennet that almost every cheese requires," Willi Bühlmann told me. While we watched one of the young men guiding a "Swiss harp," a long-handled wire-stringed tool, to slowly agitate the liquid, he explained that a natural gas is developed by these bacteria, and it collects in pockets of the cheese mass.

Instead of being ladled out to drain on mats, the curds in the round copper vats are lifted out by slipping a large piece of cheesecloth under the clotted mass and pulling the corners together to make a sack holding more than 300 pounds. The heavy, dripping curds are then hauled out on a crane guided by workmen who deposit them in a circular wooden form

to which steady pressure must be applied to squeeze all moisture out. When almost dry, each great wheel of cheese thus formed must be turned periodically while still in its wooden hoop. Moved on to a cooling cellar, its surfaces are spread with salt, it floats for about two days in a vat of brine, then goes through a fortnight period of maturing on a shelf while it is turned twice a day and is alternately washed and lightly sprinkled with fresh salt.

The famous holes continue to form as the great wheels age in a warm cellar where they undergo further washings and fresh salt treatments as they are heaved up and down again and again. After ten weeks or so of this kind of fermentation, the Emmenthalers are ready to be shipped to wholesalers, but they aren't ready for sale until they have spent months in cool curing cellars—as little as four months for mild flavor, and up to a year or more to achieve full savor and maturity.

Switzerland, the late Michael Field once said in a burst of sentiment, has "an almost mystical reverence for cows." In his phrase there are intimations of what it takes to produce fine cheese from the milk of any animal. In England it used to be said of something in fashion and highly acceptable, "That's the cheese!" Quite simply it means "the best." Whether thin-skinned and creamy, like Camembert, or firm and holey, like Emmenthalers, real cheese should have uncompromised quality. It should be composed of milk, and nothing else but natural seasonings. No preservatives. No stabilizers. I like to think there are more than a few craftsmen, busy in dairies of various sizes and almost reverent in their treatment of milk, whose sole ambition is to implement the mysterious ways devised by nature to convert milk into its finest form. The shapes and sizes of cheeses may differ, but that only varies the mystery.

2

British, American, and Continental Firm Cheeses

Let's start with the cheese most familiar to all Americans: the "Old English" of one childhood time, the "store cheese" still loved by Yankees, so common in the United States it is often referred to as "American." It is Cheddar, of course, the best-known of all types in the English-speaking world. Creamy and firm, hard but not brittle, it is smoothly consistent in texture and, as often as not in this country, the color of a blood orange. I doubt that any cheese has been more affectionately accepted. It is the morsel described in Britain as "the cut and come again cheese," of which a surfeited Londoner said in a characteristic Anglo-Saxon understatement, "I commend it with all my heart." But actually it is only one of about a dozen closely related cheeses with British lineage, all of which were made in the past by earnest farmwives.

I know of a woman, last of her family and last of her neighbors to make cheese according to an English recipe, who lived alone on a Blue Ridge farm in North Carolina and as late as 1972 was still transforming sixteen gallons of milk each day according to the alchemy she had learned from her mother. Even in her late sixties she carried the raw milk up to her house from the mailbox where a farmer left it in two milk cans, and at eight each morning she added to it a pint of buttermilk as she began to heat it in enameled pots. When it reached 90 degrees she added rennet, and she sometimes told visitors that her mother, who had no thermometer, tested the temperature in a perfectly natural way—"When it no longer felt chilly to her elbow, she put in the rennet."

That was the way things were done when the great English cheeses like Cheddar, and its well-known relative, Cheshire, were developed— and were still being done when Britishers began to colonize America and to move down the valley of Virginia and into Appalachia. We have the word of a wary Frenchman visiting this new republic that domestic cheese then compared favorably not only with his country's Roquefort but was, as he said, "equal to the best Cheshire of England." That was an accolade.

Cheshire was by then the oldest British type on record and had been declared by John Speed, a notable chauvinist of the sixteenth century, to be "the best cheese in all Europe." It was a farmhouse cheese, and had been made by dairymaids, there is reason to believe, even before the Romans established the garrison town of Chester near the Welsh border. Like Lydia Kirby on her Blue Ridge farm, the women of the pastoral region around the market town of Chester took feminist pride in their product. "What do men know of cheese," they are said to have clucked, and records indicate that they used the other sex only to do the lifting when cheeses were as large as 300 pounds. But nothing inhibited the male appreciation of Cheshire's flavor. Underneath the pastures that surrounded Chester there were salt springs, and the resulting salinity in the milk gave the local cheese a distinctive taste, just as its deep color was encouraged, in the old days, by the carrot juice the dairymaids added in judicious drops.

CHESHIRE

THREE KINDS OF CHESHIRE   They used to make three kinds of Cheshire cheese: the so-called red, which now is tinted by the vegetable coloring called annatto instead of carrot juice; the white, which is the color of cream from Shorthorn cows; and the blue, a round loaf with interior mold that deserves fuller treatment in a later chapter. The Cheshire women shaped their cheese in cylinders as wide as they were high, usually anywhere between 10 and 20 pounds in weight. Then and now, crumbly is the word for the texture of Cheshire, and this consistency makes it ideal for melting.

In Somerset, to the south of Cheshire County, other dairywomen developed a firmer or at least more compactly textured cylinder that was given a name of confusing similarity. Cheddar was first so called for a small village in the Mendip Hills, about the time American colonists were busy clearing their first frontier and turning their own excess milk into nondescript cheese. Among all Englishmen the names and the qualities that distinguished one cheese from another were only then becoming important, and the reputation that has helped to make Cheddar a generic term was just beginning to grow.*

A Cheddar of the eighteenth century that had been carefully matured warranted epicurean respect, and by the time Nathan Bailey's dictionary was published in 1721, Cheddar village was identified as "the most noted place in all England for making large, fine, rich, and pleasant cheeses." Even more, Bailey wrote, the community was known also for having established a cooperative in which dairy workers gathered in a single room to process "all the milk of the town cows . . . and one common cheese is made of it." The term "Cheddar-club" entered the language as a result of those communing cheesemakers in the Mendip Hills, and soon humorously inclined literati (who had not heard of the farmers' cooperatives to come) had invented the "Cheddar letter," to which a number of writers contributed a paragraph apiece, mailing the unfinished epistle around England much like the chain letters of the twentieth century.

AN EDIFICE OF CURDS   I've thought since coming upon these facts that Cheshire also must have retained respect and popularity of sorts, because some Connecticut settlers took the name for their village in the seventeenth century. (It is a matter of record that a recipe for making Cheshire was brought to New Hampshire about the same time by the wife of the founder of one of the first villages.) And in Massachusetts a few generations later dairy farmers gave Cheshire's name to their market town near the New York border. By the first year of Thomas Jefferson's administration these Berkshires cheesemakers were so adept at their craft that they

---

* In 1969 a bill was introduced in the British Parliament to limit the use of the words "Cheddar," "Cheshire," and "Caerphilly" to cheeses produced in Britain. "Who would be so bold," the speaker said, "to deny that such places as Cheddar, Cheshire, and Caerphilly should not enjoy the same measure of protection afforded by law to Sherry and Champagne?" The opposition, however, declared that there was no evidence housewives were misled into buying imported cheese in the belief it was made in the United Kingdom. It was posited that Cheddar is an international word, that it did not now belong to any country, and that for more than half a century only a small part of Britain's need for Cheddar could be met by Somerset producers. "We do not insist that Brussels sprouts be imported from Belgium," said the opposition. The bill lost, 178–126.

turned one day's milk from their 900 cows into curds and used a giant cider press to shape a 1,200-pound cheese that was moved by sled, boat, and wagon to the White House.

This may have been shameless exploitation of what normally would be first-rate cheese—whether technically to be described as Cheshire or Cheddar. A parson named John Leland had talked his congregation into the stunt, and he seems unlikely to have been scornful of the publicity that would come to him. Big crowds gathered at various stopping places after the cheesemakers' enormous creation was en route, and Leland did not bypass the chance to preach, of course. For his part, Jefferson publicly cited the great edifice of pressed curds as extraordinary proof of skill in domestic arts, and he gave $200 to the congregation, even though observers reported that 60 pounds or so had to be removed from the cheese because of symptoms of decay. Leland returned to Massachusetts, where a Cheshire park was eventually named in his memory and where a replica of the giant press was erected.

Under the moniker "Chester," the true British Cheshire cheese became popular in France, though not so much so as in England, because its peculiar quality owed much to the pastures of its home county. But it remained for the cheese that took its name from the village of Cheddar to become a standard type—proliferating with abandon, and not always with attention to excellence, through the English-speaking world. Among

the reasons for this success was the work of Joseph Harding, a Somerset man whose wife and six daughters became as famous as he in the cause of standardizing the Cheddar process. Indeed it was said that one daughter promised a friend she would marry an American if one could be found who sufficiently respected the art of dealing dexterously with curds.

I can find no assurance that this union of two worlds actually took place, but the Harding system crossed the Atlantic, and the Pacific, too, when factory methods were established in the United States as well as in Canada, Australia, New Zealand, and other dominions. In the middle of the eighteenth century Rhode Island cheese was being advertised in New England newspapers, and a hundred years or so later both Vermont and New York had established reputations for exemplary Cheddars that obtain today, even though everything now is made in factories of one size or another.

English sources say there are in the United Kingdom something over two hundred farmers in the cheesemaking business, and the Milk Marketing Board of that country dates and stamps each farm-made wheel as "Superfine Grade Farmhouse Cheese," "Fine Grade," or simply "Graded," for those having small but insignificant defects. In this country most of the remaining Wisconsin small-family cheesemakers disappeared in the 1960's, and as a result the tons of Cheddar produced in that and other Midwest states come from large factories. The Department of Agriculture rates quality as "Grade AA" and "Grade A." Cheddars throughout the nation which earn either rating must be stamped with a government seal of inspection. That helps to keep up standards in impersonal commercial enterprises, but does not ensure the careful attention once paid to the product by well-run family operations, and it seems sad that those days are gone. In Vermont there is only one village dairy operating in the same way it did a century earlier. At Healdville, in the center of the Green Mountains, this barnlike building is open daily to any who want to see cheese turned out just the way, back in 1873, George Crowley first made the wheels that still bear his name.

THE ASSAULT OF CREEPING BLANDNESS   The flavor of cheese depends as much on its making as it does on the quality of its ingredients. We have no way of knowing exactly how either Cheddar or Cheshire tasted on the best of occasions in the eighteenth century. Yet we know that the manufacture of cheese in factories, no matter where in the world they may be, has taken away the surprise. Time was when opening a wheel, whose rind until then had protected it from the air, was a moment of anticipation —to be followed by a first nibble that sometimes brought awe, sometimes bewilderment. Moments like that are rare these days. Too many firm cheeses today are computerized to address the palate in standard ways. We are beset by creeping blandness, and fine factory artisans have succumbed to making Cheddars—especially Cheddars—that are composed of quality ingredients but diminished in flavor in order to appeal to the greatest number of consumers, few of whom have been sufficiently encouraged to be daring.

With one or two exceptions, the United States has not been favorably inclined toward regional types, and it is hard not to wonder how long Great Britain will retain its own distinctive country cheeses. I once bought, in a Kensington supermarket, four vacuum-packed wedges, each labeled as one of England's classics. Except for variations in color, and in spite of their being differentiated as Derby, Double Gloucester, Lancashire, and Leicester, they were, as far as taste and texture went, the same cheese, their county names having been reduced to no more than sales gimmicks.

Yet there are a good half-dozen, other than Cheddar and Cheshire, that still manage to maintain their traditional British characteristics as well as their names. Caerphilly, the white unaged cheese that bears the name of a Welsh town dominated by its sprawling, moated castle, has for years been made in a score of alien places. In fact, when my wife and I picnicked there between the castle and Nay-y-Gledyr Brook there wasn't a crumb of local Caerphilly to be bought or an active cheesemaking vat in town. Somewhat later, as a part of the celebrations of the seven hundredth year of Caerphilly Castle, local shops sold one-pound souvenir Caerphillies for a limited time, but the vast majority that bear the label, especially those coming to America, are made in such places as Swindon and Melton Mobray.

Although Welsh dairymen have crossed Offa's Dyke to help make Caerphilly elsewhere, this gentle, unaged, sourish cake—no matter the locale of its manufacture—is still most in demand among Welshmen at home, especially miners, for whom, the story goes, it was first devised. Caerphilly is easily digestible, and its fresh dairy taste plus firm texture makes it, an Englishman told me, "suitable to the packed lunch of the underground worker, who appears to prefer a mild acid-flavored cheese to a 'strong' matured one." While Somerset farmers must wait at least six months for mild Cheddars to be ready, Caerphilly is sent to English markets in five days or so (although the Caerphilly retailed in the United States is usually cured for two or three weeks). It has been described as looking like a pure-white *gâteau,* and in the old days it went to Cardiff shops to be dressed with white powder made from rice.

Outstanding among the warm-toned cheeses of Cheddar affinity, most getting their color now from annatto, is Double Gloucester, which has been made for at least a couple of hundred years on farms in the valley of the River Severn. "Put a crumb of it, no bigger than a pinhead, on your tongue," a chronicler of English cheeseways wrote, "and it will fill your whole mouth with savour. Yet it is so mellow and delicate that a whole slice of it, far from being pungent, has a creamy quality—'silky' perhaps is the word." Double Gloucester, farmhouse-made and subtly matured, is hard to find. Yet mass-produced Double Gloucesters are being exported, and they are fine-looking shallow wheels of England's current best. They should be sampled, but patience may be necessary before you find among this country's imports a Double Gloucester as exquisite as this type once was.

WHAT CHEESES OWE TO WOMEN As it happened, Double Gloucester had virtually disappeared by the end of World War II, and food rationing had so disrupted the cheese business that many new housekeepers had never tasted a number of the other English varieties of their heritage. Thus the postwar challenge of the Milk Marketing Board was to bring the old ones back into the market, but in the case of Gloucester no valid recipe could be found. Experiments to reproduce something like the old product continued to be disastrous until one day, answering the general call for help, there appeared at the factory an old lady who was eighty or more and wearing her years heavily. She seemed to have exhausted her energy long before, but after smelling and tasting the factory experiments, declaring them no good at all, she set about showing the workers step by step how to make real Double Gloucester. She stayed with them until they had mastered the craft she had carried throughout her life, and then she went home, and immediately died.

I don't think there is so poignant a moment to be reported about any other British cheese. It might be said that Barbara Gilmour was the savior of Dunlop, Scotland's close relative of Cheddar, for she did secrete among her possessions her own recipe for cheese when she fled from Ireland during the religious troubles of 1688; and on the new family farm near Dunlop, in Ayrshire, she settled down to making and selling the kind of cheese not produced before by Scots. But her methods were not—as were those for Double Gloucester—considered lost when she died.* A century later her grandson was running the same farm and was by no means the only cheese-maker then producing Dunlop; it had become a Scottish tradition. As turned out in the twentieth century, it has a slightly sweeter aftertaste than Cheddar and rivals several other highly touted British cheeses for its toasting and melting propensities.

---

* In the harbor town of Kirkwall, capital of the Orkneys, the cheeses supplied to Elizabeth, the Queen Mother, are made by local farmers' wives.

CANTAL

LEICESTER

CAERPHILLY

WENSLEYDALE

SOME CHEESES FOR MELTING   On the subject of melting, one can read for instance that the pride of Lancashire was known in the nineteenth century as "Leigh Toaster." The best of this county's cheese was then produced in the village of Leigh, outside Manchester, and was still a purely farmhouse product, usually made in the kitchen and ripened on shelves near the range. The old process took two or preferably three days of preparation, on each of which the whey was separated from a new lot of curds to be combined and pressed on the third, then pressed again on the fourth before being put in an airy place to dry. Factories—strongholds of efficiency —do not have time for such niceties, but available Lancashire retains its soft texture, and it is ideal for cooking, turning custardy when melted.

Englishmen *will* stand on opinion. Ambrose Heath and Henry Stevens, two London gastronomes, writing about their preferences, both nominated Leicesters as the best melting cheeses, and Heath called Lancashire second best to Leicester for the making of Britain's classic "toasted cheese," or Welsh Rabbit. About the color of Leicester there is no argument. When you buy the real thing you'll find it is so deeply under the influence of annatto that it is still known sometimes as "Red Cheese," and is otherwise distinctive in the flatness of its cylinder shape.

White Wensleydale and Derby are Cheddar cousins from northern counties, and their factory-made versions are now being exported and sold by some better than average cheese outlets. In England, blue-veined Wensleydale is sometimes available, notably in the resort town of Harrowgate, north of Leeds (see Chapter 4). A good Wensleydale is softer, more buttery than others, and it is given credit for those doggerel lines that compare a piece of apple pie unaccompanied by a nip of cheese to "a kiss without a squeeze." Again combined with apples, Wensleydale is the distinctive factor in Dale pudding, an old favorite in Yorkshire. And partygoers in the United Kingdom know the Wensleydale dip, which is not a new dance step but a mixture of four ounces of cheese, four chopped walnuts, four tablespoons of warm cream, a little onion juice, chopped watercress, a pinch of cayenne, and salt to taste. The light-colored cheese from County Derby, in the English Midlands, is the mildest of them all, "a good working man's cheese, and even more than that," according to Ambrose Heath; "and the difficulty of obtaining it generally may yet make it an epicure's discovery." That might have been blessedly true when Derby was made in a dairywoman's kitchen. But the factory version is without particular distinction; at Christmas time, however, the eating of Derby, especially infused with the flavor and color of sage, is still a British tradition.

In France, "Chester" (pronounced Chestaire) has become a term to describe the Cheshire-like, brushed-rind cylinder now made in Castres, in the Tarn region. Not far away, in Auvergne and Cantal, is the home of Cantal, a Cheddar-like wheel usually even firmer than the original from Somerset. It is also large, 14 to 18 inches across and 14 to 16 inches high, weighing from about 75 to 100 pounds. When Cantal has been carefully handled it is an excellent foil for fruits such as apples and pears.

In American wine country one of the most widely known California dairy products is Monterey Jack, a distant relative of Cheddar developed from the traditional *queso del pais* (cheese of the country) made by Spanish padres who arrived in the eighteenth century. Although it has been imitated far and wide, this cheese was made for decades exclusively in the Monterey region south of San Francisco. I have the word of Henry Downey, long curator of the nearby Historic Carmel Mission, that a distinctly new cheese evolved under the aegis of a Scot named David Jacks, who dominated Monterey dairy farming throughout the years after the Gold Rush. The shipping point and the name of the shipper (minus the *s*) were stamped on cheeses going to other markets, and they became almost inextricably entwined—although away from the West Coast there is a tendency to label cheeses of this type "California Jack."

Actually there are two sorts of Jack. "Dry Jack," which is hard and considered a cook's cheese, is fine for grating. The other, called by technicians "High Moisture Jack," is a semihard, firm loaf that by definition has

DRY MONTEREY JACK

a moisture content of at least 44 percent but less than 50 percent; and the butterfat content is also high, with a minimum of 50 percent. It can be compared with another firm American dairy product that comes from mid-continent.

Thirty-odd years ago, Cornhusker cheese was announced with fanfare at the University of Nebraska's Agricultural Experiment Station, and it continues to be made in limited quantities for distribution in the Middle West. In introducing it, the creators named it for the college football team, but have since dropped the "corn." Husker was developed, they said, because of "an increasing demand for a mild-flavored, rather soft-textured type of cheese" and because "a great many consumers prefer this . . . to a well-aged, firm-bodied, natural cheese." Husker uses the same equipment needed to produce Cheddar, but the result is a more flexible texture and a blander flavor.

Colby, named for a small town in Wisconsin's dairy country, is another variant of Cheddar developed late in the nineteenth century by Ambrose and J. H. Steinwand, and it has become a very popular American cheese that is also manufactured in Australia and a number of European countries. Like Camosun, a cheese made by the stirred-curd method in Washington State, Colby is also related to Plymouth Cheese, produced in limited quantities in the Vermont town of that name and using a process described as "granular curd." These are all variants of cheeses made by the American technique known as "washed curd," developed in early New

York dairies. For the undiscerning they are products that look like Cheddar, and they are often sold as "American Cheddar" or sometimes simply "American Cheese."

I have tasted one American cheese that is unlike any Cheddar or any of its variants. It has been made, for about half a century, by the Mossholder family, just outside of Appleton, Wisconsin. Shaped in a long, square-cornered loaf, longer than a loaf of sandwich bread, it is sometimes sold fresh and sometimes when it is two or three months old; in the latter stage it has its own resonant character. You can ask the Mossholders how they make their cheese, but they won't give away the secret. What they will tell you is about how the first Mossholder got started. He had no cheesemaking background, so he called in his neighbors to help him. On the first day, one neighbor made Swiss Cheese; on the second another made Brick; on the next day the third made Cheddar. Mossholder cheese is a combination of all three. What could be more American than that?

STORE CHEESE

NEW YORK CHEDDAR

VERMONT CHEDDAR

3

Thin Skins
and Creamy Centers

In Normandy, that green damp land stretching along the top of France, and in the old Pays de Brie, the dairy region to the south and east of Paris, there are many who swear by a basic philosophy: the best thing to happen to excess milk is for it to be transformed into naturally fermented, or soft-ripened, cakes that are creamy and vulnerable in their interiors, rather than supple throughout like Munster, or firm from edge to edge like Cheddar.

From Norman farms, and from those of the Île-de-France, come Camembert and Brie—the world's two most notable cheeses with thin skins and creamy centers. They are downy-white disks, one about four and a half inches in diameter, the latter twice (sometimes more than three times) as wide. They are delicate, so delicate that each must be handled with knowing tenderness by both maker and consumer. They share much in common. In fact, one version of that imaginative Marie Harel legend binds Brie and Camembert together as closely as siblings. Mme. Harel, this folktale would have us believe, was the daughter of a Pays de Brie farmer who left her ancient homeland in the Île-de-France to marry, and she created Camembert by trying to make Brie in Normandy, using the smaller molds of her new neighbors.

Although rejected by historians, it is a tempting story, for Brie and Camembert are products of France deeply embedded in the past. Both have ancient importance—Brie, indeed, focused Charlemagne's attention on dairies in the Île-de-France. Camembert, for its part, also has medieval lineage, including the fact that the particular forms which give it its famous circular confinement were borrowed from an even more ancient cheese of the same region of northern France.

Today Camemberts are made in a district 280 miles wide in which almost one hundred dairies produce half the French fermented soft cheeses —a list that once included thirty-two so-called Norman types, from Camem-

bert and Carentan to Livarot, Petit Lisieux, and Pont l'Évêque.* The places of manufacture vary from the old-fashioned workrooms of Daniel and Simone Courtonne, and of Mme. Marcel Pinot, one of a handful turning out farmhouse Pont l'Évêques, to spotless laboratory-like factories such as that of Jean-Pierre Buquet, whose family has been exporting Norman dairy products for more than one hundred years.

MARKS OF QUALITY Camemberts come from the "Road of Great Cheeses," as the Normans say, which is compared to Burgundy's "Road of Great Wines" that runs from Gevrey-Chambertin to Meursault. Normandy's highway of epicurean delight may not be quite so literal a thoroughfare, but the road that passes the Courtonne farm goes south from the English Channel, through the cheese towns of Pont l'Évêque and Livarot, to Vimoutiers and, with a slight detour, to Camembert. This trail runs through the valley of the Auge River, and the words "Spécialité de la Vallée d'Auge" on any maker's label signify the quality considered best by Normans. The label V.C.N. (veritable Camembert of Normandy) is reserved for top-notch products from the departments of Eure, Calvados, Seine-Maritime, Orne, and Manche. Just as is true of Brie, and of cheeses of other dairy countries, there are mercantile agreements that limit the region in which true Norman Camemberts can be made.

Commercial imitations are manufactured in several countries, including Australia, Austria, Denmark, Germany, Holland, Iceland, Ireland, Japan, New Zealand, Norway, Sweden, and Switzerland, as well as the United States; and in Camembert factories I have visited—in Chambois, not

---

* Others: Neufchâtel, Rouenais, Incheville, Villedieu, Aurore, Triple Aurore, Gournay, Trappiste, La Bouille, Bonneville, Pavé de Moyaux, Lucullus, Brillat-Savarin, Hayons, Providence, Le Roy, Isigny, Bondon, Double Bond, Notre-Dame, Mon Carré, Maromme, Trouville, Lisieux, Bricquebec, Quittebeuf, Fin de Siècle, Excelsior.

far from Vimoutiers, and in Van Wert, Ohio, and Petaluma, California—
the difference is not visible to the average eye. It is the fresh milk of Norman cattle that gives the distinctive flavor to the region's unpasteurized
cheeses, and of course it is the grass nurtured by salt air and long days of
rain that flavors the milk. Because U.S. law requires the pasteurization of
imported dairy products, it is impossible to buy a freshly matured French
Camembert or Brie in America. Exported soft-ripened cheeses may have
downy crusts and supple interiors without any chalklike centers; but they
smell slightly of innocuous mold, and their flavor is often bland and milky.
On the other hand, when a farmhouse Norman cheese is opened *à point*
(at the point when it has achieved its moment of perfection) its crust has a
white velvety surface spotted with russet flecks, and there is a poignant
bouquet followed by a subtle tang in the aftertaste when it is eaten.

BRIE

THE MAKING OF CAMEMBERT AND BRIE   The look of Bries and
Camemberts leads some to think they have been cooked, as if they were
custards contained in powdery white pastry. They are, in fact, exposed
only to enough heat to reach the temperature of a typical hot summer day.
They are not pressed under weights as are many other cheeses; they are
shaped only by open-ended, circular metal forms of specific diameter. Both
are ripened partly by molds and bacteria that grow on the surface, forming
the thin skin within which the curds, drained to a granular consistency, are
allowed to mature delicately so that they become smooth and fluent. The
problem of distinguishing between the two best-known soft-ripened types
is as difficult as trying to explain the technical difference between Bur-
gundies and Bordeaux.

In both Brie and Camembert, health-giving spores of the penicillium fungus bring about bacteriological changes. An account in the town history of Vimoutiers relates the cheese of Normandy to medical research that occurred considerably before Sir Alexander Fleming identified penicillin as an antidote against infectious organisms. In 1926 Dr. Joseph Knirim of New York turned up in Vimoutiers to pay tribute to Camembert as a saver of lives. His experiments with patients suffering from stomach trouble, he is said to have told the local pharmacist, had resulted in cures when he kept his charges on a diet of Camembert and pilsner beer. He had proved not merely that cheese was good for the healthy, he said, but that it contained the same curative properties that later helped penicillin to have so important an effect on postwar medicine.

The story seems to add another dimension to the beneficence of cheese, but it also alludes to factors that make both Brie and Camembert tricky to handle and more perishable than other varieties. Because of risks of spoilage in shipping—and because these cheeses begin to lose their best qualities the minute they are cut—many of those exported are "stabilized" by a process devised to make them more uniform and to have, as retailers say, longer life. The term misleads, for cheese is a living substance, and what stabilization does is to prevent the continuance of natural life. A stabilized Brie, for instance, arrives on a retailer's shelf in soft

condition and will stay that way; instead of continuing to mature, with the interior becoming increasingly pliant, the arrested cheese takes on a bitter taste when it has been around too long.

A FEW CLOSE RELATIVES   Other surface-ripened cheeses have longer natural lives because of ancient differences in their formulas. Two of these take their names from the villages of Pont l'Évêque and Livarot, not far from Camembert. Both are related to the early cheeses known as *angelots* (the word for a medieval French gold coin) because their crusts turned a rich, reddish color. The handsome, dull-gold coatings of Pont l'Évêque and Livarot are similar to *angelots,* and they are still made in traditional ways. Daniel Courtonne's neighbor, Mme. Marcel Pinot, drains the curd for her Pont l'Évêques in their square molds, removes the growth on the surfaces, and washes them periodically in slightly salted water during their process of maturing. Sometimes a little coloring is added to Pont l'Évêques to achieve a creamier effect, yet the finished product is considerably firmer than Camemberts. Similar steps are taken in maturing the close relatives of Pont l'Évêques which are called Pavé d'Auge, Pavé de Moyaux, Petit Lisieux, and Carré de Bonneville.

Not far from Lisieux, on the wide Road of Great Cheeses, one can find Pavé d'Auges being made at St.-Julien-le-Faucon; and at Ste.-Marguerite-de-Viette is the establishment of an *affineur* at which Livarots—that other descendant of the ancient *angelots*—are salted, washed, and ripened after being brought in from the farms around the market town of Livarot. These are round, about the size of Camemberts, but the longer period of curing makes them firmer and gives them a smoother crust which results from the several washings in salty water and which nowadays takes some of its color from a brushing with an annatto solution. Fresh air is not permitted in cellars where these cheeses get their special treatment, and it has been a traditional kind of insurance to mix hay with the mortar on the cellar walls as an encouragement to natural bacteriological changes. When the exteriors of Livarots are smooth, somewhat glossy, and well colored, they are sent off to market by the ripener, or *affineur*.

Affineurs also are important in the making of farmhouse Bries in the Île-de-France and the region of Champagne, to the east. In Tournan, on the road from Paris to Champagne, I talked with a man whose life had been dedicated to Brie since boyhood. "One knows that the fresh cheeses from the cows of one farmer must be handled slightly differently from those of another farmer," Robert Rouzaire said in his curing cellars. "My family and their families have been doing business together for generations, but nothing is certain about cheese. All I can tell you is that to be the best, Brie has to be made in the Île-de-France. It may be called Brie and it may have taste acceptable to some people, but only Briards know how to make the cheese of the Pays de Brie. And even then a cheese will fail if just once it is mishandled."

THREE KINDS OF BRIE   In this region, where cheeses traditionally are taken as seriously as wine, *le Brie fermier* has definite seasons and is at its best in the period from November to May. These flat farm cheeses from the Pays de Brie are larger than others, measuring sometimes as much as 16 inches in diameter though only 1 inch thick. Their proportions, the very thinness of the layer of curds maturing over so large a circumference, have much to do with the unique and subtle flavor of a perfectly cured Briard farmer's product. Unlike those made in factories, they may not seem "pretty" to the eye; in fact, they should have an uneven appearance, their surfaces flecked with red.*

* "The very shape of Brie—so uncheeselike and so charmingly fragile—is exciting," Sheila Hibben wrote in *The New Yorker*. "Nine times out of ten a Brie will let you down—will be all caked into layers, which shows it is too young, or at the over-runny stage, which means it is too old—but when you come to the tenth Brie, *coulant* to just the right delicate creaminess, and the color of fresh, sweet butter, no other cheese can compare with it."

BRIE

Frenchmen classify Bries in three categories: the pancakelike Brie de Meaux, which takes its name from the market town just up Route N36 from Tournan; the slightly thicker Brie de Melun, which is about 10 inches across; and Coulommiers, most often available in a size very similar to that of Camembert. In addition the region produces comparable cheeses known as Fougeru, Cevru, and Ville St. Jacques, as well as Explorateur, with exemplifies the exceedingly rich soft-ripened cheeses called by the French *double crèmes* or *triple crèmes*.

These soft, rich disks acquire their distinction through liberal additions of cream, and they are legally defined. The law in France declares that a cheese must have at least 60 percent fat in dry matter to warrant use of the term "double cream"; those described as triple creams must have at least 72 percent fat. Thus these cheeses have a range of 10 percent to 25 percent more butterfat content than Bries or Camemberts. It takes about twenty-four hours for the cream-enriched milk to coagulate, and the drained curds are then treated with a mold that ripens inward from the outside, forming a downy crust after ten days to two weeks of maturation.

Double crèmes were first made in Normandy at the end of the nineteenth century and the type now includes, among those intermittently imported in this country, Monsieur Fromage, Caprice des Dieux, and Fol d'Amour from France, as well as the Swedish Hablé Crème Chantilly. Among the magnificent *triple crèmes* available in specialty stores are Excelsior and Explorateur, having 72 and 75 percent butterfat respectively. In the mid-1970's others included Brillat-Savarin and Suprême, which differ in size and shape but do have the pale velvety looks of well-made Bries and Camemberts.

IMITATIONS AND VARIATIONS   The look of any of these cheeses is emulated by American cheesemakers. In the United States visitors can see Brie and Camembert being made in small "family-size" dairies in Petaluma, California, and in the Midwestern small town called Lena, in northern Illinois's rich dairyland. Large plants in other dairy states like Ohio and Wisconsin also make domestic Camembert and Brie, according to formulas that are really adaptations of the methods used in French factories to turn out the square surface-ripened cakes called Carré de l'Est. American versions are also made of pasteurized milk, of course, and they take slightly longer to ripen and have a blander, factorylike uniformity of flavor. In supermarkets they are often packed in semicircular boxes that bear a stamped date and contain triangles of cheese wrapped in foil. Such cheeses are said to be fully cured within two weeks of the date they bear, but much depends upon the temperatures at which they have been kept refrigerated. It may even take a bit of luck to pick the right moment to open and serve a date-coded product. Too often, these cheeses become over-ripe before their terminal date.

In Stephenson County, Illinois, the Kolb family developed its own way of making soft-ripened cheese fifty years ago. Kolb Bries, sold under the trademark Delico, are admirable when properly attended. Molded in eight-inch circles and weighing about two pounds, they have downy crusts and the same fluent and creamy interior that is characteristic of their French originals. Pierce Thompson's Petaluma Bries, labeled Rouge et Noir, are available throughout the West Coast and, like those produced by Kolb-Lena, are sold by mail (see Mail Order Sources). As if to prove these Americans have been on the right track, a long-established French dairy

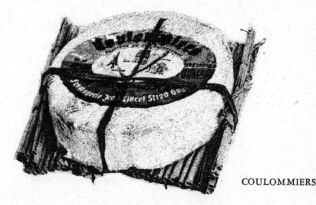

COULOMMIERS

in 1974 began to make both Brie and Camembert—in Le Sueur, a Minnesota town with an appropriately French name—in a plant hard by the valley of the Jolly Green Giant.

In France, there is no vogue for imitating the cheeses of other lands. Carré de l'Est, "the square cheese of the east," is an industrial product of the regions of Champagne and Lorraine that some gourmands think rivals Camembert and Brie, but it is not a mimic. The town of Chaource, once the most important market in Champagne, gives its name to a soft-ripened cylinder now made in factories; the average Chaource measures two and a half inches in diameter and is just as high, and its name is protected under a 1970 French government decree. Champagne is as rich in cheeses as it is in its incomparable effervescent wine. From the village next to Chaource, for instance, comes a similar cheese known as Ervy-le-Châtel, after its hometown. And the ancient province boasts many soft cheeses classified as *cendrés* because their skins are coated with edible ashes, sometimes produced by burning the vines of wine-bearing grapes.

It is not surprising that throughout the wine country of eastern France there are many local cheeses, all possessed of special affinity for local vintages. The Burgundy town of Époisses gives its name to a luxuriously soft flat cylinder that is washed in the lees of wine and is remarkable not simply because Brillat-Savarin called it *le roi des fromages* but because even today it is a cow's-milk cheese of great richness and special flavor. Many others of the region are products of goat's milk—and their turn comes in a later chapter.

CHEESE TO EAT WITH A SPOON   Wines are frequently employed in curing cheeses, including a soft-ripened type known as Vacherin that is produced on both sides of the France-Switzerland border. The name is derived from the French word for cow and, confusingly, applies also to a dessert made of cream and meringue. Vacherin Cheese as I saw it made in the Swiss town called Les Charbonnières, on Lac de Joux, is just as rich. It is full of cream, too, for it is made in winter when the mountain cows are fed on the last hay crop—when the milk yield is too low for the making of giant Gruyères but the milk fat content is substantially higher than usual. Vacherin Mont d'Or, as this variety is called, has a thickish rind, which builds up during frequent brushings with white wine, but an interior so richly fluid that it is often eaten with a spoon.

Vacherins like those I was shown at Les Charbonnières by a Swiss *affineur,* Victor Golay, seem very rustic compared with Bries or Camemberts. The unripened Vacherins come to cellars like M. Golay's shaped not by metal molds but by narrow hoops of spruce or wild cherry bark fastened sometimes with crude thongs, sometimes by rubber bands. The cellars in which I first encountered them were permeated by a woodsy aroma of tree sap. "Curing," my Swiss host said, "takes about three months in a very humid atmosphere. And the finished Vacherins weigh about a pound."

"Do you know the difference between these and Fribourg Vacherins?" he asked me. *"They* weigh sometimes twenty, sometimes thirty pounds, a little like the cheese used for raclette. To make the fondue in the style of Fribourg, people melt pieces of the big Fribourg Vacherins half and half with Gruyère. But our own small cakes don't have to be melted. Not at all. When these become mature they will be so smooth and *coulant* on the inside they are already like a fondue that needs no fire to make it melt."

In addition to copies of Brie and Camembert, and aside from their international reputation for the weighty Emmenthaler and Gruyère wheels, Alpine cheesemakers not far from Lac de Joux produce a soft-ripened factory disk called Tomme Vaudoise that is supple and dense with cream, not unlike Camembert itself. Another near-Camembert has the savor of herbs permeating its surface; a third is marketed as "Swiss Dessert," and reminds me of Chaource.

Even the Russians flatter the creators of Camembert by making the white cakes they call Loubitelski and Zakoussotchnyï by way of the same industrial process now common in France. All the Scandinavian countries turn out versions of French cheeses, but it was in Denmark that Henrik Tholstrup, a third-generation cheesemaker, set out to devise a formula that would result in a Brie-like texture without any possibility of a chalky center. His achievement, known as Crema Dania or Crema Danica, comes boxed in the form of two rectangular downy-white cheeses that weigh 6 ounces apiece. The flavor is more delicate than either farmhouse Brie or Camembert, and its consistency is fluent, like Brie—or honey too tepid to be poured. A version called Crème Royale is divided in cubes instead of sticks.

Whether modern creations frankly imitative of ancient farm products, or the result of family traditions like those of Daniel and Simone Courtonne, these cheeses with thin skins and creamy centers are the most popular in many countries. No one is born with the knack of invariably picking a perfect example of such a cheese. It takes practice. "Poking the rind, testing the elasticity of the cheese, predicting what it will be like is a bit like dowsing," the great French writer Colette once said. To those who have made these soft-ripened delicacies so popular, acquiring the knack of selection is worth all the effort. For cheese demands affection. As Colette also wrote: "If I had a son who was ready to marry, I would tell him, 'Beware of girls who don't like wine, truffles, cheese, or music.' " I agree—and not necessarily in that order.

4

The Blues

Veined cheeses—those that are mottled with blue (or sometimes greenish) whorls—are no more dependent on the substantive changes brought about by molds than any other cheeses. But the handsome contrast in color is the visible result of the work of *Penicillium glaucum* (from *glaucos,* the Greek word for bluish gray) or *Penicillium roqueforti* (from Roquefort-sur-Soulzon, a village in southwest France). These fungi, along with invisible yeasts and bacteria, are factors in forming or changing the character of the cheeses we call blue.

"Molds," in the words of Paris gastronome Robert Courtine, "are microscopic mushrooms which develop on the surface of certain cheeses and in the interior of certain others." I see them as *agents provocateurs* composed of branching filaments bearing spores that infiltrate and change the future. Without them England's Blue Vinny would have remained a simple cheese called Dorset. Without them we should have no royal blues like Stilton, Gorgonzola, or Roquefort.

Molds, long before they were understood by scientists, helped provide mankind with food to keep healthy and well fed. The ability of certain kinds of fungus to transform curds into handsomely mottled cakes persuaded mountain shepherds two thousand years ago in the realm called Languedoc that dry cheese took on flavor unlike anything else after being left for days on a piece of bread in a cliffside grotto. Among the caves of Mount Combalou, where the tile-roofed village of Roquefort-sur-Soulzon now clings on a precipitous slope, the discovery that bread mold could be used to work its wiles on curds resulted in a cheese already famous when Roman colonizers occupied Gaul.

THERE IS ONLY ONE ROQUEFORT Roquefort is so well established in the twentieth century that no other cheese distinguished by blue mold may legally claim the name of its home village, and the manner in which the cheese turns blue remains faithful to the original method discovered by accident. *Penicillium roqueforti* has been isolated as a commercial mold produced from bread. Fresh loaves made of rye and wheat flour are inoculated with a pure culture of the mold, and under laboratory conditions they are penetrated by blue growth when left in a humid atmosphere for four to six weeks. Then the loaves of mold are crumbled, dried, ground, and sifted to a fine powder that bears the spores.

When *les fromagers* of Combalou make their cheeses, dipping the curds of sheep's milk into the Roquefort forms, this powdery culture is sprinkled in layers, and as the curd solidifies it is punched with needle holes to permit air to reach the interior of the cheese so that the mold can grow, like mushrooms in fertile soil. Blue mold can be made to develop in curds at any time or place when the temperature and humidity are right, but that of Roquefort assumes its special character in the unique Combalou caves.

Thousands of visitors each year make pilgrimages to Roquefort village. They are French, or mostly French, and they drive their small cars up the steep mountain road, or tumble, stretching their legs, from the charter buses that stop at a depot from which the rest of the short climb is made on foot. Some of them were just leaving when my wife and I, one September evening, parked our Peugeot 104 in front of the Grand Hotel, in which the dining room, according to the posted menu, specialized in Palets Prinsky au Roquefort, a cheese-laced pastry. We walked up the cobbles and a steep stairway to the entrance of one of the fourteen com-

ROQUEFORT

mercial societies that control the caves, each packaging its own independently trademarked Roquefort cheese.

From a modernly appointed but cavernlike waiting room we were led deep underground through vaulted space that sometimes seemed ecclesiastical. There were man-made arches, some of which had been constructed under early Roman rule. And as the result of geological upheaval, the caves' natural walls are peculiar; the rocks break vertically, and there is a slight but constant condensation overhead. A continuous though rather faint current of air moves subterraneously through fractures in the rock walls, and through tiny vertical cracks, called *fleurines,* that reach through the stone mass from the high plateaus to the river flowing at the foot of Combalou.

NATURAL AIR CONDITIONING, UNIQUE FLAVOR Horizontal crevices had also been formed between the caves and the vertical fissures, nature providing a perpetual crosscurrent of cool moist air throughout the underground domain. Winter and summer, this natural air conditioning maintains the ripening Roquefort cheeses at a temperature that varies only a degree or so. Here the combination of slight humidity, gentle movement of air, and consistent coolness so influences the maturation of the Roquefort mold that a flavor is developed which has not been duplicated no matter how skillfully dairy scientists have manipulated modern equipment.

In the caves of Combalou, under the rough stone arches, table after table holds rows of white curd cylinders, standing on edge but turned regularly in order to keep their shape. These developing cheeses are cleaned every two or three weeks by scraping and brushing. "They have already been salted—twice in a week's time," a guide told us. "That retards the growth of microorganisms and foreign molds. They also have been punched—so the mold develops and turns a special Roquefort blue." The color is a subtlety not always discernible to the average eye. The guide added that it takes from three to six months in the caves before the 6-pound cheeses are ready to be shipped, each one wrapped carefully in foil. Each must be stamped with a drawing of a sheep, printed in red ink, a guarantee that it is a genuine product of the caves at Roquefort. (It is a mark, incidentally, that under international agreement cannot be used on any other blue cheese made elsewhere in France or in the rest of the world.)

A couple of hundred years ago Casanova said he had found the combination of Roquefort and the wine of Chambertin was an incomparable stimulant to the revival of a waning love or an inspiration for a newborn

STILTON

BLEU DE BRESSE

GORGONZOLA

ROQUEFORT

DANABLU

passion. Rabelais, practicing medicine in the region, said he always had some Roquefort within reach, to serve as a fillip to drink—romantic thoughts aside. "Roquefort," said the French epicure Grimod de la Reynière in a loftier sentiment, "should be eaten on one's knees." Still, there are other French Blue Cheeses worthy of salute.

Some of these veined loaves are made in mountain chalets near the Swiss border, some on Périgord farms, and others in spick-and-span mechanized factories. Of this various lot, Bleu de Corse, like Roquefort, is a product of sheep's milk, while a few are sometimes made of goat's milk, and others are based on the milk of cows. On the spot in Auvergne you can titillate the palate with samples of Bleu des Causses and Bleu de Laqueuille in summer and fall. And what a grand tour there is to be made out of a town like Chamonix to visit the mountain villages where Persillés des Aravis (so called because they look as if the curd had been mixed with parsley) and various assertive Blues of the Savoy are worth the hunting. Not far north, in Servas and Grièges, are the cheese cooperatives that turn out pasteurized Bresse *bleus,* sometimes labeled Pipo Crem', Pipo Nain, or Uni-Bresse; these are to be found the year around and, like Saingorlon, which is made in Auvergne, they are sometimes described as French imitations of Gorgonzola.

ORIGINS OF GORGONZOLA   There is, however, only one cheese that has earned authentic designation as Gorgonzola—despite the use of the name by American and other factories. Gorgonzola got its start, Italians believe, in Roman times when cows that had been pastured in the Lomellina Valley, south of Milan, were driven north to the mountains for the summer. To break the long journey, the dairymen of Lombardy halted at the village of Gorgonzola for milking. As a result, the villagers, faced with an excess of milk, made cheese, and they took it to age in mountain caves in the Valtellina.

In Gorgonzola's maturation the curd is left until a natural mold begins to appear, and the ripening cheeses are turned frequently on racks. Copper wires are used to ventilate the cheeses nowadays, thus inducing and ensuring speedy growth of mold throughout the curd. The Gorgonzola method turns out pungent wheels in large curing houses at Milan, Vercelli, Novara, Lodi, Como, Cuneo, Cremona, Pavia, Brescia, and Valsassina. Other cheesemakers in Italy export a very small, veined cylinder called Moncenisio; and fine handmade Castelmagno, a little-known Italian Blue, is made at Caraglio, north of Turin, by Signora Domenica Donadia and her sister Caterina.

Nothing irritates Italian cheesemakers so much, I've been told, as a Frenchman who compares Gorgonzola with Roquefort. The two are distinct varieties, and Italians shudder at the thought not only of ewe's milk but of blue veins that must be induced by moldy bread. Not for them. There is, they say, one great Blue Cheese, native to northern Italy, and it is known of course as *il Re de Formaggio.*

The title "king of cheese" has many claimants, and not the least of these is the British favorite bearing the name of Stilton (a village in which, incidentally, it was never made). I doubt many Englishmen would admit much argument. John Bidwell, one of London's best-known cheese masters, put it to me this way: "We always reckon that English blue-veined Stilton is 'king of all cheese,' and I have never met an American or any other person from overseas who has quarreled with this opinion."

THE BEGINNINGS OF STILTON'S REPUTATION   Stilton's reputation for excellence was widely known at least as early as the reign of George II, and the principal cause seems to have been its popularity at the Bell Inn, a coach stop in Huntingdonshire; from there guests who devoured it with flagons of ale took more of it back to London.* Nobody knows who developed the Stilton recipe, but a woman who had been

---

* A few years later, in the reign of George III, various British cheeses had become so popular in London that two cheesemongers named Paxton and Whitfield opened a shop (it remains today in Jermyn Street) and became purveyors to His Majesty.

housekeeper in Quenby Hall is said to have taken the formula with her when she married and settled not far from Melton Mobray in Leicestershire. Mrs. Orton, as she was known, was sufficiently monopoly-minded to let the rumor spread that her cheese could be made only with the help of cows fed on her husband's small meadow called Orton's Close. Her method stayed in the family for a while, the story goes, and one of her daughters, who became the wife of the innkeeper at Stilton, sold the cheese at the Bell Inn. There it got its reputation and its name.

Stilton differs from Roquefort and Gorgonzola in texture and in the wrinkled, dull crust that reminds some of the skin of a melon. The cheese is taller than it is wide, and it matures while tightly bound in a cloth bandage on which white mold and dry patches begin to appear. If the curds have developed the right acidity and moisture content, along with a porous, open texture allowing air into the interior, Stilton can evolve blue mold without injection of commercial penicillium, but the only way to be sure of so naturally matured cheese is to know the maker, or to have absolute confidence in its purveyor.

Some Britons eat Stilton during its early ripening, at four to six weeks, but most consider it best when left to fully mature and develop blue mold, at four to six months. Now made in numerous English factories, it is available all year round, but connoisseurs have firm notions about Stilton in its season. "I should no more want Stilton on a hot August day," Sir John Squire wrote, "than I should want boiled silverside and dumplings; Stilton is essentially a thing for cold months, when appetites are robust and in want of warming up."

A BLUE CHESHIRE FOR HEROES   With other ancient Blue Cheeses of England it has not been a matter of picking one's favorite season but of being grateful to have them whenever they appear. There are factory versions of Cheshire Blue on the market, but the real thing—once described as "fit only for heroes"—is a gift of nature resulting from unusually high acidity in the milk and sufficient openness of texture to encourage the healthy natural growth of mold. It has been said that a genuine Cheshire Blue happens only about once in a thousand times, and then only under the right stewardship. Geoffrey Hutchinson was famous in the twentieth century for his knack of being on hand when such things happened. He spent fifty-six years as a Wiltshire entrepreneur, forging a career on his ability to recognize among immature Cheshires those that would develop a natural blue quality. He traveled the countryside selecting farmhouse cheeses with "loose over-acid curd and high moisture content," then supervised their maturation in his very humid cellars in Whitchurch.

I haven't traveled the countryside in such pursuit, but I know of a British writer who chased from pillar to post one season a few years ago in search of the legendary Blue Vinny. He started in Dorsetshire, where the local cheese on rare occasions would transform itself with lovely mold. The first false leads had him going from Dorchester to Sherborne, then to three small villages, with no avail. He was sent on to a pub in the beautiful Tudor village of Cerne Abbas, where he was sold a cheese but was told he would have to drive across the moors to Wells if he wanted it certified as true Blue Vinny. There, after much to-do at the government Cheese Grading Centre, he was notified that his prize was no more than "substandard Stilton," and that he had been the victim of charlatans who exploited the mystery about Blue Vinny so they could pass off Stilton rejects as the folkloric Dorset cheese so many connoisseurs hankered after.

A WORLD WITHOUT BLUE VINNY   According to British writer John Arlott, Dorset Blue Vinny possessed—when authentic—"essentially a male taste," and it was his considered opinion that no one who had "a relishing palate" should leave this world without having known the sublime delight of his favorite cheese. To have tasted a Blue Vinny made "by a well-to-do farmer for himself and a very special friend, is to be spoilt for ever more," said André Simon, founder of the Wine and Food Society. An even greater pity, it seems to me, is that Blue Dorset itself is spoiled forevermore, the victim of modern times when too few things are permitted to happen naturally. A beautiful Dorset cheese, white as chalk and with, as Simon suggested, a royal vein of Cordon Bleu running through it, is virtually a thing of the past. Now, candid cheesemongers will tell you how rare they are.

For Ambrose Heath, another eloquent Briton, the accolade "finest of all blue cheeses" went to Wensleydale, now fairly easily available without the visible mold. At the time the Normans arrived in York, however, the monks who established Jervaulx Abbey in North Riding brought the French recipe for veined cheese to their Cistercian retreat, and it was passed on from generation to generation of farmers after the abbey was destroyed in the sixteenth century. Blue Wensleydale was originally made of sheep's milk. Today, it looks a little like Stilton, has the same shape, and is made of cow's milk; it can also seem creamier than its onetime rival, and sometimes has a little more tang.*

* Blue Wensleydale is a specialty at Standings, a shop which opened in Harrowgate, Yorkshire, a century ago and is known among some Londoners and other epicurean Britishers as the "Fortnum and Mason's of the North"—a tribute to the excellence of its gastronomic inventory, including a wide range of cheeses. As for the Blue Vinny of Dorset, there is said to be a monthly ration available to those who move quickly, at Wells Stores, Streatley, near Reading.

Of course most blue-veined cheese that is easily available today is produced in spotless modern factories, and much of it is made according to formulas arrived at by talented dairy scientists, who often believe the old methods of chance have been vastly overrated as guarantees of superlative cheeses. Dr. George Reinbold of Iowa State University has said that "if we had milking sheep running over our campus" he and his fellow faculty technicians could produce a blue-veined cheese "practically identical to Roquefort." What they have produced is a recipe widely used throughout the United States for turning cow's milk into a cheese with handsome, mottled color distinctions, and with dependable uniformity. Made in a number of states and sold under several trademarks, it is apt to lie sharply rather than zestily on the taste buds, and therefore is not the paragon to serve as dessert that good farmhouse blues can be.

The average Blue to be found in a supermarket dairy case is often good in salad dressings, can add zest to cocktail dips based on sour cream or Cream Cheese, or becomes a mellow spread when mixed with sweet butter. The best of these come from such natural caves as those along the Mississippi at Nauvoo, Illinois, at Faribault, Minnesota, or from the milk of Oregon cows which is turned into a Blue often rated by enthusiasts as somewhere between Roquefort and Gorgonzola in flavor. Midwest manufacturers also produce a domestic veined cheese that bears the name of its Italian original.

BLUES FROM OTHER SOURCES   Among European Blues are Sweden's Ädelost, which has 50 percent fat and weighs two and a half kilograms, and a slightly less salty variation to which the English name Stilton is gratuitously given. Denmark also produces two with marbled color—the widely distributed Danablu, which its makers sometimes refer to as (here we go again) "the king of the blues"; and Mycella, about twice the size of Danablu, slightly creamier in appearance, and with a greenish rather than a bluish cast. One of the best from Denmark is sold in America under the label Blue Castello. The result of a combination in a single cheese of two molds, Penicillium camemberti and Penicillium roqueforti, it is a smooth, buttery, and delightful dinner cheese. When Minnesota and Wisconsin food scientists produced a similar two-mold formula in the 1950's they found themselves ahead of the times. "They were quite successful," George Reinbold said of these innovators, "but the public was not ready for a white 'Blue.' " It was just as true that commercial cheesemakers of that period found the process expensive and apparently not worth the necessary effort at promoting the new product.

Blues are turned out in all the cheese-producing countries of the world, including Czechoslovakia, Finland, Iceland, Israel, and South Africa.

In southern Quebec, a short drive north of Vermont's ski country, there is an isolated monastery whose steeples are reflected in the clear blue water of Lake Memphremagog. There in the basement of the Abbey of St. Benoit du Lac the Benedictine monks sell cheese they make in the long dairy building just down the slope. They have named their creamy blue cheese Ermite, as if in honor of the order's founder, who had been a hermit in the Apennines. Like many commercial Blues, it may not have the gentle grace of evening vespers, but its tang and aftertaste recommend it to accompaniment by a country wine of France or, perhaps, the mellow cider also made by the monks of St. Benoit.

The making of mold-mottled cheeses is no longer purely a matter of trial and error, as it has been in the past; that is clear. There is an abundance now manufactured in various degrees of flavor. But a faultless blue cheese is hard to come by, no matter in what country or by whom. And when it comes to those few good ones that are still made by hand, it may be a matter of luck. As a Stilton maker named Mrs. Musser said of her cheeses, "Except for the fact they make no noise, they are more trouble than babies."

5

Holey
Cheeses

The mountain republic of Switzerland is even more distinguished for its cheeses than it is for its watches. Watches may be made in every other country in the world without claiming to be products of Swiss workmanship. But a cheese with well-shaped holes, no matter where it is turned out, is usually assumed to be—or indeed is advertised as—Swiss cheese.

In truth, "Swiss cheese" is a misnomer. The two best-known cheeses made in Switzerland are properly differentiated as Emmenthaler, the large flat wheel with holes that are large and regular of contour, and Gruyère, not nearly so large and with fewer, smaller holes, and a rind that is wrinkled instead of smooth as is that of Emmenthaler. The virtually universal popularity of Emmenthaler has created so great a market among consumers that there seems never to be quite enough of it. The country Byron called "the most romantic region in the world" has produced the most imitated of cheeses, and yet the great 200-pound wheels from the Emmenthal, with their great round holes, have proved themselves to be unduplicatable, however hard the copyists try.

It is not that Alpine cheesemakers have more experience. Although they do like to remind visitors that when the mountain land was known as Helvetia their dairy techniques were eons old, they were not the first to make cheese by a long shot. But by the time the Romans conquered Helvetia the cheese discovered by the invaders was so good it became a famous export immediately, known by the Caesars and their cooks as Caseus Helveticus, or Swiss cheese. Swiss dairymen seem to prove the adage that the more things change the more they remain the same.

The difference is subtle. If that term, Swiss cheese, is used to describe any cheese with holes, the boast in the valley of the Emme River is that "anybody can make the holes . . . only Switzerland can make the flavor." Similar claims about taste are made for other cheeses, as we have seen, but the Emme Valley, running north out of the heart of Switzerland, has its own climate and its distinctive Swiss cows that graze on high pastures, rich in aromatic grass and the flowers of Alpine meadows. These are the factors that may have an effect on flavor rather than on the development of holes. Yet that development, caused by natural pockets of gas, is a vital part of the making of a cheese that has the texture, consistency, and taste of a well-produced Switzerland wheel.

All these characteristics help to make Emmenthaler the superior cooking cheese that it is, as well as distinguishing it among table cheeses. It takes eight to twelve weeks to properly develop the "eyes," as dairymen describe the gas pockets, and it takes an expert, thumping the outside of the wheel and listening to the sound, to know just when the eyes are sufficiently open. These holes are the evidence of perfect fermentation. Perfectly aged cheeses undergo months in high humidity and under controlled temperature, and a wise consumer should make his purchase in bulk, patronizing a cheesemonger whose word about age can be accepted. For those who don't care about well-developed flavors, Emmenthalers that have aged only two months often are sliced and packaged in vacuum-sealed envelopes for sale in mass-oriented retail markets—where blandness of all kinds prevails.

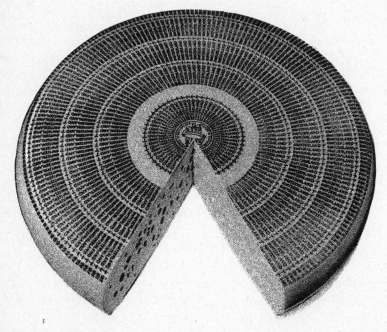

EMMENTHALER

HOLEY CHEESES IN THE UNITED STATES   An effort to reproduce good Emmenthalers in the United States began about 1850 when Adam Blumer, a man from Switzerland's German-speaking region, homesteaded in southern Wisconsin. He milked five cows, local records indicate, and he made big wheels airy with holes in the old-country way—as eventually did many other Swiss who also pioneered in Green County. Blumer's five cows multiplied, and so did Wisconsin dairymen. The Midwest became a thriving agricultural region that for half a century or so produced fine rind-cured cheeses that were Swiss in almost everything except their place of manufacture.

Similarly, other immigrants from the Alps have been among the cheesemakers who produce domestic "Swiss" in Ohio, Illinois, Iowa, and other prairie states. In Pennsylvania, Amish farmers make a "Baby Swiss," rubbery in texture, that is considered by some to be highly flavored. In Utah and Wyoming, where the landscape is more assertive than in the horse and buggy Mennonite regions, there are mountain dairies whose operators pride themselves on having cows that graze on pastures as high in the Rockies as any in the Switzerland cantons from which their ancestors may have come. One of those dairymen summed it up: "The flavor and texture of our Swiss cheese," Wallace Parrish of Utah's Cache Valley said, "speaks loudly of the pure, sweet, fresh milk—I suppose you could call it 'mountain milk' because it's made of ice cold, crystal clear mountain water and grasses that grow in high meadows."

But the old mountain methods of transforming milk were foreign to what had become the American way. New factory equipment made it possible to triple production of domestic "Swiss" cheese in the thirty years after World War II. Instead of the traditional patient brining and brushing of round, flat cheeses, the factory system turned out holey cheeses in giant, rindless blocks which could be efficiently stored and transported, and which —having no rind—eliminated "waste."

WHAT "IMPORTED" MEANS   In many cases the use of the words "Imported Swiss" on packages means only that the country which produced it was not the United States; much of such cheese is manufactured in rindless blocks and is essentially no different from copies made in America. Denmark's Samsoe may also look like Emmenthal, but its flavor is considered closer to Edam. One of the best of the imports is called Jarlsberg, a very open Norwegian cheese that still comes to this country in wheels and has a flavor all its own. But, according to one of New York's most active retailers, Jarlsberg has become so popular that distributors began to "price it out of its league." This man said he had begun to recommend

Irish "Swiss" to consumers interested in less expensive versions. But the Irish product is softer and slightly grainier. In Europe, the Swedish-made Grevéost, almost identical to Jarlsberg, is another readily available substitute. In Sweden itself, one of the most popular dairy products is Herrgardsost, the "Elite" version of which is compared favorably to Switzerland's best. Other factory copies of genuine Emmenthaler—somewhat rubbery and certainly not to be confused with the original—are produced from Iceland to Australia, including an Israeli variation called Promised Land.

The same economic pressures that caused some Swiss to emigrate to America impelled others to cross the Alps into France, and Emmental Français (as it is known to Frenchmen) has been made for one hundred years in the mountains of Savoy, Franche-Comté, Burgundy, and as far west as Brittany, the method being an almost exact copy of the Swiss original. Until this emigration the common "Swiss cheese" of France had not been a version of Emmenthal, and it had been known generically as Gruyère.

The name comes from Switzerland's Gruyère Valley, not far from Lausanne, where French-speaking Swiss dairymen were making big wheels of cheese in the Middle Ages. By the reign of Louis XI the techniques had been spirited west and Frenchmen had perfected versions known as Gruyère de Comté, after the mountainous part of Burgundy, and as Beaufort, named for the French town not far from Lake Annecy. As the original of these, the Gruyères of Switzerland are wheels weighing 77 pounds, or less than half that at which Emmenthalers tip the scales. Gruyères are fermented at lower temperatures and therefore produce less acid, thus forming fewer and smaller holes. The special fruity flavor and bouquet is the result of the briny, slightly moist rind that develops in contrast to the dry exteriors of Emmenthalers. The small holes in Comtés make them near look-alikes for their Swiss cousins, but in Beauforts the holes are almost nonexistent.

The cheeses from eastern Switzerland called Appenzeller or Appenzell (sometimes translated as abbot's cell, referring to the Abbey of St. Gallen) have very few scattered eyes, only about the size of a pea, and a subtle tang in their taste that is caused by the use of wine and spices in their curing. This spirited daily washing results in a deep rind and a softer interior than either Emmenthal or Gruyère. Appenzell is a superlative cheese for lusty nibbling, having fruity flavor, and it is eaten in its home canton, and that of St. Gallen, accompanied by caraway seeds and mustard, often washed down with Alpine cider or apple juice.

All of these cheeses are important in the national cuisine. In fact,

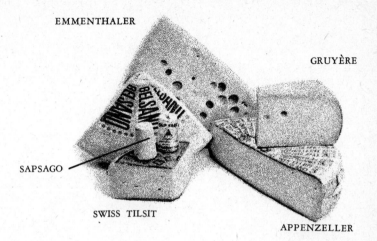

EMMENTHALER

GRUYÈRE

SAPSAGO

SWISS TILSIT

APPENZELLER

as one small Swiss cookbook from Berne says, "There is no other country in the world which can offer so many different kinds of regional cheese dishes," adding modestly, "in so small a space as Switzerland." There are dozens of cheese soups, of which the Swiss in their wintry wisdom are so sensibly fond; dozens of fritters and croquettes; Swiss steaks that contain no meat; scores of pies and tarts and cakes and fondues in variety, none of which taste quite as good as when they are prepared in Switzerland of native cheese.

EATING MELTED SWISSES "Fondue," says the little cookbook, "should really head the procession of cheese dishes by reason of its fame." Popular as it now is in the Western world, fame may have come late to fondue. It was known in the seventeenth century, according to Brillat-Savarin, but wide acceptance seems to have come only after the publication, in 1824, of *The Physiology of Taste,* in which the noted French epicure gave the fondue recipe of a Swiss friend. Gradually readers passed the word, and in the two hundred years since millions have made the melting of cheese a convivial indoor sport.

The popularity of skiing brought Americans a new term, *après ski,* which heightened interest in fondues as well as a simpler way of serving molten cheese called raclette. Those who as children had read Johanna Spyrie's *Heidi* may have been reminded of a scene in a mountain chalet when the old grandfather melted cheese at the fireplace. That was the raclette of the nineteenth century. But even before World War II the Swiss balloonist Jean Picard introduced raclette on the campus of the University of Minnesota, and his guests were fascinated as he performed the simple ceremony of melting and scraping.

Raclette is a festive thing when half a wheel of cheese is systematically melted before an open fireplace. The word "raclette" comes from the French and means "scraper." Fromage à Raclette is made by mountain farmers in the canton of Valais (called Wallis by the German-speaking Swiss), which is south of the Gruyère and Emmenthal country. A large-size wheel is called Walliser-Raclette-Käse. In wheels of 20 pounds or so such cheese is often labeled Bagnes, after a village a few miles west of the Matterhorn; another form is known as Gomser. Any one of these mountain cheeses can be used in an assortment served at the end of dinner, but any one of them also may be the *pièce de résistance* when it boils like pale-gold lava on a sizzling hot plate, accompanied by new potatoes, white onions, and sourish gherkins.

On many tourist trails through Switzerland there are dozens of cafés or restaurants at which to try raclette, and the only variation in the recipe is the source of heat. At one of the upstairs restaurants in Berne the gas flame was at counter level; the chef skillfully poised half of a Valais cheese before the flickering heat and deftly scraped cheese onto a hot plate as the melting progressed. When he had a creamy, bubbly mass he added steaming white potatoes and dispatched a waitress with a serving that was still seething when placed before the guest. In a procedure not so colorful, a 500-degree oven can take the place of an open fire and the cheese can be sliced and melted directly on heat-resistant plates, then rushed to the table.

RACLETTE

MAKING RACLETTE

In Geneva, particularly, numerous restaurants offer *beefsteak au fromage,* which is innocent of meat. It is composed of ample half-inch slices of Gruyère, sometimes dipped in a beer batter to which egg whites have been added for extra lightness. Thus encased, the cheese is fried in very hot oil and is served, in an ornate version, topped by sautéed mushrooms and baked eggs.

The thing to remember in following any recipe that calls for the use of one of Switzerland's cheeses is the need to have a cheese that has been carefully matured. Young Emmenthalers and Gruyères don't melt as well as older ones; they are apt to separate into rubbery strands. To get Emmenthaler at its best, be sure you see it cut from a wheel that has been stamped radially with the word "Switzerland" repeated over and over again. Be sure the Gruyère you buy is certified "Natural Gruyère," as opposed to processed Gruyère. Look the cheese in the eyes; they should have a *slight* gleam—no more.

Swiss law has established rigid standards, and cheesemakers are paid according to the number of points scored by each ripened wheel in government tests. Flavor and body and color are equally important, but so are the number, size, shape, and placement of eyes. Holey cheeses are judged according to aesthetic values, as well as those of content. They are, Dr. George Reinbold once told me, "truly for artists, gourmets, gourmands, epicures—and appreciative gluttons."

6

Telling the Goats
from the Sheep

In regions of rugged or arid terrain, where cows could not survive, sheep and goats still make possible the production of cheeses that are among the world's best, and most luxurious. They cost more because of the relative scarcity of the milk—cows give more than five times as much as goats, for instance. Therefore the cheeses that result are fewer in number and higher in price. Yet the piquancy of flavor and aroma of the best of them is so appealing that production has been stretched to its limit and beyond.

Today millions of gallons of sheep's milk go into the making of Roquefort, and two-thirds of all the world's goat cheeses are made in France. Yet it is in the Middle East that both animals were first domesticated, and where sheep and goat cheeses are still more common than those made from the milk of cows. For thousands of years, around the Mediterranean littoral, most of the cheese of each of the countries has come from goats, sheep, or Asiatic buffaloes.

The Berber tribes of northern Africa make Touareg, whose soft curds are coagulated with leaves of the korourou tree, then dipped on mats and dried in the sun. The national cheese of Egypt is called Domiati and is popular in other sunstruck countries where Arabic is spoken. It is often made from the milk of buffaloes and, when not sold fresh, is pickled in salt-whey or salt-milk brine, a technique for preserving cheese that is common to most of the countries of the Middle East. In Turkey, cheese manufacturers stimulate milk production by advancing money to their farmers to tide them over from fall to spring so that plenty of milk from ewes, buffaloes, and cows will be at hand for the making of tubs of white Peynir, or a sharper, veined cheese called Tulum, named after the goatskin in which this crumbly but buttery, gray-white cheese matures.

GREECE'S MOST COMMON EXPORTS Small quantities of Turkey's Peynir are exported to Greece, but that is a little like carrying coals to

Newcastle. Almost every rural Greek family owns a goat and makes its own cheese. In addition, commercial production recently has increased to the extent that exports to the United States more than tripled in the 1970's. The two most common types—both available in many American shops— are Feta and Kasseri. Traditionally made of goat or sheep milk, Feta is essential to Greek cookery. If you are really lucky enough to have a store that knows its Mediterranean gastronomy, you may be offered mature Feta that is rich and creamy, like that which is turned out in small quantities in the hills around Delphi and Mount Parnassus.

As one of the so-called pickled cheeses, Feta is white, somewhat soft and porous, and quite salty; it crumbles easily with a fork. The best Feta to come to this country travels in kegs of milk in which the cheese sloshes to keep it from dehydrating. It is also canned or bottled in household amounts, and there are small rounds from Zanthe that are matured in vats of olive oil.

Some tyrophiles consider Kasseri, Feta's companion, to be best when made of sheep's milk, but there is an acceptable cow's-milk version made in America. It is interesting to note that it is not always perfect in its native habitat—some travelers in Greece have found Kasseri (in Turkey a related cheese is called Kaser) to be so soapy in texture as to be almost inedible. To be good it should be just as white as Feta but harder (somewhat like an immature Parmesan), so it slices well. Kasseri and other hard Greek cheeses like Haloumi, Kashkaval, and Kefalotyri are delicious when cut into cubes and grilled over charcoal, or under an indoor broiler, or fried in oil or butter, then served exquisitely hot with a squeeze of lemon juice.

Claudia Roden, who grew up in Egypt, tells us in her superlative *A Book of Middle Eastern Food* how such cheeses were treated in the nineteenth century. The instructions for sizzling cheese tidbits stipulated that they be wrapped in genuine silver paper before putting them on the fire; when the paper glowed with heat one knew the cheese was properly done. A Turkish cookbook, she adds, specified that this sputteringly hot morsel was considered the kind of stimulant that would enhance the sex life of married men.

Unexposed to heat, these Mediterranean favorites are all especially good cheeses to serve as snacks, and they have their counterparts in many Old World countries. Sirene is the Balkan version of Feta and is available in America labeled "Bulgarian white-brined cow's-milk cheese." Bulgarian Kashkaval, made of sheep's milk, is also exported, and there are local versions of this pale-yellow loaf throughout the Middle East and in Russia as well. The fresh soft goat's-milk cheese of the Balkans and Central Europe is known as Bryndza. Hungary's Liptó is also soft and the product of sheep, and it is the basis for the authentic Liptauer, which combines

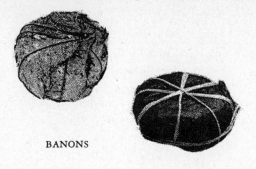

BANONS

cheese, butter, rosy paprika, mustard, caraway seeds, grated onion, and anchovy paste. In America we have adapted the recipe as a cocktail spread, called Liptauer, made by mashing and seasoning small rectangles of cream cheese, and millions consider the result a New World idea.

In Europe generally, many soft, spreadable goat-and-sheep cheeses are available, and they are in most cases the initial form taken by unformed coagulated curds that, when allowed to ripen, may mature into cakes firm enough to slice or, eventually, they become so hard they are ideal for grating. Pecorino Toscano, for instance, is very soft and mild in the early fall, but it moves on to adolescence and adulthood, just as Parmesan does. The generic term for this rural cheese derives from the Italian word for sheep. The firm, creamy-white cylinders made near Rome, labeled "Pecorino Romano," are those most commonly exported to this country. Nearly half of all the Pecorino produced in Italy comes from sheep of the province of Lazio, south of Rome, and from Sardinia, where each shepherd makes cheese that is known sentimentally as the "flower of Sardinia." This Fiore Sardo is made anywhere that sheep may be grazing, and goes to market in the handmade individual baskets in which it drains.

On the island of Corsica herdsmen habitually make Broccio (or Brocciu), a fresh sheep-and-goat cheese that is redolent of herbs. Sometimes it is stuffed in freshly picked tomatoes, or used as a filling for ravioli. It also is served in springtime by Corsican cooks with a sprinkling of sugar, or it is mixed with fruits or compotes, and often blended into a local cake called *Le friadone*. Spaniards, for their part, often mix their fresh white goat cheeses with wild honey.

THREE KINDS OF MILK IN A SINGLE CHEESE On the Spanish northern border, in the mountainous province of Asturias, goat milk and sheep milk are combined with that of cows, pressed into round forms in farm kitchens, salted, aged in limestone caves until they look like France's

Roqueforts—but, as one English traveler put it, "taste more like Stilton" when they are eaten with a draft of country cider. This Queso de Cabrales is named for a village, hidden among the trout streams of the Cantabrian Alps, called Areñas de Cabrales. Most of it ends on local tables, but some appears in distant markets, wrapped in leaves.

In France, especially in the south-central highlands, the farmhouse goat cheeses take the shape of small rustic disks and are also wrapped in leaves. Again like those of the Spanish border, many French cheeses are made from several kinds of milk. In Provence, those called Banons are made alternately of milk from goats or sheep—or cows—depending upon seasonal availability. So are the Cabécous, still produced on farms in the old domain of Eleanor of Aquitaine. In the French Basque country sheep's milk gives aroma and tangy flavor to medium-size wheels under such classic names as Laruns, or Esbareich. The small disks called Picodons are properly made only of goat's milk, but the Provence delicacy known as Poivre d'Âne, sprinkled with herbs, is made of sheep's milk in spring, of goat's in summer, and a cow's-milk version is available throughout the year. In the French Alps, and Savoy, sheep's-milk cheeses that develop interior molds are called *bleus de brebis,* and those of goat's milk are classified as *persillés,* because their greenish mottling suggests the leaves of curly parsley.

THE INCREASING DEMAND FOR GOAT CHEESES   Regardless of whether or not these cheeses turn blue (or green), they are increasingly dependent on cow's milk. On his mountain farm above the village of Appenzell, near the Swiss-Austrian border, Alois Koch has maintained an old tradition by making Ziegenkäse every summer. Most of his cheese combines the milk of goats with that of cows, yet it is one of those types that once was made of either goat or sheep milk exclusively. Koch and his teenage son, Meinhard, today might be turning out pure goat's-milk cheese in their Alpine dairy were it not for the fact that the demand exceeds the supply. More and more, cheeses bearing a "goat" or "sheep" label are being diluted with the more easily available cow's milk. Yet paradoxically the demand for goat's-milk cheeses, particularly, is increasing. Epicures cry out for them, and there is also the fervor of true believers —many health food addicts prefer goat's-milk cheese because it has smaller fat globules and a higher mineral count.*

The interest in natural foods that increased so in the 1970's sharpened the appetite for cheese in general and—as it encouraged experiment and search for variety—it widened the market for many cheeses that always before had been local delicacies to be sought by knowledgeable travelers. The jet-age travel boom helped to stimulate such appetites, and imported foods of various kinds gained more and more space in retail outlets.

MONTRACHET DUSTED WITH CINDERS

NEW DOMESTIC PRODUCTION Newly educated palates also sparked American producers in the last quarter of the century, and for the first time there was domestic goat cheese available across the country. In Oregon's Willamette Valley, in eastern Iowa, and in south-central Wisconsin it was produced for wide distribution. In the latter dairyland Daniel Considine, who started raising goats as a 4-H project with one Toggenburg doe (of the breed that originated in the Alpine district where the Kochs make cheese), built up his herd in a few years to two hundred and thirty, mainly because of the new cheese markets. "Seventy-five percent of our milk goes into cheese," he observed one winter day. "Much more work goes into

---

* Goat's milk, Raymond Sokolov has written, "has the peculiar odor and taste you may already know from having tasted feta or some other goat cheese. There is an edge to it. You are, in fact, tasting three fatty acids with the goaty names caproic, caprylic, and capric. . . . Dairymen say that most cow's milk is a hard-curd milk, while the milk of goats is a soft-curd milk. . . . This is why goat's milk has long been prescribed for infants with sensitive digestion. And it explains the normally softer, more crumbly texture of goat cheeses, which do not harden as cow's-milk cheeses do when they are completely drained and have the whey pressed out of them."

CHÈVRES:

PYRAMIDE

MONTRACHET

CROTTIN DE CHAVIGNOL

each gallon of goat milk than is needed for cow's milk, and there's the problem of seasonal breeding, besides. Does breed from the end of August through January, and that means almost no milk those months. But goat cheese is great cheese—that makes it worth doing."

The Considine cheese, like some other domestic versions, is made according to an American Munster recipe; it is cured in salt brine and ripens as a small semihard wheel. Goat's-milk Cream Cheese is made in Westminster West, Vermont, among other places; some originates in Runnemede, New Jersey. Another made in Pennsylvania follows the formula for Brick cheese. Goat Cheddar is produced in California. And in Winger, a town in northern Minnesota, Clayton Rawhouser in 1975 began producing a goat's-milk Cheddar type, a goat's-milk Colby, and others seasoned with onions, hot peppers, or toasted soybeans. The American types lack the musty aroma of most European goat products, as well as the traditional French forms of truncated pyramids, squat cones, or log shapes that are pierced by a horizontal stick to help hold them together.

Neither do they hint at the unique character that makes some Scandinavian goat cheese anathema to those who haven't spent a lifetime in the Arctic ski regions. The Norwegian Gjetost (goat cheese), for instance, is laced with all kinds of energy reinforcements. But it is also uncheeselike— brown, sticky, sweetish in flavor. Properly made, it is a combination of boiled goat's-milk whey, caramelized lactose, added fats, and sometimes brown sugar. It seems to me unfortunate that it has no taste of cheese as most of us have come to think of it, nor even of candy. Perhaps, as someone said, it demands a palate to be acquired only in the fjords.

Gjetost's smell is not as pungent as the most assertive cheeses, but then all such morsels deserve to be in a class by themselves.

7

Assertive in Flavor and Aroma

No cheese is more assertively American than the neat, moist, rosy-orange-skinned parallelepiped with a garland of a name, Liederkranz. The German word for "wreath of song" has become an American label that often causes travelers whose own countries produce exemplary cheeses to speak admiringly of this New World "original"—that is, a cheese at least as different from its relatives as is the average American citizen from his Old World forebears.

Its likeness—the quality that reminds one of other products—is its pronounced aromatic smell emanating from strong, pungent flavor. Liederkranz belongs to the category that includes, among others, Limburger, Bierkäse, aged Brick, German Handkäse, Livarot, Maroilles, Munster, and Romadur. All announce themselves without modesty to the olfactory glands, and each leaves its own distinctive aftertase on the palate. But Liederkranz (mildest in this group) has a singular genesis. Its beginning stems from the popularity of cheese among German immigrants in New York toward the end of the nineteenth century.

In Switzerland, Germany, Austria, and other countries of Central Europe, strong cheeses have been popular for uncounted generations. To appease this appetite the owner of a Manhattan delicatessen ordered supplies from abroad and also maintained a partnership in a small cheese factory not far away in Monroe, New York. There, among expert dairymen, worked Swiss-born Emil Frey, destined to become the originator of one of America's most famous products.

Frey once shared his memory of this time with an acquaintance. "My boss, Mr. Todi, had a good demand for an imported cheese called Bismarck Schlosskäse," he said, "but three out of four times when a shipment of this cheese arrived in New York harbor it was so badly spoiled that it had to be thrown away. When he asked us to try to duplicate the German cheese, I started on this project, and I worked at it whenever I had time outside my regular duties."

In 1892, after three years of experimenting, Frey finally arrived at a formula for a cheese that Todi considered even better than the Schlosskäse he had been importing. For a year or so, he sold the new cheese without name or label to an increasing number of his delicatessen customers. "Then Mr. Todi gave packages of the cheese as presents to members of a singing society to which he belonged," Emil Frey remembered. "They were so taken with it that we called it after their club, the famous New York Liederkranz—and that's how our cheese got its 'foreign' name."

But as the name became more American with the increasing acceptance of the cheese throughout the country, the need for more milk increased, making it necessary to move the Liederkranz factory west, where dairy farms were more productive. This American cheese has thus been made in Van Wert, Ohio, for more than a half-century, and Liederkranz workers feel so closely identified with some of the soft-ripened cheeses of Europe that they put up the money which paid for the statue of Marie Harel in Vimoutiers, Normandy, the market town for Camembert.

The Liederkranz process is a variation on that of several Normandy products. After the curd takes shape and drains in rectangular forms for several days, the block of soft cream cheese that has evolved is removed from the mold, salted regularly, and cut in smaller rectangles. About three weeks after the milk arrives at the Van Wert dairy, packaged Liederkranzes are ready for shipment and are stamped with a "pull date," to indicate the maximum age for appetizing eating. It is the responsibility of Liederkranz representatives to check the coded dates on the packages, replacing outdated cheeses when necessary. When fully ripened, Liederkranz has an assertive aroma but its taste is mellow and smooth, its center creamy, and even the rind should be delicious. Far more than Schlosskäse, after which it was modeled, it is a cheese for everyone.

LIMBURGER

Schlosskäse, the strong-flavored German cheese whose name means castle cheese, is the prototype in the dairyland along the German-Austrian border, versions of which are made in Hungary as well as Bavaria and the Austrian Alps. On the West Coast, Schloss cheese is produced in Marin County, California, and is dated, like Liederkranz, while a delicately flavored relative, called Old Heidelberg, is made in Lena, Illinois. Americans also produce strong cheeses with other ethnic backgrounds. Among Scandinavians who settled in the Middle West it was once traditional to make Gammelost (old cheese) in farm kitchens. Dave Wood, who grew up in rural Wisconsin, once wrote that his mother's old cheese "smeared on hot homemade bread and served up with black coffee brought each of us closer to Valhalla than any of us deserved." The making of Gammelost, he said, was an annual ritual which usually began on a cold day in January, and the process was as simple as making any Pot Cheese.

"After a week and a half," Wood wrote in a memory of his Wisconsin boyhood, "the cheese began to 'work,' and we began to eat. It was still white, like cottage cheese, but kind of gooey. The smell was pungent, but not bad, reminiscent of old Limburger." And, like Limburger, this Norwegian farm cheese developed more character with each passing day. Cheeses like these lend themselves to nostalgic memories.

Recalling an upstate New York boyhood, Maurice Brockway told of a German-American neighbor who made Limburgers and aged them in his own natural cave. "Water from natural springs dripped down the walls and ran off in shallow trenches dug into the floor. The dampness was all-important to the proper curing of the cheese, which was arranged on countless shelves. . . . Grandfather selected his cheese from the six-weeks-old shelf, and he always bought one for me from the two-weeks old." Today German-American Limburgers are made in the same region and distributed throughout the country, to be eaten with pumpernickel bread and washed down with beer by connoisseurs who may or may not have European backgrounds.

THE MAKING OF LIMBURGERS   It may be true that it takes a certain kind of temperament, as well as an insatiable appreciation of beer, to be thoroughly persuaded by Limburgers. But it is also true that these aromatic, strong-tasting cheeses are bad only when badly handled. They originated on the farms of eastern Belgium and take their names from the old province of Limburg, where the teutonic Flemish culture is prevalent.

There are variations in the methods of different cheesemakers, but all Limburger is categorized as a surface-ripened cheese. It is usually brushed with brine during a curing period of eight weeks and conditioned to last several months if kept under refrigeration at about 40 degrees Fahrenheit. Microorganisms ripening on the surface, some experts explain, are responsible for the characteristic flavor and scent. The development of acid-producing yeast is followed by the extensive growth of *Bacterium linens,* which gives the small rectangular cheeses a luxuriant surface mold; and because this external growth is not removed before the cheese is wrapped in parchment or foil or wax-coated paper, the strong pungent flavor of Limburger is enhanced.

Cheese with similar traits was made by Belgian monks in the Middle Ages, and even today many Walloon cheeses have too much character to be easily tolerated beyond their town gates. The cheese that is named for the city of Herve is "much too rambunctious," a Belgian living in New York said, to cross the Atlantic. A good Herve is a cube of soft buttery paste weighing about a half-pound, with a rosy ocher crust (somewhat like Liederkranz) and *odeur puissant,* a term used by its makers without apology.

A good deal of Herve is produced in Belgium, but most of the exported Limburger comes not from its native heath near Liège—it is shipped from factories in Austria, Germany, and Switzerland, and the variations of Limburger include Allgäuer, Backsteiner, Harracher, Hochstrasser, Kremstaler, Romadur, Schützenkäse, Schwarzenberger, and Weisslacker.

Switzerland's cheesemakers, who set such high standards for flavorsome wheels with limpid holes, are also adept at copying the products of other dairymen. Their Romadur, produced from a formula that originated in Germany, is described by some as "a little more discreet in taste" than Limburger. And so it is. Whether it is made in Austria, Bavaria, or Hungary, Romadur is also less salty than Limburger; it is apt to have color added to the milk and to have less smear on the surface. In the United States it has been imported from a cheesemaker near Munich (among others) who wraps his Romadurs in red and gold paper that bears the Kasimir trademark.

STRONG CHEESE OF FRANCE   In the early 1970's a new trademark for a strongly flavored product of Auvergne, from whence come also Cantals, *bleus,* St. Nectaires, Murols, and Gaprons, is Paillor, a word that refers to the straw mat with which the cheese is packed. Shaped like a small discus, the brine-washed Paillor, exuding a musty pungency, was said to have been developed as "a cross between Limburger and Pont l'Évêque."

Livarot, made in Normandy, is also often compared with Pont l'Évêque, from the neigboring Auge Valley. Generally bound with split

LIVAROT

LIMBURGER

reed ties to support their cylindrical shape, the Livarots that come from the Calvados town of that name are assertive cheeses, even if less pointedly so than some from Belgium and Germany. The curing cellars for Livarot are not ventilated, and the aromas thus contained help give the cheese its strong, piquant flavor. A British expert on cheeses, T. A. Layton, described the smell as "like the odor of slowly rotting apples, combined with ammonia, a whiff of ripe Camembert and a slight suggestion of seaside ozone."

Needless to say, Livarot tastes far better than any such attempt to define its smell would indicate—it is among the best of the world's cheeses when properly attended. Whether sampled in its normal quarter-pound size or in miniature cylinders, Livarot is appreciated by many people who remove the crust before spreading the firm but creamy interior paste on bread; then they eat it while sipping Calvados, the one drink that may be sufficiently abrasive to mate well with an aggressive morsel.

Livarot is one of the very oldest of French cheeses. One of the newer ones, created after the Second World War, is made in the Laonnais country of the north and is called Baguette Laonnaise or Baguette de Thiérache. It is a French version of Herve, or a Limburger with a little higher fat content. This tangy Baguette is also comparable to Maroilles (sometimes spelled Marolles), which in its turn is somewhat similar to Pont l'Évêque, though stronger. The name comes from the Abbey of Maroilles, and years ago the cheese was dubbed Vieux Puant—"old stinker"—by appreciative epicures.

Several other similar creations of French dairymen—Quart, Mignon, and Sorbais—are produced in the same region. Gris de Lille is in a class by itself, having a scent that needs no translation: *très violent de fermentation.* And the village of Rollot in Picardy is the home of a strong-flavored cheese that usually bears the hamlet's name, but is known sometimes as Guerbigny when it is packaged in heart-shaped form. In Franche-Comté, the dairy school at Mamirolle has been experimenting with a version of Limburger that has a fine, rosy exterior, very little aroma, and a taste that is described as gentle and strong at the same time.

Another variant of Limburger, called Void after a market town in Alsace-Lorraine, was popular locally but is made less and less. Mondseer Schachtelkäse is said to be Austria's counterpart of Limburger, but it has been much tamed for import into this country; too often, in fact, the Mondseer made available in New York has been nondescript.

With the exception of Liederkranz, the best of these cheeses are to be found in the United States only under rare circumstances. But for the victims of the mercantile campaigns for blandness in flavors—to please the greatest number—there may be hope in the proliferation of cheese specialty stores across the United States. A taste of one mildly assertive cheese deserves another, and suggests a progressively increasing appetite for heightened flavor. Therein may be the way to influence importers and cheesemongers. There is, of course, nothing like being assertive.

8

Monastery Products, and Related Types

There is reason to think that the poet who cherished "wealth of fruitful meadow, blessings of dew and shade" had cheese on his mind. Pastures that shimmer with dampness in the dawn and offer islands of foliage as escape from the heat of the day provide the contentment that encourages grazing animals to produce an abundance of milk. And it is that abundance which in its turn encourages cheesemakers, whether they be dairy-minded monks or ordinary farmers. In the Middle Ages dozens of agrarian cloisters throughout Europe began to develop firm, sliceable cheeses that have become models for commercial producers. In pastoral countries like the Netherlands excess milk long ago brought about the classic semihard cheeses known as Gouda and Edam. More than other things, they symbolize the wealth Dutch dairymen find in the meadows they believe to be especially endowed.

It may seem romantic to some, but there are at least a few sober, white-jacketed scientists for whom this vision has the validity of analytic geometry. The Dutch government not so long ago set some chemists to the task of determining the factors that make Holland's semihard cheeses what they are. The august commission's findings confirmed a belief long held in the Netherlands that only cows nourished by the lush pastures of the provinces of Noordholland and Friesland can produce milk of the specific quality and character necessary for semihard cheese like Edam. They moved the same cattle to other fields, established identical milking conditions, and followed the same cheesemaking procedures absolutely. The results were satisfactory in a way, the scientists reported, but the cheese that lacked the influence of the proper fruitful meadows lacked the unique Edam taste.

Influences that are more technical also have their effect as well; there's no doubt about that. Any semihard Edam with an impeccable, mellow, mild flavor may have something in common with an alluring

EDAM

perfume: just as a perfect blend of scents requires an expert known in the fragrance trade as "The Nose," so makers of Edam depend on a master cheeseman whose title is "The Ear." He earns the distinction in Holland after a quarter-century of maintaining accuracy, judging a cheese by the sound it makes when thumped. A man with a good ear knows that a hollow sound, resulting from a rap of the knuckles on ripened Edam, means insufficient curing or too many air pockets—a dull thump is the sound by which a perfect cheese is judged.

Cheesemaking in Holland has been traced back more than eight hundred years. As the age of sail began, the semihard Dutch cheeses from the towns of Edam and Gouda became the first to find markets abroad, their mild and satisfying flavor appealing to consumers throughout Europe. Edams had further appeal as the only sphere-shaped cheese, which made them instantly recognizable. But wheel-like Goudas are richer in content. The chief difference between the two is that Edams make use of skimmed milk and Goudas are products of whole milk. In the Edam process, curds that combine morning milk with fat-free milk of the evening before are wrapped in cheesecloth, then hand-stuffed into round-bottomed metal or teakwood molds. A similarly rounded top section is attached, and pressure is applied to force out whey while shaping the cheese. The balls are removed from the forms, dipped in warm whey, smoothed on the surface, and pressed again to improve the shape and consistency. (Some say the spherical forms developed so that ripened Edams could be rolled from warehouses to the nearby wharves.) Gouda, retaining all the milk's butterfat, does not coagulate as speedily as Edam does, and therefore is too moist in its early stages to hold the shape of a ball.

PIGLET SHAPES FROM BUFFALO MILK   Most semihard cheeses are wheel-shaped. Among the charms of Italy, however, are the food shops where Provolones can be seen in all sorts of figures—even, occasionally, the shape and size of toy piglets. These cheeses are commonly molded like blunted footballs, melons, pears, sausages, flasks, truncated cones, and cylinders. They are formed by hand and looped with vegetable fibers for hanging. Firm of texture, like Holland cheeses, they have smooth, thin, shiny, wheat-colored rinds, and creamy interiors. There are two varieties: *provolone dolce* and *provolone piccante.* Mild Provolone has a buttery flavor, and the other is, of course, piquant, and can be biting. Provolone is used as a table cheese up to nine months of aging—even longer for those that weigh a hundred pounds or so—and then it is good for grating. It is usually lightly smoked.

Buffalo milk was once needed to make Provolone, as well as to make other Italian dairy products, including Mozzarella. Water buffaloes were brought from India in the seventh century as dairy animals, and they still graze in large numbers in the pastures of Campania, where *mozzarella di bufalo* has been for centuries almost as important to life as pasta. But this is fresh cheese, to which more attention will be given later. Provola and Provatura are also close relatives of Provolone, and they remain important buffalo-milk products, often being smoked as well.

Caciocavallo, a word that comes from the Italian for "cheese on horse-back," is an ancient cheese, now made of cow's milk, whose name is reflected in the Balkan words "Kashkaval" and "Katshkawlj," transliterated variously in English. Traditionally, Caciocavallo has been shaped like two saddlebags looped together. The process of making it is the same as that for Provolone, and its somewhat salty taste is usually rather lactic, though much loved in Italy. It is not my favorite Italian product, but other travelers have liked it; the French poet Paul Valéry is said to have found it "parfait, le meilleur de royaume."

FORMULAS FROM MONASTERIES   Having to choose, I am tempted by Taleggio, a buttery, flat, square cake of mild piquancy when it can be found in America, but runny and soft in its Lombardy homeland. There one can also find it in more powerful versions variously kown as *taleggino, robiola,* and *robiolina.* The Taleggio most often exported comes from a large manufacturer responsible also for the easy availability of Bel Paese, a copy of which is produced in the United States under license. The imported Bel Paese has a wrapper distinguished by a map of Italy, and its quality makes it worth searching out; the other has a map of North and South America. Both have a likeness of Antonio Stoppani, an Italian priest

PROVOLONES

whose best-selling book for young people was entitled *Bel Paese*. The cheese itself, milder than Taleggio, derives from a monastery formula, and there are Italian variations under such commercial names as Bella Alpina, Bella Milano, Bel Piano Lombardo, and Fior d'Alpe. In other parts of Europe similar cheeses are branded as Schönland, Königkäse, and Fleur des Alpes, and the Butter Cheese of Canada is much like it.

Some of the plump brothers M. F. K. Fisher saluted were responsible for one of the oldest of monastery cheeses, indeed the one that bears the generic name Munster (the word is related to the Latin *monasterium*). Munster was developed at least as long ago as the early Middle Ages, and

the best of it is faithful to the methods used by Benedictines who established an abbey in the seventh century not far from Colmar in the Vosges Mountains. In France it is known as *munster fermier,* and its milk comes from cows grazing the high, stubbled grain fields above the Alsatian wine country. It is cheese with a heart of great tenderness, with a smooth, shiny, brick-red rind, and connoisseurs consider its best seasons to be summer and fall.

Highly acceptable year-round Munsters are made of pasteurized milk, as are variations labeled Chaumont and Géromé. American Munster, most of which comes from Wisconsin and Illinois, is mild in flavor—in fact is a different cheese entirely. It has nothing in common with the original except the name, which reminds one that resourceful European monks, in days when much of the joy of ordinary layman's gourmandizing was denied them, seldom failed to find ways to make simple foods seem—indeed, taste —like delicacies.

TRAPPISTS MAKE CHEESE IN MANY COUNTRIES The same Benedictine monks who make blue-veined rounds at the Quebec abbey on Lake Memphremagog produce Le Moine, a subtly flavored, thickish-skinned cheese of monastery character. The most famous of such cheeses on this side of the Atlantic is made farther up in Quebec, at the Fromagerie de la Trappe, just upriver from Montreal. This Canadian Oka, as it is called, after the nearby village, is one of several cheeses produced by Trappist monks according to a secret recipe brought to France shortly after the French Revolution. The basic formula, zealously guarded by various monasteries since those French Trappists came out of exile in the Alps in 1815, has been used by members of the order in several American states and in various monastic establishments in Europe.

The exiles began their dairy venture at L'Abbaye de Notre Dame du Port du Salut when they settled at Entrammes, outside Laval in northern France. When the monastery finally offered the cheese, called Port du Salut, to the Paris market in 1875 it became an immediate success. But it also caused other cheesemakers to try to imitate it, with results so disconcerting that it took a lawsuit to stop the piracy, and the trademark "Port Salut" was assigned exclusively to the monks. Meanwhile, however, the demand so increased that the hard-working brothers could not meet it, and they sold the formula and trademark rights to a commercial dairy after World War II; but, for regional distribution only, they went right back to making their own tangy rounds that bear the religious designation Trappe d'Entramme.

Much confusion still exists. French factory adaptations of the original are labeled Abbaye and St. Paulin, for instance, and the terms Port Salut and Port du Salut are both used. Cheeses claiming these antecedents are made in many countries, including Iceland, and in Denmark a copy which once bore the original name is now distinguished as Esrom and is good enough to stand on its own merit.

Meanwhile other Trappist brothers are using the monastic recipe in scattered but cloistered dairies. Two Trappist cheeses are produced in Brittany abbeys, and others by French clerics in Bricquebec, Chambarand, Citeaux, Echourgnac, Monte-des-Cats, and Tamié. The Trappist product is turned out in Belgian monasteries, along with commercial St. Paulins and the robust Maredsous, a rectangularly shaped skim-milk cake made by Benedictines of the abbey of Maredsous in the valley of Molignée. Variations come from monasteries and from commercial plants in Australia, Austria, Czechoslovakia, Germany, Hungary, and Yugoslavia. All of them are good regional cheeses.

ANFROM

PORT SALUT

REBLOCHON

The French factory-made Beaumont is often put in the same class—it compares favorably with good St. Paulins, and is also related to commercially produced Reblochons, from the region around Lake Annecy. Reblochon, now made in several sizes—much of which is exported to New York—is an ancient product of the French Alps, fondly referred to as "the mountain dwarf." St. Nectaire, a cheese of central France that earned accolades from Louis XIV in the sunniest days of his kingdom, bears likenesses to both Reblochons and Trappists and, like them, should be judged on qualities that prevail when it is a genuine *fermier*.

The Danes, who had the good sense to give their Port Salut its own identity by renaming it Esrom, have done the same for their variations on other European cheeses. The Danish adaptation of Tilsit has been called Havarti since the nation's dairymen decided to honor their great cheese heroine, Hanne Nielsen, whose home bore this name. She who had traveled through much of Europe, taking meticulous notes on the myriad variations of cheesemaking, got Denmark started imitating the best products of other countries. In the late nineteenth century she enlisted the help of Joseph Harding, the many-daughtered Englishman who did so much to perfect the craft of cheddaring. In the hundred years since, Denmark has become one of the most important exporters of cheese in great variety.

MIGRANT DAIRYMEN ORIGINATE NEW VARIETIES   Denmark's Havarti is one of several versions of Tilsit now made in various places. The original Tilsit (which takes its name from the East Prussian town where Napoleon made an uneasy peace with the Russians) evolved from a recipe brought to Germany by emigrant farmers from Holland. Some time after their cheese had gained fame under its Prussian name, one of the emigrants moved on to northeast Switzerland, and eventually Tilsit was produced from the milk of mountain meadows in the cantons of St. Gall and Thurgau. The recipe has traveled to America and as far north as Norway's mountain dairies, and Tilsit is also made under the Central European name Ragnit. Sometimes its flavor is compared to that of typical monastery cheeses.

Across the Swiss mountains on the southern slope of the Jura range, the monks of Bellelay turn out other round cheeses, not unlike Tilsit in flavor, which sometimes bear the place name and sometimes are called Tête de Moine, because custom required a head count of the cassocked dairymen and the distribution of one cheese to each monk. Today Tête de Moine is also made by commercial dairies in western Switzerland. Other dairies have adapted the basic Tilsit recipe to produce a cheese known as Glarus (the canton of that name is so called because of the clarity of its air); its flavor is somewhat sweeter, its consistency softer. Just as Havarti is a Tilsit variation, so is a product of Austria's low meadowlands that has been marketed on this side of the Atlantic as Doret, and is also known among its makers as Ziegel (brick) because of its shape.

THE ORIGIN OF BRICK CHEESE IN WISCONSIN   The Brick cheese that is considered one of the few American creations began in Wisconsin, where the current annual output of this semisoft loaf is more than 20 million pounds. The formula was worked out in 1877 by a Dodge County farmer named John Jossi, and his brick-shaped achievement has a rather pungent yet sweet flavor that has been termed mild and nutlike. The rectangular loaves measure about 3 by 10 by 5 inches and average 5 pounds apiece; they have smooth texture that slices easily without crumbling, and small irregular holes are scattered throughout the interior. A slightly bitter rind develops during the aging process, which requires a maximum of two to three months.

The American appetite for cheese in this general category was responsible for a buttery cheese with a very American name: Gold'n'Rich. With the help of a French expert on Port Salut it was first made in Elgin, Illinois, during the Great Depression to provide a market for milk producers in the Middle West. Another regional development of this period, without as much tang but equally smooth in texture, is retailed as Baronet. And there are others, with various trade names, all apparently aimed at palates not yet courageous enough for cheese with strong character.

Cheesemakers everywhere seem to take seriously the sensibilities of fledgling gastronomes—or those others who keep a morning eye on the bathroom scales and maintain a resolute attitude toward too much intake of things as luxurious and, yes, comforting as cheese. The Swedish version of the Italian Fontina is a pale imitation, but it has won a host of aficionados who like its bland, pastiche quality and who might not otherwise have much to do with cheese. In a way, something similar applies to the problem of calories. There has been a rush to temper the butteriness of some old standbys, and a lot of innovative work with skim milk. In the Department of

Food Science at the University of Minnesota, technologists labored imaginatively and long to come up with an appetizing creation that is now manufactured for (among other outlets) a Minneapolis specialty food store as "Minnesota Slim." It has real cheese flavor and, indeed, *is* cheese rather than processed cheese, or "cheese food." It may not be considered with epicurean awe, but it pleases a mighty group which takes note of the fact that it has 30 percent less fat content than a normal Colby, say, without loss of protein or other good things.

Cheeses made of milk that has been skimmed of its fat are not new by any means. Thrifty farmers' wives were making them hundreds of years ago, and there are now dozens from which to choose. Even the good brothers of Port du Salut sometimes used partly skimmed milk. And after all, as Clifton Fadiman has written, "there is no such thing as a *bad* cheese. A cheese may disappoint. It may be naïve, it may be oversophisticated. Yet it remains cheese, milk's leap toward immortality."

9

Parmesan and Other Hard Cheeses

The Italians have a word for hard cheese. It is *grana,* as in grain, and it means in its ultimate definition that the exposed flank of the world's best cooking (and eating) cheese is a pinpoint honeycomb of tiny holes showing the hard, finely grained texture which indicates impeccable quality when the cheese has been flawlessly aged.

Hard cheese is not just cheese that has been allowed to dry out. If it deserves the name Parmesan—the well-earned term for the Italian grating cheese for centuries considered the best—it is a large wheel that has been treated with as much care and skillful attention as is given to the great wines in France. And just as wines have helped to give the French a distinctive cuisine, Parmesan has helped to make the cooking of Italy as subtly flavored as the best of it is. Cheeses made in several parts of the world are called Parmesan, but only those from certain legally defined areas of northern Italy can be stamped Parmigiano-Reggiano; this means that they conform to the high standards developed in the Middle Ages by the dairymen of the Duchy of Parma in the Enza Valley, between the cities of Parma and Reggio. Their manufacture is limited to the seven months from mid-April to mid-November, when the grass of these northern plains is lushest and the milk is richest.

Other *granas,* often wrongly called Parmesans, are produced the year around. In Italy such cheeses made in certain Lombardy and Piedmont regions are defined by law as Grana Padano, but there are many habitual terms that make use of the name of cheesemaking centers, like Grana Lodigiano for that which is made in Lodi. Aside from the fact that the milk is not so rich, these all are usually larger than the original Parmesans from Parmigiano-Reggiano country.

The fame of the cheese from Parma is due to its richness of flavor and to its failure to form strings when used in cooking. In the era when

Italian hard cheese was known simply as *cacio duro,* this quality helped establish ready markets as far afield as Flanders, to which it was exported by monks of the Milanese Abbey of Chiaravalle. By the beginning of the sixteenth century it was recorded by a forgotten observer that "in our day, Italy's greatest glory comes from Parmesan cheese"; and faraway Englishmen so appreciated Parmesan that during the great fire of London in 1666 Samuel Pepys described the digging of an enormous pit to bury a store of Italian cheese and thereby save it from the consuming heat.

PARMESAN

ASIAGO

ROMANO

LESS FAT, MORE SALT The cheese so prized is made from skim milk, and the whey drained off in its making feeds many Italian pigs from which come Reggiano sausages or Parma hams—almost as famous among epicures as the cheese itself. When perfectly cured it has 10 percent less moisture than Cheddar or Cheshire, about 5 percent less fat, but is slightly saltier. It is aged a minimum of fourteen months. "It is the world that hardens Parmesan," Hillaire Belloc wrote in a gustatory mood. "In its youth, the Parmesan is very soft and easy—and is voraciously devoured."

Thousands of people salute Parmesan as a table cheese as well as one of ideal consistency for grating. In Italy some choose to wait at least three years, when the descriptive word is *stravecchio* (very old), while many more Italians prefer *grana stravecchione,* at least four years in maturation and perhaps as many as twenty—the older, some say, the better. As if in proof, in her *Classic Italian Cook Book,* Marcella Hazan, a critic of cheeses in both America and her native Italy, says: "There is no more magnificent table cheese than a piece of aged, genuine *parmigiano-reggiano,* when it has not been allowed to dry out and it is a glistening, pale-straw color. It is frequently combined with the fruit course and eaten together with peeled pears, or with grapes." A couple of hundred years earlier, Parmesan had found appreciation in America, but it was hard to come by in the colonies. Benjamin Franklin wrote a friend that if only he could find "a receipt for making Parmesan cheese, it would give me more satisfaction" than almost anything else.

As hard to get today for most Americans is the Italian cheese called Asiago, which takes its name from a castlelike village east of Lake Garda in the province of Vicenza. True, Asiago is made in an American version by Michigan and Wisconsin dairymen, but the best of it, like Parmesan, must be found in its native Italy. It is a cheese that some people think resembles, in consistency and flavor, the splendid Cantal of central France, and as a younger cheese it has been compared to Battelmatt, the Tilsit-like wheel from the Italian cantons of Switzerland.

Asiago, however, reaches its zenith as a grating cheese, and should have its own characteristic flavor. Categorizing Parmesan as "a sweet type," David Frigo, a Connecticut cheesemonger whose family claims six generations of Asiago makers, told me, "We call Asiago's character *piccante*— it sort of tells you it's been around a long time, has that extra taste." It is sharper than Parmesan and is therefore favored by some cooks for the accent it adds to risottos and other dishes typical of Veneto, but is also a fine dessert cheese.

THREE KINDS OF ROMANO   One of the sharpest of the hard cheeses is Romano, traditionally made of sheep's milk (see Chapter 6)—as was the original Asiago—but produced increasingly of cow's milk in Italy, as well as in the United States and other countries. In addition to the generic Pecorino Romano, Italians speak of the version made from goat's milk as Caprino Romano, and of that from cow's milk as Vacchino Romano. Authentic Romano is whiter than Parmesan or Asiago, and is usually made in smaller cylinders that in Italy are ripened about eight months, and in this country for as little as one hundred and twenty days. It is a much-favored cooking accent, and in Lazio, outside Rome, according to Waverley Root in *The Food of Italy,* a variety of Romano called *caciotta di pecorino* provides a local specialty when used to season broad beans.

Among the hard cheeses of Switzerland that are used principally for cooking is a medium-size cylinder, weighing between 30 and 45 pounds, that is known as Spalen. Now exported to the United States from the mountains of Nidwalden and Unterwalden, it is a grainy cheese with a tangier flavor than that of Parmesan. Unlike the Italian prototype, it is made of whole milk, but it ages about the same time for use as a grating condiment, and when really venerable and extra hard it is shaved off with a razor-sharp blade and served as a first course. In some areas of Switzerland, and elsewhere, Spalen is known better as Sbrinz, a name that derived from the town of Brienz in the Bernese Oberland. The cheeses are round and flatter than most, and a vertical cut shows striations, as if the interior were made of fragile tightly pressed layers. In fact, *fromages à rebibes,* as the Swiss sometimes say, are narrow sheets of Sbrinz sold in rolls for munching with apéritifs and good wines.

HEIRLOOM CHEESES   This idea springs from ancient custom. The market town of Saanen, in the resort country near Gstaad, gives its name to a similar wheel that gets harder and harder as it ages for five to seven years or even more. It ages so well, it is true, that Swiss families began to keep such rounds as heirlooms, making a cheese on the birth of each child, to be eaten when that young person married; or it was saved for cutting into at the funeral of an old one. Some mountain families kept cheeses in their cellars as a proof of affluence and held onto them through several generations. So hard and firm did they become that a special plane, or *hobel,* had to be used to serve them, and they became known as Hobel-käse, plane cheese, served up in thin shavings.

GRATED PARMESAN

10

Fresh
and Creamy

Mrs. Isabella Beeton, whose *Book of Household Management* was the bible of housewives of the English-speaking world in the nineteenth century, defined the simplest of cheeses with her characteristic simplicity: "Cream cheese, although so called," she wrote, "is not properly cheese, but is nothing more than cream dried sufficiently to be cut with a knife."

Fresh and creamy cheeses are, in fact, produced in various ways, and there is a wide range of character and individuality among them. Some are easy enough to make in a small apartment kitchen; some are more sophisticated. The term "cream cheese," as used a hundred years after Mrs. Beeton, describes fresh cheeses very simply prepared with a "starter" like sour cream or buttermilk, or with the rennet also used in the soft, fluent cheeses that require aging. (The same term is used for those ultrarich, ripened products, to which extra cream is added, described in Chapter 3.)

"Would you make soft cheese?" a nineteenth-century Briton asked in an instructive poem. "Then I'll tell you how," he went on, spelling out the formula in rustic meter:

> *Take a gallon of milk*
> *quite fresh from the cow.*
> *Ere the rennet is added,*
> *the dairyman's daughter*
> *Must throw in a quart of the*
> *freshest spring water.*
> *When perfectly curdled,*
> *so white and so nice,*
> *You must take it all out of the dish*
> *with a slice.*
> *And put it 'thout breaking with*
> *ease in the vat,*

With a cheese-cloth at bottom,
be sure to mind that.
This delicate matter take care not
to squeeze,
But fill as the whey passes off
by degrees.
Next day you may turn it,
and do not be loth
To wipe it quite dry with a fine
linen cloth.
The cheese is now finished,
and nice it will be
If enveloped in leaves from the
green ashen tree.

Cottage Cheese is the common term in England and America used to describe fresh curds produced as the lines above indicate. Sometimes called Dutch Cheese, Pot Cheese, or Schmierkäse, and made from skim milk or nonfat dry milk solids, it is simple enough to master at home. In fact, numerous standard cookbooks include directions for beginners, and easy-to-follow instructions worked out for home kitchens are given in Chapter 12.

Commercially, when Cottage Cheese curds are large and flaky, they are packaged and sold in some communities as popcorn cheese, because that is the shape they take. When the preparation of Cottage Cheese results in smaller, more granular curds the result is frequently labeled country style, or farm style. The so-called Creamed Cottage Cheese, according to law, has added cream and a minimum fat content of 4 percent or more. But in America the greatest interest in this sort of fresh cheese is among calorie counters, and therefore the total amount annually produced and sold is enormous—over a billion pounds according to recent figures.

FRESH CHEESES IN GREAT BRITAIN   Fresh cheeses are coveted around the world. In Scotland, the type of Cottage Cheese once made as a matter of course by crofters is called Crowdie. Although it disappeared during the Second World War, when all dairy products were under strenuous rationing, its revival by Susannah and Reg Stone on their Ross-shire farm turned up eager fans in many countries. Crowdie is a high-protein and fat-free cheese traditionally eaten on oat cakes by Highlanders. The name derives from the Lowland word for curds, and a luxury version, called Crowdie and Cream, is a combination of two-thirds curds from skim milk and one-third fresh double cream.

In England the ancient unripened cheeses are called Colwick, Slip-cote, and York (also known as Cambridge). As made at the Cheshire School of Agriculture, the Yorks are soft curds, approximately one-third butterfat, one-third milk solids, and one-third moisture. They are ready to eat as a spread for bread in slightly over twenty-four hours, having what is described as a soft, junket-type texture and piquant lactic flavor.

FRESH CHEESES IN FRANCE . . . Fresh cheeses, marketed in the small baskets in which they drain, can be found in almost every region of France and are typically served—as is Brittany's Crémet Nantais—at the end of a meal or with fresh fruit. Perhaps the simplest is Fromage Blanc, or drained, unsalted curds which are often later sprinkled with salt and pepper. When the drained curds are kneaded into a paste to which cream and sugar are added before being put in wicker molds, this rustic cheese is called Fromage à la Crème. And it becomes the classic dessert Coeur à la Crème (see Recipes, page 178) when curds are drained in heart-shaped molds, then turned out on a plate and adorned with a coating of heavy cream and sugar.

The fresh cheese called Neufchâtel, after the Norman city on the Seine River, is among the best-known, often having been ripened about three weeks in the Camembert manner. But Neufchâtels are also popular in France when unripened. A hundred years ago fresh cheeses from this

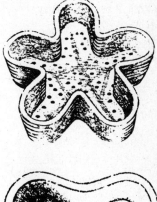
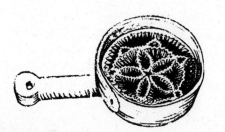
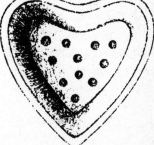

region were speeded to market by horse and wagon, then sent on to Les Halles in Paris by train. It is said that a Swiss dairyman working on a Normandy farm was the first to develop a fluffy combination of curds and rich cream, which is now famous as the flat, cylindrical Petit-Suisse and, like the well-known Gervais, is sometimes frozen for export.

. . . AND IN ITALY   Italy's Ricotta is also much exported and—more pointedly—much copied in various countries, especially the United States. It bears such names as Céracée, Recuite, Schottenziger, Serac, and Ziger, and is a product of whey, having originally evolved from the process of making Mozzarella or Provolone. It now is also made from the liquid residue of Cheddar and Swiss-type cheeses, and in this country has an addition of 10 percent whole milk, with live steam frequently injected to clarify the curd. If it is to be marketed as dry Ricotta, the curd is placed in perforated forms and pressed to make it firm. Ricotta's parent cheese, Mozzarella, is also a fresh cheese of the plastic-curd, or *pasta filata,* category which requires lengthy kneading to achieve its resilient yet somewhat stringy texture. It is widely used in cooking because it melts well. The great herds of water buffalo from whose milk Mozzarella is properly made are disappearing from southern Italy, and much cheese sold as Mozzarella is really Fior di Latte, made from cow's milk. But fresh Italian Mozzarella, quite unlike that known by Americans, is roughly ball-shaped and at its peak when eaten moist and dripping its own buttermilk on the day it is made. (Italo-Californians make Tuma, a fresh cheese drained in baskets.)

In central Italy the farmers of Abruzzi and Molise traditionally produce the fresh cheese known as Scamorze. Like Mozzarella, it once was made exclusively of buffalo milk, and it also is eaten when soft and plastic. The surface has a yellow tint, and its flavor is mild but tasty; sometimes it is toasted, or fried with an egg. Dairymen of Lombardy are famous for the fresh curds known as Mascarpone, which is so smooth some people relate it to whipped cream, eating it with fresh berries, while others spread it on chocolate cake. The Italian Incanestrato is, as its name suggests, a basket-formed cheese, eaten fresh at times, and also pressed and salted for curing several months.

THE GOOD COPIES IN AMERICA   So natural, so free of the need for either long practice or great skill, fresh and creamy cheeses are made—one very much like another—in every dairy country. That such simple and delicious concoctions became more and more sophisticated in France is no secret, of course. And French cream cheeses were among the first to invite imitation. Americans were producing good copies of Neufchâtel as

COTTAGE CHEESE

early as the mid-nineteenth century in an effort to supply the domestic market with a cheese that then couldn't be easily exported. In New Orleans, however, the French influence that affected life generally had little to do with the making of a simple fresh cheese called Creole, which was sold on the streets by women who carried covered baskets containing a number of perforated tins in which their homemade cheese was formed. They also carried a can of fresh cream to pour over the cheese when it was turned out in a customer's dish. Essentially, Creole Cheese consisted of a single large curd, and the added cream served as a natural sauce when it was eaten for breakfast or lunch. It is now made commercially in Louisiana dairies.

Dairymen in other parts of the country did their best to make closer copies of the well-known French classic versions of fresh cheese. In the process, a formula for one of the world's most popular dairy products was hit upon. One firm, William E. Lawrence of Chester, New York, is given credit for originating the rectangular cakes that characterize American Cream Cheese. By 1906, in this Orange County town which then supplied New York City with much of its Grade A milk, the Lawrence dairy had established an impressive annual production of Neufchâtel and their own Cream Cheese.

On the other side of the Catskill Mountains, in South Edmeston, another New York dairyman had devised an almost identical formula and considered his creamy product elegant enough to name it after Philadelphia, a city of well-founded gastronomic pretensions. Within fifty years the manufacturers of Philadelphia Cream Cheese had proclaimed it to be the world's largest-selling packaged cheese, and by 1972 the total annual production of Cream Cheese in American factories had reached 127,428,000 pounds.

The fact that this kind of Cream Cheese in its silver-foil wrapping presents few problems to stores and is no trouble in home refrigerators helps to account for its wide acceptance. "Cream cheese as it is made today," one cheesemaker pointed out, "is vastly different from that made originally, or even thirty years ago, because new methods of manufacture have doubled or tripled the shelf life." Those which last the longest have a preservative (as the wrapper will tell) that is called carob or locust bean gum, from the leguminous tree that is said to have kept John the Baptist alive in the wilderness.

Cream Cheese often is the first cheese tasted by children—the pale, bland, buttery flavor is the taste that opens the future for more adventurous eating. It may start a childhood career of Cream Cheese and jelly sandwiches, or a lifetime enthusiasm for that great American institution known as cheesecake. Or it may lead to an appetite for Cream Cheese enhanced by the contrasting accents of herbs, spices, or spirits—as we shall see in the following chapter.

11

Spiced
and Spirited

Cheese has become another symbol of affluent living. Like wine, it demands the development of a sensitive palate, and this fact has led dairymen over the centuries to tamper with the natural flavor of certain bland cheeses by adding herbs, spices, spirits, and other seasonings. In fact, some experts believe that a bland cheese into which further flavors are introduced often leads neophytes to become confirmed tyrophiles who will relish both the delicacy of perfectly matured Brie and the brilliant character of Roquefort. Some people, they say, just naturally love cheese in its pure forms, whereas others need to be lured by nondairy additions.

The flavor that results from exposing cheese to wood smoke is now among the most popular of such allurements, but the process began—as a practical matter, of course—because smoke was once one of the chief methods of preserving foods. Perhaps earlier, as one theory would have it, cheese toasted over a blazing fire became (coincidentally) saturated with smoke, providing a pleasing new taste. Fumed cheese became so popular during the rule of the Caesars that many patrician houses in Rome had ovens expressly designed for making this treat, and there were similar public facilities. According to Martial, the first-century epigrammatist, "It is not every smoke that is suited to cheese; but the cheese that imbibes of the smoke of the Velabrum [the popular Roman shopping center] is excellent."

It is still a good idea to consider the source of smoky flavors. The United States Department of Agriculture reports that "only good-quality cheese should be smoked," and government experts list three methods currently in use: "(1) A chemical or so-called liquid smoke may be added to the milk from which the cheese is made, or to the curd shortly after it is cut. (2) The cheese may be salted with so-called smoked salt. However, this sometimes gives the cheese a streaked appearance. (3) The cheese may be smoked in the same way as meat. The smoking facility," the government pamphlet continues, "consists of two rooms. In one room, wood—preferably hickory—is burned slowly, in a smothered condition. An opening or pipe conveys the smoke to the second room." There the cheese, most often in small rectangles resting on open shelves, is exposed to fumes for a full day.

THE BEST WAY OF SMOKING   Smoking cheese with the same respectful attention to detail as smoked meats require is, it seems to me, the only method that is really satisfactory; and if the cheese is natural Cheddar or a similar type that is seared with the smoke of nut and fruit woods, as is the tradition in Vermont, the result can be a rewarding culinary experience. In Italy smoked Mozzarella enhances the flavor of lasagne and other pasta dishes, and *provolone affumicato*—shaped like fruits or sausages or even miniature pigs—may well be the twentieth-century version of the products of Velabrum two thousand years ago.

Ham-shaped cheeses, called Ostiepky (or Ostypka), are characteristic of Central Europe's smoked dairy products, and in America these are available, along with a Hungarian favorite labeled Parenyica, at Paprikas Weiss, a New York import house. Edward Weiss, the third generation of this family to deal in such matters, refers to Parenyica as "ribbon cheese" because the curd is shaped in long strips and wound up like a jelly roll before it is smoked.

RIBBON CHEESES

An equally distinctive European cheese, too perishable for export, is low-fat cheese from Denmark's Fyn, the island where Hans Christian Andersen was born. This is a smoked acid-curd cheese to which caraway flavor may be added before the cheeses are formed into rectangular or round loaves. After twenty-four hours, during which period they are turned several times, the delicate Fyn cheeses "are placed on an iron grid over a fire of hay or straw, grass or fresh nettles," according to Jan Reeslev, Danish cheeseman. "They are smoked a couple of minutes on both sides till the surface is slightly brown, with stripes from the grid; then they are sprinkled with caraway seeds, and are ready for sale."

SEEDS AND HERBS FOR FLAVOR   For hundreds of years various kinds of seeds have been used to flavor cheeses made in Scandinavia and Central Europe. A Swedish caraway-accented wheel exported to America is called Riksost. Caraway is also sometimes added to Norway's Nökkelost, which in its native habitat is usually as round as a Gouda, but when made in the United States comes loaf-shaped and weighs 5 to 7 pounds. The word *nökkel* is Norwegian for "key," and it is said that Nökkelost originally was stamped with St. Peter's crossed keys, the symbol of the city of Leiden. It is most often found here labeled as "Leyden." (See Lexicon.)

The Dutch cheese that bears that city's name is one of the most famous spiced cheeses, its assertive flavor usually the product of cloves, anise, or cumin seed, as well as caraway. Munster, one of the best of all imported cheeses when carefully treated, is occasionally produced with caraway seeds mixed into the curd before aging; but this flavor combination is at its best, I'm certain, when the mature Munster is very soft, pungent only with dairy flavors, and sprinkled with caraway seeds just before eating.

John Coolidge, the president's son, adds caraway to some of the wheels of Vermont cheese made in the village of Plymouth; and his small factory, like those of other cheesemakers in the Green Mountains, turns out a goodly quantity of green cheese seasoned, he says, "with hand-rubbed sage"—a type for which Vermont has been famous for a century and a half. It's a sad fact that most sage cheese, according to the Department of Agriculture, is now flavored with a synthetic sage extract. The appearance of fresh sage is produced by a substitution described in a government handbook: "Succulent green corn is cut fine, and the juice is pressed out. This juice is added to a small part of the milk, which is made into curd in the usual way."

This procedure, quite understandably, amounts to heresy in the minds of those who swear by traditional standards. Not far from Plymouth, in

the bustling hamlet of Weston, Vermont, one of the better sage cheeses
I have eaten is sold by Vrest Orton, a Vermonter famous for his efforts
to preserve the verities of his native state. Mr. Orton does not hesitate
to tell his customers that the shipments he makes are "simply our good
aged Cheddar with leaves of real sage for flavor."

SAGE CHEESE FOR CHRISTMAS   Among British food lovers for
hundreds of years this kind of sage cheese has been a traditional part
of the Christmas celebration all over England. The chopped herb, spread
between layers of curd, looks very appealing and adds a fittingly green
yuletide aspect to the Derby cheeses.

As a year-round variation, an eighteenth-century recipe stipulates that
two handfuls of sage and one of marigolds and parsley be bruised and
steeped in milk overnight. The next morning curds are to be made from
the resulting green milk, as well as a separate batch from plain milk.
Sometimes, the recipe states, the green curd is cut with metal patterns,
and the shapes thus made are arranged on the outside of the form to
produce a three-dimensional design of green and white cheese.

Eye appeal may have as much as anything to do with the current
success of all the flavored cheeses, but the art of adding accents to cheese
is virtually as old as dairying itself. On their Ross-shire farm in northern
Scotland, the enterprising couple Susannah and Reg Stone, who some years
ago revived the making of Crowdie, have brought back the ancient tradition of using wild garlic as a subtle seasoning, and the bulb is now gathered
for them by children from the town of Tain. The resulting blend bears
the old Scottish name Hramsa—a fresh cheese with an almost unidentifiable
flavor and a pleasing aroma.

Switzerland's Sapsago has its own delicate fragrance and is as green
as Vermont Sage, but it is a cheese better for use in cooking than to eat with
bread and crackers. Taste and color come from a kind of clover the Greeks
called honey lotus, now cultivated in mountain fields expressly for Glarus
dairymen. Pressed into very hard truncated cone shapes, Sapsago is a green
grating cheese known in Europe as Schabzieger, Glärnerkäse, or Grünerkäse. Widely used to season salads, soups, sauces, and herb butters, it also
gives a special green accent when grated onto hot pasta. Numerous green
herbs are being used to accent more and more cheeses available in American
markets and specialty stores. In recent years the Boursin factories in Normandy and the Île-de-France have exported snow-white fresh cheeses that
are vibrant with noncheese flavors. In the same category are Tartare and
Margotin, which are made in Périgord. The French government is also
promoting goat's-milk cheeses with herbs added. Wisconsin produces the
herbed-cheese called Rondelé.

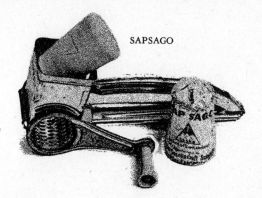

SAPSAGO

ACCENTS OF WINE OR NUTS   And then, of course, there are the varieties that take their character from the grape itself—when it is fermented, that is. Windsor Red Vein cheese looks at first glance a little like a whole Stilton whose blue mold has turned scarlet. Instead, Windsor Red Vein is simply British Cheddar laced with British red wine from vineyards in southern England. Stilton that has been mixed with port—after maturation rather than in the early stages—is looked upon askance by the cognoscenti. "My very strong view," said the London entrepreneur John Bidwell, "is that Port should never, repeat never, be mixed into the cheese, but drunk separately from the glass." Nevertheless, of the thousands of cheese gift packages sold by mail, or to be found at cheese counters, many include Cheddars (usually of inferior quality) subjected to baths of port, sherry, or other spirits.

In France kirsch brandy is blended into processed Gruyère with a resulting consistency that seems artificially smooth and has a flavor with mysterious appeal for some knowledgeable cheese fanciers. But the Gourmandise, as this is called, that is exported to the United States must be flavored with cherry extract instead of alcohol; it is even sweeter, therefore, and a concoction something less than cheese—perhaps it is in the category of ice creams that taste as if they had been emulsified. Another French import called Grappe is also composed of Gruyère *fondu,* but its flavor is very bland and what interest it has lies in its coating of grape seeds and, sometimes, grape skins. Most often the coating of seeds has been treated to make a crusty exterior that comes off in rough sections and is not intended to be eaten. It is not exotic—if that is the quality its appreciators think fits.

Also popular among nibblers who approach pure cheese gingerly are items adorned with nuts—ball-shaped, cylindrical, or shapes so ornate that

PEPATO

LEYDEN

GRAPPE

VERMONT SAGE   BOURSIN AU POIVRE

they are difficult to distinguish from cakes made by a patissier. There is, for instance, a long-established Lorraine cheese to which pistachios are added. But this should not be confused with the prevailing enthusiasm for decorating wheels of flavored processed cheese with walnut halves or stuccoing fist-sized spheres with crushed nut meats—merchandising measures that are still gathering momentum. It is interesting that Herkimer County in New York, once famous as the home of one of the New World's best Cheddars, is now better known for a neatly packaged ball that is a mélange of Blue Cheese, Cheddar, nuts, and whey. Perhaps even more eyebrow-raising are the "chocolate cheese creams" made in Mayville, Wisconsin; they look like candies but have centers in which Wisconsin Edam is a principal ingredient.

Black peppercorns provide an even more common means for embellishing cheese. Pepato is a traditional Romano variety produced in Sicily, southern Italy, and now in northern Michigan that has pepper arranged in layers and sometimes mixed into the curd. Dried chili is churned into several American cheeses as the result of a popular trend that began in the West and Southwest.

As often as they add interest, such embellishments cause problems. Unless the manufactured cheese is very fresh the flavor of the herbs or spices becomes stale; faded garlic, particularly, can make cheese seem rancid. The way to avoid problems like these—and to minimize the high cost of products with added seasonings—is to choose one's own herbs, and other flavors, and to season a cheese you have made yourself from scratch, or to blend your choice of additives into basic fresh types like the various kinds of Cottage Cheese, Cream Cheese, or even to grind or finely grate tired leftover cheeses and mix them with cream or butter and appealing accents of one kind or another.

I often try this as a form of entertainment, a kind of therapy, if you will. Cheese lends itself to amateur handling about as well as any food I can think of. Certainly it is too expensive to waste, and the remnants to be found in the icebox, the seasonings to be found at the windowbox or on the herb shelf, the urge to unwind with an indoor sport that is mostly manual—all these can combine to make a tempting "new" cheese. Or, so I've discovered, you can make a cheese that is really your own, starting with milk and little more than the will to do so. As the saying goes, it's a whole new world.

Part Two

Some Practical Matters

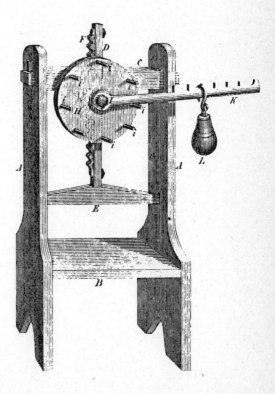

12

How to Make Cheese

Driving south on the Swiss autobahn from Fribourg to Bulle, then a couple of miles farther on Route 77, you can pull into the walled town of Gruyères with its fifteenth-century castle, its rutted streets, painted houses, and blossom-filled flower boxes, and at the model *fromagerie* you can take a short course in how to make cheese. The town is surrounded by sloping green pastureland on which Brown Swiss milk cows graze; there are snow-capped peaks in the distance, tumbling waterfalls, and a scattering of gingerbread chalets to accent this idyllic setting.

In most of the world's dairy regions there are instructive tours of commercial factories open to the public. In Battice, Belgium, a token admission fee is charged to watch (and sample) the assertive Remoudou in the making. Nearer home, scores of schools induct children into the craft of cheesemaking as special term projects. In a YMCA evening class in Minneapolis not long ago a candidate for a doctorate in geography taught a group of adults how to make cheese with minimal equipment that included a large pail, a large pot, a thermometer, a knife, cheesecloth, and an ingeniously contrived homemade press. In Idaho, at the "School of Country Living" on a Potlatch River farm, a cheesemaking workshop offered instruction in the winter of 1975–76—in the same way hundreds of cooking schools have set serious gastronomes on the way to creating their own haute cuisine.

And in the mountains of the northwest corner of North Carolina the novelist John Ehle and his actress wife have been making various cheeses for several years; a side result of this activity has been Ehle's fine book, *The Cheeses and Wines of England and France,* which is recommended to anyone who takes this present chapter seriously. Cheesemaking is, in a sense, a form of cooking, for it employs heat and a few basic kitchen implements. As cooking can sometimes seem more difficult than it is, so it is with making cheese, but cooking and cheesemaking are both skills easy to acquire through a minimum of patience and persistence.

THE BASIC TECHNICALITIES   Cheese is made by heating milk to a point sometimes called the coagulation temperature, which varies according to the type of cheese to be produced; it may be as low as 70 degrees or as high as 100 degrees Fahrenheit. The milk is warmed to provide a hospitable climate for lactic acid organisms which help to separate curds and whey. At the prescribed temperature, the addition of these organisms in one form or another, called "the starter," produces acid in the same kind of chemical change that causes the souring of milk. Primarily *Streptococcus lactis* and *Streptococcus cremoris,* these "starter" bacteria, which exist in cultured buttermilk or yogurt, for instance, are allowed to grow in the warm liquid until the milk has reached the degree of acidity necessary to speed the action of enzymes. At this point, the enzyme rennin is added in the form of commercial rennet extract from the stomach of young calves. In this step the coagulation of the milk is brought about as the protein called casein is separated from the liquid, or whey.

Rennet produces clotted milk. It breaks down the protective barriers of protein, and with the aid of acid and slow gentle heat, 95 percent of the water in the milk is released, and the remaining curd draws together in a mass of granules. The manner and degree in which the curds are drained influences the final moisture content and, indirectly, the texture and body of the cheese, thus determining the finished characteristics that separate one type from another. The process called ripening or curing also results in distinctions in flavor and texture.

THE BASIC EQUIPMENT   Two kettles are necessary—one of 1½-gallon capacity; a second large enough to hold the first so that it can be surrounded by water. A wire cooking rack on which to set the smaller kettle is needed. A thermometer must be used to measure the heat of liquids up to 150 degrees or more. A straight knife—one made for slicing ham, for instance—must be long enough to touch the bottom of the kettle. You should have a slotted spoon and a measuring cup that is graduated to ounces, a package of cheesecloth, and a colander of 1-gallon capacity.

HOW TO MAKE COTTAGE CHEESE   To make large-curd Cottage Cheese, put one gallon of whole or skim milk in the 1½-gallon pot; put the pot on the rack in the larger vessel, then carefully pour hot water into the larger pot until it reaches the level of the milk. Turn on the heat under the pots and slowly bring the milk to 72 degrees Fahrenheit. Stir in ¼ cup fresh cultured buttermilk and rennet as prescribed on its package (some is compounded for one-gallon lots of milk; other commercial rennet must be diluted according to manufacturer's instructions).

Maintain the temperature of the milk at 72 to 80 degrees for twelve to eighteen hours, or until firm clabber forms and a little whey appears on the surface. Test by inserting a knife at the side of the pot and pull the curd toward the center; it should break cleanly away from the pot, having a consistency somewhat like gelatin.

When the curd is firm it must be cut in small pieces. Insert your long knife about three-quarters of an inch from the side of the pot, holding the knife vertically straight as it touches bottom, then drawing it so you make a straight cut close to the curve side of the pot. Make another vertical cut parallel to the first at a three-quarter-inch interval, and repeat until all

of the surface of the curd is divided by parallel, vertical cuts. Turn the pot at right angles and repeat slices so that surface of curd is now cut into small squares. Turn the kettle back to its original position, and this time slant the knife at a 45-degree angle to follow the original cutting lines, thus separating the curd mass into small pieces. The cutting helps the release of whey, and the pot and its contents should stand for ten minutes. During this interval, use a slotted spoon to lift any pieces of curd that settle on the bottom, thus gathering all solids to the top of the whey.

Now slowly heat the water in the outer kettle, while watching the temperature of the whey. It should take about one minute for the whey to gain one degree of heat, then it should gain one degree at one-minute intervals until it reaches 110 degrees. Test the curd for firmness by pinching it very gently between your thumb and forefinger—it should not be mushy, but firm enough so it does not disintegrate easily. If it is not firm enough at 110 degrees, continue heating until temperature reaches 115 or even 120 degrees in order to achieve the proper consistency.

Now dip off the whey on top of the curds. Line a colander with several layers of cheesecloth. Carefully pour curds and whey into lined colander and let curds drain about three minutes. Fill one of the pots with clean cold water. Gather edges of cheesecloth to form a loose bag holding the curds, and dip this into the pot of cold water. Slosh this around so the water reaches all the curds, then pull out the bag and put it back in the colander to drain. Meanwhile, empty the pot and fill again with clean cold water, adding one or two dozen ice cubes. Dunk the cheesecloth bag containing the curds into the ice water, hanging edges of the cloth over the sides so you can work the curds with your fingers to expose every bit to the ice water. Return curds to the colander and leave to drain an hour or more, shaking the colander periodically to keep curds from sticking to each other. Now you have fresh Cottage Cheese.

Salt may be added at the rate of one teaspoon for every pound of curds. To make creamed Cottage Cheese, mix the salt with two ounces of heavy cream for each pound and stir into curds. Your cheese is now ready to be eaten, or to be chilled in a covered dish or jar. Under refrigeration it will keep as long as milk or cream.

HOW TO MAKE CREAM CHEESE WITHOUT RENNET Put one quart of light cream in a two-quart saucepan with one cup of whipping cream. Heat over very low heat until thermometer reads 72 degrees; stir in one tablespoon of cultured buttermilk. Cover pan and put in a place where temperature of liquid will remain at 72 degrees up to eighteen hours. After about fourteen hours, the cream will coagulate and will split before your finger when you run it one way and then the other through the curd.

Put the pan in another pan of hot water, and heat slowly for forty-five minutes until a thermometer inserted in the cream shows 130 degrees. Turn off heat and let the curds, now looking like thick soup, cool to 90 degrees. Stir in one tablespoon of salt, then put in refrigerator for four to five hours.

Make ready a piece of muslin or worn towel about 18 inches square; turn the curds into this cloth and let drain over the sink or into a bowl by tying edges to form a tight sack. Continue draining about two hours, squeezing the contents occasionally to speed up release of whey.

Put a colander in a shallow rectangular pan, and arrange eight or ten ice cubes to make as even a surface as possible across the bottom. Put the bag of curds on top of the ice and place a small foil (or other) plate upside down on top of the bag. Fill a quart jar with water and put it on the inverted plate. Spread around the jar as many ice cubes as possible. Now put the whole assembly in the refrigerator for twenty-four hours or less, until the curds are smooth and rather firm.

When the consistency is firm enough to cut with a knife, it is ready to be salted lightly. Add a little at a time, mixing well, to your taste. Pack the cheese about one and a half inches thick into square plastic containers that have covers, and it is ready for storing, or for immediate eating. To

remove from containers, turn upside down and run very hot water over so cheese slips out, maintaining its rectangular shape. If not eaten immediately it must be kept under refrigeration, for homemade fresh Cream Cheese has no emulsifiers, stabilizers, preservatives, or so-called antibacterial agents. Its maximum storage time is three weeks or less. To accent your Cream Cheese with herbs, spices, or other additives, see Recipes.

HOW TO MAKE FIRM, AGED CHEESE   This cheese will not be in a technical sense Cheddar, but it will be very much like Colby or, as the saying goes, American Cheese; it will be, when successful, eminently slice-able and may have pungent flavor, depending upon the aging.

To make a finished cheese about four inches in diameter and three inches high, begin with one gallon of milk, heated in a 1½-gallon pot surrounded by water in a larger pot. The milk should be unskimmed. Turn on heat under pots and let the milk gradually reach 86 to 88 degrees Fahrenheit. Add six to eight ounces of buttermilk, stirring thoroughly to ensure that the starter is well mixed into the milk. Keep the milk warm and stir repeatedly during the ripening period of about thirty minutes. If you want your finished cheese to have color, add rennet according to package directions, and stir well. Dissolve a quarter of a rennet tablet (or follow directions and proportions given by the manu-facturer) in a glass of cold water, and stir until rennet solution is thor-oughly mixed. Stir rennet into warm milk, making certain it is completely blended, then cover the pot and leave it where it can maintain a constant temperature. In about thirty minutes the curds should have coagulated, and should be cut in the same fashion as for Cottage Cheese (see page 97).

Heat carefully to bring the temperature of curds and whey to 100 degrees over a period of about thirty minutes. Stir just enough to keep curds from sticking to each other. Hold the temperature at about 100 de-grees (absolutely not more than 102) for an hour, until the curds can be squeezed without clinging together afterward. Lift the pot out of the hot water and set aside.

Remove whey by carefully ladling until the mass of curds rests on the bottom of the pot. Line a colander with cheesecloth, pour in curds to drain, and cover with a hot, damp cloth. As the colander cools, lift the curds with your fingers to keep them separated. Taste one. If it makes a squeaky sound when you chew, it is ready for salting. At three separate intervals, add one teaspoon at a time of noniodized salt, stirring each spoonful well into the mass. Cover again with the cloth and set aside for twenty minutes. The cheese is now ready to be pressed.

If you don't possess a commercially manufactured press you can make one by cutting out the ends of a coffee can or one similarly shaped. Cut two wooden rounds just enough smaller than the diameter of the can to easily slide up and down inside. Cut a zinc bolt the same length as the can and bore holes in each wood round to allow the bolt to pass through. Thread a wing nut onto one end of the zinc bolt and slip one of the wooden rounds over the bolt; fit this assembly into the can with the wood piece resting against the wing nut at the bottom. Line the sides of the can and the wooden round with cheesecloth. Spoon in the drained curds, pressing them down after each addition. Press the ends of the cheesecloth down over the curds, slide on the second wooden round, and push down against the cheesecloth. Thread on the second wing nut, then tighten both nuts, thus pressing both wooden rounds against the cheese. Leave the filled cylinder on its side to drain for about fifteen minutes, then tighten the rounds at each end to exert maximum pressure while squeezing out more whey. Stand the cylinder on end and let it drain three or four hours, then turn it over and continue to drain a similar amount of time.

Remove the cheese from the press and carefully take away the cheesecloth, and smooth the surfaces with a clean towel before putting the finished cheese, uncovered, in the refrigerator's vegetable crisper overnight. Next day melt about one-quarter pound of paraffin in a double boiler large enough to immerse half the cheese at one time. Dip it evenly for about ten seconds, then turn over and dip the other half. Make sure you leave no uncovered spots. Label the cheese with name and date and return to refrigerator crisper for at least three weeks to develop a flavor. In sixty days, more character develops, but this is not a cheese to age as long as Cheddar, for instance.

HOW TO MAKE BLUE CHEESE AND ITS MOLD AT HOME   Bluemold spores may be bought at several cheese suppliers, but the usual minimum amount is enough for about one hundred 5-pound cheeses. At home, however, you can make enough *Penicillium roqueforti* to inoculate twenty gallons of milk by simply spreading a slice of open-textured homemade-type (preferably rye) bread with Roquefort Cheese. Put it in a widemouth jar, stretch several layers of cheesecloth across the top, and secure with a rubber band. Put the jar in the bottom of your refrigerator for a week or more—long enough for the texture of the bread to be thoroughly penetrated by the Roquefort mold. Cut the slice in quarters and let them dry at room temperature until they can be crushed into dry crumbs.

To make about three and a half pounds of Blue Cheese, start with five gallons of fresh whole milk. (Follow the procedure outlined on page 100.) Heat it to 84 degrees Fahrenheit and stir in seven tablespoons of lactic starter or three-quarters of a cup of buttermilk; continue stirring about five minutes. Add only about a quarter of a teaspoon of liquid rennet, or just enough to set the milk in one and a quarter hours. Blend the rennet into the milk for about five minutes and set aside the pot in a warm place until it is coagulated.

When the milk has coagulated, cut the curds into one-inch pieces (see page 97), and leave them in the pot about ten minutes. Spread cheesecloth over a colander and lift curds into it with a slotted spoon. Tie corners of the cloth together and drain the curds about an hour.

You don't need a press for this cheese, but you need an open-ended cylinder (a coffee can or stove pipe) about six inches in diameter. Stand this mold on a mat so the whey can drain away. Use a large spoon to put slabs of curds into the mold, and when the bottom is fully covered with curds, sprinkle on a little of the blue-mold bread crumbs. Repeat with a layer of curds, a sprinkling of blue mold, until all the curds are used as the top-most layer.

In the next two hours, turn the curd-filled mold upside down at least five times, making sure it is not in a draft that will cool the cheese too quickly. Wait two more hours and turn the cheese again; then wait another two hours before turning. Now leave it several hours or overnight in slightly cool room temperature, about 65 to 80 degrees.

When the cheese has contracted slightly from the sides of the mold, slide it out and rub all its surfaces with salt, repeating once each day for a week.

The growth of the blue mold in the cheese requires ventilation, therefore it must be skewered to let air into the interior. Use a kitchen skewer or knitting needle or a piece of 1/8-inch wire, and pierce both top and bottom of the cheese about twenty times each. Put the cheese on its side in the refrigerator vegetable crisper, turning it every few days so it doesn't go flat. Continue this operation for about six weeks, scraping the surfaces as necessary to inhibit development of slime and extraneous mold. After three months, scrape the cheese clean, wrap it with foil, and store at 40 degrees for three more months.

13

Tips on Buying and Serving

For many years in Manhattan there was a food shop that needed no advertising. On most days, especially in hot weather, a smell pervaded the air around its corner location; the smell was rank, a musty odor that reeked of cheeses past their prime.

There were even worse things about this store. It boasted of offering a choice of hundreds of varieties of cheese, yet its proprietor indulged in the larceny of selling a Cheddar he knew to have come from New England (which he happened to have) to an unwary customer who had asked for the estimable cheese of Tillamook County, Oregon (which he did not have). To the tentative seeking his recommendation he would sell the stock he wanted most to get rid of, excusing himself in his belief that an ignorant buyer would not know the difference.

It is true that cheese may constitute the most vulnerable inventory a food merchant may handle, but it is not true that an odoriferous emporium is an indication of anything other than bad housekeeping. Good cheese stores stock a variety of items without assaulting the olfactory senses. Good cheesemongers treat their inventories with tender loving care and do not misrepresent one kind for another.

Long ago in Leicester, England, the town crier's duties included bawling out a formidable list of "awful pains and penalties to be visited upon anyone selling a cheese not up to reputed weight or standard." But a buyer today cannot expect the laws to do more than require fine print on packaging. He can, however, learn to be his own protector. Cheese buying is, most of all, a matter of tasting and trying—a continuing adventure.

An experienced buyer can tell by feeling whether or not a Camembert is, as the Normans say, *"bien fait,"* meaning "well done." As with all soft cheeses, it should be felt tentatively, from edges to center, because the fermentation starts at the outside and moves in. Pressing gently, one should find the center as resilient as the edges. Similarly, an experienced buyer can look at a wedge of firm cheese like Cheddar and note the deepening of color near the rind that denotes drying out. It is perceptiveness based on repeated trials that is always important.

HOW TO SHOP WITH CONFIDENCE But it is also always important to have a retailer to whom one can turn confidently for guidance. Every buyer should have a reliable shop, of course, but it is particularly essential for beginners to start their serious seach for knowledge by locating a good specialty shop where questions can be asked with the assurance of getting specific answers about the flavor of various types, for instance, or suggestions about new varieties to add to one's repertoire.

Sampling before making a decision is the only sure way to tell whether you like the flavor, or whether the choice you have made is in acceptable condition. With the increased interest in cheese in the 1970's, many cheese shops and departments in large stores began a practice of setting out small pieces of cheeses as they introduced new varieties. Good stores have no reluctance in offering tastes before purchase. Nor will they push a sale on the unwary in order to get rid of stock that is over the hill.

European exporters, without being direful, try to guide retailers to handle their stock so that it never is too old to sell. From each dairy country there come frequent brochures containing delicately phrased admonitions about the various kinds of cheese, almost as if the cheeses were little orphans about whom surrogate parents should be told in the kindest terms. In a booklet entitled "The Art of Selling French Cheeses," the government agency in Paris called Sopexa mentions that it is at the point of sale that the most important stage in the aging process takes place. "The client buys cheese with his eyes," a Swiss Cheese Union sales manual adds in amplification.

In France, with its hundreds of indigenous varieties, the proprietor of a cheese shop has traditionally seen to it that his sign identified him as *"fromager affineur"*—cheese seller and "finisher." In such stores cheese is bought not from a merchant who considers it just another item in the store's stock but from one who knows it to be, in the traditional phrase, "a living substance" to be brought to the peak of its maturity as the result of skill and concern.

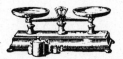

CHEESES NEED REFINING   A Paris *affineur*—long trusted with his handmade Camemberts by Daniel Courtonne—is named Hubert Schoonwater. It had been this man's life's work to take in adolescent cheeses— he had been supplied at one time by as many as three hundred dairymen —for careful aging before offering them to his own customers. Every three days he washed the brick-colored rind of the Burgundy cheeses known as Époisses in a mixture of salt water and marc (the distilled residue of wine). His Maroilles, the monastery cheese from Flanders, were washed in beer to bring them to perfection, and the mountain cheeses called Vacherins developed their own crusts in regular baths of white wine and herbs. Others were nurtured toward just the right-colored mold, and all were turned repeatedly to ensure consistent development of their interiors.

The steady disappearance of those devoted to the perfection of cheeses is a result of the new dairy economy. Farmers all over the world have been persuaded that it is more sensible to sell their milk to large factories than to be tied down to making cheeses seven days a week. The economy of world markets now demands pasteurization, and in many cases the addition to the curds of a stabilizing agent to keep the product in saleable condition for a longer time. For Hubert Schoonwater the change meant, as he said, "working with dead cheese."

After a lifetime of buying and finishing cheeses, the internationally known *maître fromager* Pierre Androuët wrote a book, *Guide du Fromage,* in which he said, "Tastes change. Today people prefer products that are guaranteed to be hygienic, even if the taste suffers; this despite the fact that products lacking such guarantes are not the least bit harmful, and are far more authentic in taste." Later Androuët told Joseph Wechsberg in an interview, "There is much nonsense said and written about germs and such. Naturally, the finest flavored cheese is made from fresh milk."

Nevertheless, Pierre Androuët accepts pasteurization as the fact of life it is, and supplies his customers with certain pasteurized cheeses during the seasons when those varieties in their raw-milk versions would not otherwise be available. "I stock pasteurized cheese only in certain seasons," he wrote, pointing out that by paying careful attention to his selections, he could offer special clients favorite cheeses whose taste had not been altered entirely by the pasteurization process. But he remained certain that the flavor of a natural cheese can only be approximated under factory conditions.

Below his shop and that of Hubert Schoonwater there are aging cellars that have been divided into rooms in which both temperature and humidity are controlled at levels suitable to various types of cheese. Along one wall at Chez Androuët hundreds of Camemberts are stacked neatly on wooden shelves; near the stairway there are red-skinned Edams, round orange Mimolettes, goat cheeses in various shapes and sizes, and platter-size Bries, powdery-white and separated from their shelves by straw mats. American shops, in contrast, are not equipped for the craftsmanship of the *affineur.* Glass-doored or other types of cooling units keep various categories of stock at temperatures designed to prevent spoilage and retard excess development.

WHAT TO LOOK FOR   For a shopper frustrated by a supermarket, a delicatessen, or another store unwilling to offer samples of cheeses, the best recourse is to look for a shop at which cheese is sufficiently in demand to ensure that most do not languish on their shelves beyond their time. You may have the greatest confidence in buying bulk cheeses so displayed that you can see their condition, and you should approach foil-wrapped items cautiously—at least at first.

Look for descriptive labels. Aged Cheddar is no different in appearance from young, and therefore mild, Cheddar, but each should be identified as "aged," "sharp," or even "medium sharp"; if the Cheddar is young and mild in flavor, it should be so indicated. No Cheddar should be cracked and dry-looking, and it should show no external blemishes or mold.

Blue-veined cheeses, on the other hand, wear mold as a badge of merit, but they too should not be dry or bear brownish traces near their edges—a sign that they are overly ripe. England's blue-veined Stilton has more fat content than either Gorgonzola or Roquefort, but its texture is more like that of a good Cheddar, while Gorgonzola has a more buttery look. To recognize a so-called Blue Cheese made by modern automated methods, look for the small, sharp straight lines adjacent to the spots of mold that show the manner in which the mold is injected.

Swiss Cheese, as Willi Bühlmann pointed out, is only a genuine product of the Alpine republic when it is packaged as "Switzerland Swiss," or when it has the word "Switzerland" stamped repeatedly on its rind like spokes of a wheel. "Imported Swiss," as some cheese with holes has sometimes been marked, may be the product of another country altogether. Cheesemakers in Wisconsin, and elsewhere, make a copy of Switzerland's Emmenthaler; there is in addition a great deal manufactured according to a recent formula that turns out "large-eyed" cheese in large blocks without the nutty texture and taste of the original. Look carefully at the label when buying, and note the shinier surface of the machine-made block cheese.

A sin that passes for a convenience is the packaging of ground Parmesan and Romano. The magnificent Italian grating cheeses, which include Asiago, Pecorino Toscano, and others, should be bought in small chunks about a pound in weight and grated at home each time you use some, as the stuff that comes in small jars or plastic envelopes has little, if any, flavor and is no more succulent than sawdust. If necessary, look for an Italian neighborhood store to find the real thing. And look for the words "Parmigiano-Reggiano" stenciled on the rind of bulk pieces, or the labels "Italian Parmesan" or "Imported from Italy" on the package.

A WORD ABOUT IMITATIONS . . . Another much-copied Italian cheese is Fontina, the great wheels from the Piedmont that take their name from Mount Fontin, not far from the Swiss border. It is the basis of *fonduta,* in which melted cheese, butter, milk, and beaten egg yolks are mixed and crowned with leaf-thin slices of white truffles, then poured sometimes over slabs of polenta. Genuine Fontina is the deep ivory color of Emmenthal and its texture is very supple, with a natural rind a shade darker in color. A substitute that is much more common in the United States is bright red on the outside, bright yellow inside, and has mild, innocuous flavor.

Life may seem equally confusing for shoppers confronted with two kinds of Munster. The original, from eastern France, is soft, creamy in texture, and full of flavor; the American version, of which thousands of tons are sold to contented buyers, is not as moist and is much milder. In the same category, Port du Salut has been described as "between Cheddar and Limburger" in flavor. Experiment is recommended because this cheese, which is called either Port du Salut or Port Salut, is apt to vary in consistency, taste, and maturity, depending on where and how it is made. Port du Salut, when imported from France, is usually a good buy for those seeking flavor with gentle piquancy. Similar attributes apply to the related cheeses known as Esrom, made by the Danes. Less assertive among other such semisoft cheeses are Holland's Edams and Goudas, which have Scandinavian imitations called Fynbo and Elbo.

. . . *AND ABOUT SOFT-RIPENED*   Soft-ripened types—Brie, Camembert, some of the double and triple creams, Pont l'Évêque, and others —require special attention from buyers. Brie is now made in several parts of France, in Central Europe, Scandinavia, Ireland, Australia, Canada, and the United States. On its native heath, it is made in the traditional large flat disks weighing three and a half to four and a half pounds and varying in diameter from 9 to 14 or more inches. But Brie also is now manufactured and packaged to look almost exactly like Camembert, as if no difference recognizable to the amateur had validity. The niceties that in the past distinguished the Bries of connoisseurs have disappeared, except for those who are devoted to the search. The average shopper who does not want to settle for a small packaged Brie should look for a store in which wedges of this once superlative cylinder are wrapped in cellophane and so displayed that the sides cut and exposed by the knife reveal the consistency within. If a Brie bulges against its cellophane constraint it is so ripe it should be eaten immediately—it may not even make a short trip home—and it certainly will be running all over the plate if left at room temperature for an hour or so. In a condition so fluent, this is a cheese to buy only from an absolutely trustworthy supplier. If its appearance seems good but its taste is rank, a good dealer will replace it.

Camembert is boxed and usually wrapped, but it should not be bought without testing its resiliency. Don't be afraid to open the box. The cheese within should seem slightly plump to the touch, slightly springy, an indication that it does not have a heart of chalk. A Camembert made in Ohio is widely available and often good and, like the Liederkranz made in the same town, it is stamped with a date that indicates its prime; select one of either cheese and eat it a day or two in advance of the pull date to get it at the right degree of ripening—after the white center has disappeared and before it is either too runny or too rank. If the flavor is overly strong and the tang has become bitter, return it for refund or exchange.

Beware of stores that keep dated products on the shelf after—sometimes long after—the manufacturer stipulates. Beware also of stores unwilling to accept the return of cheeses you have found bad once you have taken them home. The responsibility for one gone bad before its terminal date is the retailer's. This is one way to tell the degree of dependability of the dealer. If he won't make good on a cheese that has gone bad through no fault of the buyer, you might as well know it—and avoid repeating the disappointment.

There is something equally important to be said about establishing a friendly rapport with your cheese dealer, especially if you have only one store that is conveniently located. Recently, a friend who lives in a remote New England community suggested the value of "cultivating" such people. "They have a difficult life," she said. It is a good point. A great deal of attention as well as a steady flow of customers is required to maintain a variety of cheese in stock. "I think dealers respond to customers who express pleasure and interest and who are willing to discuss what types they might buy," she continued. In other words, there is much to be gained from having a single supplier with whom you have a relationship based on trust and candor.

This sort of thing is impossible when dealing with the so-called

cheese clubs or the packagers who offer gift assortments that are shipped from warehouses. Despite the blandishments of mail order brochures it is difficult to be sure of getting what you think you have ordered until you are knowledgeable about many types of cheese and many imitations. It is one thing to use the mail order service of a cheesemaker or retailer who deals in special selections on which he stakes his reputation, and quite something else to deal with a "club" that offers bargains or "discoveries" purported to be made available to a select clientele.

SELECTIONS FOR ENTERTAINING   In America in the 1970's the serving of cheese to guests became increasingly popular. In a decade the per capita consumption jumped more than 50 percent, and the amount of cheese imported from Europe doubled, with Denmark, Italy, Switzerland, and France supplying about 75 million pounds a year. More and more people took to the European habit of offering an assortment that included a balance of soft and hard varieties. With so many kinds available throughout the country, selection of a small array for serving at or near the end of a meal became easy. A small revolution in menu planning was one of the results.

The idea was not new, of course, and in considering it I'm reminded of a passage in James Beard's *Delights and Prejudices,* a book full of temptations, published in 1964: "I am grateful to have learned young that cheese has an important place in a menu. It isn't something to serve with apple pie, and it isn't something to cut into nasty little cubes and serve with crackers. Early in life I learned to see the beauty of great slabs or rounds of cheese on the table, and I still respond to the sight of a well-stocked cheese tray properly presented."

Slabs or rounds can be arranged attractively, and they deserve careful selection. For instance, as a dinner course with or after the salad, you might match a perfectly finished Camembert with a Stilton, a Bel Paese, and a wedge of real Emmenthal. A presentation of cheese as a part of a dinner menu should give guests a variety of consistency as well as flavor. Another assortment might include a creamy Boursault, a Vermont Cheddar, Taleggio from Italy, and a Blue Castello. Or, perhaps, Caerphilly, a wedge of Brie, a French goat cheese.

The number of selections offered may depend upon budgetary considerations, of course, but three, four, or even more are in order for a dinner in which the rest of the menu has been planned with love and consideration. Think of contrast in color—as in the chance to match the mottled green of Vermont Sage against the reddish crust of Liederkranz, the mellow, pale gold of Cantal or St. Nectaire, and the pristine look of Caprice des Dieux. Such compositions need handsome service: a well-shaped cheese board, veins of subtle color in a marble plate, or a simple, unpatterned platter that will provide appetizing support. A separate knife for each cheese is also advisable, so that one is not mixed with another. Many cheese stores have added serving paraphernalia to their stock, and offer assortments of knives, wire slicers, and peelers to shave off wide curls from a smooth, firm loaf. For those who have discovered the magnificence of aged Parmesan when served as one of the choices in a cheese course, or separately as an accompaniment for fresh fruit, there are special knives with rounded points—designed not to cut but to plunge into a side of the cheese and pry away small pieces, following the natural grain of the cheese.

THE COCKTAIL HOUR   With such weaponry, there are many who like to serve cheese at the cocktail hour, with whiskies, gin, vodka, and other so-called hard drinks. Aside from choosing a whole cheese, from which guests can appease their appetites as they see fit, there are almost infinite variations of canapés—hot or cold—which are based on cheese. A three-pound wheel of sharp Tillamook or Crowley (among domestic Cheddar cousins), a whole Brie, a Stilton for those whose taste for cheese is as expansive as their thirst, or a whole Havarti is a good choice for hungry drinkers. And the many kinds of cheese easily available make it easy to arrange cheese buffets—assortments that might include one or two soft-ripened cheeses, slices of caraway-flavored loaves, and so on. Cheese balls, or logs—highly American devices—are available where good cheeses are sold or, better yet, can be mixed at home combining Cream Cheese with Stilton or Roquefort, Cheddar with pimientos, chilies, or nuts; various combinations are to be found in the Recipes, pages 123–9.

The generically American cocktail party has gone abroad, and the ubiquitous cheese dip has found a hospitable climate in Europe. "New York and Chicago have come to Paris," Simone Beck wrote in her magnificent *Simca's Cuisine,* "and the cocktail party is very common . . . with some special differences, a strong French accent." As a dip for raw vegetables to be served with drinks, Mme. Beck invented a combination of Philadelphia Cream Cheese, peeled, seeded, and grated cucumber, hard-boiled eggs, and tomato paste that is accented by capers, garlic, chives, shallots, parsley and basil or dill, Tabasco, and a little cognac. She gives another French touch to bite-size sandwiches of Emmenthaler and ham (the classic snack called *Croque Monsieur*) that are dipped in egg and bread crumbs, then baked in a hot oven.

Prevalent in this country, and not to be confused with dips and other mixtures created at home, are manufactured combinations called "cold pack," or "cold pack cheese food," sold in crocks, jars, or variously shaped plastic wrappings. Somewhat like processed cheese, which is achieved by use of an emulsifying agent, these products were devised as ways to market cheeses with minor defects by working salt, color, and spices, along with a reducing factor, into cheese that has been finely ground. Aptly, such products have been termed "the TV dinners of the cheese world."

THE CARE AND PRESERVATION OF CHEESE   Real cheese demands, and deserves, far more care than do such concoctions. It is susceptible to temperature changes and to exposure to air. No matter how it is wrapped at point of sale, there is reason to treat it with care when you bring it home. It may be wrapped with foil smoothed against all surfaces to force out air, then folded tightly or crimped along the edges. But clear plastic wrap serves a dual purpose by sealing the cheese as well as showing what it looks like, so one kind can be recognized from another without opening. The important thing is to wrap each piece tightly. Put several pieces so wrapped in a plastic bag and tie it shut. Then put the cheese in the warmest part of your refrigerator. In our experience, the bottom shelf is ideal. Before serving, remove it from the refrigerator soon enough to bring each piece to room temperature—except when the weather is exceedingly hot. An hour and a half is about right for whole cheeses of most kinds, but Camemberts and Bries, and others like them, usually require somewhat less time and should be carefully attended so they don't run out of their crusts. As soon as dinner is over, wrap every leftover piece tightly and return to refrigerator for future use. Even though it may have been ineptly cut, cheese is too precious ever to throw out.

And if it is cut well there will be less excuse for casting remnants aside. In fact, the times when all the cheese you serve will be consumed at one sitting will be very few. Hence, what is left should be in shape to serve again. For reasons of flavor, as well as aesthetics and conservation, it is important to treat cheese with respect at home, or in a public eating place; therefore, here are some drawings of various types of cheese and various shapes:

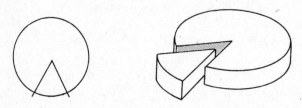

Round cheeses should be cut in the same way and with the same care as a cake or pie.

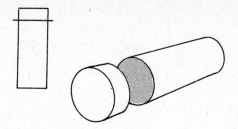

Log-shaped types, like the French goat cheeses, should be sliced to make individual rounds.

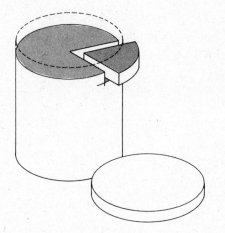

Stiltons are sometimes opened at the top and spooned out, but the more accepted British way requires slicing horizontally about a quarter of an inch from the top, then cutting thinnish pie-shaped pieces and replacing the top slice as a lid.

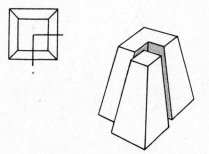

Pyramidal-shaped cheeses, like Valencay, should be cut in neat quarters.

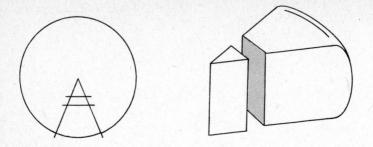

Large wedges cut from big wheels, like Cheddar, should be cut across the point, with additional cuts forming parallel slices.

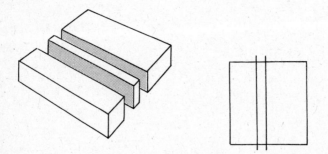

Square types, such as Livarot or Carré de l'Est, should be cut parallel to one side; divide the piece at right angles if a smaller size is desired.

Imported Italian Parmesan is never sliced, when properly served. Instead, small pieces should be pried away, following the natural grain of the cheese (see Selections for Entertaining, page 110).

FREEZING FRESH CHEESES Experience persuades us that virtually any cheese that is fresh and in good condition can be frozen. In fact, one New York purveyor freezes the Bries he selects for a distinguished client on the West Coast, then packs them in dry ice for shipment by air. In our kitchen we have stored cheese we can't eat immediately in the freezing compartment of the refrigerator by simply wrapping it tightly in plastic film and putting it next to the ice trays. Whole wheels can be frozen, or they may be cut into halves, quarters, or any other size; make sure each piece has air-tight wrapping, for this preserves flavor, texture, and moisture content. For best results, remove the cheese from the freezer and leave it in the refrigerator for 24–48 hours of slow, steady thawing. If you plan to keep grated cheese for any length of time, it is also better to store it in the freezer than the refrigerator.

14

Good
Drinking Companions

"The true wine lover is also a connoisseur of cheese," the late Helen Evans Brown wrote in a treatise she called *Wine and Cheese, the Perfect Partners*. Mrs. Brown went on to reiterate that there is nothing like cheese to prepare the palate for the enjoyment of wine. "And wine repays the compliment," she said, "for it brings out the best in a natural cheese." A lifetime in the vineyard state of California only made it easier for Helen Brown to find this home truth early in life, for the partners she wrote so lovingly about were brought together as soon as each was discovered by man. Cheese and wine have been found side by side among the tokens of comfort provided in the earliest Egyptian tombs. No journey beyond this world—it was recognized even ten thousand years ago—should be made without the best of food and drink.

Certainly, at any fine meal nothing is pleasanter than the course—just after salad and just before the dessert—when a selection of cheese is served as a kind of tribute to the wine. Between a green salad and a fruit tart, for instance, you might serve a fine Camembert and the same Bordeaux you have chosen to enhance the meat course, and it will inform your taste buds anew. Or if you have chosen a white Graves to accompany fish or seafood, you may find (as some Frenchmen do) that Roquefort is one cheese that goes as well with a white wine as with a red.

There are as many theories for mating a cheese bearing one set of traits with a wine that has a perfect affinity as matchmakers have for selecting brides and bridegrooms incontestably attuned to each other. In simple truth, however, there is no secret to picking a wine to go well with cheese. In a country like France, so rich in both, the local wines—renowned or otherwise—are preferred as matches for local cheeses; there is natural affinity between two products of the same district. It is so in all wine-producing countries. In Switzerland, for example, any of the mountain cheeses are popularly served with Swiss white wines like Neuchâtel, Dézaley, Aigle, Mont, Fendant, and La Côte, while in the Italian-speaking region known as Ticino other Swiss eat their cheeses of goat's and cow's milk with the local reds from Pinot Noir, Gamay, or Merlot grapes.

Leaving out other persuasions, it is worth a trip abroad to sample together cheeses and wines that have matured side by side, so to speak. There are small wines in the Savoy that are just right for cheese from those high meadows, or you may find in the French Rhône Valley local wines that are perfect with the *chèvres* of nearby cheesemakers. Before the advent of swift transportation and refrigerated storage, many cheeses never were to be found outside their native regions. Because that is true to some extent today, the easiest way to get to know certain rustic cheeses is to come to them, in their own territory, and wash them down with their own vintages.

Enterprising people at Swissair have assured me that the "Wine and Cheese Discovery Tours," begun by the airline in the early 1970's, have attracted more and more Americans each year from each of the states, as well as hundreds of travelers from everywhere in Europe. The tours take students of wine and cheese into remote Alpine chalets where the vineyards were planted in the days of the Romans and the cheeses were being made even earlier than that. Some of the itineraries take you on to eastern Austria for the gusto of Steiermark cheese and spicy Schilcherwein, and down to the vineyards and pastureland of Yugoslavia. Still, though an organized trip to Europe may be fine for such out-of-the-way discoveries, it is much simpler to begin on home turf.

It is a good idea to keep things, under any circumstances, just as uncomplicated as is the matching of regional wines and cheeses on their native heath. In the same way that white wines are traditional accompaniments for fish and poultry, red wines enhance hearty red meats and game—and most cheese. Nothing is more subjective than a choice of wine for a specific kind of cheese, and that makes experiment necessary to please your own palate. No travel is required to try to find the right Burgundy wine to go with the cheeses—say, Époisses or Explorateur—that come from that region. In fact, a full-bodied Burgundy is as good a choice as a Bordeaux red to bring out the flavor of any sensitive morsel—Brie, for instance, or Camembert. Cream cheeses like Boursault and Crema Dania go well with lighter red wines, as does the rich Italian Taleggio. (Try the latter with a Valpolicella from its home ground.) French goat cheeses may, in their own regions, be accompanied by local white wines, rosés, or reds, but certain connoisseurs would insist on Sancerre or Chablis to serve with the small local Loire disks called Crottins. The white Seyssel liked by skiers in the French Alps is considered a boon companion of Reblochon.

In the Normandy apple country, cider accommodates Camembert perfectly to the native taste, just as it is habitually served by some Britons with Cheddar and other English cheeses; for others in the United Kingdom the drink to take with your Ploughman's Lunch is beer or ale. With Stilton the average Britisher will want a glass of port (and the fastidious will frown upon pouring it onto the cheese itself). Sherry is often served with Stilton and other blue-veined types, and Roquefort is in good hands, at least in southwest France, when mated with Gewürztraminer and even more appreciated by others who marry Château Yquem, "the greatest of Sauternes" in their opinion, with Roquefort, "the greatest of *les bleus*." Madeira, also, sometimes satisfies the palates of those who are deeply moved by the eloquence of well-made marbled cheeses.

Because the confirmed wine lover is by nature a philanderer among cheeses, he soon finds that no food better prepares the taste buds for the appreciation of subtleties in wine than does cheese in any of its myriad manifestations. The great vintages become even more worthy of esteem and modest bottles are seemingly changed in character when served with one or another of the world's good choices among cheeses. Conversely, wine often heightens distinctions of flavor among the cheeses. Together, the two provide a reason as inviting as any for gathering with friends.

GIVING A WINE AND CHEESE PARTY   A "cheese and wine tasting" is a kind of party that grows more popular in America and is one that gives a distinctive reason to bring friends together. One learns by tasting in company, and at the same time gets more satisfaction. If hosts and guests are serious about learning the differences among cheeses, as well as wines, the evening can be one for which no big meal is planned. Both wine and cheese should be selected as seriously as you would plan a menu for a good dinner.

HOW MUCH TO BUY· Inviting between eight and a dozen guests, you ought to have almost as many kinds of cheese, no less than three-quarters of a pound of each—enough so that each person gets a sample of each cheese offered and more of those he or she is taken with. Don't worry about leftovers. If, by chance, you should have remainders when the party is over, turn to the Recipes.

One wine will do if the party is really an introduction to new cheese tastes. But a combined "cheese and wine tasting" suggests at least a taste for everyone of (a) a full-bodied red wine, (b) a light, fruity red, (c) a dry white, (d) a dry sherry.

WHICH CHEESES TO BUY The greater variety, the more fun the party is apt to offer guests. The selected cheeses should include one or two blue cheeses for comparison (and to make up your own mind about the mighty Roquefort); two or three goat cheeses; two or three soft-ripened; two or three supple, rinded wheels; and a sampling of semihard types. You might get guests to rate Danish Blue against a Michigan wheel that takes the name of Gorgonzola; or compare an imported Gorgonzola against a Bleu de Bresse. From the goat types choose one of those shaped like a pyramid, or a Ste. Maure. The soft-ripened category should include a big wheel of Brie from which you have cut a wedge just as the guests arrive, and rounds of Camembert, Coulommiers, a square of Carré de l'Est. Supple, rinded cheeses are well represented by Beaufort, Oka from Canada, Port Salut, Reblochon, or a youthful Appenzeller.

For smaller parties, it may be amusing to announce a Brie-tasting party at which a real Brie, fresh off the plane from the Île-de-France, is matched with its imitators from Denmark, Germany, Ireland, Lena, Illinois, Petaluma, California, and so on. There are more variations of Camembert to inspire discussion among wine tasters, including the domestic from Van Wert, Ohio, and various other American dairy regions.

Van Wert's most famous product, Liederkranz, could spark a beer or ale drinkers' gathering at which it could be compared with Limburger, Schloss, Old Heidelberg, imported Munster, or Brick.

A FONDUE AND WINE PARTY There are plenty of kits and various paraphernalia of all sorts available for making fondues, but all that is really necessary is a source of heat, an enamel or Teflon-lined pot, something to spear the cheese (wooden-handled 10-inch three-pronged forks are traditional), and a basket or plate to hold the bread. Any good dry domestic wine such as Chardonnay, Chenin Blanc, French Colombard, Gray Riesling, Monterey Gewürztraminer, Pinot Blanc, Sauvignon Blanc, or a jug labeled Mountain Chablis can be used as both an ingredient and an accompaniment. However, this Swiss cheese and wine party will seem more authentic if you choose one of the white wines from western Switzerland: Aigle, Dézaley, Fendant, Mont, or Neuchâtel. There are a number of ways to vary the consistency and flavors of fondues, but the basics are wine and cheese—and sometimes the accent of kirsch (see Recipes). In Italy the variation of such a party's *pièce de résistance* is called *fonduta,* a mélange of diced Fontina that has steeped in milk several hours before being melted and served with thin slices of white truffles from the Piedmont, and it is worth trying with a glass of Barolo from the Piedmont, or a Barbera from the Napa Valley.

A SKIERS' WINE AND CHEESE RESPITE   A raclette party calls for winter, an open fireplace, if you're lucky enough—and a zestful appetite that follows a day of skiing may not be necessary, but adds to the enjoyment of this mating of wine and cheese. To serve raclette to a large group you should buy half a wheel of the firm, creamy cheese that bears this name, or another Swiss mountain cheese like Bagnes, Delalp, or Gomser. You will need heatproof plates that can be made sizzling hot, plus underplates or wooden or wicker plate holders. Put the semicircle of cheese next to the glowing coals of a fireplace (or other heat source) in a vertical position; heat the plates and put one of them under the cheese as it melts. When it begins to ooze hotly and freely, scrape some cheese onto one plate and serve while it is still bubbling, accompanied by buttered boiled potatoes, tiny boiled or pickled onions, and tart gherkins. Keep the cheese hot and melting, and repeat the servings one at a time. Serve a Swiss white wine like Fendant, or a hearty French wine like Les Murets, or a California bottle you like.

Our refrigerator, which for years has sagged a bit with its burden, has never been without a choice of cheeses on its bottom shelf. My wife and I not only finish virtually every dinner with a cheese course, but we use many kinds in cooking. We have found that while good cookbooks give useful directions for well-known dishes using cheese, there is still much room for a fertile imagination—to be sparked, perhaps, by some of the ideas in the following section.

Part Three

Recipes

*Unless otherwise indicated these recipes would
generally serve four, but they are meant to be
informal and flexible, it being obvious
that a dish used as a first course
will stretch farther than if it were served
as a main entrée at lunch or supper.
Use your own judgment.*

Appetizers for Drinks, or for Meals

Not only can cheese be turned into plain and puffed appetizers, canapés, tidbits, quiches, turnovers, and other pastries (see Index), but such luscious things can be made from leftover nubs no longer presentable on the cheese board. Two or more cheeses that have seen their best days can be melted together. Sharp cheese that has been allowed to dry out can be ground to add accent to creamy cheese spreads. The underdeveloped chalky core of Camembert (or Brie, Liederkranz, and so on) can be made into a thick béchamel, as Simone Beck has suggested (see page 171), then formed into morsels and dipped in bread crumbs to be fried. Cream Cheese, of course, makes a fine stuffing for rolled slices of ham, chipped beef, or sausage, and even zestier combinations result when the Cream Cheese is accented by the mixing in of cheese that has sharper flavor; or use Cottage Cheese or Farmer Cheese as a base for similar mixtures. In the recipes that follow, Cream Cheese is the common base—for which you may choose your own substitute, for there is much room for invention.

CHEESE PISTACHIO

1 cup heavy cream
1 scallion, minced
1 Tbs. applejack (or other brandy)
1/3 cup finely ground pistachio nuts

1/2 tsp. salt
freshly ground pepper
8 oz. Cream Cheese (or Farmer),
    room temperature

Whip cream until stiff, stirring in minced scallion and applejack, ground nuts, salt, and 8 to 10 turns of pepper grinder. Mash cheese with a fork and combine with whipped cream mixture. Shape into an attractive mound, decorated, if you wish, with additional pistachios, and chill before serving.

CARAWAY CREAM COCKTAIL CHEESE

This is especially good on fingers of pumpernickel, and a perfect companion for cold beer. Another time, try substituting Liederkranz for the Cream Cheese.

4 oz. Cream Cheese	1/2 tsp. caraway seeds
1 cup creamed Cottage Cheese	1 tsp. Dijon mustard
3 scallions, finely minced	1 Tbs. grated Parmesan
1 tsp. capers, drained	1 Tbs. flat beer

Put all ingredients in a mixing bowl and beat until well blended, then cover and ripen in the refrigerator about 48 hours.

JEANNETTE SEAVER'S BOURSINOISE

I sometimes mix up herbed cheeses on impulse and with the help of whatever ingredients come easily to hand. This recipe, however, is from a book full of ideas called *Jeannette's Secrets of Everyday Good Cooking;* it is the next best thing to dinner at the Seavers'.

8 oz. Cream Cheese	1 clove garlic, minced very fine
1/3 cup sour cream	2 tsps. dried thyme
1/2 cup whipped cream	1/2 cup finely chopped parsley
4 shallots, minced very fine	salt
1/2 cup finely chopped chives	freshly ground pepper
(or scallions)	

In a bowl, thoroughly mix with a fork all the ingredients, seasoning to taste. Refrigerate until ready to serve, either in a pretty crock or reshaped on a platter. It can be eaten as soon as you have made it, but refrigeration will give it added firmness.

GARLIC CHEDDAR–CREAM CHEESE ROLL

1 lb. sharp Cheddar	1/2 tsp. sugar
1/2 lb. Cream Cheese	salt
3 cloves garlic, finely minced	cayenne
1 tsp. lemon juice	

Grate Cheddar into a bowl and mash Cream Cheese into it, then add garlic, lemon juice, and sugar, mixing until smooth and thoroughly amalgamated. Taste and add a dash of salt if needed, then mix in a dash of cayenne. Divide mixture into four equal parts and roll into uniform shapes; wrap separately and put into refrigerator to mature 2 or 3 days. Slice thinly for use on crackers (or see page 164 for other uses).

CHILI-FLAVORED CHEESE LOG

1/4 lb. Cream Cheese	2 Tbs. minced parsley
1/4 lb. white Cheddar, grated	1 1/2 tsps. chili powder
1 clove garlic, minced	1 Tbs. minced watercress
1/4 cup finely minced shallots	1 tsp. paprika
3 Tbs. pine nuts	

Beat cheeses together with a fork, then blend in garlic and shallots; cover and chill 2 hours so flavors meld. Scrape mixture onto a piece of wax paper, and shape into a log about 1 1/2 inches thick. Stir together remaining ingredients; spread this out on the wax paper and roll the log over it until the cheese is encrusted on all surfaces. Wrap carefully and chill 2 to 3 hours before serving in slices to be eaten on crackers.

WENSLEYDALE DIP

1/2 lb. white Wensleydale (or mild Cheddar), grated	3 Tbs. finely minced watercress
1/2 cup heavy cream	3 Tbs. finely chopped walnuts
1 1/2 Tbs. onion juice	cayenne
	salt

Put grated cheese in a mixing bowl. Heat cream, but do not let it come to boil; beat it into the cheese, adding onion juice, watercress, nuts, a pinch of cayenne, and salt to taste.

ANCHOVY-MOZZARELLA CROSTINI

8 thin slices white bread	oregano
2 small cans anchovy fillets	1/4 lb. butter
1/2 lb. Mozzarella, room temperature	

Trim crusts from bread and cut each slice into four strips. Soak anchovies in warm water about 10 minutes, then drain and pat dry. Cut Mozzarella in flat strips just a little smaller than the bread. Top bread fingers with cheese and sprinkle lightly with oregano. Arrange in a shallow baking dish and put in a hot oven for about 7 minutes, until cheese begins to bubble. Meanwhile chop the anchovies and heat with the butter, stirring to make a sauce; pour over sizzling cheese strips, and serve at once.

DEEP-FRIED MOZZARELLA CROQUETTES

These are affectionately known in central Italy as "telephone croquettes" because the melted cheese strings out when bitten into as does a wire hanging from the phone when one puts the receiver to his ear. Some say that they were originally made of buffalo-milk Provola, but Mozzarella is most commonly found in the centers of these deep-fried balls that are often made with leftover risotto; some cooks (who occasionally substitute Bel Paese) add a little ham to the cheese. Many Italians find them an attractive dish for a luncheon first course.

2 cups cooked rice
2 eggs, beaten
½ lb. Mozzarella, cut in ½-inch dice

3–4 slices prosciutto (or other ham), cut in ¾-inch squares
¾ cup fine bread crumbs
oil for deep frying

Combine rice and beaten eggs, making sure each grain is covered. Put 1 tablespoon of coated rice in the palm of your hand, press into the center a few pieces of cheese and a square or two of ham, then put 1 more tablespoon of rice on top and shape into a ball, completely enclosing the ham and cheese. Roll the ball in bread crumbs to cover entirely. Heat oil to 375°, and fry four or five balls at a time, turning them over and around for about 5 minutes to make an even crust all over. Drain on paper towels and keep warm in the oven until the entire batch is finished.

MOZZARELLA MILANESE

1 lb. fresh Mozzarella
flour
1 large egg, well beaten
1–1½ cups fresh bread crumbs

2 cups tomato sauce, flavored with anchovy
oil for deep frying

Cut the cheese in slices ¼ inch thick and preferably 2 inches wide and 4 inches long. Dredge slices in flour, covering all surfaces. Dip each slice in beaten egg so it is thoroughly covered, then in bread crumbs. Cheese must be thoroughly sealed by the three coatings. Heat oil to 375°, and add cheese slices, turning up heat slightly to maintain temperature. Watch carefully so bread crumbs do not burn, nor cooking take so long that cheese oozes out. After 3 minutes, turn coated slices over; fry 2 more minutes, or until crusty outside is golden. Drain on paper toweling, quickly transfer to very hot platter or, better, plates, and serve with hot anchovy-flavored tomato sauce.

PUFFED-UP CHEESE CANAPÉS

1½ cups grated semisoft or firm
    cheese
1 egg, lightly beaten
few drops Worcestershire or
    Tabasco

optional: mustard
6–8 slices homemade-type bread
    (Cheese Bread, page 174,
    is excellent)

Mix grated cheese, egg, and Worcestershire or Tabasco to taste. Remove crusts and cut two small rounds from each slice of bread. Brush a little mustard on the rounds if you wish. Place generous amount of cheese mixture on each, mounding toward the center. Broil carefully under hot broiler until puffy and lightly browned. Serve hot.

AJOQUESO: GARLIC–MONTEREY JACK SPREAD

½ cup minced onion
2 large cloves garlic, minced
4 Tbs. olive oil
4 Tbs. green chili peppers, seeded
    and minced

2 Tbs. flour
1 cup light cream
½ lb. Monterey Jack (or Colby or
    mild Cheddar), shredded

Sauté onion and garlic in oil and stir in peppers. Blend in flour, stirring about 3 minutes. Off heat, add cream and stir until smooth. Return to heat, stir in shredded cheese, and let it melt. Serve in a chafing dish with tortillas as an accompaniment for drinks.

CHEESE STICKS

This is a fine way to use up any bits of pastry after you have trimmed a pie; the sticks are particularly good made with the Cream Cheese Pastry Dough on page 176. All you do is sprinkle the pastry board generously with grated Parmesan and over it roll out whatever dough you have on hand as thinly as possible. Then, using a ruler as a guide, cut strips about ¼ inch wide. Transfer to baking sheet, brush lightly with egg glaze (1 beaten egg mixed with 1 tablespoon water), and sprinkle with more Parmesan. Bake in 350° oven for about 10 minutes or until golden brown. Transfer the sticks carefully to a rack and let cool.

SAPSAGO COCKTAIL SPREAD

8 Tbs. sweet butter   ½ cup finely grated Sapsago

Whip butter until light, then blend in cheese to make a smooth, pale-green mixture. Mold it attractively on a serving plate, and chill about 2 hours. Arrange crackers around the spread when serving.

FILLED PASTRIES AND PUFFS

For bite-size appetizers to go with drinks, nothing beats a cheese filling spooned into tiny precooked pastry rounds or boats (made of your favorite basic pie dough, or the Cream Cheese Pastry Dough, page 176, or the puff pastry described in the Feuilletée recipe, page 146), then slipped into a hot oven. Or a cheese filling can be baked in the center of a little turnover. Or stuffed into an already baked pastry puff made of *pâte à choux*—the dough used for cream puffs and éclairs. Any of the fillings for Crêpes and Omelets described on pages 142–3 would do nicely, but remember that with these small mouthfuls, the filling should have a bity flavor, surrounded as it is with pastry; so don't be afraid to sharpen the accent in any of those fillings by adding, perhaps, a more assertive cheese, a dash of Tabasco, or a bit of anchovy, particularly with tomato. Here are suggested fillings, particularly good for a sizzling pastry appetizer.

SWISS CHEESE AND SAPSAGO: Mix one part soft sweet butter with two parts grated Swiss, Emmenthal, Gruyère, or other good firm mountain cheese, and just enough cream to make a smooth but firm paste. Add enough grated Sapsago to give zest. For a variation, try using a soft-ripened cheese (in this case less butter is needed) with Romano, Asiago, or Pecorino.

BLUE CHEESE CREAM: Mix about ½ pound Blue Cheese with 1 beaten egg and about ⅓ cup heavy cream (or a combination of cream and sour cream). Add salt and cayenne pepper to taste.

CAMEMBERT AMANDINE

Nothing could persuade me to tamper with Camembert *fermier* when tenderly nurtured toward maturity, but many imported, factory-produced Camemberts stand to benefit from imaginative doctoring. *Camembert au Vin* is most simply made when the wheel of cheese is set aside to stand in white wine overnight, then is rolled in crumbs of melba toast and chilled. It is served at room temperature. *Crème de Camembert* is an extension of the same recipe—extending, in a sense, the amount of cheese, as well as offering a way to retrieve a Camembert that is chalky at its heart: the thin white rind is scraped away and the cheese marinated in Chablis or Muscadet for 6 to 8 hours; then it is blended with ⅓ cup of unsalted butter, reshaped, and coated with crumbs before being put in the refrigerator to gain firmness. Best of all such Camembert embellishments is this one, calling for almonds.

1 whole Camembert	*about ⅓ cup finely chopped*
white wine to cover	*almonds*
¼ lb. unsalted butter	

Soak the cheese overnight in white wine; drain, scrape off any discoloration, and thoroughly blend the cheese with butter. Chill when perfectly smooth, then reform to look like Camembert. Cover top, bottom, and sides with chopped nuts, pressing them in lightly. Chill but remove from refrigerator about 1 hour before serving.

Soups

Few things seem more evocative of the manifest glory of soup than the onion-and-cheese-laced broth of Paris market workers. Recipes usually call for drifts of grated Gruyère, but as Paris gastronome Robert Courtine says of French onion soups, "Cheese? Yes, but the kind doesn't matter. There are at least 100 recipes, and there is only one." Onions are not essential to cheese soups, but the flavors go hand in hand, no matter what proportions are used. And other members of the onion family have an affinity for cheese in soup—leeks, scallions, shallots, as in the case of Alice B. Toklas's bouillon with shallots and cheese. Any stock may be used, or the base can be milk, cream, even water; the trick is not to let the cheese boil. A quarter-cup of grated cheese to one cup of liquid is an acceptable rule of thumb, but the variations are numberless—some adding garlic, some mixed vegetables. The kind of cheese called for in most recipes can be replaced with another of your favorite types, or with anything on hand in the refrigerator.

BASIC CHEESE SOUP

4 Tbs. butter
1/2 cup sifted flour
2 cups milk
2 cups cream (or chicken stock)
1 1/2–2 cups chopped sharp Cheddar

salt and pepper
1/2 tsp. dry mustard
opional: crumbled bacon or
    chopped hard-boiled egg

Melt butter in saucepan, then gradually stir in flour, making a smooth paste; cook about 5 minutes while heating milk and cream (or stock). Stir in hot liquid. When mixture is creamy, add cheese and cook over low heat just until cheese is melted. Season to taste, and garnish with crumbled bacon or chopped egg if desired.

EMMENTHALER SOUP

"No Swiss," an Alpine saying goes, "has ever refused his soup." Every canton has its own cheese soup specialty, and in less hurried times when wood fires burned in mountain kitchens and soups of various ingredients were simmered for hours, those made without the addition of cheese in cooking were served with small hills of grated cheese in side dishes. Traditionally, *Käsesuppe* was a meal in itself, often a mixture of bread and cheese in which a spoon stood upright and just as often containing more calories than a dinner of several courses. Croutons are common enough in the soups of Switzerland, and several of these potages are made with leftovers—pancakes cut into strips, or crumbled rolls, added to the stock with fried onions, chives, or parsley. Others, however, have a rich foundation of browned flour.

4 Tbs. butter	*freshly grated pepper*
3/4 cup flour	*1 garlic clove, minced*
4 cups beef stock, heated	*2 eggs, beaten*
1 Tbs. caraway seeds	*3/4 cup cream, heated*
freshly grated nutmeg	*1 cup grated Emmenthaler*
salt	*3–4 Tbs. minced parsley*

Melt butter in a good-size saucepan and add flour, stirring almost constantly over low heat 10 minutes or more, until flour turns a rich brown without burning. Stir in hot stock, blending until smooth and adding caraway and a liberal grating of nutmeg, salt and pepper to taste, and the minced garlic. Simmer over very low heat 1 hour or a little less. When the mixture has thoroughly cooked and is as thick as porridge, stir in the beaten eggs. Pour the hot cream into a heated tureen and sprinkle in the cheese; add the soup and serve very hot, with a scattering of parsley on each bowl.

LIEDERKRANZ CHEESE–BEER SOUP

1/3 cup butter	*4-oz. pkg. Liederkranz Cheese,*
2 Tbs. finely chopped onion	*cubed*
1/3 cup flour	*salt and pepper*
2 1/2 cups milk	
1 1/2 cups beer (12-oz. can), room	
temperature	

Melt butter in a saucepan, add chopped onions, and sauté until tender. Stir in flour and cook 3 to 4 minutes, then gradually stir in milk, letting the mixture thicken over low heat; blend in beer, add cheese, and stir constantly until cheese is melted. Season to taste.

SWISS VEGETABLE-CHEESE SOUP

1½ Tbs. butter	1½ cups beef stock
1 small leek, chopped	¼ cup diced carrots
1 small onion, chopped	¼ cup diced celery
1½ Tbs. flour	½ cup grated Gruyère
1½ cups milk	

Melt butter in a saucepan and sauté leek and onion (2 onions if leeks are unavailable) until tender. Blend in flour to make a smooth paste, then gradually add milk and stock, stirring until smooth; cook about 5 minutes. Add carrots and celery and simmer 20 minutes. Stir in the cheese and serve.

SCANDINAVIAN FISH-CHEESE SOUP

3 Tbs. butter	1 lb. haddock or halibut, flaked
1 carrot, finely chopped	1 cup grated Jarlsberg (or other
1 parsnip, finely chopped	firm, mild cheese)
1 large onion, finely chopped	2 tsps. salt
3 Tbs. flour	freshly ground white pepper
4 cups fish stock, heated	1–2 Tbs. minced parsley

Melt butter in a saucepan, add chopped vegetables, and cook over low heat, stirring occasionally, about 5 minutes. Stir in flour, eliminating lumps, and cook slowly about 3 minutes. Add hot stock a little at a time, stirring until smooth, then let mixture cook until it begins to thicken slightly. Add flaked fish and simmer 5 minutes; then stir in grated cheese a little at a time. When cheese has all melted, season soup to taste. Serve in hot soup bowls, sprinkling each with minced parsley.

Meat and Fish Dishes

Even though good cheese is expensive today there is a particular advantage to using cheese in meat and fish dishes because the little that you use (and, again, it can be a leftover) goes a long way; it not only stretches the meat but extends the protein content of the finished dish. The prime purpose, of course, is to add subtle flavor as well as contrast in texture—a trick long practiced by most European cooks, particularly the Italians. Hard cheese can be grated into meat mixtures, a soft cheese can provide a melting center, a zesty cheese can make a delicious topping for grilled steaks and chops and fish fillets. All kinds of cheeses can be used in stuffings, and fresh white cheese can often provide a binder, eliminating the necessity for a rich sauce.

BEEF-OATS-MOZZARELLA MEAT LOAF

Here a mild, easily melting cheese, like Mozzarella, is layered into the meat loaf to give a striped look when the loaf is sliced.

For more than 4

1½ lbs. ground lean beef	1 tsp. dried oregano
1 cup tomato sauce	½ tsp. dried basil
¾ cup rolled oats	½ tsp. dried rosemary
1 large onion, minced	freshly ground pepper
1 clove garlic, minced	½ lb. Mozzarella (or Bel Paese,
1 egg	Brick, American Munster),
1½ tsps. salt	thinly sliced

Combine ground meat with sauce, oats, minced onion and garlic, egg, and seasonings. Put some of the meat mixture in a ½-inch layer on bottom of a 1-pound loaf pan. On top of this lay thin slices of cheese down the middle. Repeat with ½-inch layer of meat, pressing down to enclose cheese on sides and ends. Lay thin slices of cheese on top, covering again with meat, to make three layers of cheese and four of meat. Bake at 350° about 1 hour.

BLUE CHEESE MEATBALLS

1½ lbs. ground lean beef	¼ lb. Blue Cheese, cubed
1½ tsps. salt	flour
1 small garlic clove, minced	4 Tbs. butter or cooking oil
1 large egg	1 cup red wine

Put meat in mixing bowl and mix thoroughly with salt crushed with minced garlic; blend in egg. Shape pieces of meat around each cube of cheese, then roll each meatball lightly in flour. Heat butter or oil in skillet and sauté meatballs, turning frequently until well browned. Add wine and simmer, covered, about 10 minutes.

PORK SAUSAGE–CHEESE STRATA

1 lb. pork sausage meat	½ cup half-and-half or light cream
4 slices white bread	½ tsp. salt
¼ lb. Emmenthal (or other mild,	freshly ground pepper
firm cheese), grated	freshly ground nutmeg
2 eggs, beaten	Tabasco
1 cup milk	

Brown the sausage meat and use a little of the fat to grease a shallow rectangular baking dish; line this with bread slices side by side—the dish should be just large enough to hold one layer. Drain the sausage and spread over the bread. Sprinkle with cheese. Combine the remaining ingredients and pour over the cheese. Bake at 350° for 30 to 35 minutes, until custard puffs and is firm.

TYROLEAN ROAST BEEF WITH CHEESE

For more than 4

1 beef fillet	½ tsp. dried marjoram
2 Tbs. butter	½ tsp. dried basil
1 carrot, finely chopped	salt
1 stalk celery, finely chopped	freshly ground pepper
1 large onion, chopped	3–4 Tbs. white wine
1 garlic clove, minced	12 oz. Austrian Swiss (or other
½ tsp. dried rosemary	Swiss cheese), sliced

Remove fat and sinews from beef. Cut lengthwise on one side and open fillet out flat. Sauté in butter all vegetables and herbs for 5 minutes; then add a sprinkling of salt and pepper, and white wine. Simmer until wine is almost evaporated. Chop four or five slices of cheese, stir quickly into cooked vegetables, then spread through center of open fillet. Roll up and tie securely. Put rolled meat on rack in shallow pan and roast about 40 minutes, basting with juices from meat and adding a little water to bottom of pan as necessary. Remove strings from roll; cover top with cheese slices, and return to oven long enough for cheese to bubble and turn slightly golden.

ROAST CHICKEN STUFFED WITH GRUYÈRE AND NOODLES

For more than 4

1 chicken, about 4 lbs.
salt
8-oz. pkg. wide noodles
1 qt. chicken broth
1/4 lb. mushrooms
1/4 lb. butter
1/2 cup freshly grated Gruyère

1/2 cup heavy cream
freshly ground pepper
1/2 tsp. dried sage
1 carrot, cut in 1/4-inch slices
1 onion, coarsely chopped
Mornay Sauce (page 170)

Wipe the chicken with a damp cloth and sprinkle a little salt inside. Cook the noodles 4 to 5 minutes in broth, until about half done. Wipe mushrooms with a damp cloth, trim hard edge, and mince stems with a sharp knife; slice caps thinly. Sauté both in 4 tablespoons of butter in a large saucepan. Drain noodles well (reserving broth), and stir into mushrooms. Mix in Gruyère and 4 tablespoons of the cream, adding salt and pepper to taste and the sage. Stuff the chicken with the noodle mixture, scraping juices from the pan; skewer openings and truss legs and wings. Put remaining butter in a roasting pan with carrots and onions, and heat until the butter melts. Roll the chicken in the butter until it is well coated, then put the roasting pan in the oven at 450°, adding from time to time a little hot broth from the drained noodles. When the chicken begins to brown in the oven, turn it breast side down and cover the roasting pan. Reduce heat to 325° and continue roasting 25 minutes, basting frequently with more hot broth and pan juices. Remove cover from the pan, salt and pepper the chicken lightly, and cook about 30 minutes longer. Serve with Mornay sauce thinned with remaining cream.

LIEDERKRANZ- AND HAM-STUFFED CHICKEN BREASTS

Several kinds of cheese are singled out by good cooks for use in combination with ham and veal, or with ham and poultry. In Italy the cheese is as often grated Parmesan as it is Mozzarella, which is used in the classic veal cutlets of Bologna. In the Italian Piedmont sliced Fontina is combined with prosciutto as a topping for broiled chicken breasts, while in other regions the stuffing combination is dominated by prosciutto and Mozzarella and the chicken breasts (sometimes turkey) are baked in a tomato sauce. Almost any cheese can be adapted to this style of cooking, and in the recipe below the American Liederkranz gives a subtlety of flavor not easy to detect.

2 whole chicken breasts, skinned and boned	*salt*
4 thin slices cooked ham	*freshly ground white pepper*
4-oz. pkg. Liederkranz	*4 Tbs. butter or cooking oil*
4 Tbs. all-purpose flour	*1 cup chicken broth*
½ tsp. dried tarragon	*½ cup dry white wine*
½ tsp. paprika	*1 cup thinly sliced mushrooms*

Separate halves of chicken breasts and put them between two sheets of wax paper; then flatten them with the side of a cleaver until they are ⅓ inch thick. Trim ham as necessary to fit one half of chicken piece, then place it on top. Cut cheese lengthwise into four pieces and put a slice on each piece of ham. Fold chicken piece over and skewer edges together to make a neat package. Combine flour, tarragon, and paprika with about ½ tsp. of salt and a turn or two of the pepper grinder. Dredge chicken in this mixture, shaking off and reserving excess. In a skillet large enough to hold all four pieces, melt butter or oil over medium heat and sauté chicken until golden on all surfaces. Remove to shallow baking dish just large enough to hold them. Stir reserved flour mixture into fat remaining in skillet, blend well, and cook a few minutes. Now, off heat, stir in chicken broth. Return to medium heat and cook gently, stirring continuously, to make smooth sauce. Add wine and mushrooms and continue cooking over low heat about 5 minutes, until sauce thickens. Pour over chicken in baking dish and bake 45 minutes at 350°, until chicken is very tender.

CHEESE-, SPINACH-, AND RICE-STUFFED BREAST OF VEAL OR LAMB

For more than 4

1½ lbs. fresh spinach (or 1 pkg. frozen chopped)
2 Tbs. olive oil
2 garlic cloves, peeled
1 cup cooked rice
2 oz. Mozzarella, cut in small cubes
⅓ cup grated Swiss Cheese
2 Tbs. grated Parmesan
salt and pepper

freshly ground nutmeg
4–5 lbs. breast of veal or lamb
2 Tbs. vegetable oil
2 carrots, scraped and sliced
2 onions, sliced
½ cup vermouth
¾ cup veal or chicken stock
¼ tsp. dried thyme
2 bay leaves

If spinach is fresh, wash and chop it; if frozen, defrost slightly and cut in blocks. Heat oil and garlic in skillet, stir in spinach; cook, stirring and tossing, 5 minutes. Remove garlic and add rice, the cheeses, and salt, pepper, and nutmeg to taste. Make a pocket in the veal or lamb breast, fill it with spinach stuffing, and close the opening with skewers and string. Brown meat in hot oil, add vegetables and brown slightly, then splash in liquids. Sprinkle thyme, bay leaves, salt, and pepper over the meat. After bringing to the boil, cover and braise in 325° oven for 2 hours. Remove to a platter, mashing vegetables into the braising liquid for sauce.

BROILED FISH WITH CHEESE

From Coquilles St. Jacques to Lobster Mornay, there are many recipes that call for cheese to accent the special flavor of one or another fish. No good recipe uses cheese to dominate a bland taste, but inventive cooks find deft combinations in piscatorial cuisine. For instance, the Restaurant Dorrius (sometimes called the only hostelry in Amsterdam to feature "Dutch" food) serves Sea Bass Gratiné as both an appetizer and a main dish. Fillets are sautéed, then topped with fried rings of leek and hollandaise sauce over which is generously sprinkled grated aged Gouda cheese before the whole is slipped under the broiler. Some English cooks bake two-inch-thick turbot or halibut steaks in wine, then cover them with puréed mushrooms and a rich Cheddar cream sauce before broiling. The recipe below is equally good with split, cleaned mackerel, or bluefish.

2 lbs. turbot fillets	dry white wine
butter	Vermont or New York aged white
salt	Cheddar
freshly ground white pepper	tomato slices

Wipe fish with damp cloth. Butter broiling pan, and put fillets side by side. Broil about 3 inches from heat for about 3 minutes, until golden, then turn, sprinkling lightly with salt, a few turns of pepper grinder, and 3 or 4 tablespoons of wine; broil 3 more minutes, until golden. Cut thin slices of cheese to fit surface of fish and lay on fillets. Top with thinly sliced tomato, and return to broiler about 5 inches from heat. Cook until cheese melts and tomato browns slightly.

GHARITHES: GREEK SHRIMPS WITH FETA

3 Tbs. olive oil	1½ Tbs. brandy
2 onions, chopped	¼ cup red wine
3 cloves garlic, minced	salt
4–5 tomatoes, peeled and chopped	freshly ground pepper
minced parsley	1 lb. cooked shrimps
2 tsps. dried mint	1 tomato, thinly sliced
¾ cup sliced mushroom caps	¼ lb. Feta, thinly sliced

Heat oil in a skillet and sauté onions and garlic about 3 minutes, then add tomatoes and cook about 10 minutes. Stir in about 2 tablespoons of parsley, the mint, mushrooms, brandy, and wine, and simmer about 10 minutes. Sprinkle in salt and pepper to taste. Pour this sauce into a shallow baking dish, covering the bottom, and arrange cooked shrimp on top. Lay tomato slices over shrimp, and top with sliced Feta. Bake at 450° about 8 minutes, until cheese begins to melt. Sprinkle with minced parsley and serve immediately.

CHICKEN AND FARMER CHEESE CROQUETTES

Here is a way to make a croquette that is both quicker—you don't have to make a cream sauce base—and less rich than the usual type. It can be made with any leftover meat or fish; ham is particularly good, and so is shrimp. Serve piping hot, either plain or if you like with a mushroom or fresh tomato sauce.

2 cups ground cooked chicken
(or other cooked meat or fish)
2 scallions, finely chopped
½ cup fresh Farmer Cheese
1 tsp. chopped fresh basil (or
½ tsp. dried)
1 tsp. chopped fresh tarragon

salt and freshly ground pepper
flour
1 egg, lightly beaten
1 cup fresh bread crumbs
2 Tbs. grated Parmesan (or other
sharp grating cheese)
oil for deep frying

Mix chicken, scallions, Farmer Cheese, and herbs. Season to taste. Form into four ovals or sausage shapes. Roll in flour to coat lightly, dip into beaten egg, then roll in a mixture of bread crumbs and grated cheese to cover all sides. Refrigerate at least 30 minutes. Heat oil to 375°. Place croquettes in frying basket and lower into hot oil. Fry about 4 minutes, until golden on both sides. Remove, drain, and serve hot.

MUSSELS AND SPINACH GRATIN

6 lbs. mussels
3 lbs. fresh spinach (or 2 pkgs.
frozen chopped)
2 Tbs. chopped shallots or
scallions
½ cup dry white wine
3 Tbs. butter

3 Tbs. flour
½ cup cream
generous pinch saffron
salt and pepper
2 cups loosely packed grated
Fontina (or other mild
cheese)

Scrub the mussels well. If spinach is fresh, wash it and shred it; if frozen, let it defrost slightly and cut in small blocks. Scatter shallots or scallions over the wine in a large pot, bring to a boil, add spinach, then the mussels, cover tightly and boil about 5 minutes or until all the mussels have opened. Remove them and scrape the meat from the shells. Drain the spinach well, reserving the liquid. Make a sauce by melting the butter, adding the flour, blending and cooking a minute or two, then straining in about 1 cup of the spinach-mussel cooking liquid and about ½ cup of cream, to make a fairly thick cream sauce. Stir in saffron, salt, and pepper to taste. In a casserole make a bed of the well-drained spinach, put the mussels on top, pour sauce over, then scatter grated cheese on top. Bake in a 400° oven 10 minutes and then slip under the broiler to brown the top.

LONG ISLAND OYSTERS BAKED WITH CHEESE

1/4 lb. butter	36 large oysters
2 Tbs. flour	1 cup bland cracker crumbs
2 cups cream	1 cup diced semisoft cheese
2 tsps. anchovy paste	(American Munster, mild
salt	Cheddar, or Colby)
freshly ground white pepper	minced parsley
grated rind of 1 lemon	
2–3 Tbs. red caviar (or minced	
pimiento)	

Melt the butter in a saucepan and stir in flour, until paste is smooth. Off heat, stir in cream to make a smooth mixture, return to heat, and cook until it thickens. Blend in anchovy paste, very little salt, pepper, grated lemon rind, and caviar (or pimiento). Put one-quarter of this sauce in a buttered 2-quart baking dish, then arrange 18 oysters over it. Sprinkle with a layer of crumbs, diced cheese, and parsley. Pour another quarter of sauce over this, then arrange the remaining oysters on top. Sprinkle with another layer of crumbs and remaining cheese. Pour in remaining sauce and top with crumbs. Bake about 10 minutes at 375°, and scatter minced parsley over the top crust before serving.

SHRIMP AND GREEN BEANS

A way of using white cheese as a binder, adapted from a description in *The New Yorker* of a Michel Guérard recipe for his *cuisine minceur*.

1 lb. unpeeled shrimp	2–3 Tbs. lemon juice
3 cups fish stock*	1 Tbs. finely chopped shallots
1/2 lb. fresh, young green beans	2–3 Tbs. chopped fresh parsley,
3 oz. warm Armagnac or cognac	tarragon, or basil and chives,
4 oz. (1/3 cup tightly packed)	mixed
Farmer Cheese	salt and pepper

Cook the shrimp in the fish stock, boiling gently for 5 minutes covered,

* If you do not have fish stock, improvise by simmering 1½ cups water, 1½ cups white wine, ½ cup clam juice, 1 small slice onion, pinch thyme, and ½ bay leaf for about 20 minutes.

then let cool in the liquid. Meanwhile snip the ends off the beans and cook them whole in a large kettle of boiling, salted water for 5 to 10 minutes as size and freshness warrant; don't overcook—they should be somewhat crisp. Drain immediately and refresh with cold water. Remove shrimp from stock when cool enough to handle and peel. Boil down the stock to about 2/3 cup until a bit syrupy. Pour the warm brandy into the pan, set aflame, then swish well around, scraping any coagulated juice from the pan. Now pour this juice into the blender with the cheese and lemon juice, and blend until smooth and fluffy. Mix in shallots and herbs, then season to taste. Toss the shrimp and beans with this dressing, mixing well. Let stand 5 to 10 minutes to exchange flavors before serving.

LASAGNE OF CHEESE AND SEAFOOD

1 lb. shrimp, cooked and shelled	1 1/2 cups tomato sauce
1 lb. cooked crab meat	salt and pepper
4 Tbs. olive oil	2/3 lb. lasagne noodles
1 Tbs. minced parsley	1/4 lb. Mozzarella, thinly sliced
1/2 tsp. dried oregano	1/2 lb. Ricotta
1/2 tsp. dried basil	4 Tbs. freshly grated Parmesan

Chop shrimp coarsely, and flake crab meat. Cover bottom of a skillet with oil, stir in shrimp and crab meat, and cook about 2 minutes. Add parsley, oregano, basil, and tomato sauce, and cook about 15 minutes. Taste for seasoning. Cook lasagne noodles in boiling water; drain. Oil a shallow baking pan, and put half the noodles on the bottom. Cover with half the tomato sauce, half the Mozzarella, and crumble half the Ricotta over the surface. Repeat the layers, and sprinkle the top with the Parmesan. Bake in 375° oven for about 30 minutes.

Breakfasts, Brunches, Lunches, One-Dish Meals

Whether it is Cottage Cheese in America, Gruyère in Switzerland, or Frühstückkäse in Germany, cheese in itself or in cooked form makes a fortifying start for the day—just as it can be a major factor in a simple lunch, the mainstay of supper, a family casserole, or a deliciously exotic enterprise like the Middle Eastern Moussaka (page 150). For breakfast and brunch try a mixture of applesauce, Cottage Cheese, and yogurt on potato pancakes, for example, or thin out Cream Cheese, add fresh berries and a mite of sugar, and serve on crêpes; or work out cheese-based stuffings of your own to use in crêpes, omelets, and pasta (see recipes that follow).

FILLED CRÊPES, OMELETS, ET CETERA One of the most satisfying ways we have found of using up odds and ends of cheese is to make a delicious filling—for a thin pancake, for an omelet, or for pasta, such as cannelloni, manicotti, rigatoni—sometimes combining the cheeses with other bits of cooked food (known as leftovers), sometimes letting the cheese serve as the principal filling ingredient. Here are some ideas that we have tried, which we hope will inspire you to make imaginative use of the cheese you have on hand.

RICOTTA- AND HERB-FILLED CRÊPES

CRÊPES
1 cup flour
½ cup milk
½ cup water

3 eggs
3 Tbs. melted butter
¼ tsp. salt

FILLING
1 cup Ricotta (or Cottage Cheese or
  fresh Farmer Cheese or a
  combination)
3 Tbs. minced scallions, including
  green part (or combination of
  onion and chives)
2–3 Tbs. chopped herbs (fresh
  parsley and basil or tarragon or
  savory)

salt and pepper
optional: a little heavy cream
melted butter
4 Tbs. grated Parmesan, aged
  Cheddar, or similar dry, flavorful grating cheese

Spin all the crêpe ingredients in a blender for at least a minute. Let batter stand several hours before using. To bake: brush butter or oil over a hot skillet (4, 6, or 8 inches, depending on size crêpe you want to make), pour in just enough batter to coat the bottom, and tip pan to distribute evenly. Cook over medium-high heat until bubbles appear on surface, then flip crêpe over and cook about a minute on the other side. Stack and keep warm in foil in low oven until ready to use. (Crêpes may also be refrigerated or frozen and warmed up again in foil.)

Mash the Ricotta, scallions, and herbs together, season to taste, and add just enough cream, if the cheese is dry, to make a spreadable consistency. Distribute evenly among eight 6-inch crêpes, roll them up over the filling, place in a shallow buttered casserole, brush the tops with butter, and sprinkle with grated cheese. Bake 10 minutes in a 400° oven, then run under the broiler to brown.

Note: Also good as a pasta stuffing, served with a fresh (not too strong) tomato sauce and topped with Parmesan.

TOMATO AND MOZZARELLA FILLING: To each cup of seeded, peeled, chopped tomatoes, cooked with a clove of crushed garlic and a little basil until just tender, add ¾ cup coarsely grated Mozzarella and 1 tablespoon grated Parmesan. Use for stuffing and rolling crêpes, as a filling for an omelet, or spread filling over each cooked crêpe and stack like a layer cake, spreading a little more tomato on top and sprinkling with more Parmesan before baking.

RICOTTA (OR FARMER CHEESE) AND SPINACH: Mix equal parts of Ricotta and cooked chopped spinach. Season with nutmeg, salt, and pepper. Good as either a crêpe or an omelet filling accented with some grated Swiss Cheese on top.

MUSHROOMS AND CREAMY CHEESE: Mix equal parts of *duxelles* (finely chopped mushrooms that have been sautéed in a little butter and minced shallots) and a creamy cheese—Cream Cheese or Farmer—accented with a little leftover Camembert or Brie or even Liederkranz, if it is not too strong, or Crema Danica. Taste for a good balance of flavors, add a pinch of tarragon, and salt and pepper to taste.

CRÊPES FOURRÉES AU CAMEMBERT: A French dish very similar to the stuffed manicotti on page 155 is made by rolling thin pancakes around enough Camembert to plump them out, sprinkling them with grated Gruyère, then with a blanket of rich tomato sauce and a gratiné of cheese before heating them in a medium oven.

CHEESE-VEGETABLE FRITTATA

One evening in Seattle a distinguished native Italian and professor at the University of Washington mused aloud as I watched him cook; he was making a frittata with fresh eggs and even fresher spinach from his own garden, just a pebble's throw from his house. "The name is Italian," Angelo Pellegrini said that night. "Literally, it means 'a fry,' but it is more precisely a special kind of omelet." I learned that in Italy eggs so cooked are sometimes called *frittate maritate,* married omelets, which are unions of eggs and cheese, various vegetables, and leftover meat, fish, or sausage. A frittata looks like a portly, puffy pancake in which chopped ingredients are scattered throughout the beaten eggs, and the top is a mottled golden brown.

8 eggs
3–4 oz. boiled ham, cut in ½-inch
    squares
½ cup crumbled cheese
½ cup chopped cooked zucchini
    (or summer squash or other
    leftover vegetable)

2 tsps. chopped herbs (such as
    parsley, chives, basil, or
    oregano)
salt and freshly ground pepper
4 Tbs. butter
1 large onion, chopped
2 cloves garlic, minced

Beat eggs and add ham, cheese, chopped vegetable, herbs, and salt and pepper to taste. Sauté chopped onion and garlic in about half the butter until translucent, then scrape all into egg mixture. Melt remaining butter in shallow 1-quart baking dish that will take direct heat (or an iron-handled skillet works well). Turn dish to cover sides with butter, and pour the egg mixture into it. Cover and cook over low heat about 10 minutes, until egg has begun to draw away from sides. Then finish cooking about 6 inches below broiler heat so that top of frittata becomes golden and firm.

CHEESE PANCAKES

1 cup grated, firm, tasty cheese
    (such as Cheddar or Swiss)
2½ Tbs. flour
grated rind of ½ lemon

salt and freshly ground pepper
dash of cayenne or fresh nutmeg
⅔ cup sour cream
3 egg yolks, beaten

Combine all the ingredients thoroughly. For each cake scoop up a table-spoonful of the batter and drop onto well-greased hot skillet. Spread out with the back of spoon, turn heat down, and bake the pancakes some-what slowly, 4 to 5 minutes on each side to cook well through. Handle gently and don't crowd the pan. Keep warm until all are done. Serve hot.

QUICHES The original Quiche Lorraine surprisingly did not include cheese, but this famous custard tart lends itself to the use of so many different kinds of cheeses blended with other tidbits that a quiche to most people today almost automatically spells cheese. Incidentally, a Yankee Cheddar Cheese Pie—store cheese pudding baked into a pie shell—is basically the same thing as a cheese quiche, which is one more proof that wherever there is good cheese good cooks find ways to put it to good use. Here are a number of combinations we have used to fill a 9-inch shell. Try the recipe for the Cream Cheese Pastry Dough, page 176—it makes a delicious rich dough for quiche—and partially bake before filling as directed on page 177. Or any basic pie crust can be used. The same fillings are good, too, in small 1-inch tartlets to serve as hors d'oeuvre.

CHEESE AND HAM QUICHE

9-inch pastry shell, baked 10 minutes	1 cup grated cheese (if very sharp cheese, 3/4 cup)
2 tsps. mustard	salt and pepper to taste
3–4 oz. ham	1 Tbs. chopped parsley and chives
3 eggs	or celery leaves
1/2 cup milk	optional: 1 Tbs. grated Parmesan

Paint the bottom of the pastry with mustard, then cut ham in small pieces and scatter them over it. Mix all the other ingredients, reserving the optional Parmesan to sprinkle on top if the type of cheese you are using needs that additional accent, and pour into the shell. Bake in a 350° oven for 30 to 35 minutes, until custard is set and lightly browned.

ROQUEFORT FILLING: Mix 2 egg yolks with 2 whole eggs and 2/3 cup cream. Add 3/4 cup crumbled Roquefort (or other blue cheese, adding more or less depending on its strength) and pour filling into shell. Bake as above.

SPINACH AND FETA (OR SWISS CHARD AND CHEDDAR): Mix 2 egg yolks and 2 whole eggs with 1 cup cooked and well-drained chopped spinach (or Swiss chard) and 1/2 cup crumbled Feta (or Cheddar or Monterey Jack). Season to taste with salt and pepper and a little nutmeg. Fill shell and bake as above.

TOMATO (OR OKRA OR ASPARAGUS) AND SWISS CHEESE: Spread 1 cup of cooked, drained, seasoned chopped tomatoes (or make a spoke pattern of cooked whole okra or asparagus) over the tart shell. Mix 2 whole eggs and

2 egg yolks with ⅔ cup cream and ½ cup grated Swiss Cheese, season with salt and pepper, and pour over the vegetable. Sprinkle with grated Parmesan or Romano and bake as above.

CHEDDAR, ONION, AND BACON: The proportions are somewhat different in this American version of the quiche, but the principle is the same. Mix 8 slices of cooked, crumbled bacon with 1 cup chopped sautéed onions, 2 beaten eggs, 1 cup milk, ¾ pound grated sharp Cheddar mixed with 1 tablespoon of flour, and salt, pepper, and cayenne to taste. Fill tart shell and bake as above.

GLAMORGAN SAUSAGES

My friend Jane Grigson says in her fine book *English Food* that the Welsh "serve these sausages with potato, but I think this is too much stodge. They are delicious on their own, or with grilled tomato, as a supper dish, or first course." In New York we sometimes have them for a Saturday or Sunday family lunch, and we use Caerphilly—although there is nothing wrong with substituting Cheddar, or Lancashire.

1 cup grated Caerphilly	*1 whole egg*
1½ cups fresh bread crumbs	*2 eggs, separated*
¾ tsp. dry mustard	*salt*
½ tsp. thyme	*freshly ground pepper*
½ tsp. rosemary	*flour*
½ tsp. basil	*1 cup dry bread crumbs*
2 Tbs. grated onion or finely minced leek	*vegetable oil*

Put cheese, fresh crumbs, mustard, herbs, and onion in a bowl and mix well. Beat the whole egg and two yolks until lemony, and stir into cheese mixture, seasoning to taste. Whip whites until frothy. Take about 2 tablespoons of the mixture and shape into small sausages; roll in flour, dip in the frothy egg white, then in dry crumbs. Cover bottom of a skillet with about 1 inch of oil; when it is hot fry the sausages, turning frequently until they are crisp and golden.

PÂTE FEUILLETÉE AU ROQUEFORT

Many years before we visited the caves of Combalou at Roquefort-sur-Soulzon, I tasted for the first time the supreme delight of a perfect Pâte

Feuilletée au Roquefort at the Chanteclair. I was writing a story for *Sports Illustrated* about this Manhattan French restaurant, which happened to be a rendezvous for racing car enthusiasts, and after tasting this Roquefort specialty of theirs, I wanted the recipe. So I went down to the kitchen and watched Jacques Jaffry, the chef, prepare his version. But after I put the recipe on paper, the magazine decided it was too complicated for the average cook. I don't agree; it is one of those rare treats well worth the effort, and I hope the account below will inspire others who have never attempted puff pastry to try it.

2½ cups flour	*7 oz. (or 14 Tbs.) butter*
½ tsp. salt	*1 egg beaten with 2 tsps. water*
¾ cup cold water	*¾ lb. Roquefort*

With Chef Jacques's instructions fixed in my head, I started by putting the rolling pin in the refrigerator to chill. Then I washed my Formica working surface (if you have marble, which our kitchen has since acquired, so much the better) with ice-cold water and dried it thoroughly. Adding the salt to the flour, I sifted it into a mound on the cold surface, and in the center of this mound I made a well with my fingertips. I took a cup three-quarters full of very cold water in my left hand and poured it little by little into the well, using my right to mix the flour and water together as rapidly as possible. When the dough was finally smooth, but not stiff, I formed it into a ball and put it in the refrigerator to rest for 30 minutes.

Then I sprinkled the working surface with flour and rolled the butter (which I let stand at room temperature about 15 minutes so that it was pliable but still cold) into a cylinder about an inch in diameter.

After the dough had rested, I put it on the floured surface and with the chilled rolling pin rolled it into a rectangle about 5 to 6 inches wide and 12 inches long. In the center I put the cylinder of butter. I folded in the ends and sides of the dough to seal the butter completely. Picking up the folded dough, I dusted the rolling pin and the surface with flour and turned the dough upside down so that the folded edges were on the bottom. I rolled it out lengthwise to about 15 inches until the butter just began to show through. Then I quickly folded the dough in thirds by bringing the farther end toward me and folding the nearer end over that, making three equal tiers. This then went into the refrigerator to rest for 20 minutes.

This process of rolling, folding, and resting 20 minutes was done six times altogether. Then I was ready to add the cheese and bake the pastry.

I made two rectangles of the dough by dividing it in half and rolling each piece out again to a rectangle about 12 inches long, 5 to 6 inches wide, and about ½ inch thick. I put one of these on a baking sheet, which I'd moistened slightly with water, and brushed the top of the dough with beaten egg. I crumbled the cheese and distributed it evenly over the surface, leaving a margin of ¾ inch on all sides and adding another brush of beaten egg to the edges. Then I set the second rectangle on top, pressing the edges of both rectangles together with the tines of a fork to seal thoroughly. Finally I brushed the top with the rest of the beaten egg and made four 3-inch slashes across its width. My Feuilletée au Roquefort was now ready for baking, and I put it in a 400° oven for 10 minutes, reducing to 350° for 35 minutes more. The result was a splendid thing—puffed to thrice its original height, golden on top, the pastry separated into buttery, flaky layers, and the cheese inside molten and tangy.

SOUFFLÉS

Cheese soufflés can vary greatly. There is the more solid type with a good, old-fashioned cheesy flavor and a more puddinglike consistency; this is usually cooked slowly in a pan of water—a style you are more likely to encounter in old basic English and American cookbooks. Then there is the French soufflé, so airy that it is supported for its final ascent by a paper collar. Some cooks insist on a very mild and delicate cheese flavor, for which Gruyère is best recommended. Some like a runny center. So don't be enslaved to any one recipe. What follows is a basic approach that can be varied. Above all, a soufflé is a lovely way to use up all kinds of lingering cheeses, and there is no reason not to combine flavors. We've made a superb soufflé out of leftover Blue Cheese tempered with a little Bel Paese (the proportions would be about 1 cup of Blue to about 4 tablespoons of a milder creamy cheese). The last of a very assertive cheese can be mixed with a bland Cream Cheese; Parmesan, Asiago, and Romano are always good foils for a mild type. The point is to play around with what you have in the fridge.

4 Tbs. butter	*freshly ground nutmeg*
⅓ cup flour	*8 egg yolks*
1¼ cups milk	*1¼ cups grated cheese*
¼ tsp. salt	*9 egg whites*
freshly ground pepper	*1–2 Tbs. grated Parmesan*

Melt the butter, blend in the flour, and cook over low heat a few minutes. Off heat, stir in milk, then whisk over low heat until mixture is very thick and smooth. Season, adding pepper and nutmeg to taste, then one·by one beat egg yolks into the sauce, and finally, off heat, stir in cheese. Beat egg whites until they form soft peaks. Fold into soufflé base. Butter a straight-sided 2-quart baking dish, then sprinkle Parmesan over bottom and sides, shaking out excess. Pour batter in and place in preheated 400° oven, turning down to 375° as soon as soufflé is in. Bake 30 minutes for more runny interior, 35 to 40 for more firm. Serve immediately.

SOUFFLÉ ROLL

This lovely, light cheese-flavored roll is literally a fallen soufflé that can be made with different kinds of cheese and wrapped around a variety of fillings. Note that the proportions and the basic procedure are almost the same as for the preceding soufflé recipe, except that you double the basic sauce ingredients because half of the sauce goes into the filling. Both Julia Child and Simone Beck have splendid recipes for the *roulade* on which this recipe is based. See *From Julia Child's Kitchen* and *Simca's Cuisine* for their recipes and more detailed instruction.

For more than 4

SOUFFLÉ ROLL

1/4 lb. butter
2/3 cup flour
3 cups milk
1/2 tsp. salt
freshly ground pepper

1 cup grated Cheddar (or Colby
    or Swiss)
freshly ground nutmeg
8 eggs, separated
1/2 cup fresh bread crumbs

FILLING

1 Tbs. butter
2 Tbs. finely chopped scallions or
    shallots
1/2 lb. mushrooms, finely chopped
1/4 lb. country ham or prosciutto,
    finely chopped

1 1/4 cups cooked chopped spinach
    (or 1 pkg. frozen), drained
1/3 cup mild cheese (Swiss or Colby
    or mixture of Cheddar and
    Mozzarella)

Following the procedure for cheese soufflé, melt the butter, add the flour, blend in the milk, and cook until you have a thick sauce. Season, adding pepper and nutmeg to taste. Then set aside half to add to the filling. Continue the next steps: to the warm sauce add the egg yolks one by one, then the cheese. Finally fold in the beaten egg whites. Now butter a standard jelly-roll pan (17 by 11 inches), line it with wax paper, then butter and flour the paper, knocking off excess. Pour in the soufflé batter, smoothing to reach into the corners, and bake in a 400° oven for 15 minutes.

While soufflé is baking, prepare filling by sautéeing in the butter chopped scallions or shallots, mushrooms, and ham together for about 5 minutes. Add the well-drained spinach, the remaining soufflé base sauce, and cheese. Correct seasoning and keep warm.

Remove the soufflé from the oven, sprinkle the top with a few tablespoons of the bread crumbs, and place wax paper on top overhanging slightly, then a large flat cookie sheet on top of paper, and turn the whole thing over, dislodging the soufflé. Let it rest for about 5 minutes, then peel off the paper used in baking. Now spread the warm filling over the soufflé and roll it up, log-fashion, using the paper overhang to help roll it over. Garnish with a sprinkling of the rest of the bread crumbs, toasted lightly, if you like.

MOUSSAKA:
EGGPLANT BAKED WITH MEAT AND CHEESE

For more than 4

2 medium eggplants	4 Tbs. minced parsley
salt	1/2 cup red wine
1/2 cup olive oil	2 cups milk
4 Tbs. butter	2 Tbs. cornstarch, dissolved in 1/4
2 onions, chopped	cup water
3 cloves garlic, minced	4 eggs, lightly beaten
2 cups ground beef (or lamb)	1 cup grated Kefalotyri (or
1 1/2 cups chopped peeled tomatoes	Parmesan)
1/2 tsp. dried oregano	ground cinnamon
1/2 tsp. dried rosemary	

Peel eggplants vertically, leaving 1-inch stripes of purple skin; cut into 1/2-inch slices. Sprinkle slices with salt, leave in colander to drain 15 minutes, then slap dry with paper towels. Put slices side by side on oiled cookie sheet, and brush lightly with oil. Bake in preheated 400° oven for 15 minutes. Meanwhile heat 3 tablespoons butter in a skillet, and sauté onions and garlic about 3 minutes, then stir in ground meat, tomatoes, herbs, and wine; simmer 10 minutes. Now in a saucepan bring milk and remaining butter to boiling point, add dissolved cornstarch, and stir until it thickens. Off heat, stir beaten eggs into the mixture with a wire whisk, then salt to taste. Oil the bottom and sides of a square or rectangular cake pan, and arrange a layer of eggplant slices. Spread the meat filling over them. Arrange remaining eggplant slices in another layer, brushing with oil; cover the egg plant with white sauce. Distribute cheese evenly over the top, and sprinkle liberally with cinnamon. Bake at 325° for 45 minutes. Cut in squares when serving.

PASTA AND RICE   The Italians, to whom the world is indebted for macaroni, spaghetti, and dozens of other forms of pasta, usually forgo cheese as an accompaniment only when seafood is involved (for an exception to this rule see page 141). Pasta and cheese are natural partners, providing a splendid repast when brought together in a dish like *fettucine al burro,* which, in its authentic form, adds only fresh unsalted butter to the combination of Parmesan and noodles. Other grating cheeses like Asiago, Caciocavallo, Pecorino Romano, and Ragusano often give a serving of pasta and one or another kind of sauce the edge that makes it seem sublime. And Mozzarella and Ricotta are equally well mated with various kinds of pasta, while outside Italy, Cheddar and various American-made cheeses are as important to macaroni, for instance, as ham is to eggs. Similar things could be said about the affinity between rice and cheese. It is easy to forget meat when cheese is combined with either rice or pasta—cheese may enhance the sauce, but it often is the principal ingredient that supplies more than adequate amounts of protein in addition to appetizing flavors.

MACARONI AND CHEESE

The secret of good macaroni and cheese is to make plenty of sauce—the macaroni seems to drink it up—generously flavored with a good tasty cheese.

2 cups macaroni
salt
4 Tbs. butter
4 Tbs. flour
2½ cups milk
salt
freshly ground black pepper
½ tsp. dry mustard

cayenne
*3 cups grated flavorful cheese (such
    as Cheddar or aged Monterey
    Jack)*
½ cup fresh bread crumbs
1–2 Tbs. melted butter
paprika

Cook the macaroni in 3 quarts of rapidly boiling salted water for 10 minutes. Meanwhile melt the butter over low heat, blend in the flour, and cook slowly a few minutes. Off heat, add the milk, return to medium heat and whisk until smooth. Season to taste with salt, pepper, mustard, and a pinch of cayenne, then toss in all but 2 tablespoons of the cheese, removing from the heat as soon as it has melted. Drain the macaroni, mix with the cheese sauce, then turn into a 2-quart, lightly buttered casserole. Bake in 350° oven 20 minutes covered, then turn up the oven to 450°, scatter bread crumbs on top, drizzle melted butter over, and sprinkle with paprika and remaining cheese. Bake uncovered 5 minutes, or slip under the broiler, until golden on top.

STUFFING FOR CANNELLONI, MANICOTTI, OR RAVIOLI

1 lb. Ricotta	2 Tbs. chopped Italian parsley
1/4 lb. Mozzarella, diced	3 eggs, beaten
1/2 cup freshly grated Parmesan	freshly grated nutmeg
1/2 cup freshly grated Romano	1 tsp. salt
3 Tbs. finely chopped walnuts	freshly grated black pepper

Break up Ricotta with a fork and stir in other cheeses, the walnuts, parsley, beaten eggs, a little grated nutmeg, salt, and several turns of pepper grinder. Blend well and use in filling cannelloni, manicotti, or ravioli.

ITALIAN NOODLES . . . WITH FOUR CHEESES

1/2 lb. butter (preferably unsalted)	1/4 lb. Fontina, diced
3/4 cup freshly grated Parmesan	1 cup heavy cream
1/4 lb. Bel Paese, diced	freshly grated pepper
1/4 lb. Gorgonzola, crumbled	1 lb. Italian noodles or spaghetti

Melt butter in a large saucepan, then add cheeses, stirring constantly until they dissolve into a rich mass. Add cream slowly, and continue steady stirring until a smooth sauce results. Add pepper to taste, then set aside in a warm place. Cook pasta in boiling salted water, stirring to keep strands separate, for about 8 minutes. Drain well, return to pot, and pour in cheeses over low heat; stir until pasta is mixed with sauce, and serve immediately.

. . . WITH CREAM CHEESE, EMMENTHAL, AND PARMESAN: Cook noodles as in preceding recipe. Melt 1/2 pound butter with 1/2 pound Cream Cheese, adding several tablespoons of pasta water while stirring the mixture over low heat. Sprinkle with a little salt and a few turns of pepper grinder. Drain pasta thoroughly. Toss with cheese-butter mixture, adding ½ cup freshly grated Parmesan and ½ cup freshly grated Emmenthal. Serve with more grated cheese on the table.

RICE BAKED WITH PROVOLONE, BEL PAESE, GRUYÈRE, AND PARMESAN

1 cup long-grain rice	*½ cup chopped ham*
⅓ cup chopped Provolone	*salt*
⅓ cup diced Bel Paese	*freshly ground pepper*
⅓ cup diced Gruyère	*butter*
⅔ cup freshly grated Parmesan	

Boil the rice in 3 quarts of rapidly boiling water for 15 minutes, until almost done; drain. Mix Provolone, Bel Paese, and Gruyère with half the Parmesan and all of the ham. Stir a little salt and pepper into the cooked rice, then butter a 1½-quart casserole. Put a third of the rice in the casserole, covering it with a layer of half the cheese-ham mixture. Repeat with a layer of rice, the remainder of the cheese-meat mixture, and a third layer of rice. Top with bits of butter and remaining Parmesan. Cover and put the casserole in a pan of hot water, then bake about 20 minutes at 350°. Remove the lid and continue baking 5 minutes, or until top layer of cheese turns golden.

GREEN RICE WITH PARMESAN

2 Tbs. butter	*1 cup finely minced parsley*
1 small onion, chopped	*1 tsp. dried basil*
1 clove garlic, minced	*1 cup freshly grated Parmesan*
1 cup long-grain rice	*½ tsp. salt*
2 cups chicken broth	*freshly ground pepper to taste*

Melt butter in a skillet and sauté onion and garlic. When onion is translucent, stir in rice until coated with butter. Pour in broth and bring it to a boil, then stir in remaining ingredients. Transfer to a 2-quart buttered casserole and bake about 30 minutes at 350°, or until rice is tender. When all liquid has been absorbed and rice is done, fluff up with a spoon and serve immediately.

ARROZ VERDE CON CHILIES RELLENOS: In Mexico, cheese is not cooked in the rice mixture. Instead, green chilies are stuffed with cheese and inserted into the casserole.

4 large canned green chilies, peeled   *½–¾ lb. Monterey Jack or Colby*

Cut the chilies open on one side and remove all seeds. Cut the cheese to fit the chilies and stuff well. When the rice (preceding recipe) has cooked about 15 minutes, set the stuffed chilies into it with the open side upward. Cover the casserole and bake about 15 more minutes.

TWO-CHEESE MACARONI-VEGETABLE CASSEROLE

For more than 4

1½ lbs. (4 or 5) small eggplants
salt
6 Tbs. vegetable oil
1 medium onion, finely chopped
1–2 cloves garlic, minced
4–5 ripe tomatoes, peeled, seeded,
*   and chopped*
2 Tbs. minced fresh basil

sugar
freshly ground pepper
½ lb. shell macaroni (or other
*   shape)*
½ lb. Mozzarella, in ½-inch cubes
½ lb. hard salami, in ¼-inch cubes
6–8 Tbs. freshly grated Parmesan
butter

Peel eggplant, cut in ½-inch slices and sprinkle with salt; set aside to drain about 30 minutes. Cover bottom of large skillet with oil and sauté drained slices until soft and slightly brown. Drain on paper towels. Sauté onion and garlic in same pan, adding oil as necessary. When onion is translucent, add tomatoes, basil, and a pinch of sugar; add salt and pepper to taste. Meanwhile cook macaroni 8 to 10 minutes and drain. Turn cooked tomato mixture into a large bowl and combine with drained pasta, Mozzarella and salami cubes, and 4 tablespoons of the Parmesan. Butter a shallow baking dish large enough to take eggplant slices in one layer. Spread macaroni mixture over layer of eggplant, and sprinkle thoroughly with more Parmesan; dot surface with butter. Bake 25 minutes at 375°, until Parmesan turns golden.

MANICOTTI: PASTA TUBES
STUFFED WITH RICOTTA AND HAM

8 manicotti

4 Tbs. olive oil

1 large onion, chopped

3 cloves garlic, minced

1/4 lb. mushrooms, chopped

3 cups ground cooked ham (or
    other meat)

1/2 lb. Ricotta

1/4 lb. Mozzarella, grated

1/4 lb. freshly grated Parmesan

salt

freshly ground pepper

4 cups tomato sauce

Cook manicotti about 6 minutes until just undercooked; remove from boiling water one at a time and lay side by side to drain so that they don't stick together. In a saucepan heat oil and sauté onion, garlic, and mushrooms about 5 minutes without burning; stir in ham. Blend Ricotta, Mozzarella, and 1/2 cup Parmesan in a mixing bowl, then stir into it the ham mixture. Salt to taste; add several turns of pepper grinder. When manicotti is well drained stuff the tubes with cheese-ham mixture; arrange them side by side in a buttered shallow baking dish, preferably rectangular. Heat the tomato sauce and pour it over the manicotti, spreading well, then sprinkle with remaining grated Parmesan. Bake at 350° about 30 minutes, or until sauce is bubbling and the Parmesan has formed a golden crust.

PASTITSIO: PASTA WITH LAMB
AND KEFALOTYRI

1/2 lb. ziti or elbow macaroni

4 Tbs. olive oil

1 large onion, chopped

1 clove garlic, minced

1/2 lb. ground lamb

salt

freshly ground pepper

ground cinnamon

1/4 cup red wine

1 cup tomato sauce

3 Tbs. butter

2 1/2 Tbs. flour

1 1/2 cups milk

2 eggs, beaten

bread crumbs

1 cup freshly grated Kefalotyri (or
    Parmesan or white Cheddar)

Cook pasta, rinse it under hot water, and set aside to drain. Heat oil in a skillet, and gently sauté onions and garlic about 2 minutes, then stir in meat. When meat loses its redness sprinkle it with salt, a little pepper, and a dash of cinnamon, then add wine and tomato sauce and simmer about 15 minutes. In a saucepan melt butter and stir in flour to make a smooth paste. Off heat, stir in the milk, eliminating all lumps; return to heat and let it thicken, then set it aside to cool. Beat the eggs into the cooled sauce. Butter sides and bottom of a rectangular baking pan, and sprinkle with bread crumbs. Spoon in half the drained pasta, cover it with meat sauce, and sprinkle some of the grated cheese over all. Add remaining pasta, and pour the egg sauce over it. Top with remaining cheese and sprinkle with cinnamon. Bake 45 minutes at 350°, until top is golden.

SPANAKOPITTA:
GREEK CHEESE-SPINACH PIE

½ lb. filo sheets	*salt*
1½ lbs. fresh spinach (or 1 pkg.	*3 eggs, well beaten*
frozen chopped)	*6 Tbs. olive oil*
½ lb. Feta (or mild Cheddar or	
Cottage Cheese)	

Bring filo to room temperature about 2 hours before beginning to prepare the pie. Wash spinach and blanch 5 minutes, then drain and chop (or simply thaw out the frozen). Drain Feta and break it into small bits. (If you are using a substitute, add salt to taste.) Stir the cheese into the beaten eggs. Paint the bottom and sides of a 9-inch square baking pan with oil. Unwrap the sheets of filo and smooth them out flat. Sprinkle each sheet with oil as you arrange half of them on the bottom of the oiled pan; let the pastry overlap the edges to the height of the pan. Top with a layer of the spinach and cover it with the crumbled cheese, pressing the cheese into the spinach. Put a layer of filo over this mixture and sprinkle with oil, repeating layers until you have used all the filo. Tuck pieces in all around the sides to enclose securely. Brush the top and edges with oil, and bake at 350° for about 50 minutes. Cut in 2- to 3-inch squares and serve very hot.

FONDUES   It was more than a hundred years after Brillat-Savarin, author of *The Philosophy of Taste,* published a "Recipe for Fondue" that the dish achieved something like mass popularity—a reception, indeed, that is deeply warranted. There are dozens of recipes in Switzerland, where fondues originated, and variations to be found elsewhere. The traditional utensil is a clay pot called a *caquelon,* glazed on the inside but not on its exterior. The principal ingredients are cheese—at least two kinds in Switzerland—wine, a little kirschwasser, a whiff of garlic, and abundant pepper and nutmeg. In Italy, where eggs habitually are added (as Brillat-Savarin's recipe also required), the molten sauce is called *fonduta,* is made with Fontina, and is accented by bits of white truffles from the Piedmont. Italians often pour their *fonduta* over slabs of polenta, and in Aubusson, France, the local *fondu* is based on local cheese and served with hot potatoes. In the Alps, a fondue party is limited to no more than four or five persons, a way of ensuring plenty of elbowroom when the *caquelon*'s contents bubble in the center of the table and each guest is armed with a long-handled fork. Anyone who lets a bread cube, once coated with cheese, fall from his fork must pay a round of kirsch, with one for the cook, of course. Most Swiss serve a bottle of the white wine with which the fondue is mixed, but there are those who think drinking anything cold as accompaniment brings on indigestion—some self-styled "gourmets" opt for unsweetened black tea, finishing it off with a glass of kirsch.

CHEESE FONDUE

1 clove garlic
1½ cups dry white wine
1 Tbs. lemon juice
1 lb. coarsely grated Swiss cheese
   (Emmenthaler, Gruyère, or
   combination with a little
   Vacherin)

freshly ground pepper
freshly grated nutmeg
optional: 1 oz. kirsch
1 long loaf French bread
optional: additional warm white
   wine

Rub the interior of an earthenware fondue pot or chafing dish with the cut sides of a clove of garlic. Set the vessel over medium flame and heat the wine and lemon juice, but not to boiling. When hot, start adding cheese by the handful, stirring constantly in one direction with a wooden spoon. Each handful of cheese should melt and become thoroughly incorporated before adding more. Make sure that the heat is distributed evenly; otherwise the cheese can coagulate in the center. If this happens, it is better to stop and start over rather than risk ruining all of the cheese. When all the cheese has melted and the mixture has become smooth and creamy, season with pepper and nutmeg to taste and add kirsch if you wish. Cut the bread into thick slices and then into quarters so that each piece has crust on one side. Keep the fondue warm over low heat as everyone dunks bread in and coats each piece with the bubbling cheese mixture. If it gets too thick, add additional warm wine and stir until smooth.

Note: Should there be some of the fondue left over, pour it into a plastic container or bowl and keep it covered; one use we have found for this residue is as a foundation for cheese-accented soups—cut up the chilled fondue in small dice or cubes and pour hot soup over. Delicious.

WELSH RABBIT

I like the story that this dish, so much like fondue, got its name when Welsh wives, waiting anxiously, spied their husbands or sons returning from a hunt empty-handed and set cheese before the fire to melt, as a substitute for a dinner of game. But my friend Paul Leyton, indefatigable proprietor of The Miners' Arms, at Priddy, near Bristol, England, has delved into the musty past to come up with an explanation of why Welsh Rabbit is sometimes called Welsh Rarebit. In England, says Mr. Leyton, there was a time when hors d'oeuvre were known as "forebits," because they were served in advance, and the characteristic savouries that come at a meal's end on British menus were called "rearbits"—hence the rarified pronunciation "rarebit." Whatever melted cheese concoctions may be called on native ground, the most common local potable serves as the catalytic agent—when in the Highlands stout porter is mixed with Stilton or Cheshire the result is often called "Scotch Rabbit." (One difference in a Yorkshire Rabbit is that it may be served over fried sliced apples instead of toasted bread. A poached egg as a coronet turns a Rabbit into a Golden Buck.) The cooking secret that covers all recipes is in heating whatever liquid is used, and adding cheese gradually, stirring constantly in a single direction; when eggs are included particular caution to keep the heat low and even is necessary.

2 Tbs. butter, melted
2 egg yolks
½ cup beer
½ tsp. dry English mustard
1 tsp. Worcestershire
cayenne to taste

½ lb. sharp Cheddar (or
  combination of Cheddar and
  Caerphilly)
4 slices toast (toasted Cheese Bread,
  page 174, is excellent)

Have all ingredients ready at hand. If you have a chafing dish, use it; otherwise a double boiler is best for your first attempt at Welsh Rabbit. Place container over barely boiling water and add melted butter. Beat egg yolks, beer, mustard, Worcestershire, and cayenne together, and add to butter. Let this get hot, but not boiling, then start adding cheese in handfuls, stirring constantly in one direction with a wooden spoon, until all the cheese has been added and mixture is creamy and smooth. It can wait about 5 minutes. Correct seasoning before spooning over toast.

CROQUE MONSIEUR—CHEESE DREAM

"A rather fantastic name," says *Larousse Gastronomique,* "for a kind of hot sandwich which is served as an hors d'oeuvre or as a small entrée. It can also feature in the list of small dishes for lunch, tea, etc." The name of fantasy is a French conceit, but the putting together of ham (or bacon) and cheese, between slices of bread which are then fried to a crusty gold, has some universality about it. New Zealanders, among others, grate the cheese and mix it with beaten egg, as does the chef at Scotland's Fortingall Hotel. It is a "Cheese Dream" in many English-speaking regions, and there are variations known as Croque Mademoiselle and Croque Madame—Donn Pearce's recipe, from San Francisco, includes sliced mushrooms; in Paris Simone Beck's puffy feminine version is flavored with cognac, kirsch, or rum, and both are run under the broiler at the last moment. When prepared as appetizing tidbits, the sandwiches are cut up into small mouthfuls. Here is the basic recipe we use, made with whatever cheese needs using up:

8 slices bread (Cheese Bread, page 174, is particularly good)
soft butter
4 slices country ham

about 1/3 lb. cheese
clarified butter (or equal amounts butter and cooking oil)

Remove crusts from the bread slices and butter one side. Trim ham slices to cover half the bread, place on top, then cover with cheese. (If cheese is a melting type like Mozzarella or a soft-ripened variety, simply break in pieces; a firm cheese should be sliced; a hard one should be grated and mashed with a little butter to make more meltable. Any combinations can be used.) Close the sandwiches with the other pieces of bread, butter side down, and press firmly. Heat a large skillet or pancake griddle, melt several tablespoons of clarified butter (or oil and butter—straight unclarified butter will burn), and when sizzling add the Croques Monsieur. Cook on each side about 3 minutes, pressing down with the spatula and adding a little more butter before turning. Serve the golden Croques hot, cutting in quarters if they are to be used as appetizers.

Vegetables

Vegetables can be turned into "one-dish meals" by cheese, or they can be delicately accented by gratinés or sauces. Strong-flavored root vegetables, which some people never touch, can be so transformed that their assertive nature is pleasantly modified. Parmesan, as the best of all cooking cheeses, adds a little zest to almost any leafy, stalky, or tuberous food from the garden, and so does Gruyère. Don't, however, overlook the chance to experiment with any cheese you have on hand, including those in the refrigerator that may seem a little old for table service—or variously flavored cheeses, like those perked up by seeds or spices. Ways of dressing vegetables in Mornay sauce are well known; so are methods of glazing cauliflower, endive, and such. What follows are ideas for using various cheeses in complement to other vegetables, some not so commonly transformed in these ways.

ROMANO- AND ANCHOVY-STUFFED ARTICHOKES

4 large artichokes
2 cups dry bread crumbs
freshly ground black pepper
2 cloves garlic, minced
1 cup grated Romano
1 tsp. dried oregano

1 tsp. dried rosemary
2–3 Tbs. minced parsley
6 anchovy fillets, finely chopped
olive oil
2 eggs

Trim base of artichokes to stand upright; snap off tough outer leaves and snip off points of remaining leaves. Boil in salted water 5 minutes, then drain and cool. Remove center choke carefully. Mix bread crumbs, several turns of the pepper grinder, minced garlic, cheese, herbs, anchovies, and about 4 tablespoons of olive oil. Blend in eggs. Gently pull back outer leaves and begin stuffing artichokes, working toward the center. Pour about 2 more tablespoons of olive oil and ½ cup water into a shallow baking pan and arrange artichokes in it upright. Cover tightly with foil and bake at 350° for 30 to 40 minutes (or until a leaf pulls out easily).

JERUSALEM ARTICHOKES
FRIED IN CHEESE BATTER

Jerusalem artichokes are very good when cooked in a Cheddar cream sauce, sprinkled with more Cheddar, and glazed under the broiler. Cooked, marinated, then deep-fried in batter, as below, they are hard to beat as a vegetable dish.

1½ lbs. Jerusalem artichokes
1 small onion
milk
¼ cup olive oil
1 Tbs. vinegar
salt and freshly ground pepper

½ tsp. dried basil
12-oz. can beer
1 cup flour
1 Tbs. paprika
½ cup grated Parmesan
oil for deep frying

Pour boiling water over artichokes and rub off skins. Put them in a saucepan with onion and enough milk to cover thoroughly; bring to the boil and then simmer 20 minutes. Drain artichokes, cut in slices while still warm, and marinate immediately in olive oil, vinegar, salt and pepper to taste, and basil. Meanwhile prepare batter by mixing beer and flour sifted with about 1 tablespoon salt and paprika. After 30 minutes or more, drain and dry artichoke slices, and dredge them in the grated cheese. Dip in fritter batter and fry until golden brown in hot oil.

REFRIED BEANS WITH CHEESE

1 lb. pinto beans
6 strips bacon
½ cup diced cheese (Cheddar,
    Monterey Jack, Sardo)

salt and freshly ground pepper

Wash and sort beans. Put in deep saucepan, cover with cold water, and bring to a boil. Cook slowly 5 to 6 hours, adding more boiling water if needed. Meanwhile chop bacon in squares and fry until crisp. Pour off most of the fat, then add the cooked beans, spooning to distribute bacon evenly. (Beans may be mashed, if you prefer.) When heated through, stir in the diced cheese, mixing until just melted. Season to taste.

BEETS, CHEESE-FLAVORED

We've found Roquefort beets delicious as a cold dish after the beets have been cooked and peeled, then covered with a sour cream and Roquefort dressing (about 1 tablespoon of cheese to 4 of sour cream). The same dressing can be used on warm beets, with the mixture just poured over them. In Tuscany tiny cooked beets are baked whole, with a little salt and pepper, minced chives, and a sauce of one part grated Parmesan to two parts heavy cream, the surface then dotted with butter before going in a hot oven just long enough for the cheese to melt and bubble. Here is a Swiss cheese variation:

2 cups hot diced cooked beets	*1/4 cup grated Emmenthal*
1/3–1/2 cup sour cream	

Mix prepared beets with sour cream and pour into buttered baking dish. Sprinkle cheese over top and broil about 4 inches from the heat until cheese melts.

CAULIFLOWER, TOMATO, AND CHEESE CASSEROLE

1 medium cauliflower	*1/2 cup grated Gruyère*
2 cups puréed tomatoes	*salt and freshly ground pepper*
6 Tbs. butter	

Cut cauliflower into pieces and boil in salted water for 10 minutes. Drain and put half in blender with half the puréed tomatoes; spin until smooth. Repeat with remaining cauliflower and tomatoes, adding 4 tablespoons of the butter. Spread remaining butter on sides and bottom of 1½-quart casserole. Combine vegetable purée with all but 2 tablespoons of the grated cheese, and season to taste. Pour into casserole, sprinkle with remaining cheese, and bake at 350° for 10 to 15 minutes.

CYPRIOT EGGPLANT AND TOMATOES BAKED WITH CHEESE

1 large eggplant	*freshly ground pepper*
salt	*1 cup diced Cream Cheese (or*
about 1/2 cup olive oil	*Farmer or Ricotta or yogurt)*
2–3 large tomatoes, sliced	*1/2 cup grated Kefalotyri or*
1 tsp. dried oregano	*Parmesan*
3 scallions, finely minced	

Slice eggplant into ½-inch slices, salt on both sides, and leave spread out in a colander 15 minutes to sweat. Pat dry and sauté quickly in hot olive oil, a few pieces at a time. Put a layer of sliced tomatoes in bottom of a buttered casserole, sprinkle with a little salt, some oregano, some scallions, and pepper. Then make a layer of half the eggplant slices and half the cheese. Repeat: tomatoes, seasonings, eggplant, cheese, scattering any remaining oil over, and finish with tomato and remaining seasonings, topping with grated cheese. Bake about 45 minutes in 350° oven.

EGGPLANT PARMIGIANA: This more famous eggplant, cheese, and tomato dish is made in various ways in this country, with the eggplant heavily breaded and layered with a tomato sauce often laden with strong tomato paste. But it is at its best, we find, made almost the same as above, using fresh tomatoes, substituting 4 to 5 ounces of sliced Mozzarella for the Cream Cheese, and topping with freshly grated Parmesan.

BAKED CORN WITH CHILIES AND CHEESE

2 Tbs. finely chopped onion
1 clove garlic, minced
3–4 Tbs. butter
6 canned green chilies, peeled
2 cups corn kernels

1/4 lb. Monterey Jack (or mild
    Cheddar or Colby), diced
salt and freshly ground pepper
garnish: sour cream

Sauté onion and garlic in butter until soft. Cut chilies in strips, add to onions, and cook about 5 minutes, then mix with corn, cheese, and a little salt and pepper. Transfer to 1½-quart casserole, scraping in all of butter. Cover tightly and bake at 350° for 20 minutes. Serve hot with sour cream.

BRAISED FENNEL WITH TWO CHEESES

4 small heads of fennel
3 Tbs. butter
1/4 cup freshly grated Italian Fontina
    (or similar mild cheese)

2 Tbs. freshly grated Parmesan
salt and freshly ground pepper
chicken stock
minced parsley

Trim away hard base and stalks of fennel, and slice bulbs into ¼-inch pieces. Drop in boiling salted water for 5 minutes. Drain well. Butter a baking dish and arrange half the slices on bottom. Dot with butter. Mix cheeses and sprinkle some lightly over fennel. Add a touch of salt and a few turns of pepper grinder. Repeat with remaining fennel and butter. Pour over enough hot chicken stock to just cover, then bake in 325° oven, covered, for 30 minutes. Remove cover and sprinkle fennel with remaining cheese. Bake about 15 minutes more at 425° until cheese is golden and brown. Sprinkle with minced parsley and serve immediately.

ENDIVES BAKED WITH TWO CHEESES

8 medium Belgian endives	*salt and freshly ground pepper*
½ cup grated fresh Parmesan	*1 cup heavy cream*
1½ cups shredded Swiss or Gruyère	*paprika*

Trim and wash the endives. Drop into boiling water, bring to boil again, and cook slowly for 10 minutes. Drain, cool, then squeeze each to force out as much moisture as possible. Place in baking dish just large enough to hold in one layer, and sprinkle with two cheeses, adding just a touch of salt (Parmesan is salty) and a few turns of the pepper grinder. Pour cream over all, and bake in top third of 375° oven for 30 minutes. Sprinkle paprika on top.

HOMINY GRITS WITH GARLIC CHEESE

½ cup hominy grits	*salt*
1½ cups boiling water	*cayenne*
¾ cup milk	*2 eggs, beaten*
3 oz. processed garlic cheese (or	*butter*
* Garlic Cheddar–Cream Cheese,*	*optional: grated Parmesan*
* page 124)*	

Stir grits into boiling water, add milk, stir, and cook until thick, about 30 minutes. Stir in cheese until well blended; remove from heat. Add salt to taste, a dash of cayenne, and beaten eggs, stirring well to amalgamate. Pour into buttered 1-quart casserole, and sprinkle with Parmesan if you like. Bake in 350° oven about 40 minutes.

BROILED CHEESE-STUFFED MUSHROOMS

16 medium mushrooms	*1 cup soft Italian bread crumbs*
2 Tbs. unsalted butter	*olive oil*
2 Tbs. Blue Cheese	*optional: 6 cherry tomatoes, 1 green*
3 Tbs. freshly grated Parmesan	* pepper*
1 small clove garlic, minced	

Wipe mushrooms clean and remove stems. Mix butter, two cheeses, minced garlic, and bread crumbs. Pack into mushroom caps, dribble oil on top, and broil 10 minutes. To broil on skewers, press two stuffed caps together to enclose stuffing, and alternate on skewers with cherry tomatoes and parboiled pieces of green pepper.

ONION-POTATO SCALLOP WITH CAERPHILLY

1½ lbs. potatoes
¾ lb. onions
3 Tbs. butter
salt and freshly ground pepper

1 cup freshly grated Caerphilly
   (or other semisoft cheese,
   preferably light-colored)

Peel potatoes and onions, and slice both rather thinly. Butter a 2-quart casserole and put a layer of potatoes on the bottom; dot with butter and sprinkle with salt and pepper. Arrange a layer of sliced onion over this and sprinkle well with cheese. Repeat, ending with a layer of potatoes, dotted with butter and seasoning. Bake, covered, at 350° for 1 to 1½ hours.

ONIONS STUFFED WITH LIEDERKRANZ

4 large onions
4-oz. pkg. chilled Liederkranz
   (or other soft-ripened cheese)

2 cups fresh bread crumbs
⅓ cup finely chopped green pepper
4 Tbs. melted butter

Cook onions in boiling salted water about 15 minutes. When just tender, remove and drain. Then scoop out all but the three outside layers to make a firm hollow cup of each onion. Cut cheese into small cubes and toss with bread crumbs and chopped green pepper; stir in all the melted butter but enough to coat bottom of shallow baking dish. Stuff onions with cheese mixture, arrange in dish, and bake at 350° about 15 to 20 minutes, until stuffing bubbles and turns light brown on top.

SALSIFY (OYSTER PLANT) IN CHEESE SAUCE

1 lb. salsify
1 Tbs. lemon juice
2 cups Cheddar Sauce (page 170)

minced fresh basil
paprika

Scrape salsify roots and cut them into rounds or lengths of equal dimensions. Drop them into 3 cups of boiling water with lemon juice and cook 7 to 10 minutes, until just tender. Drain and fold gently into hot Cheddar sauce. Serve dusted with basil and paprika.

BAKED OKRA, TOMATOES, CORN, AND CHEESE

1 lb. fresh okra
2 cups cherry tomatoes
4 chopped scallions
½ cup chopped green pepper
3 cups semisoft cheese, diced (such
*   as combination of Feta and*
*   Port Salut or Cheshire)*

1 cup cream-style corn
salt and freshly ground pepper

Cut tops and tails off okra, and split cherry tomatoes. In a buttered 2-quart casserole make a layer of half the tomatoes, then half the okra. Sprinkle with some scallions and green pepper, then add half the corn and cheese. Season to taste. Repeat with another layer until everything is used up, ending with cheese. Bake in a 350° oven for about 45 minutes.

CHEESE-FILLED RÖSTI POTATOES

We once used a very fragrant, almost over-the-hill, imported Munster to make this version of the famous Swiss potato dish, and ever after we have reserved only our good smelly cheese for it—a dish that makes a meal-in-itself done this way.

4 medium Idaho baking potatoes
5 strips bacon
salt and freshly ground pepper
about 6 oz. ripe Munster (or
*   Livarot, Limburger,*
*   Leiderkranz)*

2–3 Tbs. chopped parsley

Scrub and boil the potatoes 15 minutes (or 5 minutes in pressure cooker). Peel and grate coarsely. Meanwhile cook the bacon in a large skillet until crisp, remove to drain, then dump the grated potatoes into hot fat. Season and let brown well on the bottom before turning. Grate or break up the cheese, then spread over the potatoes along with the crumbled bacon. Put under a hot broiler to melt on top. Flip half the potatoes over onto the other half and turn the pancake onto a hot platter. Sprinkle with parsley.

ALIGOT: POTATOES PURÉED WITH CHEESE

There are dozens of recipes for accenting potatoes with cheese, of which a number come from France. This one, known in patois as *l'aligot*, comes from the Auvergne in southwest France and has been called an "exquisite" blending of potatoes and fresh cheese by the gastronomical experts Gault and Millau. Elizabeth David, writing of French provincial food, gives a recipe she discovered at the small town of Entraygues, in which she substituted Caerphilly when she made the dish in England. In this country the grainy-textured Farmer Cheese made in New York is a good, fast-blending choice. A dry, close-packed Ricotta might also be used. (This mixture also makes wonderful potato croquettes.)

2 lbs. potatoes	*1 clove garlic, minced*
7 1/2-oz. pkg. fresh Farmer Cheese	*salt*
3–4 Tbs. butter	*freshly ground white pepper*
1 cup cream	*minced parsley*

Cook potatoes in boiling water until tender, then peel and put through a sieve or ricer. Meanwhile bring cheese to room temperature. Put butter and cream in a large saucepan and heat gradually until butter is melted. Stir in garlic. Blend potatoes into the hot cream, then add the cheese in small dollops, stirring the mixture with a whisk until all is well amalgamated. Season to taste. Transfer quickly to a hot serving dish, sprinkle with minced parsley, and serve immediately.

GRATIN OF SLICED TOMATOES

1 lb. ripe, firm, peeled tomatoes, sliced	*1/2 cup heavy cream*
4 tsps. dry sherry	*3/4 cup grated Cheddar (or almost any other, except soft-ripened cheese)*
fresh basil, minced	
salt and freshly ground pepper	*minced parsley*

Divide tomato slices among four buttered 4-inch gratin dishes and dribble 1 teaspoon of dry sherry over each. Sprinkle each with a little minced basil and bake 30 minutes in 300° oven. Give each dish 2 tablespoons of cream, then sprinkle evenly with 3 tablespoons each of grated cheese. Bake 15 minutes more and serve hot, garnished with parsley.

CHEESE- AND MUSHROOM-STUFFED ZUCCHINI

4 small zucchini (about 6 inches)	3–4 oz. Cream Cheese
3 Tbs. olive oil	1 egg, beaten
½ cup finely chopped onions	½ cup grated fresh Parmesan
1 clove garlic, minced	½ cup minced parsley
½ cup finely chopped mushrooms	salt and freshly ground pepper

Cut zucchini in half lengthwise and scoop out centers, leaving ¼-inch-thick shell; chop pulp. Heat oil in skillet and sauté onions until translucent, then add garlic, chopped mushrooms, and zucchini pulp. Cook 5 minutes, then turn up heat and cook, stirring, until juices are absorbed. Add Cream Cheese, beaten egg, all but 1 tablespoon of Parmesan, and parsley, and cook slowly, stirring constantly, about 5 minutes. Season to taste. Divide mixture among zucchini shells and sprinkle with remaining Parmesan. Arrange in baking dish and bake at 350° for 10 minutes, then slip under broiler to brown tops.

TIAN OF ZUCCHINI, RICE, AND CHEESE

4 small or 3 medium zucchini	2 cups cooked rice
1 Tbs. coarse salt	salt and freshly ground pepper
4 chopped scallions	2 Tbs. chopped parsley and fresh
3 Tbs. butter	basil
1 small clove garlic	2 Tbs. fresh bread crumbs
½–¾ cup heavy cream (or	1 Tbs. grated hard cheese
combination of sour and heavy	
cream)	
1¼ cups grated mild semisoft	
cheese (such as Bel Paese	
or Oka)	

Trim the zucchini and grate it coarsely. Toss with salt and let sit in a colander to drain for about 30 minutes. Squeeze dry and sauté with the scallions in butter for about 5 minutes, tossing and stirring. Add a whisper of garlic by scraping some of the juice from a small clove (or if you want more, add the whole clove minced—it can overpower this delicate dish); add cream and simmer another 5 or 6 minutes. Now stir in the grated cheese, the cooked rice, and salt and pepper to taste. Heat through, add herbs, and turn into round shallow buttered casserole (the tian). Mix bread crumbs and grated cheese, sprinkle on top, and brown under the broiler.

Salads

Perhaps the most talked-of salad in America in the years between World Wars I and II was the combination of romaine, garlic, anchovies, croutons, and Parmesan that is said to have been first achieved in Tiajuana, on the Mexican border, and named for Caesar—in this case the creator, Caesar Cardini. In his Connecticut inn called Stonehenge, Chef Albert Stockli created a remarkable salad of cheese and beef, and there are dozens of possible combinations that include both cheese and ham. In devising a salad, Parmesan or other grated cheese may be added as a condiment—crumbled Roquefort is often used this way—or a mild, supple cheese may be cut in strips to make a principal ingredient. Cottage Cheese, sometimes shaped in herb-flavored balls, often pleases salad eaters; or it makes a fine filling for ripe red tomatoes, or can be packed into green peppers and thinly sliced to serve with salad dressing. There are many recipes for vinaigrettes or mayonnaises accented with Blue Cheese. More interesting to me is the Italian way of dressing shredded smoked Mozzarella by tossing it with olive oil, freshly ground pepper, and minced basil. Mme. Jehane Benoit, famous in Canada for her knowledge of all kinds of food, once told me that she sometimes served as a first course Gruyère cubes that she marinated four hours or so in a mixture of oil, lemon juice, a little grated lemon rind, fresh marjoram and parsley, salt, and freshly ground pepper; it might be served with greens as a salad course. In Greece, Feta is often tossed with lettuce salads, and a Danish mélange is made with thinned mayonnaise accented with mustard, sliced tomatoes and cucumbers, juliennes of ham, lettuce leaves, and cubes of Danbo. The possibilities for cheese salads are no more limited than your imagination.

Sauces

Almost any cheese lends itself admirably to the making of sauces for a variety of purposes—northern Scandinavians, for instance, blend grated whey cheese with cream and seasonings, then simmer reindeer steaks in it. Blue Cheese and butter make a flavorsome adornment for broiled beef, and thinned with cream the same cheese may be used on delicate fish. The kinds of vegetables that can be made more interesting with one or another variation of cheese sauce are too numerous to mention. The sauce below serves to enhance vegetables, spaghetti, fish, or meat loaves. Substitute any firm cheese in place of Cheddar if you have something else on hand.

CHEDDAR SAUCE

4 Tbs. butter	1 cup grated Cheddar Cheese
1/4 cup flour	1/2 tsp. salt
2 cups milk	freshly ground white pepper

Melt the butter in a saucepan and blend in the flour, stirring over low heat for a few minutes. Heat milk, then stir into flour mixture until a smooth sauce forms and thickens. Stir in cheese and add salt and pepper to taste.

MORNAY SAUCE

A classic Mornay (see Lexicon) is made from a béchamel, prepared with veal stock and cooked long and slowly to reduce. This is a simpler version, but it should still cook long enough for the milk to reduce and thicken to a rich cream-sauce consistency.

1 small onion, sliced	1/4 cup grated Parmesan
2 cups milk	salt and freshly ground white pepper
3 Tbs. butter	2–3 gratings freshly ground nutmeg
3 Tbs. flour	optional: heavy cream
1 cup grated mild Cheddar, Swiss, or Gruyère	

Let the onion simmer in the milk about 10 minutes. In a heavy 1-quart saucepan melt the butter, stir in the flour, then cook slowly 3 to 4 minutes, stirring constantly. Strain in the hot milk, discarding the onion, and stir until smooth, then lower heat and let cook about 10 minutes until fairly thick. Add the cheeses, stirring until well blended, then add salt and pepper to taste, and nutmeg. Add a little heavy cream if you want a creamier consistency.

SIMONE BECK'S UNRIPENED CAMEMBERT CHEESE SAUCE

"When you open a piece of Camembert there are times when the center is hard and chalky, indicating that the cheese is not yet ripe," writes Simone Beck in *Simca's Cuisine.* "This part is not good to eat because it has not developed the proper texture and flavor; and it will never develop once the cheese has been cut into, because at that point the maturing process is arrested. During the war, the Germans often took the good Camembert, and one day I took that hard center and used it in making a Mornay sauce, which turned out to be unusually flavorful. On another day, I was using the chalky center of a Camembert to make a béchamel sauce, and I found that it made a very, very thick sauce—so thick that it was no longer really a sauce. I took it by spoonfuls, rolled it in bread crumbs, and fried it in deep fat, and it made a wonderful little bouchée to serve with drinks."

WHITE CHEESE SAUCE

This is a delicate sauce recommended for fluffy forcemeat balls of chicken, veal, or fish.

2 Tbs. butter	salt
2 Tbs. flour	1/2 cup Farmer Cheese
1/2 cup chicken or fish stock	1/2 tsp. dried chervil
1 cup milk or cream	freshly ground pepper

Melt the butter in a saucepan, stir in the flour, and cook gently a few minutes. Add stock off heat and stir. When mixture is smooth, blend in milk or cream, return to heat, and cook gently as it thickens. Taste and add salt, depending upon saltiness of stock. Break up the cheese and stir it into the sauce with a wire whisk, adding chervil (or another herb of your choice) and a few turns of the pepper grinder.

MUSHROOM-CHEESE SAUCE

1/4 cup minced shallots　　　　　　2 cups heavy cream
1/2 cup butter　　　　　　　　　　1 cup grated Gruyère
1 lb. mushrooms, chopped　　　　　1 cup grated Romano
3/4 cup flour　　　　　　　　　　　salt
2 cups milk　　　　　　　　　　　freshly ground black pepper

In a saucepan sauté shallots in 3 tablespoons butter about 5 minutes. Add remaining butter and mushrooms, gently cooking about 10 minutes. Blend in flour. Off heat, stir in milk to make a smooth texture, then stir in cream, return to heat, and simmer until sauce thickens. Stir in the cheeses and about a teaspoon of salt, depending on sharpness of Romano. Add pepper to taste.

BACON-CHEESE SPAGHETTI SAUCE

1/2 lb. bacon, chopped　　　　　　freshly ground black pepper
3 cloves garlic, minced　　　　　　1/2 cup grated Romano

Fry chopped bacon about 5 minutes, then stir in minced garlic and cook without browning. Grind in plenty of pepper, then scrape out bacon, garlic, and fat, spreading over hot, freshly made spaghetti. Sprinkle immediately with the Romano, and toss.

CHILLED BLUE CHEESE SAUCE FOR FISH

1/2 cup crumbled Blue Cheese　　　cayenne pepper
1 cup heavy cream

Put cheese and cream in blender and spin until smooth and fluid; add cayenne to taste. Chill 2 hours or more.

PESTO

This classic Italian pasta sauce that exudes the heady fragrance of fresh basil is bound and accented by grated cheese—Pecorino or Parmesan or a combination thereof (there are partisans for each choice). Your preference may depend on what's in the fridge. In any case, make the pesto base and blend in the cheese at the end, using three parts of the basil mixture to one part freshly grated cheese.

3 cups basil leaves	2/3 cup olive oil
3 cloves garlic	2/3 cup freshly grated Pecorino or
1/3 cup pine nuts	Parmesan (or a combination)
1 tsp. coarse salt	

Wash the basil leaves, if necessary, and dry well. Spin them in a blender (or food processor) along with the garlic, pine nuts, salt, and olive oil until you have a smooth paste. Fold in the grated cheese. Serve tossed with hot cooked spaghetti or thin noodles—approximately 1/3 cup per serving but more if wanted. Pesto is also excellent as an accent with certain bland fish and meats—just brush a bit over before broiling or baking, according to your taste.

MILD PESTO WITH RICOTTA: Substitute 3 tablespoons chopped Italian parsley for the garlic in the preceding recipe, omit the pine nuts, and use twice as much salt and half as much oil. Mix with 1 1/2 cups drained Ricotta and 1/4 cup freshly grated Pecorino.

CREAM CHEESE–CHILI STEAK SAUCE

1 Tbs. minced canned green chilies	1/2 cup wine vinegar
1 onion, minced	salt
4 cloves garlic, minced	1/4 cup crumbled Cream Cheese or
1/2 cup olive oil	fresh Farmer Cheese

Mix chilies, onion, and garlic with oil and vinegar; stir in about 1/2 teaspoon salt, or to taste, and let mixture mature about 3 hours. Stir in the cheese, and pass with barbecued steaks or other barbecued meat, or with steaks broiled in the kitchen.

Breads

CHEESE BREAD

This deliciously chewy and flavorful cheese bread can be baked either in a bread pan, making a loaf that is wonderful for canapés, sandwiches, toast, and croutons, or in a free-form French loaf, which is superb served warm for dinner. Both are so good that we like to make one of each at the same time, and this recipe is geared for that.

1 pkg. active dry yeast (or 1/2 oz. fresh)
1 3/4 cups warm water
4–5 cups unbleached flour
2 1/2 tsps. salt

1 cup grated sharp Cheddar (or 1/4 Parmesan—or other dry, strong cheeses like Romano or Asiago —and 3/4 Swiss cheese)
softened butter

Dissolve yeast in 1/4 cup of warm water. Mix 4 cups of the flour with the salt, then add dissolved yeast and remaining water. Mix, turn out on floured surface, and knead at least 10 minutes, adding more flour as required. Place in a large bowl, cover, and let rise slowly at average room temperature until triple in bulk. Punch down and let rise again until doubled in bulk this time. Turn out, kneading just long enough to work in the grated cheese. Butter an 8-by-4-by-2-inch bread pan and fill it two-thirds full of dough. Roll remaining dough into a loaf about 10 to 12 inches long and place on cornmeal-sprinkled baking sheet. Let both doughs rise to double, then bake in 450° oven (brush or spray the French loaf lightly with water once as it goes into the oven and again in about 2 minutes). Remove long loaf after 20 to 25 minutes, when done, and give the pan loaf another 5 to 10 minutes at 350°.

HELEN EVANS BROWN'S CORN, CHILI, AND CHEESE BREAD

In this marvelous rich cornbread from California, the cheese is a subtle ingredient but it helps to keep the bread moist and gives an ineffable flavor.

Mrs. Brown would have used Monterey Jack, but just about any firm cheese with good flavor will do.

For more than 4

about 1 cup corn kernels
1 cup yellow cornmeal
2 tsps. salt
3 tsps. baking powder
1 cup sour cream
¾ cup melted butter

2 eggs, beaten
¼ lb. Monterey Jack or similar
    cheese, finely diced
4-oz. can green chilies, peeled and
    finely chopped

Mix the corn with the rest of the ingredients. Pour into a well-buttered baking pan, about 9 inches square, or a similar-size shallow round baking dish. Bake in 350° oven for 1 hour. Serve warm with melted butter.

CHEESE POPOVERS

Makes 8

1 cup flour
¼ tsp. salt
2 eggs
1 cup milk

few drops of Tabasco
1 cup grated sharp, dry cheese
    (Cheddar, Asiago, Romano)

Sift flour and salt into a bowl. Beat eggs and milk together, then add to flour, beating until quite smooth. Add Tabasco. Lightly oil 8 Pyrex custard cups. Spoon a tablespoon of the batter into each, then a tablespoon of grated cheese, alternating until both are used up and cups are about half full. Place in cold oven, then immediately turn heat to 400°. After 30 minutes lower heat to 350° and bake another 25 to 30 minutes. Serve right away.

CHEESE BISCUITS

Really baking powder biscuits with cheese added, which makes them so much more tasty, particularly when served with something fairly bland like clear soup, or a salad, or scrambled eggs. They can be made with the cheese worked into the dough as in this recipe; or mix equal parts of soft butter and cheese and spread a teaspoon or so over the top of each biscuit before baking, in which case you could use just about any leftover bits of cheeses.

Makes about 1 dozen

2 cups flour
3 tsps. baking powder
½ tsp. salt
4 Tbs. butter or shortening

1 cup grated cheese (almost any
* kind firm enough to grate, with*
* good pronounced flavor)*
¾ cup milk

Sift flour, baking powder, and salt together. Work in the butter or shortening and the cheese until both are of the consistency of oatmeal. Then blend in the milk, turn out, and knead on floured surface for 30 seconds. Pat or roll out to ½-inch thickness, cut into rounds, and bake on ungreased sheet at 450° for 12 to 15 minutes.

Desserts

Long ago, in 1772, the Oxford antiquary Thomas Hearne noted in his diary that "nae healthy man has ony use for mair than half a dozen dishes at dinner—soup, fish, flesh, tairts, and cheese." Nevertheless it is the way of things in the United Kingdom to end a dinner with both a savoury and a dessert, as often as not a cheese course after a fruit-filled "tairt" or some other sweet. Indeed, it is hard to top the combination of well-aged Stilton and a juicy pear. In every country there are such affiliations of cheese and fruit, just as the fresh white regional cheeses have been used in various ways as fillings for sweet desserts. Cream Cheese can also be worked into pastry as a shortening that makes an excellent rich crust, and other cheeses can be used in similar ways in cookies.

CREAM CHEESE PASTRY DOUGH

3-oz. pkg. Cream Cheese
¼ lb. butter

1½ cups flour

Bring Cream Cheese and butter to room temperature and then blend thoroughly. Sift the flour into the cheese and butter. Work in well until thoroughly mixed, then wrap and chill a few hours before rolling out. This is enough dough for an 8-inch pie pan or for about 24 tartlet molds.

FOR QUICHE: The same recipe will fill a 9-inch shallow quiche mold. It is better to partially bake the crust before adding the quiche filling. Line the quiche mold with rolled-out pastry (there should be just about enough to fill it), then line the dough with buttered foil. Fill with dried beans or rice and bake 8 minutes in 425° oven. Then remove foil, prick bottom all over, and bake another 2 to 3 minutes.

FOR FRUIT TARTS: Prebake as for quiche, then spread the bottom with apricot or currant glaze and bake another 15 minutes at 375° for a fully baked shell.

FOR FRUIT PIES: Double the amount of dough to make enough for a top crust. Sprinkle the bottom with bread crumbs before adding fruit, which will help keep the dough from getting soggy.

BRONWYN'S CHEESECAKE

There are so many versions of cheesecakes that a book could be devoted exclusively to the subject, and one recipe—that of the old Lindy's restaurant in New York—added much to that Broadway rendezvous' reputation; more recently a Vermont cheeseman has made Lindy's cheesecake the foundation of a thriving business. The method here described has been handed from mothers to daughters and daughters-in-law for several generations. It might just be that a good cheesecake recipe is the way to a man's heart.

For more than 4

8 double graham crackers, crushed
    into crumbs
1½ cups sugar, plus 2 Tbs.
cinnamon
¼ lb. butter, melted
2 lbs. Cream Cheese, room
    temperature

4 eggs
1½ Tbs. lemon juice
1½ tsps. vanilla
1 pint sour cream

Stir crumbs, ½ cup sugar, a sprinkling of cinnamon, and melted butter until well mixed. Press the mixture evenly over the bottom of a spring pan or flan ring. Bake at 300° for 8 to 10 minutes, or until crumbs are lightly toasted; remove, and turn oven up to 375°. Beat the cheese until smooth and fluffy, then add 1 cup of sugar gradually, mixing well. Add eggs one at a time, beating after each addition. Stir in lemon juice and 1 teaspoon of vanilla, and pour the mixture over crumbs in baking pan; bake at 375° about 40 minutes, until done. Make a topping by mixing sour cream with 2 table-spoons of sugar and ½ teaspoon of vanilla, and spread over top of cake. Bake at 475° for 5 minutes. Remove cake to cool, and put in refrigerator overnight.

COTTAGE CHEESE PANCAKE GÂTEAU

8 crêpes (page 142)
½ lb. Cottage Cheese
¾ cup apricot jam
⅓ cup glacéed fruit (orange, grapefruit, figs)
½ cup light-brown sugar

1 Tbs. water
¼ cup orange juice
2 Tbs. thin strips of orange peel
¼ cup condensed milk
1 cup orange segments

Butter a baking dish just slightly larger than the size of the crêpes, and put one crêpe on the bottom. Combine cheese, jam, and glacéed fruit, then spread a little of it on the crêpe, repeating with remaining crêpes separated by layers of cheese-fruit filling, and ending with last crêpe on top. Cover with foil and bake 15 minutes at 350°. Meanwhile dissolve brown sugar with water, simmering about 4 minutes. Blanch strips of orange peel in boiling water 10 minutes. Drain and add to simmering sugar water. Stir in the condensed milk or cream, and add the orange segments; when this sauce is hot, pour over the pancake gâteau and serve hot, cutting in wedges like a pie.

COEUR À LA CRÈME AMÉRICAINE

2 cups Cottage Cheese
2 cups Cream Cheese
2 cups heavy cream

1 pint fresh strawberries
light cream

Line heart-shaped basket molds with dampened muslin or several layers of wet cheesecloth. Force both cheeses through a fine sieve, then beat until smooth with a rotary beater. Whip the cream until it peaks stiffly and fold it into blended cheeses. Pour the mixture into the prepared molds, drawing the cloth over the top and placing a small weight on each basket; let the molds drain on plates in the refrigerator for several hours. Unmold onto chilled plates, surrounding each serving with strawberries and a little light cream.

RUTH LOWINSKY'S CAMEMBERT ICE CREAM

Any embellishment of Camembert may strike you as a case of gilding the lily. If it doesn't, you'll find this recipe from Mrs. Lowinsky's *Lovely Food* (London, 1931) delicious and worth the effort. The method is from Jane Grigson's *Good Things*.

1 Camembert, soft and mature but not overripe	cayenne or Tabasco
	salt
½ cup heavy cream	water biscuits
½ cup light cream	

Mash up (or put in blender) the cheese with the two creams. Season well with cayenne or Tabasco and salt to taste. Freeze until just firm, but not hard. No need to stir. Serve sliced on a bed of cracked ice cubes with water biscuits that have been thoroughly heated.

SWEET BOUREKIAS WITH CREAM CHEESE

Flavored Cream Cheese is used variously in the Old World. It is the basis of this classic Mediterranean dish, and is the filling in *Queijadas de Évora*, the sweet cheese tarts of central Portugal, which have small flaky shells instead of being bundled in filo.

¼ lb. filo sheets	ground cinnamon
4 oz. Cream Cheese	unsalted butter, melted
1 rounded Tbs. honey	confectioner's sugar
1 tsp. granulated sugar	

Bring filo to room temperature about 2 hours before beginning to make the bourekias. Use a rubber spatula to mix Cream Cheese with honey and granulated sugar; stir in ½ teaspoon cinnamon, scraping mixture from sides of bowl until all is well amalgamated. Cut six sheets of filo pastry into four rectangular strips about 3 inches wide. Brush the strips, one at a time, with melted butter. Put a teaspoon of filling near one end of a strip. Fold one corner over the filling, making a triangle, then fold the triangle over and over again, maintaining the three-cornered shape, until the strip is folded into a single triangular bundle. Repeat with each other strip, and brush each bundle with melted butter, then sprinkle with confectioner's sugar and a little cinnamon. Butter a baking sheet and arrange bourekias on it. Bake about 30 minutes at 375°, until crisp and golden.

LISL'S CHEESE COOKIES

¼ lb. grated cheese (*Emmenthaler, Cheddar, or similar type*)
1 cup flour

¼ lb. butter, room temperature
1 egg yolk
optional: cumin seeds

Mix the cheese, flour, butter, and egg yolk together until well blended. Chill until firm enough to handle for rolling. Then roll the dough out to a thickness of ¼ inch. Cut into rounds with a cookie cutter. Place on ungreased cookie sheets and sprinkle cumin seeds over some or all the cookies if you like. Bake in a 325° oven for about 20 minutes.

SOMERSET APPLE CHEESE PANCAKES

¼ cup raisins
¼ cup sherry
1 cup soft fresh white cheese
   (*Farmer, Cottage, or local variety*)

1 medium apple, peeled and chopped
grated peel of 1 lemon
8 crêpes (*page 142*)
confectioner's sugar

Let the raisins plump in the sherry and a little warm water for half an hour or so. Drain and mix with the apple and grated lemon peel. Divide the filling among the crêpes, then roll them up and sprinkle with confectioner's sugar.

Savouries

Escoffier, who presided over the cuisines of the Savoy and the Carlton in London at the end of the nineteenth century, regarded the English savoury as food for barbarians; highly seasoned dishes served after dessert, he said, should not be tolerated. Nevertheless, the British love for the savoury course at the end of dinner persists and is justified by some as a way to whet the palate for the round of port which often follows. Various cheese delicacies (see Welsh Rabbit, page 158) are among the more popular recipes for a savoury ending to an English meal, including a whole Camembert embedded in aspic. In an anthology called *Food for Pleasure*, the gastronomically talented Ruth Lowinsky credited the aspic idea to her friend Lady Jeckyll and suggested it (among menus headed "Little Dinners for the Girl Who Lives Alone and Has a Guest") as the last course of a meal beginning with baked eggs and featuring beef stroganoff. Mrs. Lowinsky contributes a much better idea, I think, for dessert with Camembert Ice Cream, page 179.

CHUTNEY CHEESE SAVOURY

2 cups grated Cheddar	1 Tbs. chopped cucumber pickles
2 Tbs. milk	1 Tbs. chutney
½ cup butter	freshly ground pepper
2 Tbs. beer	toast triangles, hot and buttered
1 tsp. English mustard powder	

Put cheese in a saucepan over low heat and add milk, butter, and beer, stirring constantly until creamy. Stir in mustard, pickles, chutney, and several turns from a pepper grinder. Serve immediately on hot triangles of buttered toast.

FRIED CAMEMBERT SAVOURIES

In the International Wine and Food Society's *Guide to Cheese and Cheese Cookery*, T. A. Layton, once the redoubtable proprietor of The Cheddar Roast restaurant in Great Russell Street, London, asserts that "a delicious savoury to begin or end a meal can be made with Camembert." Such British ways with French cheese include dipping small pieces of Camembert in beaten egg (*à l'anglaise*) and deep-frying them a minute or two in hot fat at 375°. Sometimes the morsels are dipped in bread crumbs before going into the sizzling fat. Obviously, these could be served as a hot canapé with drinks, but in England they are still apt to be part of dinner. In Minnesota some immigrant Anglo-Saxons serve Camembert croquettes with salads.

1 Camembert	1 egg, beaten
½ cup plus 2 Tbs. butter, softened	2 tsps. olive oil
4 Tbs. flour	1 Tbs. milk
2 egg yolks	½ cup fine bread crumbs
½ tsp. paprika	oil or fat for deep frying
½ tsp. cayenne, or dash of Tabasco	freshly grated Parmesan
salt and pepper	

After scraping off thin rind, beat cheese with butter, flour, yolks, and seasonings; knead three times and shape into a ball, then let it stand 2 hours. Roll out to ½-inch thickness on a floured board and cut into desired shapes. Mix beaten egg with olive oil and milk. Dip the cheese pieces in and then roll in crumbs. Fry in hot fat at 375°. Dust with Parmesan and serve hot.

LOCKETS' SAVOURY

Not far from the House of Commons in London, Lockets is so typically a British restaurant that visitors from abroad are often taken there for meals unadulterated by the so-called Continental touch. A specialty of the house is this combination of fruit and cheese baked to a molten state and fragrant with contrasting flavors.

8 slices white bread	12 ozs. Stilton (or Blue), sliced
1 large bunch watercress	freshly ground black pepper
4 ripe Comice pears, peeled and	
thinly sliced	

Trim bread into neat rectangles and toast, then put one slice in each of four small ovenproof dishes. Cut off watercress stems and arrange leaves evenly over the toast, then cover with sliced pears and top with cheese slices. Bake 10 minutes in 350° oven, just long enough for cheese to melt. Garnish with freshly ground pepper.

Part Four

An International Cheese Lexicon

A FRENCHMAN'S ODE TO CHEESE

. . . Whether from Parma or from Jura heights,
Kneaded by august hands of Carmelites,
Stamped with the mitre of a proud abbess,
Flowered with the perfumes of the grass of Bresse,
From hollow Holland, from the Vosges, from Brie,
From Roquefort, Gorgonzola, Italy!
Bless them, good Lord—bless Stilton's royal fare,
Red Cheshire, and the tearful, cream Gruyère.
Bless Tomme de Chèvre, and bless the Leiden round,
Where aniseed and other grains are found;
Bless Edam, spherical, and Gouda then,
And those that we salute with "Sir," like men.

—translated by J. Bithell

I have tried here to identify and describe briefly as many of the world's cheeses as possible, and to include other definitions important to anyone interested in the subject. In doing so I have encountered—as has every other cheeselover—recipe innovations, as well as modifications in manufacture, that result in "new" cheeses and therefore new names, if not wholly new types. While this evolution continues, it is impossible to keep up with all the changes. It is also impossible to include every one of the hundreds of traditional French variants. Experts in France say it is "a land of 350 cheeses," but a count of all those for which some individuality is claimed would easily double that number.

If you are traveling in France, you will be able to "discover" cheeses in scores of small villages surrounded by dairy country. Although the variations may seem slight, *fromagères* of one locality are certain their product is as distinct from those of another as their own village differs from its neighbor. And they are right. My trouble is a limitation of space; so I have tried to cite as many from every region, from every cheese-producing country, as would help to show the surprising, ever increasing variety in the world of cheese.

The American appetite for cheese had increased so much by the end of the first quarter of 1979 that there has been a commensurate increase in stores specializing in the sale of imported cheeses and, indeed, an ever-widening choice of cheeses with unfamiliar names. One of the best of the new products is a two-mold cheese called Saga, developed in Denmark; it makes you think of eating a perfectly ripe Gorgonzola and a molten Brie at the same time. Under various new labels, there are more Goat Cheeses than ever before—in various shapes and sizes. There are also seemingly uncountable variations of rich and creamy French cheeses that have fat contents running from 50 to 75 percent, just as there are new products low in fat, designed for the diet-conscious market. Revidoux, for instance, comes from Lorraine, has 62 percent fat, and is soft and gentle yet tasty (as its manufacturer tells you on the label). Saint-Albray is the name of a new variation (50 percent fat) of cheese that is traditional in the western Pyrenees. Triomphe Creme is a brand name for one of the plethora of Cream Cheeses accented by garlic and herbs, and it comes from Austria.

In addition, among French products particularly, names of localities in dairy regions have recently been used as generic labels for cheeses very different from those once known exclusively under the same names. As an example, there is a soft, flavorful Cream Cheese possessing no rind which is sold as "Soumaintrain"—that name traditionally has been the label of a Burgundian disk with a shiny red-brown washed crust and a penetrating aroma. Cheese buyers are well advised to shop where a knowledgeable salesperson can offer accurate information about new products—and where sample tastes of new cheeses are cheerfully offered.

E. J.
May 1979

A

ABERTAM (sheep) Assertive, hard; originated in farm dairies of Bohemia, near Karlovy Vary (Carlsbad), Czechoslovakia.

ABONDANCE (cow) Called also Vacherin d'Abondance, this brushed-rind farm product takes its name from a Savoy valley near Thonon les Bains; similar to other mountain cheeses of the Alps and Pyrenees.

ÄDELOST (cow) Blue-veined, Swedish factory product of pasteurized milk.

ADMIRAL'S (cow) English Stilton blended with port.

AETKEES (cow) Tiny, square, rindless, this ancient fermented Belgian cheese is made in Brabant and around Louvain. Popular among Brussels gastronomes and sometimes called Fromage de Bruxelles, it has strong aroma and is wrapped in parchment, but was once put up in cabbage leaves at the St. Clary market.

AGRAFA (sheep) A Greek imitation of Gruyère is sometimes marketed under this name.

AGRINI TICENESE (cow) A fresh cheese found locally in southern Switzerland.

AISY (cow) Also called Cendré d'Aisy for one of the many Burgundian cheese villages, this is a soft washed-rind cheese cured for two months in marc, then stored in vine ashes until it matures.

AJOQUESO Mexican cheese mixture (literally "garlic cheese").

AKUREYRI (cow) The port of Akureyri, in north-central Iceland, gives its name to a factory Blue Cheese made by Arctic dairymen.

ALCOBACA (sheep) Named for the town north of Lisbon; a variation of Portuguese Serras in the form of a small, flat disk.

ALENTEJO (sheep) In Portugal's farmlands of the Alentejo, small cylinders of three different sizes are made from sheep's milk with the addition sometimes of a small amount of goat's milk or, more frequently, cow's milk. The smallest are 2 ounces, usually produced from a mixture. Pure sheep's-milk Alentejos weigh either 1 pound or 4 pounds and are ripened for a few weeks to be eaten when soft. A mountain cheese of the same name, once made of milk coagulated by thistle flowers, developed its best flavor when aged about two years.

ALIGOT (cow)   French mountain product, similar to Mozzarella, made in small chaletlike dairies called *burons* of the area that turns out Cantals. When not eaten within 48 hours, it becomes the base of Cantal and Laguiole.

ALIGOT   A purée of potatoes and cheese. (See Recipes, page 167.)

ALKMAAR   Cheese market town in northern Holland to which bright yellow balls of Edam (those for export have red exteriors) and wheels of Gouda are brought from farms.

ALLGÄUER BERGKÄSE (cow)   Made in Bavarian Allgäuer district, just across the Swiss border from St. Gall, by the Emmenthaler techniques; it thus resembles and often is virtually as good as Emmethal. It is sometimes called Allgäuer Emmenthal, sometimes Allgäuer Rundkäse.

ALPKÄSE (cow)   Made in the Austrian Alps; a smaller variant of Emmenthal.

ALTAISKI (cow)   Factory-made Russian cheese that matures in six months and is firm in texture.

ALTE KUHKÄSE (cow)   One of the German "Hand" Cheeses (see below); also called Berliner Kuhkäse.

ALTENBURGER (goat)   Wheel-shaped; made in Thuringia, Germany.

ALTIER (goat)   On Lozere farms in southwestern France the word meaning "lofty" is applied to a small rustic but creamy disk.

ALVERDE (sheep)   Portuguese rounds sometimes made with addition of goat's milk.

AMBERT (cow)   See Fourme d'Ambert.

AMBROSIA (cow)   Mild, slightly tart and aromatic, soft and porous product of the provinces of Halland and Småland in southern Sweden; sometimes called Svensk Tilsiter.

AMERICAN (cow)   Loosely used term for American-made Cheddar and similar types; often applied to processed products. A reputable cheesemonger will describe U.S. cheeses accurately: Brick, Colby, Monterey Jack, New York Cheddar, Tillamook, Vermont Cheddar, etc.

AMFROM (cow)   See Anfrom.

AMISH BABY SWISS (cow)   Not to be confused with traditional "Swiss" loaves with large holes, this product of Ohio Amish farmers is pliant and mild; it is sometimes smoked for retail sale.

AMOU (sheep)   Named for the market town east of Biaritz and one of the best types made in Gascony; a table cheese, used for grating when hard.

AMPU (cow)   Rare, local farmhouse type of southwest France.

ANARI (goat or sheep)   Fresh, and known by Cypriots as Anari Analati;

eaten with sugar, honey, or preserved fruit within a day or two of making. The heated curds are stirred with a ladle called an *anaro-kanni*, to which a clean thyme bush is attached, and then drained in small baskets called *talaria*, made from reeds native to Cyprus. It is sometimes preserved in salt.

ANDECHS (cow)   A version of Allgäuer mountain types developed at the Andechs monastery on Lake Ammer, outside Munich.

ANDORRE (cow)   Mountain cheese of Andorra.

ANDROUËT   Family of *fromages maîtres* whose Paris cheese shop and restaurant is internationally known. Pierre Androuët is the author of *Guide de Fromage.*

AÑEJO (cow)   see Queso Añejo.

ANFISSIS (cow)   Buttery farmhouse type from Thessalonia.

ANFROM (cow)   Considered a commercial version of the Trappist Oka; supple and mild with slightly acerbic aftertaste, it is manufactured in the Montreal suburb of Anjou, and is sometimes spelled Amfrom.

ANGELOT (cow)   Ancient cheese of Normandy.

ANNATTO   Yellowish red dye stuff made from the pulp around the seeds of the tropical tree *Bixa orellana,* annatto is used in Latin American cooking and as a coloring agent for Leicestershire and many American versions of Cheddar.

ANNIVIERS (cow)   A mountain cheese of Switzerland used in making raclette, produced in Val d'Anniviers, Valais; when aged it is grated for cooking.

ANNOT (goat)   Of mild, slightly nutty flavor, firm, resilient texture, and smooth brushed rind; made on mountain farms in the upper Var Valley, high above Nice.

ANOST (goat)   Named for a village in Burgundy, and sometimes a mixture of cow's and goat's milk. See Charolles.

ANSÓ (sheep)   Named for Pyrenees town in the province of Huesca, Spain; supple, semihard, yellow-rinded wheel.

ANTHOTYRO (goat, sheep)   The term meaning "flowery cheese" is applied to soft cheese of Crete when flavored with dill; Kretiki island Greeks eat it with honey.

AOSTIN (cow)   Soft, buttery, washed-curd type from Val d'Aosta in northwest Italy; when matured about three months in special salt brine which develops flavor it is sometimes known as Salmistra.

APPELLATION D'ORIGINE   French laws protect certain cheese just as others define legal use of wine designations. Look for these words on wrappings of Bleu de Gex, Bleu de Septmoncel, Cantal, Gruyère de Comté, Maroilles, Reblochon, Roquefort, St. Nectaire. In 1951 the international convention (see Stresa Convention) resulted in agreement to refrain from calling imitations of classic cheeses by the names of the originals. Hence, for instance, Danish-made Port Salut is known as Esrom.

APPENZELLER (cow) Appenzell, the name of a canton in eastern Switzerland, is also used in mountain patois for the isolated family groups who make cheese in Alpine chalets. (It derives originally from *Abbatis cella,* "abbot's cell," in reference to northeastern Switzerland's Abbey of St. Gallen.) Wheels bearing the name have a thickish, tan, inedible rind and a special flavor that results from the wine and spices used in maturation. Imitations are made in Bavaria and Baden. See St. Galler Alpkäse.

APPENZELLER-ZIEGENKÄSE (cow, goat) Made in summer of two milks (when goat's milk is scarce) and sold locally under this name.

APPETITOST (cow) Danish sour-buttermilk type.

APPLEWOOD (cow) British Cheddar smoked in applewood fumes; see Smoked.

ARAGATSKI (cow, sheep) Sour-buttermilk type produced by Caucasian farmers in the U.S.S.R.

ARASTAL (cow, goat, sheep) Hard Portuguese mountain type containing 75 percent sheep's milk, 12½ percent cow's milk, and 12½ percent goat's milk; salty flavor that sharpens as it matures.

ARAVIS (goat) See Persillé.

ARBER (cow) Creamy, yellow, semihard; made in Sudetenland mountains.

ARDI-GASNA (sheep) Basque word for "local cheese" applies to firm, supple wheel from border mountains above St.-Jean-de-Pied-de-Port in the western Pyrenees; also known as Arneguy, for a market town.

AREQUIPA (cow) Local Peruvian cheese named for the mountain city near the Chilean border.

ARLES, TOME D' (sheep) See Camargue.

ARMAVIR (sheep) Somewhat like the German "Hand" Cheese (see below); made from acidified ewe's milk with sour buttermilk or whey added, it is a specialty of the western Caucasus.

ARNEGUY (sheep) See Ardi-Gasna.

ARRAN (cow) One of Scotland's firm types, named for the island in the Firth of Clyde, Arran is sometimes colored with annatto, sometimes left naturally cream-colored.

ARRIGNY (cow) Named for a town in the French province of Champagne; a version of Carré de l'Est.

ASADERO (cow) The Mexican term meaning "fit for roasting" is applied to a white highly meltable type produced in Chihuahua, Jalisco,

Michoacán, as well as Oaxaca, where it originated. See Oaxaca.

ASCO (sheep or sheep and goat)   A Corsican shepherd's cheese named for a village near the famous gorge in the northern part of the island.

ASIAGO (cow)   Pungent *grana* type once made from sheep's milk in the Veneto village that gave it its name; now made from partly skimmed cow's milk throughout much of northern Italy, and also in Michigan and Wisconsin. *Asiago di taglio* is cured not more than 60 days and served as table cheese. When it matures six months or more, it is one of Italy's superior grating types.

ASIN (cow)   Washed-curd type common on northern Italian farms and in small mountain dairies; soft, buttery, white, sparingly ripened.

AULUS (cow, sheep)   Much is consumed by frequenters of the cure town of Aulus-les-Bains in the Pyrenees north of Andorra; produced from either cow's or sheep's milk and matures to firm texture and tangy flavor. See Bethmale.

AUNIS (cow, goat)   Named for an ancient region in western France; traditionally triangularly shaped, and very rare.

AUOSI (cow)   Rustic Pyrenees herdsman's cheese, cylinder-shaped, and usually eaten fresh.

AURA (cow)   Finnish Blue Cheese, produced in small wheels.

AUTUN (goat)   See Charolles.

AZEITÃO (sheep)   Small Cream Cheeses from Portugal's Setúbal peninsula; often served as appetizers.

B

BACKSTEINER (cow)   Brick-shaped but otherwise different from U.S. Brick Cheese; a north German version of Romadur, somewhat milder and smaller.

BACON-FLAVORED (cow)   Term applied to Cheddar first made at Woodford, Queensland, Australia, by Ken Grehan, who added ham bits to Cheddar curd produced at Caboolture Cooperative.

BAGNES (cow)   One of the firm, pliant Valais types from Switzerland, named for an Alpine valley, and used in making raclette, a melted cheese dish. When not used in raclette, it is a delicious table cheese, served often with Switzerland's paper-thin dried beef and Valaisan bread.

BAGOZZO (cow)   Grating type sometimes called Grana Bagozzo, made in smaller wheels than Parmesan; it is also classed as a Caciotta, and sometimes called Bresciano after the city of Brescia in northern Italy.

Flavor and aroma are strong, interior yellow, and rind often colored red.

BAGUETTE LAONNAISE, BAGUETTE DE THIÉRACHE (cow)   The latter name refers to a French loaf of bread; it is often called Baguette Laonnaise after the city in Champagne; character is reminiscent of Maroilles.

BAKER'S (cow)   Made specifically for commercial use from skim milk; sometimes produced from spray-dried nonfat solids with a texture similar to Cream Cheese but not sticky. It is packaged often in polyethylene-lined tin cans.

BANBURY (cow)   Hard-pressed cake aged in shallow molds; made in Shakespeare's time and so characteristically thin it is used as an ephithet against Slender in *The Merry Wives of Windsor*.

BANDAL (cow)   One of India's soft Cream Cheeses, eaten fresh or lightly smoked over wood fires.

BANDON (cow)   Oregon-made Cheddar, exclusively of Jersey milk.

BANON (cow, goat, sheep)   Commercial plants now produce Banons from cow's milk, but farmhouse versions, following the original prescription of sheep's milk in spring and summer, or goat's milk in late spring, summer, and autumn, are superior. Banon is a provincial market town in the Alpilles, the rocky hills covered with wild herbs that account for the cheese's characteristic flavor; Banons are sometimes wrapped in leaves, sometimes dipped in eau de vie and wrapped again in chestnut leaves, tied with raffia and, traditionally, matured in earthenware jars.

BANON AU PEBRE D'AI (goat)   See Poivre d'Âne.

BARBEREY (cow)   A Camembert-like cheese that takes its name from a town near Troyes, in Champagne; cured in ashes. Also called Fromage de Troyes.

BARONET (cow)   Bland, buttery American type.

BARRILITO (cow)   Vanished Cuban table cheese.

BASKET (cow)   Fresh curds molded in baskets.

BASSEZ (goat)   A classic small cake from Rouergue, France.

BATH (cow)   Production discontinued; originally 9 inches square, 1 inch thick, mature in one week, with piquant flavor.

BATTELMATT (cow)   Small version of Gruyère made in the canton of Tessin (Ticino), Switzerland, but more supple in texture and sometimes compared to Tilsit.

BAUDEN (goat)   Czechoslovakian relative of Harz, somewhat bigger and shaped both in conical form and in a 2-pound wheel by herdsmen in Sudeten mountains; also known as Koppen.

BAUGES, VACHERIN DES (cow)   Mountain dairymen of Les Bauges, near Aix-les-Bains, Savoy, make a thinnish, mild cylinder shaped by spruce bark; see Vacherin.

BEAUCERON (goat)   The fertile plains of Beauce, adjoining Normandy and Île-de-France, produce much good food, including the goat cheese of Dreux, north of Chartres.

BEAUFORT (cow)   Made in Dauphine and Savoy and sometimes known as Gruyère de Beaufort because of resemblance to Swiss Gruyère; the best, labeled Beaufort de Montagne, is produced in mountain chalets and matured six months in cool Alpine caves.

BEAUMONT (cow)   A version of St. Paulin developed by Jeremie Girod, whose surname appears in blue ink on the wrapping of Beaumonts sent to the U.S.; factory-made, it resembles commercial Reblochons.

BEL   French international producer of Baby Bel, Bonbel, Kiri, La Vache Qui Rit, with factories in Algeria, Belgium, Denmark, Italy, Japan, and Spain; a U.S. affiliate in Kentucky makes a Cheddar called Albany.

BEL LAGO (cow)   Factory-made, semisoft, firm consistency, ripened; compares with Belle Suisse, Doulce Gruyère, Fleurs des Alpes, Fromage Roth, all produced in Switzerland.

BEL PAESE (cow)   Italian term for "beautiful country" was the title of a children's book by Father Antonio Stoppani, whose picture appears on packages of semisoft type made in several countries under license. Stoppani's friend Egidio Galbani devised a factory formula after studying methods for Bella Alpina and other cheeses. Bel Paese produced at Melzo, near Milan, bears the map of Italy, whereas that made in America has a map of the Western Hemisphere.

BEL PIANO LOMBARDO (cow)   A Lombardy prototype of Bel Paese.

BEL PIEMONTE (cow)   Similar to Bel Paese; see Fior d'Alpe.

BEL VAL (cow)   Similar to St. Paulin; made by monks at the Abbey of Bel Val, Picardy, France.

BELLA ALPINA (cow)   Italian forerunner of factory-made Bel Paese.

BELLA MILANO (cow)   Local Milan forerunner of Bel Paese.

BELLE BRESSANE (cow)   Bresse cheesemakers in the vicinity of Grièges, an important French cheese town, devised this thick 8-inch blue-veined disk that has a 3-inch hole in its center. It has 50 percent fat and a smooth, creamy texture, and reminds some of a cross between Gorgonzola and other French *bleus*.

BELLE ÉTOILE (cow)   Île-de-France double-cream type produced at Chapelle-aux-Pots; sometimes with spice.

BELLE SUISSE (cow)   See Bel Lago; some Belle Suisse is produced in Austria.

BELLELAYE (cow) See Tête de Moine.

BELO VRHNJE (cow) Croatian Cream Cheese from Sestine, Yugo-slavia.

BELSANO (cow) An Austrian factory-made Fontina type.

BENIR (goat, sheep) An ancient term still used in Romeli region of central Greece for rustic types.

BERGKÄSE (cow) A German term for mountain types from south-western Bavaria, part of a dairy region stretching over the Alps toward the valley of the Emme River, which gives its name to Em-menthaler; see Allgäuer. So good is the best Bergkäse that wealthy connoisseurs of Czarist Russia habitually stored each new year's Allgäuers like vintage wines. In Switzerland and Italy the classifica-tion covers Battelmatt, Fontina, Gruyère, Montasio, and Walliser.

BERGQUARA (cow) A Swedish version of Gouda.

BERGUES (cow) A low-fat product of Flanders farms near Dunkerque and Bergues; it resembles Holland cheeses in form but has sharper flavor.

BERKELEY (cow) A yellow marbled cheese still made on British farms, but not often stocked by cheesemongers.

BERLINER KUHKÄSE (cow) See Alte Kuhkäse.

BERNADE (cow, goat) The flavor is distinguished by 10 percent goat's milk plus a seasoning of saffron; Bernade is produced in northern Italy, where it is sometimes known as Formagelle Bernade (see Formagelle).

BETHMALE (cow, sheep) A firm-textured local mountain cheese of France's Pyrenees country.

BÉTHUNE, FORT DE (cow) A strong-smelling variant of Maroilles (see below), Fort de Béthune comes from a small French industrial town near the Belgian border; connoisseurs know it affectionately as "old stinker," or "old gray."

BGUG PANIR (sheep) Armenian shepherd's product of skimmed milk accented with herbs; known also as Daralag (see below).

BIANCO (cow) Also known as Bayerischer Schnitzkäse, this has a mild Tilsit-like flavor and multiple tiny holes.

BIAROM (cow) Semisoft, part skim milk, Biarom is a mild type pro-duced at Waging-am-See, Bavaria.

BIBBELSKÄSE (cow) An Alsatian farm specialty made of whole-milk curds mixed with horseradish and fresh herbs.

BIERKÄSE (cow) The term is often translated in the U.S. as "Beer Cheese"; it is best known in Germany as Weisslacker because of its white interior. Made in Bavaria, Belgium, and Wisconsin, it has affinities with American Brick and Limburger. *Bierkäse* is also the term used for a Munich custom of dissolving cheese in beer as a thick and pungent potable.

BIFROST (goat)   A mild, white Norwegian type.

BILLINGE (cow)   Factory-made, firm, white Swedish product with a scattering of round holes; mild but mellow flavor.

BILLY (goat)   Named for a French village not far from the Selles-sur-Cher; this rustic farmhouse type is wrapped in plane-tree or grape leaves and matured in small stone pots.

BIQUET (goat)   The name means kid, and the cheese is shaped like a Camembert, a product of the cooperative *fromagerie* at Reparsac, not far from Cognac, France.

BITTO (cow, goat)   Named for a valley near Sondrio, on the Italian-Swiss frontier; it resembles small-eyed Swiss table cheeses and is used for grating when hardened by age.

BIZA (sheep)   A product of Iraqi herdsmen, using skim milk without rennet, and flavored with onion and garlic; also called Fajy. It is so similar to the Scottish Hramsa (see below) that the latter has found a market in the Middle East.

BLADEN (cow)   A mild cheese from Dorsetshire; British cooks find it good for cooking, and it is popular with children.

BLANC DE MAI (cow)   "May cheese" of Holland is produced in the spring as soon as cattle go from barns to meadows; it is very fat and creamy.

BLARNEY (cow)   Semisoft, usually mild and a trifle moister than Cheddar, this is an original Irish cheese of which some of the best comes from County Cork. It has small holes, red skin, and is sold in "Baby Blarney" wheels and in 26-pound cylinders.

BLEU (cow, goat, sheep)   With the exception of Roquefort, considered to be in a class by itself, internal-mold cheeses of France are known generally either as *fromage bleu* or as *persillé;* certain others are distinguished by the word *fourme,* as in Fourme d'Ambert. The penicillium that causes the mottling differs from that necessary in the making of, say, Brie and Camembert, mainly in the fact that the resulting mold becomes visible. In addition to Roquefort, a few internal-mold types are made exclusively of sheep's milk; some of the *persillés* at times have a percentage of goat's milk, which is also the base of the rare Bleu d'Aveyron.

BLEU D'AUVERGNE (cow)   Many blue-veined cheeses are produced in the French region of Auvergne, and the best are protected by legislation and come to U.S. stores wrapped in foil that bears a green band.

In the general area of central France others with reputations include: Bleu de Bassignac, Bleu de Bassilac, Bleu des Causses, Bleu de Cayres, Bleu de Costaros, Bleu de Figeac, Bleu de Loudes, Bleu de Quercy, Bleu de Salers, the farmhouse Bleu de Thiezac, the sheep's-milk Bleu de Tulle, and Bleu de Velay.

BLEU DE BRESSE (cow)   After Roquefort and Fourme d'Ambert, Bleu de Bresse is considered the best of French *bleus;* many believe it a match for Italy's Gorgonzola. It was created in 1950 when the method for producing Saingorlon in small wheels was developed at the Servas dairy cooperative in the bountiful Bresse country near Lyon. Copies called Pipo-Bleu and Pipo Crem' are both made at nearby Grièges and are sometimes sold under the name of that town. See also Belle Bressane.

BLEU DES CAUSSES (cow)   See Bleu d'Auvergne.

BLEU DE CORSE (sheep)   On the high plains of northern and central Corsica, shepherds in isolated huts make white cheeses and send the best of them off to be finished in the ideal conditions of Roquefort cayes, near Millau. Those that remain on the island long enough to develop interior mold are either consumed in Corsica or shipped to the mainland under this label.

BLEU DE HAUT JURA, BLEU DE GEX (cow)   To legally bear the former name, blue-veined types from the Jura Mountains must be produced at an altitude of 2,500 feet. They are made in many communities, and include those known as Bleu de Gex and Bleu de Septmoncel; both of these are used in fondue Nantuatienne.

BLEU DE LAQUEUILLE (cow)   Named for a small town not far from Clermont-Ferrand where a memorial celebrates Antoine Roussel, who developed a factory method for introducing blue mold into the white cheese habitually made in the area.

BLEU DE LAVALDENS (cow, goat)   One of the local blue types of the French Savoy; considered outstanding when produced from goat's milk.

BLEU DE SASSENAGE (cow)   Similar to Bleu de Gex, Sassenage is named for its market town in Isère.

BLEU DE SEPTMONCEL (cow)   See Bleu de Haut Jura.

BLEU DE TIGNES (cow, goat)   A rustic Savoy farmhouse cheese produced in chalets using milk from Alpine pastures; it is of special interest if made of goat's milk.

BLODERKÄSE (cow)   See Toggenburger.

BLONS   A typical cheese village of the Vorarlberg Alps whose product is referred to in export markets as "Austrian Swiss Cheese."

BLUCREME (cow)   An internal-mold cheese with added cream, Blucreme is produced in Denmark and is similar to Danablu but smoother and creamier; it is manufactured to order in 10-pound loaves.

BLUE (cow, goat)   While attempts to make a product like Roquefort were being perfected in Denmark by Marius Boel, U.S. experiments met with success in 1918. Methods were developed to use the mold *Penicillium roqueforti,* and efforts of the Department of Agriculture and California Experiment Station resulted in a method of making Blue Cheese from goat's milk. Research at universities of Iowa, Minnesota, Washington, and Wisconsin helped to perfect current commercial production of cow's-milk Blue Cheese. Loosely the term is used in reference to include certain English types (see following entries), Scandinavian veined cheeses, and several manufactured in the U.S., including Maytag, Nauvoo, Oregon Blue, and Treasure Cave.

BLUE CASTELLO (cow)   Creamy Danish invention that looks somewhat like Gorgonzola but has both visible and invisible interior molds.

BLUE CHEDDAR (cow)   Very rarely, internal mold develops in farmhouse Cheddars when they are aged in humid caves. So few Cheddars turn blue that they are much coveted by cheeselovers.

BLUE CHESHIRE (cow)   Once thought of as an "accidental" transformation, the internal mold that caused certain Cheshires to be referred to as "Old Blue" resulted from conditions in curing cellars rather than deliberate inducement. Adequate Blue Cheshire is produced by factory methods, and farmhouse Blues are increasingly rare.

BLUE DORSET (cow)   See Blue Vinny.

BLUE STUART (cow)   Forsyth's in Princes Street, Edinburgh, considers this the best blue-veined Scottish type.

BLUE VINNY (cow)   By 1935 the marbled cheese of Dorsetshire was rare, and now it is seldom made. West Country people use the word *vinny* to describe any mold on food, and the name of the cheese developed out of affection for the hard, crumbly, country cheese of Dorset that once in a while became mottled with blue-green veins.

BLUE WENSLEYDALE (cow)   Monks who founded the Jervaulx Abbey in Yorkshire after they arrived in the Norman Conquest appear to have brought the beginnings of Blue Wensleydale with them; it has a creamy, rich, sweet taste and a texture soft enough to spread. See Stilton.

BLUEFORT (cow)   Commercial blue-veined product of Canada.

BOERENKAAS (cow)   Translated into English, the term means "farmer cheese"; it is stamped on Goudas made on farms in the dairy region of Gouda, Holland.

BOL EN BRODVORM (cow)   A Finnish "bread cheese," as mild as Edam, also known as Boule et Pain.

BOLA (cow)   Best-known of the Portuguese types; Bola is likened to Edam in form and taste.

BOM PETISCO (cow)   A trade name given to an American-made version of the common semisoft cheese of Portugal.

BONBEL (cow)   Factory-made variant of St. Paulin; Baby Bel is a small, semisoft imitation Edam. See Bel.

BONDARD, BONDE, BONDON (cow)   The French word *bonde* means "bung," the shape taken by numerous small, soft, double- and triple-cream products of Normandy and Picardy. Other related types include Briquette, Carré, Coeur Double Bonde, Double Coeur, Malakoff, Triple Bonde.

BONDAROY AU FOIN (cow)   Soft French cheese with natural crust, wrapped in hay; it is made on farms and small Orléanais dairies.

BONDOST (cow)   Mild, cylindrical Swedish farm cheese considered ideal for melting.

BONGARDS, MINNESOTA   A town that produces Cheddar, Colby, Monterey Jack, and Munster under automated conditions at the rate of over 150,000 pounds daily.

BONNEVILLE (cow)   See note, page 29.

BOSSONS MACÉRÉ (goat)   Le Bossons, a small mountain hamlet near Chamonix, France, produces small goat cheeses macerated in alcohol, olive oil, and herbs.

BOUGON (goat)   Camembert-like goat's-milk disk taking its name from Poitou village in western France.

BOULE DES MOINES (cow)   Fresh curds drained, flavored with herbs, shaped in 3-inch balls; made at the Abbey of Pierre-qui-Vire, Côte d'Or, Burgundy, by monks who may have been the first to market herb-seasoned cheese. They also make a soft-ripened type called Pierre-qui-Vire.

BOULETTE D'AVESNES (cow)   Soft, kneaded curds flavored with parsley, tarragon, and pepper, with reddish rinds, aged three months in humid cellars.

BOULETTE DE CAMBRAI (cow)   Pure-white hand-molded balls produced in Flanders in homes and on farms, with herbs added; eaten fresh.

BOULLE DE LILLE (cow)   Spherical with rind tinted red; a version of Mimolette made in Flanders and marketed in Lille.

BOUQUET DE THIÉRACHE (cow)   Local farm product found along Meuse River on the France-Belgium border.

BOURG-D'OISANS (cow, goat)   Named for a village near Grenoble; pressed curds of cow's and goat's milk.

BOURSAULT (cow)   Named for the man who began a modest dairy enterprise at Perreux, a suburb of Roanne, northwest of Lyon; a triple-cream, soft, rindless cake with an aftertaste of Brie.

BOURSIN (cow)   Named for a Norman dairyman whose factories market triple creams throughout the world.

BOUTON DE CULOTTE (goat)   Tiny cylindrical cakes taking their name from French britches buttons, which they resemble—or, as Roy de Groot wrote, looking like "nothing so much as small marshmallows, some of them toasted brown, others with a red crust."

BOX (cow)   Known in Germany in two forms: Soft Box is a mixture of equal parts of skim and whole milk to which caraway seed is added; it is hooped in 6½-inch disks and ripened about three months. Semihard Box resembles American Brick and is often labeled Hohenburg.

BRA (cow)   Named for small Piedmont agricultural town south of Turin; this hard white type, sharp and salty, was first produced by nomad herdsmen; a smaller, milder version is cured in brine by Lombardy farmers, and it is also made in Quebec.

BRACH (cow)   A fresh-curd type made on farms in Lorraine.

BRACKI SIR (sheep)   Small, very hard, this is a specialty of Brac Island, north of Dubrovnik, Yugoslavia.

BRAIDED (cow, sheep)   Rather bland and fibrous, this product of the Middle East has been discovered recently in Europe and America; it is sometimes flavored with a scattering of seeds and its consistency lends itself to separation into string-like pieces, sometimes called hair (see String Cheese, below). Separated cheese fibers are often stuffed inside flat pitta bread and baked.

BRAND (cow)   One of the German "Hand" types (see below), this is a mixture of curds slightly fermented with butter and moistened with beer.

BRANDZA (sheep)   Soft Romanian white cheese that is made for winter curing in tubs alternately filled with salt and milk; it is eaten especially at the end of Lent during "the week of cheese," an annual celebration. Brandza de Burdouf is much more piquant and is pre-

served in leather bottles or in bladders. Brandza de Cochuletz is produced from aged rustic white cheese, kneaded with salt; in certain Romanian villages aromatics are sometimes added, while in others it is shaped in hoops made of fir bark.

BRANZI (cow)   Soft cakes made on Lombardy plateaus north of Bergamo.

BRÄTKÄSE (cow)   Swiss melting cheese either toasted on a stick over open fire or cooked in a frying pan.

BRAUDOST (cow)   Traditional Icelandic Edam type, once the most popular in the country; shaped in 8- to 10-pound rectangles.

BREAKFAST (cow)   Soft-ripened, floury rind; some is produced at Petaluma, California, under the Rouge et Noir label.

BRESCIANO (cow)   See Bagozzo.

BRESSAN (cow, goat)   Soft, natural crust cakes of equal parts cow's and goat's milk shaped in truncated cones by farmers east of Lyon, France; sometimes used in local fondues.

BRESSE-BLEU (cow)   See Bleu de Bresse.

BREYIBACTERIUM LINENS   A mold that imparts reddish orange color to such types as Brick, Liederkranz, and Limburger; it is important in developing characteristic flavor in several soft-ripened cheeses. See penicillium.

BRIARDES   Type of cattle native to Pays de Brie in the Île-de-France; Brie makers consider versions of their cheese made with milk of other cattle unauthentic.

BRICK (cow)   Creamy, pale-yellow, brick-shaped loaf with semisoft texture that has many irregular holes; the salty, somewhat nutty flavor ranges from bland to a tanginess as assertive as genuine Munster. It was developed in Wisconsin and is made in Oregon, other dairy states, and Canada. Brick has been characterized as "the married man's Limburger," and dairy analysts also have likened it to St. Paulin.

BRICKBAT (cow)   Vanished Wiltshire farm product.

BRICQUEBEC (cow)   Sold as "Providence" (see below) and produced by monks of the Trappist abbey near Cherbourg; Bricquebec is similar to other monastery wheels.

BRIE (cow)   Soft-ripened cheese has been made by Briard farmers at least since the eighth century when Charlemagne ate it at the priory of Reuil in 774. The snowy crust of Brie takes on a haze of reddish brown when ripe; the three principal varieties are Brie de Meaux, Brie de Melun, and Coulommiers (see below).

BRIE D'AMATEUR   French term for Brie past its prime; strong, grayish cakes once were not discarded but saved for farm workers said to have a preference for assertive food.

BRIE DE COULOMMIERS (cow)   See Coulommiers.

BRIE, DELICO (cow)   An American version developed in Lena, Illinois, by Karl Kolb in 1928.

BRIE DE MEAUX (cow)   Genuine farmhouse Brie, labeled *fermier,* from the district around Meaux, east of Paris, is the best of the type and is produced in molds of two sizes, about 11 inches or 14 inches in diameter; it is sold in France unwrapped, or in foil, when about one month old.

BRIE DE MELUN (cow)   About 9½ inches in diameter and 1¼ inches thick, it has a reddish rind flecked with white; it matures more slowly than other Bries and is ready to eat at about 2½ months.

BRIE, ROUGE ET NOIR (cow)   An American version made on a Petaluma, California, farm by the Thompson family for three generations.

BRIE, VALMEUSE (cow)   One of the factory products to which a stabilizer is added so that cheese remains soft and pliant up to two months if refrigerated; not the real thing, but acceptable in places where good Brie is unavailable.

BRILLAT-SAVARIN (cow)   Invented at Rouvray-Catillon, near Dieppe, France, this triple cream was named for the nineteenth-century gastronome by Henri Androuët and is much like Camembert in appearance.

BRINA DUBREALA (sheep)   A Romanian pickled cheese.

BRIN D'AMOUR (goat)   Also known as Fleur du Maquis, this Corsican "morsel of love" is a soft-ripened square with rounded corners; flavored with rosemary and savory, it is at its best at about three months.

BRINSEN, BRINZEN (cow, sheep)   German terms for Bryndza.

BRIOLER (cow)   East Prussian soft cheese, compared to Limburger and Pont l'Évêque.

BRIQUE, BRIQUETTE   A group of French brick-shaped cheeses.

BRIQUE DE FOREZ (goat, cow)   Also called Cabrion; it is made in small rectangular loaves on mountain farms in central France, south of the Loire River. The rind has bluish spots of healthy mold when made from goat's milk, grayish spots when diluted with cow's milk.

BRIQUE DE LIVARDOIS (goat)   Similar to preceding, but made in Auvergne.

BRISEGOUT (cow)   A household cheese made in the same locale as Beaufort, in the French Savoy and across the Italian border.

BROCCIO, BROCCIU (goat, sheep)   Variously spelled, the name of this fresh Corsican classic is a distortion of the ancient Provençal generic term for cheese, *brousse.* Fresh, or semidry, it is eaten immediately with fresh fruits or vegetables, or used in preparing pastries and other cooked dishes.

BROCOTTA (cow)   Another name for Ricotta.

BROODKAAS (cow)   A rectangular loaf made in Dutch and Belgian factories, this "bread cheese" is a version of Gouda.

BROUSSE DU ROVE (sheep)   Similar to fresh Broccio; it is produced on the peninsula between Marseille and the Berre lagoon, and occasionally cured with salt.

BROUSSE DE LA VESUBIE (goat, sheep)   A product of the milk from high pastures of the Vesubie Valley, one of the most beautiful in southern France; it is fresh cheese similar to Broccio.

BRÛLEUR DE LOUP (cow)   Developed relatively recently, this white factory cheese, somewhat harsh in flavor, is produced throughout the Gevaudan plateau in southern France. The name recalls the reports of a supernatural beast that struck terror in the region in 1765; although the fearsome animal was determined to have been no more than a wolf with a bushy tail, the scary stories are savored by tyrophiles and many others.

BRUSHED   In French, brossé, a cheesemakers' word for rinds that have been lightly brushed by hand or by machine during the course of curing or ripening; for instance, Gruyère.

BRUXELLES, FROMAGE DE (cow)   Belgians call this their most typically regional product; made by a newly developed process in flat 2-pound cylinders, it has piquant flavor but is milder than Herve or Limburger.

BRYNDZA (goat, sheep)   Throughout the 800-mile stretch of the Carpathian Mountains dividing Czechoslovakia and Poland and running down into the Balkans, crisp white cheeses bear this name, or a variation of it. France imports an immaculately white-brined cheese from Romania that is called Brinza. In Romania itself, and in Russia's northern Caucasus and Transcaucasia, it seems to be more often spelled Bryndza. (See Brinsen, Brinzen.) In the Carpathians the curds of mountain herdsmen are taken to centralized factories, called brynziar, where they are cured in wooden casks, then cut into cubes and packed in salt. When soft and buttery the cheese is sometimes run through a roller mill, then packed in various ways for shipment. It is often compared with Feta and can be used as a base for Liptauer spread—the Hungarian-American gastronome George Lang (see his excellent The Cuisine of Hungary) recommends the Bryndza imported in New York from the Tatra Mountains.

BÛCHE FOREZIENNE (cow)   A factory-made mold type from the Auvergne region, in central France.

BÛCHE LORRAINE (cow)   A log-shaped double-cream type, this has a floury-white crust.

BÛCHE DU VERCORS (goat)   A factory-made long narrow cylinder produced from the goat's milk of the high Vercors plateau in the French Alps.

BUCHERON (goat)   Extra creamy, piquant large-size cylinder; its name means "woodsman" in Provence. Bucheron is sold in bulk rather than in individual logs, and sometimes is lightly flavored with herbs.

BUCHETTE D'ANJOU (goat)   Factory-made; an effort to reproduce the classic Ste. Maure (see below).

BUFALO   The white buffalo from India has been the source of milk and cheese in Italy and the Middle East for fourteen centuries.

BULGARIAN BRINED CHEESE (sheep)   See Rodopa.

BUOST (cow)   The Swedish version of Steppe (see below), Buost is made in the province of Jämtland; firm, with elastic consistency, it is low in fat.

BURGOS (cow, goat, sheep)   One of Spain's most popular, and served in thick slices at the end of a meal; it takes its name from the Old Castile province.

BURIELLO (buffalo)   See Manteca.

BURMEISTER (cow)   A Wisconsin factory-made Brick.

BURON   A rustic mountain cheese hut in France.

BURRINO (buffalo)   Another name for Manteca (see below).

BUTIRRO (cow)   Another name for Manteca (see below).

BUTTER (cow)   Butterkäse, made in Austria and Germany, derives its name from its butterlike texture, but it contains no butter; versions are made in Canada and the U.S.

BUTTERMILK (cow)   Produced from buttermilk, this is a fresh English cheese much like Cottage Cheese.

BUTTERMILK, CULTURED   Cultured buttermilk is made by cheesemakers, and it differs from the milk left from churning butter. It can be produced from skim milk but is more apt to be whole milk to which mixed lactic starter cultures are added before heating to a temperature no less than 70 degrees and no more than 72 degrees. It is the most popular fermented milk beverage in the U.S.

BUTTIRI (cow)   A Calabrian version of Caciocavallo, enclosing a heart of butter.

C

CABÉCOU, CABICOU (goat)   Variant spellings of Chabichou (see below), which means "little goat"; small rustic cakes labeled Cabécou are marketed at Cahors, Entraygues, Gramat, Gourdon, Livernon, and Rocamadour in Aveyron. Cabicou is the trade name of a cylinder exported by the farmers' cooperative at La-Mothe-St.-Héray, south of the Loire River.

CABOC (cow)   An ancient farmhouse product (see Kebbock); manufacture in quantity was revived by Susannah and Reg Stone on a Scottish farm near Tain, Ross and Cromarty County, and much is now exported. It is a soft unripened cylinder made from pure cream and rolled in toasted pinhead oatmeal.

CABRALES (sheep, goat)   The Spanish word for goat is given to the Roquefort-like cheese made for hundreds of years by farmers of Asturia in northern Spain. Formerly made of the milk of either sheep or goats, it is now commonly a combination that includes cow's milk as well. Aged in mountain caves two or three months, those not consumed at home are wrapped in leaves and can be found occasionally in Spain's fine food shops.

CABREIRO (goat, sheep)   A Portuguese mountain cheese from the area between Castelo Branco and the Spanish border; it is eaten fresh or is cured in a salt solution and aged about three months.

CABRION (goat)   See Brique du Forez, Brique du Livardois. Cabrion is also the name of a small disk produced in central France from milk of goats which graze high on the Morvan; it is finished in a vat of marc and wrapped in leaves from plane trees.

CACHAT (goat, sheep)   In Provence this rustic cheese is eaten fresh, dried, or well preserved in pots. See Fromage Fort.

CACHCAVAL (sheep)   Firm, mild, pale yellow, Cachcaval is one of the mainstays of life in the Romanian province of Dobrogea, on the Black Sea. See Kǎckavalj, Kashkaval.

CACHE (sheep)   A Romanian white cheese; it is aged from a week to 12 days, during which it develops a mild piquancy.

CACHE VALLEY   Dairymen of this Utah area produce several kinds of cheese, including a "Swiss" made by modern techniques.

CACIO   Not to be confused with the Italian caccia, meaning "game," or "hunting," cacio is an ancient Tuscan word for cheese.

CACIOCAVALLO (cow)   Related to Cachcaval (above) and originally spelled cacio a cavallo, "cheese on horseback," because it looks something like saddlebags, this was a cheese of nomads. As currently made, it is much like Provolone with mild, slightly smoky flavor.

CACIOFIORE (goat, sheep)   A soft, saffron-tinted Italian farm product. The curds are started by vegetable rennet which is prepared from salt water and wild artichoke flowers, *caglio fiore,* and mixed with goat's milk on the Isle of Capri, with goat's or sheep's milk in Lombardy, with sheep's milk alone in Lazio, Tuscany, and Umbria, and sometimes with cow's milk in the Marches. See Caciotta.

CACIO MAGRO   This is Piedmont Cottage Cheese that is dried to be taken by herdsmen into the mountains during long summer pasturage.

CACIO PECORINO DI MONTAGNA (sheep)   A hill-farm product from Arrezzo, Tuscany.

CACIOTTA (goat, sheep)   Small Italian farmhouse cheeses, in. considerable variety, bear this name; best known are Bagozza, Caciofiore, Chiavara, Fresa, Toscana, and Urbino. See Formagelle.

CACIOTTA NORCIA (sheep)   Fresh cheese from Norcia, a mountain town in central Italy, is considered superlative.

CACIOTTA ROMANO (cow)   A semihard, bland factory product popular in Rome.

CAERPHILLY (cow)   A crumbly, porous, white cheese once made on Glamorgan farms and named for the Welsh castle town near Cardiff, Caerphilly was described by British gastronome Ernest Oldmeadow as "an almost ideal cheese for those who love buttermilk." Made in blocks or large wheels, today mostly in Wiltshire, Leicestershire, and other English counties, it is not a long-lasting cheese, but has a fresh, tart flavor and has been for generations a favorite lunch of Welsh miners.

CAFFUTS   A French term for cheese balls—mashed cheese mixed with herbs and reshaped.

CAHORS (goat)   See Cabécou. Another cheese bearing the name of this French gastronomical capital is Bleu de Cahors, sometimes sold as Bleu de Quercy.

CAILLADES (cow)   Fresh cheeses from Corrèze, in France's Massif Central, sometimes bear this name.

CAILLEBOTTE (cow)   The name comes from the latticed shelves on which *caille,* curdled milk, is drained, resulting in a very fat, white, fresh cheese that is popular in Brittany and nearby districts; it is served with fruit stirred into it. In Cognac this term applies to fresh cheese coagulated by *chardonette,* artichoke flowers, and it is a regular item of family meals.

CAITHNESS (cow)   A semisoft Scottish cheese with mild flavor and creamy texture, Caithness is good when served with cocktails, better with fruit and a pleasant wine.

CAJASSOUS (goat)   A name sometimes spelled *cujassou* and said to be an ancient corruption of Cubjac, a village not far from Périgeux in one of France's great truffle regions; this is a variety of Chabichou.

CALCAGNO (sheep)   A hard Sicilian grating cheese.

CALEF (cow)   A washed-curd product of New York farms but aged by the Calef family in Barrington, New Hampshire; Calef is an assertive, firm-textured American cheese.

CAMARGUE (sheep)   Cheese made from the milk of Camargue sheep which summer in the low French Alps; it is very fragrant with thyme and laurel, especially when sold fresh. It is also known as Gardian, or Tome d'Arles, for the famous Roman town situated where the Rhône River divides before flowing into the Mediterranean.

CAMBRIDGE (cow)   A distinctly English, fresh, unsalted cheese that is also known as York; it should be eaten within a day or two of its making.

CAMEMBERT, BONGRAIN (cow)   In the spring of 1973 a Frenchman named Jean-Claude Bruneau opened a Bongrain factory in Le Sueur, Minnesota, to turn out Camemberts, joining Borden in Ohio, Kolb-Lena in Illinois, and Marin Cheese Company in California in emulating the Normandy original.

CAMEMBERT, BORDEN (cow)   Produced in Van Wert, Ohio, the Borden version is usually packed in semicircular cardboard boxes containing three wedges designed for individual servings. Quality and flavor are good when not mishandled in supermarkets or by cheesemongers who should know better.

CAMEMBERT FERMIER (cow)   The art of making Camemberts by hand has almost disappeared. Very soft within and floury-crusted without, Camemberts Fermier are at their best when labeled Pays d'Auge, which means they come from the heart of Normandy near the village from which they take their name. When they are labeled V.C.N. (*véritable camembert de Normandie*), they have been produced from the rich milk of Norman cows in any of the following districts: Eure, Calvados, Le Manche, Orne, or Seine-Maritime.

CAMEMBERT, FIVA (cow)   Iceland's version, comparable to the best of factory-made Camemberts.

CAMEMBERT, LATROBE VALLEY (cow)   Australian imitation made at More, Victoria province.

CAMEMBERT PASTEURISÉ (cow)   Camemberts made in factories where milk is pasteurized are produced in Normandy, and copies are turned out by the thousands in 67 departments of France, as well as in Australia, Austria, Belgium, Canada, Denmark, England, Germany, Holland, Iceland, Ireland, Norway, Sweden, Switzerland, and the U.S.

Only pasteurized versions may be imported in this country, but increased distribution has made a wide choice of floury-surfaced, creamy-centered disks available here; most from France are dependable, as are those produced in American factories (see preceding Camembert entries).

CAMEMBERT, RAHM (cow)   Extra cream is added to the milk of Allgäuer cows used in a German version that bears the trademark Edelweiss.

CAMEMBERT SUISSE   Switzerland exports thousands of Camemberts, including Camembert à la Crème, a double-cream version.

CAMOSUN (cow)   A semisoft farmhouse cheese, about 6 inches in diameter and 7 inches deep, Camosun was developed at the University of British Columbia and introduced at Washington State College in 1932 in the interests of farmers lacking a ready market for milk. The process is a simplification of that used in making granular or stirred-curd types, and therefore similar in some ways to Cheddar and Colby; but after soaking in brine for 30 hours the cheese is coated with paraffin and aged about three months. Dr. N. S. Golding, who directed the Washington laboratory work, reported that the name was taken from the Hudson's Bay fur-trade post on the site of Victoria, B.C., where Camosun College is located. "The idea," Golding wrote me, "was to make a cheese as simple as possible, for farmers to use small surplus supplies of their milk."

CAMPOS (sheep)   One of Spain's best. See Villalon.

CANCOILLOTTE (cow)   A runny, wine-flavored cheese, not unlike the dish called Welsh Rabbit, which starts with a base of Metton (see below). Making Cancoillotte has been a tradition of the French Alps, and the mixture is now produced commercially and sold in small pots.

CANESTRATO, INCANESTRATO (cow, sheep)   Taking its name from the word for basket, this Sicilian type is one of the most popular in Italy, and its exterior is imprinted with the marks of the wicker forms in which it is cured. When it is the traditional sheep cheese it is called Pecorino Incanestrato, once produced by the ancient method of using kid's rennet. Cow's-milk Canestrato (or Incanestrato) is now common in Italy and the U.S. A California version is called Tuma.

CANTAL (cow)   No cheese may legally bear this name that is not produced in the Department of Cantal, France, where exacting standards must be met. It is made on farms during the summer and in small dairies the year round, and in France may be further distinguished by names of such market towns as Mauriac, Murat, and Salers. Pressed but not cooked, it has a natural brushed rind and sometimes weighs as much as 75 to 120 pounds. The ancient cheese of the Cantal region was praised by Pliny the Elder, and in the eighteenth century Cantal was considered so exemplary that Diderot gave the recipe for it in his *Encyclopedia.* "Accidental" internal molds sometimes develop, and the best of such cheeses (Bleu de Cantal or Bleu de Salers) are coveted by connoisseurs.

CANTALET (cow)   Small rounds with piquant flavor and dry, close texture are exported under this name, and are considered worthy French relatives of Cantal.

CANTALON (cow)   As the name implies, Cantalon is a smaller version of Cantal, 6 to 8 inches in diameter, 10 to 12 inches high, and may weigh from 9 to 22 pounds; it has pronounced flavor when aged about three months.

CAPRICE DES DIEUX (cow)   Double-cream soft-ripened oval cake originated at Bongrain dairy in Illoud, Haute-Marne, southeast of Paris; commonly exported to the U.S.

CAPRICETTE (goat)   Its texture is much like other French Cream Cheeses, but it has the subtle aftertaste of the pasteurized goat's milk from which it springs; produced at Marsac, Périgord.

CAPRINO ROMANO (goat)   A characteristic Romano, differing only in the flavor derived from goat's milk.

CARASSAI (cow)   Fresh cheese is one of the distinctions of the village of Carassai, in the Italian province of Ascoli Piceno.

CARDIGA (sheep)   Portuguese mountain dairymen make this cheese by coagulating sheep's milk with cardoons, the wild thistles of the region.

CARENTAN (cow)   One of the best of Normandy's near-Camemberts was marketed at, and took its name from, the market of Carentan, near St.-Lô, France.

CARRÉ   The word for "square" in French is used as a generic term for certain cheeses that are square and flat.

CARRÉ DE BONNEVILLE (cow)   See Pavé d'Auge.

CARRÉ DE BRAY (cow)   A soft-ripened square cake from France's Pays de Bray, this is cured about two weeks and usually sold unwrapped on straw mats.

CARRÉ DE L'EST (cow)   "Square of the East" is the name of this product of Champagne and Lorraine, and some consider it to be the rectangular version of Camembert. In fact, U.S. Camemberts developed from a process closer to the method used in making Carré de l'Est than the Camembert process. Its flavor is pungent, not as subtle as Camembert.

CASEREL   One of the French words for a utensil made of clay, reeds, or wood which is used to taste cheese.

CASERETTE (cow)   A fresh Normandy cheese.

CASETTE (cow)   A Belgian product also known as Boulette, this is a soft cheese fermented at high temperature, seasoned with salt and pepper. It is kneaded and shaped by hand into balls, wrapped in walnut leaves, and encased in small willow baskets for sale, traditionally in the markets of Dinant, Hay, and Namur.

CASIDDI (goat, sheep)   In the region of steep mountains in Basilicata, in southern Italy, the small, hard, local cheese bears this name.

CASIGLIOLO (cow)   A Sicilian version of Caciocavallo, known also as Panedda, or Pera di Vacca. In Sardinia it is often spelled *casizzolu.*

CASIZZOLOS, CASIZZOLU (cow)   Mild-flavored and shaped like a large pear, this is a specialty of Nuoro province, Sardinia. When cut into strips and melted over a fire, it is drawn out into sticky hot threads and is known as *su casu imbasiau.*

CASTEL (cow)   A fresh, very rich cheese made industrially in Normandy.

CASTELMAGNO (cow)   One of the best produced in Italy's Piedmont, this is a creamy blue-mold cheese that compares favorably with good Gorgonzola; it is named for a mountain village not far from Turin.

CASTELO BRANCO (sheep)   In central Portugal the name of this city is sometimes applied to a sheep cheese akin to Spain's Roquefort-like Cabrales (see above).

CASTELO DE VIDE (goat, sheep)   The mountain people near the town of Castelo de Vide, on the Portuguese-Spanish border near Portalegre, make fine rustic cheeses, sometimes of sheep's milk alone, sometimes mixed with that of goats; what little they don't consume themselves is taken to this nearest of markets.

CASTILLON (cow)   A local cheese from mountain farms near the small town of this name, not far from Foix, in the French Pyrenees; it is similar to Bethmale.

CASU BECCIU, CASU ISCALDIDU, CASU MARZU (cow, goat)   In Sardinia's Gallura region dairymen produce a crumbly, exceedingly assertive cheese to which they give several names, sometimes calling it fondly the equivalent of "old rotter."

CEBRERO (cow)   Spanish internal-mold cheese made on mountain farms, having clear yellow rind and soft creamy texture mottled with blue; it is sharp and assertive.

CENDRÉ   Generic French term for cheeses ripened in ashes, generally produced in wine-growing regions; the vegetable ash gives the surfaces a bluish hue, as *cendré bleue,* a color used by painters.

CENDRÉ D'ARGONNE (cow)   A local, partly skim-milk cheese produced at Clermont-en-Argonne in Lorraine, France.

CENDRÉ D'ARMENÇON (cow)   Also called Aisy, for the village in which it is marketed, it is soft-ripened and has a washed crust; shaped as a thick disk or truncated cone. The aroma is assertive and the flavor tangy.

CENDRÉ DE LA BRIE (cow)   A little like a Coulommiers (see below) that has been dusted with ashes; it has very little fat content and is seldom seen off the farms on which it is made.

CENDRÉS D'ORLÉANAIS (cow)   Identified with such French places as Les Aydes, Olivet, Pannes, and Vendôme, these are soft-ripened, with natural rinds coated with ashes. "Ash-coated cheeses," according to Pierre Androuët, "are in a sense 'cheese preserves' put aside during the period when milk is abundant for use during the summer when demand will be great, especially during mowing and harvesting." They are much appreciated as farm workers' snacks.

CÉRACÉE (cow)   See Serac; another name for Ricotta.

CERTOSA (cow)   A Stracchino type, Certosa gets its name from the Carthusian monks who first produced it several centuries ago.

CERVELLE DE CANUT   A French term (literally "silk weaver's brains"), popular in Lyon, for fresh cheese seasoned with herbs, shallots, garlic, salt and pepper, and sometimes a little vinegar, white wine, and olive oil added. It is also referred to as *claqueret,* little smack.

CHABICHOU (goat)   Traditionally shaped as truncated cones about 2½ inches at base and 2½ inches high, Chabichou has a natural rind that is bluish gray, flecked with red. In addition to that made on Poitou farms, a copy with a snowy rind is made in the region by commercial dairies which also market the same cheese in long cylinders or in rectangles about 2½ inches thick. See Cabécou.

CHABRIS (goat)   A disk-shaped cake that looks like Camembert and is made of goat's milk and named for a small town in France's Cher Valley.

CHALARONNE (cow)   Densely creamy, and firm but buttery in texture, this comes in long, log-shaped loaves invested with crumbly pockets of blue mold; not much known outside of southwest France.

CHAMBARAND (cow)   A small flat disk made by Trappist monks at the Abbey of Chambarand at Roybon, south of Grenoble, Chambarand is sometimes labeled in France either Trappiste de Chambarand or Beaupré de Roybon. Its smooth rind varies from light yellow to pinkish, and it has a mild, creamy interior, often compared to Reblochon, which it resembles in shape.

CHAMBERAT (cow)   This is similar to St. Paulin, about 8 inches in diameter, 1½ to 2 inches thick, weight between 2½ and 3½ pounds. It is supple and mild, and its name comes from a village west of Vichy, France.

CHAMBOURCY (cow)   A factory-made French fresh type without much savor.

CHAMPOLÉON (cow)   Dairymen at Champoléon-les-Borels, high in the French Alps south of Grenoble, make a mixture similar to Cancoillotte that is seasoned with herbs and white wine and bears the village name.

CHANTELLE (cow)   A variation of Bel Paese produced in Canada and the U.S.

CHANTILLY (cow)   See Hablé Crème Chantilly.

CHAOURCE (cow)   Chaource was once the most important market town in Champagne, and the cheese that takes its name is rich and fat, a white cylinder that varies in size; use of the name is protected by law and by the Syndicat de Défense du Chaource.

CHARDONETTE   Artichoke flowers, still sometimes used by rural French cheesemakers. See Caillebotte.

CHAROLLES (cow, goat)   Sometimes called Charolais for the mountains above the village of Charolles, near Mâcon, France, this is a small cylindrical goat type to which cow's milk is added, or which in some cases is now made entirely of cow's milk, depending upon availability.

CHASCOL D'ALP (cow)   A product of central Switzerland and sometimes called Chaschosis, this is a very rich and creamy wheel about 20 inches in diameter, 4 inches thick, weighing 20 to 40 pounds.

CHASCOL DA CHASCARIA (cow)   A medium-size Swiss wheel made of skim milk.

CHASCOL CHEVRA (goat)   A truncated cone made by Alpine goat farmers on Switzerland's southeastern border.

CHASTEAU (cow)   This local cheese is made by hand around the village of Lugon-et-l'Île-du-Carnay, not far from Bordeaux.

CHATEAUBRIAND (cow)   Some French retailers gave this name to a triple-cream cheese made at Forges-les-Eaux, Normandy; it resembles Brillat-Savarin and Magnum.

CHATEAUROUX (goat)   A variant of Valencay, its name comes from one of the big industrial centers of France, equally famous for its gastronomy.

CHAUMONT (cow)   A soft-ripened wheel about 3 inches in diameter, 2 inches high, weight about 7 ounces, Chaumont is named for a town on the Marne, not far from Charles de Gaulle's home at Colombey-le-Deux-Églises. It has pronounced flavor somewhat like Époisses, Langres, and Soumaintrain.

CHAUNAY (goat)   A factory-made cheese of the Chabichou type.

CHAVIGNOL (goat)   The French wine village of Chavignol made its small hard cheeses famous, and the term *crottin* applies properly only to farmhouse products of Chavignol itself or the neighboring hamlets of Amigny, Bué, Crézancy, and Verdigny. Today, however, the term is used by dairymen in Poitou and other areas who produce for export imitation "Crottin-Chavignol." See also Crottin de Chavignol.

CHECY (cow)   This small cheese of the Olivet (see below) group takes its name from a village near Orléans.

CHEDDAR (cow)   The English village of Cheddar, west of Bath in Somerset, has been famous for centuries as the hometown of one of the world's favorite cheeses, some of which is still distinguished as "farmhouse," but most of which is made in factories. U.S. law restricts the importation of English Cheddar. Canadian Cheddar is usually superior, as is that of several Vermont and rural New York dairies; Cheddar is made in each of the U.S. dairy states. It is so internationally popular that it is produced in Belgian, Dutch, French, and Scandinavian factories for export, as well as in many Commonwealth countries. It is categorically a hard cheese, moister than Parmesan but firm enough to slice. In its mildest form it is aged six months, and the pungency of its flavor develops thereafter. Real Cheddar is naturally cream colored, but often in America it is turned orange by the use of annatto.

More Cheddar is consumed in the U.S. than the combined total of all other similar varieties. In addition to being the name of the type, Cheddar is the descriptive term for the most common style, a cylinder about $14\frac{1}{2}$ inches in diameter, 12 inches thick, weight between 70 and 78 pounds. Other styles, according to the U.S. Department of Agriculture: Daisy, about $13\frac{1}{4}$ inches in diameter, slightly more than 4 inches thick, 21 to 23 pounds; Flat or Twin, $14\frac{1}{2}$ inches in diameter, slightly more than 5 inches thick, 32 to 37 pounds; Longhorn, 6 inches in diameter, 13 inches long, 12 to 13 pounds; Young American, 7 inches in diameter, 7 inches thick, 11 to 12 pounds; and rectangular blocks or prints, usually 14 inches long, 11 inches wide, $3\frac{1}{4}$ inches thick, weight 20 pounds. Blocks or prints often are cut in smaller rectangles and packaged as natural rindless loaves (see below).

CHEDDARING   When the curd is drained and firm enough to be turned without breaking it is matted, or cheddared, that is, it is cut into slabs

4 to 6 inches wide; the slabs are turned frequently, and when so firm they withstand force they are piled in layers.

CHEEDAM (cow)   An Australian cheese that combines the Cheddar and Edam techniques; the result is a mildly interesting flavor and texture.

CHEESE BANKS   In Italy the Lombardy Cassa di Risparmio (bank for savings) maintains "cheese banks" in Cremona, Lodi, Montava, Novara, Pavia, Pegognaga, and Villa Po, to whose cold-storage rooms farmers bring ripening cheese in return for cash for operating expenses. When the cheeses have matured they are sold and the loans made by such banks are redeemed by their owners.

CHEESE FOOD   A form of processed cheese in which additions may be made of cream, milk, skim milk, cheese whey, or whey albumin in various mixtures or concentrates; at least 51 percent of the finished product must be pure cheese.

CHEESE-EATING SUNDAY   See Tyrofagos.

CHESHIRE (cow)   With more moisture and only slightly less fat content, Cheshire is a crumblier cheese than Cheddar, and it is probably the oldest of all in Britain, dating back to the twelfth century at least. Traditionally made in cylinders as high as they are wide, Cheshire is now produced in factories, shaped as blocks or in small individual units, although there remain a few Cheshire farmers who turn out handmade Cheshires from unpasteurized milk. Cheshire's true cheese-making center has been for generations the town of Whitchurch, not in the county of Cheshire at all but across the line in Shropshire. Most of the cheese is turned a deep orange by the use of annatto, but White Cheshire is available in England, and both can be found with internal molds (see Blue Cheshire).

CHESHIRE CHEESE, THE   Scrubbed board tables at which tourists gather distinguish this Fleet Street pub in London, made famous by the patronage of Dr. Sam Johnson in the eighteenth century. The British appetite for "toasted cheese" can be appeased here, along with the traditional steak, kidney, mushroom, and oyster pudding.

CHESTER (cow)   At Castres in southwest France a domestic factory-made version of the orange-colored Cheshire has been produced since soon after World War II under the name of the capital city of the English county. It is made in tall cylinders weighing 70 to 110 pounds, and is welcomed by French cooks as a melting cheese. A version is made in Germany, and in Mexico a light-colored cheese manufactured and sold under this name is important in much cooking, including the making of cheese-filled tortillas called *quesadillas*.

CHÈVRE   The French word for "goat" designates, by legal action of 1953, that country's cheese that is made of goat milk. *Pur chèvre,* printed on a label, indicates fine cheese made exclusively of goat's milk.

CHEVRET (goat) A small cheese made of goat's milk in the Jura Mountains; it is called Tome de Belley when sold in the market town of that name—the place where the gastronome Brillat-Savarin lived and wrote his famous *Physiologie du Goût.*

CHEVRETON (goat) In the Ambert region of central France this word is used for the rectangular-shaped goat types, more and more produced from mixed cow's and goat's milk, and better known in France as Brique de Forez. Chevretons are also made in the Loire country.

CHEVROTIN (goat) In the French Alps region of Aravis the *chèvres fermier* are known as Chevrotin and are a mixture of ripened and fresh curds. Chevrotin du Bourbonnais is the generic term for the goat types shaped like truncated cones produced in the area of Moulins, Souvigny, etc.

CHEVRU (cow) Named for an Île-de-France village, this is sometimes compared to Coulommiers, but has sharper flavor. It usually weighs about 1 pound and is about 6 inches in diameter, about 1½ inches thick.

CHHANA (cow) A sour-milk cheese made in India.

CHIAVARI (cow) A mixture of sweet and sour milk, Chiavari is named for a port on the Ligurian coast of Italy.

CHIBERTA (cow) Like others of the so-called Pyrenees types, this is cheese with open, supple texture and a sourish tang pleasant to the palate; it is a medium-size wheel about 3 inches high, weighing about 6 pounds.

CHINESE RED CHEESE Also known as Red Bean Curd cheese, Spiced Red Bean Curd, or Southern cheese, Chinese Red Cheese consists of pressed bean-curd cubes fermented in rice wine with spices and salt until it is brick-red and very pungent. Sometimes it is used to season pork, or as a side dish served with rice. See Fu-Yü.

CHINESE WHITE CHEESE This is sometimes known as Bean Curd Sauce, White Bean Curd cheese, or White Bean Sauce, and it is made from buff-colored beans; the curd cubes are pressed and fermented in rice wine and salt, and the resulting taste has been compared to that of Camembert. Chinese White Cheese is used to season fish, chicken, pork, noodles, rice, and vegetables.

CHRISTALINNA (cow) A hard mountain type from central Switzerland.

CHRISTIAN IX (cow) A firm-textured wheel weighing 30 to 35 pounds, seasoned with cumin, caraway, or other seeds, this is made in Danish commercial dairies.

CHUBUT (cow)   In northern Argentina this white cheese is made by shepherds, and it is consumed locally.

CIERP (cow)   A mountain cheese that belongs to the Pyrenees category, Cierp is named for a village near Luchon, west of Perpignan, sometimes with the addition of sheep's milk; it compares favorably with Laruns.

CINCHO (sheep)   See Villalon.

CITEAUX (cow)   A Burgundian product of the monks who farm at the Abbey of Citeaux, in the heart of the wine country, this is an excellent example of the monastery type, but not much is produced.

CLAMART, FROMAGE DE (cow)   The town, not far from the Paris market of Rungis, was once at least as well known for the cheese of the same name as for tiny peas which it made famous. Fromage de Clamart has now, however, entirely disappeared.

CLAQUEBITOU (goat)   A fresh cheese accented by herbs and garlic, this is made in the Beaune Mountains of Burgundy and consumed locally.

CLAQUERET LYONNAIS (cow)   See Cervelle de Canut.

CLOVIS (cow)   The beans that helped to make the French town of Soissons famous also inspired the oval-shaped local cheese called Clovis because the clay forms used by the *fromagères* had to be cleaved apart to free the finished product.

CLUB OF FRENCH CHEESE IMPORTERS   Promotional group organized by Foods of France, Inc., New York, to improve point-of-sale information about French cheese and increase distribution throughout the U.S.

COALHADA (cow)   Fresh and creamy, this Brazilian specialty is eaten almost exclusively with an overabundance of sugar.

COCHAT (sheep)   In the same region whence comes Bouton de Culotte (see above), a local specialty combines cheese and onions. According to Alice B. Toklas, Cochat is made of "the milk of very young ewes, and ripened in vinegar. It is then pressed under weight and served in the shell of a medium-sized onion. With this it is traditional to drink a red wine, preferably a good vintage of Chateauneuf du Pape."

COEUR D'ARRAS (cow)   Heart-shaped, washed-rind cheese that is compared to Quart Maroilles and Rollot (Rollot is sometimes the label on heart-shaped imports in New York), Coeur d'Arras comes from the town of Arras in Artois and from neighboring Picardy.

COEUR DE BRAY (cow)   Floury of skin and soft and creamy inside, this cheese heart is closely related to Neufchâtel and is produced in the same part of Normandy.

COEUR À LA CRÈME   Cheese curds assume this romantic label when they are drained in a heart-shaped basket, then turned out on a plate and covered with cream and sugar, making a simple but elegant dessert (see Recipes, page 178).

COLBY (cow)   Taking its name from Colby, Wisconsin, this is an open-textured variant of stirred-curd or granular cheese developed by a frontier family named Steinwand around the end of the nineteenth century. It is one of the most popular cheeses in the U.S. and is produced in factories around the world. A version made for several generations by the Crowley family in Healdville, Vermont, has established its own identity. See Crowley.

COLOMBIÈRE (cow)   A close relative of Reblochon, this soft cheese with a washed rind is named for highlands in the French Alpine skiing area.

COLUMELLA   In the first century A.D. the historian Columella, who entered Rome with Hannibal, gave the first detailed description of the method of making Pecorino Romano.

COLWICK (cow)   Often made in Stilton dairies, Colwick is a product of Leicestershire and Nottinghamshire, England. It is a soft-cream type, shaped in cylinders for immediate consumption. See also Slipcote.

COMTÉ, GRUYÈRE DE COMTÉ (cow)   Sometimes called French Gruyère and sometimes compared to Beaufort, Comté is made in 2-foot-wide wheels that look like millstones and weigh up to 160 pounds. Dairymen of the Franche-Comté have been making it since Roman times. It has firm, resilient texture and is fruity-flavored.

CONCHES (cow)   Almost identical with Bagnes, this is one of the Valais cheeses used in making raclette (see below), the melted cheese dish that originated in the canton of Conches. See Fromage des Alpes.

CONFRÉRIE DES CHEVALIERS DU TASTEFROMAGE   Founded in 1954 by Jean Richard, a French dairy publicist, this group of connoisseurs has branches in various countries, all of which are known to meet on occasion in celebration of the delights of cheese.

CONFRÉRIE DU REMOUDOU   This brotherhood of Belgian gastronomes has chosen to salute Remoudou, the pungent Limburger-like product of their own dairymen, as the best of all cheeses. Members of the *seigneurie* often don costumes of the era of Charles V for meetings held in Battice, not far from Liège. See Remoudou.

CONGRESS OF VIENNA, 1814–15   Talleyrand, France's great diplomat, brought Carême, his *chef de cuisine,* to the Vienna conference that changed the face of Europe, and he and his fellow ministers often talked about food. As they extolled the cheeses of their respective homelands, Lord Castlereagh lauded Britain's Stilton, a Swiss pointed out the excellence of the Emmenthal he had brought, a Dutchman praised Edam, the Italian delegate, Stracchino. Talleyrand remained silent until an aide entered and reported the arrival of a courier from Paris bearing, in addition to diplomatic papers, a case of Brie cheeses made by a farmer named Baulny. "Très bien," said Talleyrand. "Put the dispatches in the chancellery and the cheese on the table." Turning to his distinguished company, he said he had refrained from taking part in the discussion or boasting of his own country's *fromage*. "But it is here. Judge for yourselves, gentlemen." When each of the diplomats had cast his vote, the decision was unanimous in favor of Brie; they solemnly named it the king of cheeses.

COON (cow)   A well-aged American Cheddar, now produced in volume, and favored by many who like very sharp flavor.

CORNHUSKER (cow)   A bland, moist loaf, similar to Cheddar and Colby, Cornhusker was developed at the Agricultural Experiment Station of the University of Nebraska about 1940, and it is now made commercially in the Midwest. It is either hooped or shaped in blocks and sealed with wax.

CORNISH, CORNWALL (cow)   Cornish farmers once made Cream Cheese of the English type; the term now applies to a molded, firm, farmhouse type, aged six weeks.

COTHERSTONE   Once made by border farmers of the north of England, this British blue was named for a country town but was also known sometimes as Yorkshire Stilton; if still made, it is virtually impossible to buy. T. A. Layton, erstwhile proprietor of London's defunct Cheddar Roast restaurant, reported that "about 1939 a white Cotherstone could be bought which tasted not unlike a cross between a Port Salut and a Bel Paese" (see his *Cheese and Cheese Cookery*).

COTRONESE (sheep)   Taking its name from the port city of Cotrone, in Calabria, this Italian plastic-curd type is much like Moliterno (see below).

COTSWOLD (cow)   Recently developed in Leicestershire by British dairymen, Cotswold has a base of Double Gloucester liberally sprinkled with chives; it is orange-colored, flecked with dark green. Britons like it melted on toast, and they recommend it for its delicate onion flavor.

COTTAGE (cow)   In England and America simple, white, unripened cheeses of the kind once produced most frequently for home consumption are described as Cottage Cheese. They can be made with or without rennet. In the U.S. and Canada they are required by law to contain not more than 80 percent moisture; creamed Cottage Cheese must contain 4 percent or more of milk fat. Commercial versions are variously described as Large-Curd, Medium-Curd, and Small-Curd, depending upon the size of the flakes. See Pot, Popcorn, Schmierkäse.

COTTENHAM, DOUBLE (cow)   An English blue cheese once shipped from Cottenham, between Cambridge and Ely, this often was rated as better than Stilton; it disappeared sometime during World War II.

COUGAR GOLD (cow)   A Cheddar type developed at the State University of Washington at Pullman.

COULANT   The gastronomic term (literally "flowing") which describes Brie, Camembert, and similar types when the crust is mature and the interior oozes as if it were molten.

COULOMMIERS (cow)   A type of Brie, Coulommiers is a flat disk with soft white rind sometimes as large as 10 inches in diameter in France, but usually smaller; in the U.S., imported Coulommiers is slightly larger than Camembert, weighing 10 to 12 ounces. Louis XV's queen is said to have used it to make the first *bouchées à la reine*. It is now made in factories in the town which gives it its name, as well as in numerous other French localities. A Cream Cheese variant is produced in the U.K.

COURTONNE, DANIEL   The maker of Camembert Fermier de la Vallée d'Auge under the trademark Le Royal Montgommery, M. Courtonne in 1975 was the last *fromagère* using ancient techniques, including hand milking of cows and nonpasteurization; such practices, he said, neutralize the organic life that gives true Normandy character to Camembert.

CREAM (cow)   American Cream Cheeses are variations of Neufchâtel, having very smooth but firm consistency effected by the use of centrifugal separators. Gum arabic is usually added to ensure firmness and longer "shelf life" for retailers. Products sold as "imitation cream cheese," or "nondairy spread," sometimes are diluted mixtures of Cream Cheese and Cottage Cheese, or concoctions based on such things as "vegetable flour."

CREAM (goat)   An increase in raising milk goats in America has resulted in a variety of cheeses produced in many states. Natural Cream Cheese, of pure goat's milk, is made in Vermont and New Jersey. See Chapter 6.

CREAM CHEESE, SCOTTISH FROZEN (cow)   In Scotland, Cream Cheese made by thoroughly draining sour milk and cream, and seasoning it with caraway, is wrapped in nasturtium leaves, skewered, then frozen.

The cheese is served frozen as one of the popular savouries to accompany celebratory drinks.

CREMA DANIA, CREMA DANICA (cow)   Soft-ripened white-mold cheese in 6-ounce bars, this Scandinavian achievement is smooth, firm, and not runny. It has been described as "one of the truly new cheeses invented during the past few decades," and "surely the greatest triumph that Danish cheesemakers have ever had." Crema Danica was developed in Copenhagen by Henrik Tholstrup, who set out to produce something with the texture of Brie but with no possibility of a hard center. He succeeded.

CRÈME CHANTILLY (cow)   See Hablé Crème Chantilly.

CRÈME CHÂTEAU (cow)   A soft-ripened, factory-made type that is compared to Hablé Crème Chantilly, Crème Château is produced in the Swedish province of Värmland.

CRÈME ROYALE (cow)   This is a copy of Crema Danica manufactured in Denmark, sometimes packed four small rectangles to a box.

CRÉMET NANTAIS (cow)   Named for the Brittany city of Nantes, this is simply fresh, unsalted curds, drained in forms of various shapes, to which whipped cream is added in the process.

CREMINA (cow)   Like most others, Italian commercial Cream Cheese is shaped in small rectangles and wrapped in foil.

CREOLE (cow)   This mixture of clabber and heavy cream is very popular in New Orleans, where it was once peddled door to door by black women who also sold cala cakes made of rice. It is produced by Louisiana dairies like Cottage Cheese, but differs in consistency—composed of a single large curd floating in heavy cream.

CRESCENZA (cow)   Called Carsenza, Crescenza Lombardi, or Stracchino Crescenza, this creamy, mild Italian rectangle weighs from ½ to 3½ pounds; it is produced in Lombardy, Piedmont, and Veneto. In Mayville, Wisconsin, a semisoft disk weighing about ½ pound is marketed as "a natural Crescenza type" under the brand name Maybella; it is slightly salty, supple in texture.

CROQUE MONSIEUR   The French use this term affectionately for any toasted ham and cheese sandwich, but a proper Croque Monsieur can have as much delicacy as a cook is willing to put into it (see Recipes). The name derives from croquer, to crunch, hence a morsel that crackles when eaten.

CROTONESE (goat, sheep)   Unlike most Italian Pecorino types, this one from Calabria is made of mixed goat and sheep milk, accented with pepper.

CROTTIN DE CHAVIGNOL (goat)   In the French region of Berry, where

Chavignol grapes help to make the wine of Sancerre, this small cheese is one of three which legally can be called, in the sardonic humor of the farmers, *crottin* (dung). Only hard, dry cheeses blackened by age are entitled to the name. Usually they must be bought directly from the farm on which they have been dried as a means of preserving them for winter; demand has increased production to the detriment of quality. See also Chavignol.

CROWDIE (cow)   A Scottish type of Cottage Cheese with a hint of lemony flavor, this is said to go back to the era of the Vikings in the Highlands. "Crowdie" derives from the Lowland word "cruds," or curds.

CROWDIE AND CREAM (cow)   In Ross-shire, Scotland, Crowdie was the word in ancient times for well-drained and pressed curds mixed with equal parts of butter. Now it is a soft, unripened cheese of two-thirds curds and one-third double cream pressed into plaid-decked 4-ounce tubs by Highland Cheeses in Tain.

CROWLEY (cow)   Several generations of the Crowley family in Heald-ville, Vermont, were so successful in satisfying New Englanders with the cheese they made according to the Colby process that the product of their century-old farm factory is known throughout the world as Crowley cheese—open-textured, firm enough to slice well, and offering a fine tang when aged a year or more.

CUAJADA (cow)   Traditionally wrapped in banana leaves, which lend flavor, this soft and creamy Venezuelan type is much used throughout the Andes region.

CUARTIROLO (cow)   Produced in Argentina, this is a Western Hemisphere version of Italy's Quartirolo, a soft, rustic type made in the fall.

CUBJAC (goat)   One of Périgord's small-farm products, this is similar to Rocamadour and is named for a village in truffle country.

CUP (cow)   This gets its name because it is formed in handleless white china cups which traditionally were carried to farmers' markets in Pennsylvania Dutch country, then emptied out for each customer; some was made from whey. Berks Cup Cheese is the result of baking curds in the oven, with new curds added each day for a week. The baked curds are then poured into a heated pan and simmered slowly to a boil, without stirring; salt, cream, butter, and baking soda are added, and the mixture is boiled 15 minutes, during which time eggs are mixed into the curds. The cheese is cooled in cups.

CURD CHEESE   A little-used term for Cottage Cheese (see above).

CURÉ, FROMAGE DE (cow)   Stories are told that a parish priest of Nantes

(a) baptized or (b) invented—depending on which version is accepted—a small cheese in the form of a square with rounded corners that is 1½ inches thick and 3½ inches square; it weighs 6 to 7 ounces. Fromage de Curé has strong flavor, is sometimes compared to St. Paulin, and is now made in small Breton factories. It is also known as Nantais, or Curé de Nantais.

𝒟

DACCA (cow)   Common in India, Dacca is a small, lightly pressed type that matures in about two months and often is smoked.

DAGANO (cow)   Semisoft with nutty flavor, smooth texture, pliable body, and waxed exterior, this cheese was developed at Michigan State University; it is considered one of the "new Swiss" types with large holes which include Iowa-Style, Jarlsberg, Purdue-Swiss, and Sweden's Grevéost or Herrgard.

DAIRY   The word is devised from the Middle English "deirie," "deie" being the then prevailing term for female servant, or the dairymaid whose job included making cheese.

DAMEN (cow)   A Hungarian fresh cheese traditionally made by farm women, Damen is sometimes known more pretentiously as Gloire de Montagnes.

DAMIETTA (cow, buffalo)   The most popular cheese of Egypt, indeed of the Arab world, is named for the city at the eastern mouth of the Nile. Soft and white, and distinguished because it is salted before it is pressed instead of after, it can be produced from whole cow's milk, skim milk, or that of buffalo, by adding rennet after salting. It is sold fresh locally, or pickled in briny whey and cured as long as four to eight months; for export it is sealed in metal containers. The name is sometimes spelled Domiati or Dumyat.

DANABLU, DANISH BLUE (cow)   A factory-made internal-mold type developed in Denmark to compete with Roquefort for U.S. sales; the paste is very white, the flavor sharp, and the buttery consistency is the result of a process invented by Marius Boël, who used homogenized milk to this end.

DANBO (cow)   Considered by some to be a variant of Steppe, and belonging to the Samsoe category, Danbo is a mild, supple Danish cheese with a limited number of small uniform holes. It is sometimes seasoned with caraway seeds.

DANISH WHITE MOLD (cow)   Made from cream, with a floury crust and a rich, buttery consistency; it is shaped in rectangles and often packed in chipwood boxes.

DARALAG (sheep)   Herb-accented and based on skimmed milk; see Bgug Panir.

DARIWORLD (cow)   An industrial variant of Cheddar manufactured as a base to process with highly flavored types and thus produce pasteurized processed cheese spreads. See Processed.

DAUPHIN (cow)   A fancy-shaped variation of the Flanders cheese Maroilles, Dauphin sometimes has the form of a heart, a crescent, or a shield. Its name seems to derive from a visit by Louis XIV and his son, the Dauphin, to Flanders; during the royal stay the right of the prince to tax carters was lifted—perhaps because he so liked the local cheese. In any event, dairymen began to use his title to distinguish their product. It is soft and rich, has a washed rind, and is seasoned with tarragon, parsley, and spices.

DAVENTRY (cow)   Named for a Northampton village, this ancient English cheese was considered at its best when it developed blue veins that caused it to be compared with Stilton.

DELFT (cow)   One of Holland's spiced wheels that is made of partially skimmed milk; see Leyden.

DÉLICE DE ST.-CYR (cow)   One of France's triple-cream types, this factory-made disk comes from the region that produces Bries and is often compared to Brillat-Savarins and Excelsiors.

DEMI-SEL (cow)   A variation of Normandy fresh cheese for which the method of manufacture is protected by law. As with Gervais, the curds are homogenized and pressed into a small cake wrapped in foil.

DERBY (cow)   One of nine British cheeses manufactured in quantity for export, but described by the English Country Cheese Council as "the rarest of all English cheeses"; pale, with close and firm texture, it has delicate, mild flavor. In England a traditional Christmas treat is Sage Derby, and this herb-accented cheese is increasingly available regardless of season.

DESERVILLERS   This village in Franche-Comté, on the basis of evidence dating to 1288, is said to be the birthplace of the cheese that later came to be internationally known as Gruyère; archives indicate that in that year an association was formed in the village by local farmers who by then had been making it for generations.

DESSERTNYÏ-BELYÏ (cow)   A Russian fresh cheese aged about ten days, this is slightly sour in flavor and is said by some to have an aftertaste of mushrooms.

DEVONSHIRE CREAM (cow)   There is disagreement as to whether this is to be comfortably included among cheeses, but it is magnificent when eaten in Devonshire in much the way French cooks serve fresh cheese with berries. Immediately after milking—according to prevailing tradition—cream is allowed to rise for about 10 hours in shallow pans; the pans are then set over low heat until the cream reaches 175° or until the surface takes on a wrinkled appearance. Pans and their contents are cooled in running water until the cream is thick and clotted and easily skimmed off. Clotted cream is a necessity of life in England's West Country. In Cornwall, "Thunder and Lightning" is the awe-inspiring name for bread spread first with Devonshire's cheeselike cream, then with treacle.

DIL PEYNIRI (cow, sheep)   Fresh cheeses are sold under this and other names in such Turkish cities as Adana, Ankara, Istanbul, Izmir, and Mersin.

DOLCE LATTE (cow)   A factory version of Gorgonzola.

DOMIATI (cow, buffalo)   See Damietta.

DOMREMY (cow)   Square, soft-ripened and similar to Carré de l'Est, under which name it is sometimes sold. Domremy-la-Pucelle is the village in which Joan of Arc was born.

DORET (cow)   An exported version of Ziegelkäse (see below).

DORNECY (goat)   One of the truncated cones, Dornecy takes its name from a village not far from Lyon that is famous for both cheese and charcuterie.

DOROBOUSKI, DOROGOBOUKSKI (cow)   A Russian soft-ripened cheese with piquant flavor and slight ammoniacal smell, made near Smolensk and retailed in small cubes.

DORSET (cow)   See Blue Vinny.

DOUBLE BERKELEY (cow)   Double Gloucester originally was known as Double Berkeley after Berkeley Vale, south of the city of Gloucester, England.

DOUBLE COTTENHAM (cow)   Before World War II a cheese sometimes compared with Stilton, or with Wensleydale, was produced near Cottenham, a village not far from Cambridge, England.

DOUBLE CREAM, DOUBLE CRÈME   Throughout France *double crème* is the term for fresh cheeses made from cow's milk. Technically, cheeses so labeled must contain 60 percent fat in dry matter, and they are usually shaped in the Camembert form.

DOUBLE GLOUCESTER (cow)   See Gloucester.

DOUBLE-COEUR (cow)   Neufchâtel is sometimes so called when molded in heart-shaped form.

DOULCE GRUYÈRE (cow)   Factory-made semisoft Swiss cheese with firm, somewhat butterlike consistency; compare with Bel Lago, Belle Suisse, Fleurs des Alpes, Fromage Roth, all products of Switzerland.

DOUX DE MONTAGNE (cow)   One of the so-called Pyrenees cheeses, this has open texture and a tough inedible rind.

DRABANT (cow)   Mild-flavored yet piquant; rindless, square, semihard Swedish cheese with scattering of round holes, made in factories. It has been called a Swedish version of Comté.

DREIZEITIGE (cow)   See Wilstermarsch.

DREUX (cow)   A flat, round cheese with powdery, delicate crust, taking its name from the market town north of Chartres, Dreux is found in the Île-de-France wrapped in chestnut leaves when it is made on farms; increasingly it is made in small factories.

DUCS (cow)   Trademark of a round, flat, powdery-skinned, soft-ripened disk made in a factory at La Chapelle-Vieille-Forêt, near Chablis. Much is exported in distinctly marked cardboard containers.

DUEL (cow)   A small, square, soft-ripened product of Austria's dairy country.

DUNGARVAN (cow)   A southern Ireland cheese.

DUNLOP (cow)   Often likened to Cheddar, Dunlop is packaged in a number of ways—formed into 3- to 4-inch balls, for instance, or in 38-pound wheels covered with black wax. It is the legendary cheese of Barbara Gilmour (see Chapter 2); off-white in color and of firm texture, it is sometimes eaten in Scotland when seven to eight weeks old but is considered at its best at four months or more.

DUTCH DANDY (cow)   Export name for a factory-made Holland cheese that has no rind, is semisoft in consistency and golden yellow in color; its flavor is faintly reminiscent of Port Salut.

ε

ECHOURGNAC (cow)   In southwest France the monks of the Abbey of Echourgnac, near Montpon-sur-l'Isle, east of Bordeaux, make a Trappist cheese in the form of a disk with bulging sides that weighs slightly over 1 pound; it matures in about three weeks and has a mild, aromatic flavor.

EDAM (cow)   One of Holland's pair of famous dairy products since the Middle Ages, Edam is spherical and coated red for export, usually weighing about 3½ pounds in its traditional form. It is duplicated in various countries, including the U.S., and in Latin America locally made versions have been produced since early Dutch colonial rule—to such an extent that it is considered a native New World cheese. The Edam made on the Japanese island of Hokkaido is also considered excellent. Other names for Edam include Katzenkopf, Manbollen, Tête de Maure, Tête de Mort.

EDELPILZKÄSE (cow)   Produced in the Bavarian Alps east of Salzburg, this Blue Cheese whose name means "noble mushroom" has faint pocks of mold in a very creamy texture and is made in rectangular blocks of varying sizes. Its curiously strong moldy flavor, unlike any other cheese, may have inspired its name.

EDIRNE (sheep)   Shepherds around Edirne, on the Turkish-Bulgarian border, took the city's name for a soft white cheese now made throughout western Turkey in substantial quantities.

EGG (cow)   Finns in the province of Nyland, according to the USDA's *Cheese Varieties and Descriptions,* have long made Egg Cheese by mixing raw eggs either with raw milk or with drained curd. Pennsylvania Mennonites heat milk to the boiling point, then stir in eggs beaten with sour milk or buttermilk, salt, and sugar; the cheese curds which result are skimmed off and served with syrup. In North Carolina's mountains a similar cheese, to which soda is added in the process, is called Yellow Cheese. Such primitive cheeses are often shaped in handy kitchen utensils. See Cup Cheese.

ELBINGER (cow)   A cheese once marketed in the East Prussian city of Elbing; see Werder.

ELBO (cow)   Like Samsoe, Elbo is one of Denmark's mild slicing cheeses with a cream-colored to yellow interior that is rather firm. Its rind is dry and yellowish, and the loaves are often covered with red or yellow wax.

EMILIANO (cow)   Italians use this term generically for the *grana* produced in the province of Emilia; it is very hard, like Parmigiano-Reggiano. The quality is variable.

EMMENTAL FRANÇAIS (cow)   See Emmenthal. The best French copies of so-called Swiss cheese have been made in the Savoy and Franche-Comté since the immigration in the nineteenth century of Swiss cheesemakers; other copies bearing this name are now made in Charente and Brittany. The best examples look like genuine Emmenthalers (except for the stamping of the word "Switzerland"), having the same shape, size, and weight. They are probably the next best thing to the original.

EMMENTHAL (cow)   The word means "valley of the Emme," the river which flows through central Switzerland where dairymen have been making cheese since before records were kept. Emmenthal (the French spelling is usually Emmental) is the model which all makers of so-called Swiss cheese seek to emulate, and none is genuine unless the word "Switzerland" is stamped repeatedly on the rind after rigorous inspection. Wheels are about 33 inches in diameter, 9 inches thick, and weigh 176 to 220 pounds; they are further distinguished by large spherical holes evenly distributed throughout. The flavor is fruity without sharpness, and a true Emmenthaler is worth the difference in price without question.

ENGADINE (cow)   A local mountain cheese which takes its name from a valley in the canton of Grissons, in eastern Switzerland.

ENGLISH DAIRY (cow)   Very hard and made in much the same way as Cheddar, this was once known in the U.S. for its cooking and grating propensities.

ENTRAMMES (cow)   The name comes from the Abbey of Entrammes, in the French province of Maine, which is recognized as "the cradle of Port-du-Salut"; when the original trademark was sold the monks applied the name of their monastery to the cheese they now make in small quantities.

ENTRAYGUES (cow, goat, sheep)   A Cabécou cheese (see above) taking its name from a village near the Cantal country.

ÉPOISSES (cow)   The Burgundy village of Époisses was long the chief marketplace for this soft-ripened, red-skinned disk called by Brillat-Savarin "the king of cheeses." In France true Époisses is washed with Burgundy marc and is smooth and shiny on the outside and supple and creamy within; it is compared to such other Burgundy delights as Langres, Les Laumes, St. Florentin, and Soumaintrain. A creamy disk sometimes available in New York under this name is dusted to look brick-red, but although it is of pleasing texture and flavor, it is not a matured Époisses.

ERCÉ (cow)   Like Bethmale, this is a local product from the village for which it is named high in the French mountains north of Andorra.

EREVANSKI (cow, sheep)   Yerevan (Erevan) is the capital of Armenia, whose people eat cheese for breakfast, lunch, and dinner. Some Erevanski cheese is pickled. Other cheeses from the area, made mostly from sheep's milk, are known as Erevani (Eriwani), Elisavetpolen, Karab, Kasach, Kurini, and Tali.

ERMITE (cow)   The trade name for blue-veined cheese made by Benedictine monks in Canada, Ermite is usually strong in flavor and creamy in texture. It is sold in retail stores and at the Abbey St.

Benoit du Lac, Brome County, Quebec, on Lake Memphremagog. The monks also make Port Salut and a cheese somewhat like Emmenthaler.

ERVY (cow) A rare farmhouse cheese of the Champagne country of France, Ervy bears the name of a market town not far from Troyes; it should be small, round, and full of butterfat.

ERVY-LE-CHATEL (cow) Made in the shape of a truncated cone, this is a soft, bloomy-rinded cheese from the town that gives it its name; sometimes compared to Chaource and Époisses.

ESBAREICH (cow, sheep) One of the mountain products of the Pyrenees, shaped in a big flattened round and compared to Iraty or Laruns.

ESROM (cow) It is said that Esrom has been tops among cheeses exported from Denmark since 1959; sometimes it is sold as Danish Port Salut. Its texture is very open and its flavor and aroma distinctive.

ESSEX (cow) A fabled English cheese so unappealing, they say, that it caused dogs to bark.

ESTONSKI (cow) A mild, hard-paste Estonian cheese.

ETTEKEES (cow) See Aetkees.

ÉVORA (goat, sheep) A firm mountain cheese named for a market city south of the Serra d'Ossa in south-central Portugal.

EXCELSIOR (cow) Invented about 1890 in a small dairy in Rovray-Catillon, Normandy, Excelsior has 72 percent butterfat and belongs therefore among the so-called *triple crèmes*. Its flavor is mild and smooth, its rind white and downy; it is formed in irregularly shaped small cylinders.

EXPLORATEUR (cow) One of France's *fromages triple crème*, it is a luxurious 12-ounce disk made by Fromagerie du Petit-Morin, a small cheesemaker in the village of La Trétoire on the Petit-Morin River west of Paris.

F

FAISCRE GROTHA The ancient Irish term refers to Cottage Cheese firm enough, they used to say, to be carried in a woman's apron; literally "a compression of curds" in Gaelic.

FAJY (sheep) Usually a product of skim milk, Fajy is made by Iraqi shepherds without animal rennet but with wild onion or garlic as the coagulant. See Biza.

FARMER (cow)   Most often the term is applied to basic fresh cheese such as Cottage Cheese. A granular white product called Farmer in the U.S. is made of cultured skim milk fortified with cream, salt, and sorbic acid as a preservative; Friendship Farmer Cheese is made in Friendship, Allegany County, New York. In Ohio, a semisoft, part-skim-milk cheese, firm enough to slice or cube, is sold as Farmer Cheese and said to be made originally by farmers in Europe who used the skimmed-off cream to make butter. George Lang reports in *The Cuisine of Hungary* on the drying and smoking of paper-wrapped Farmer Cheese in the unspoiled pastoral land between Budapest and the Russian border.

FARMHOUSE   British cheese made on farms by expert cheesemakers is graded, under England's Milk Marketing Board system, as "Super-fine Grade Farmhouse," "Fine Grade Farmhouse," and "Graded"; none is authentic British "farmhouse" unless it bears the initials M.M.B. The cheeses are stamped with the date of making and guar-anteed to contain all the natural butterfat. According to the English Country Cheese Council, which issues special contracts for farm-house cheese, 10 percent of the U.K. total, made by 290 farmers, warrants this distinction.

FERMIER   French term for cheese produced on farms by traditional methods.

FETA (cow, goat, sheep)   The best-known of Greek table cheeses (also spelled Fétta) is very white and moist and is preserved in brine. Its sourish, tangy flavor is often used to accent salads, and it is much favored in Mediterranean cuisine as a cooking cheese.

FEUILLE DE DREUX (cow)   See Dreux.

FIN DE SIÈCLE (cow)   One of France's very rich so-called triple-cream products, given its name by Henri Androuët of the Paris cheese family. See Excelsior.

FIOR D'ALPE (cow)   Similar to Bel Paese, this is a fragrant product of Lodi, the Lombardy town from which also come *grana Lodigiano* and much fresh Cream Cheese in muslin-wrapped cylinders called *mascarpone.*

FIOR DI LATTE (cow)   In Campani province, some Italian cheesemakers distinguish between Mozzarella, properly made of buffalo's milk, and that made of cow's milk by labeling the latter either Scamorze or Fior di Latte.

FIORE SARDO (sheep)   "Flower of Sardinia" that it is, this is a shepherd's cheese made in wheels that vary between 3½ and 9 pounds; factory versions may weigh as much as 13 pounds. The crust is yellow, and the paste white or straw-colored. It is delicious as a table cheese when about two months old, and ready for grating as a condiment after six months. Traditionally, Fiore Sardo comes from Sardinia's mountains, but the same label may be found on sheep's-milk cheese from mainland Latium or Campania.

FJORDLAND (cow)   A skim-milk product, Fjordland is a "Swiss" type made in Norway and compared sometimes to Jarlsberg; properly matured, it has mellow, nutty flavor but softer texture than Emmenthal.

FLEUR DE ALPES   A trademark for a monastery type; see page 69.

FLEURINES   The French word for the natural openings in the caves of Combalou through which air currents pass, affecting the bacteriological conditions considered essential to the proper maturation of genuine Roquefort.

FLÖTOST (cow)   The Norwegian word means "Cream Cheese," but Flötost is actually made of cooked whey and resembles Mysost with slightly more fat content as the result of the addition of whole milk or, sometimes, cream.

FOGGIANO (sheep)   Milk from sheep raised on the low fertile plain, called Tavoliere, in Apulia, Italy, is turned into a plastic-curd cheese; see Cotronese; Moliterno.

FOL D'AMOUR (cow)   Soft-ripened in French factories to emulate Brie and Camembert, Fol d'Amour is shaped in ovals that weigh just under ½ pound and contain 60 percent butterfat.

FONDU   Applied to European products, this describes a cheese that has been melted down and blended with liquid or powdered milk, cream, butter, casein, or whey; sometimes flavoring is added. See fromage à tartiner.

FONDU AU MARC DE RAISIN (cow)   Known sometimes as Fondu au Raisin, or Fromage Affiné dans le Marc de Raisin, this classic French processed cheese has an artificial crust of dried grape seeds. See Grappe.

FONDUE   Applied to various dishes based on melted cheese; see Recipes.

FONDUE NANTUATIENNE   A French dish based on Bleu de Gex or Bleu de Sassenage.

FONDUTA (cow)   A bland, buttery-textured Wisconsin product.

FONDUTA   Italian and Swiss versions of fondue in which eggs are added to cheese.

FONTAINEBLEAU (cow)   Unsalted fresh cheese is mixed with whipped cream, and the result is a French classic, often served with fruit.

FONTAL (cow)   Because the term Fontina is limited by Italian law to products of Val d'Aosta, almost identical wheels made in other parts of northeast Italy and in the Ain region of France are called Fontal; they are also compared to some Swiss cheeses from Valais. Fontal is much used in fondues and raclettes. A Danish Fontal is made at Kjellerup, on the Jutland peninsula.

FONTINA VAL D'AOSTA (cow) Named for Mont Fontin overlooking Piedmont, Fontina is an ancient cheese cited as one of Italy's best as early as 1477, when a dairy encyclopedia was published by Pantaleone da Confienza. Italians say it is the milk of the Val d'Aosta breed of cows, grazing on pastures as high as 8,500 feet, that accounts for Fontina's special quality and its supple and delicate flavor. True Fontina is recognized by its pale-yellow brushed rind, and its consistency is considered essential to making a successful truffle-laced *fonduta piemontese.* The Swedish cheese called Fontina has a bright red exterior and a moister consistency. A Wisconsin imitation is labeled Fontinella.

FORMAGELLE (cow, goat, sheep) This soft cheese of Switzerland's Ticino country and the neighboring mountains of northern Italy is most often eaten fresh, with or without salting, but it is sometimes spiced, and sometimes ripened; that made near Lecco, in the district of Como, was traditionally ripened in caves of the Sassina Valley.

FORMAGGI DI PASTA FILATA Italian term for cheeses made by so-called plastic-curd or spun-curd methods.

FORMAGGIO Italian word for cheese; *formaggio di capra* is goat cheese, *formaggio pecorino,* sheep cheese, and *formaggio vaccino* is made from cow's milk.

FORT DE BETHMALE (cow) See Bethmale.

FORT DE BÉTHUNE (cow) See Béthune, Fort de.

FOUGERU (cow) A Coulommiers-like round made in Tournan-en-Brie and adorned with a fern leaf on its top surface.

FOURME D'AMBERT (cow) One of the best-known of French blue-veined cheeses, named for a town not far from Clermont-Ferrand.

FREY, EMIL American cheesemaker who developed Liederkranz. See Chapter 7.

FRIESEKAAS (cow) One of Holland's aromatic cylinders, seasoned with cumin seed. It is also known as Commitie.

FRIESIAN CLOVE (cow) This Dutch spiced cheese may be produced from partly skimmed milk with cloves added to the curd. It is similar to Leyden; see below.

FRISON (cow) Somewhat like Gouda and bearing a label of guarantee like Leyden, Frison has more salt, is spiced with a mixture of cloves and cumin, and is wrapped tightly in cloth.

FROMAGE   French word for cheese.

FROMAGE DES ALPES   Swiss classification for a group of mountain cheeses that are further distinguished by names of locations: Cantons such as St. Gall or Uri, villages such as Bagnes, Conches, or Piora.

FROMAGE BLANC   The French term for their fresh "white cheese," which they used much as Cottage Cheese is used elsewhere.

FROMAGE DE CLAMART (COW)   See Clamart.

FROMAGE À LA CRÈME   A simple French cheese dish produced by mixing curds with cream and sugar, and then draining in basket molds.

FROMAGE FORT   In parts of France it is traditional to save overage cheeses like Cachat, Bouton de Culotte, mixing them sometimes with a milder cheese like Gruyère, or with oil or butter, herbs, or wine, then sealing them so that they mature and usually develop very strong flavor and aroma.

FROMAGE À TARTINER   The French term for "melting cheese" is also applied to certain packaged processed cheeses.

FROMAGE DE TROYES (COW)   See Barberey.

FRÜHSTÜCK (COW)   Called a breakfast cheese in Germany, this is compared to Limburger and Romadur and is also produced in Belgium.

FTINOPORINO (sheep)   Macedonians use this name for a Liptauer-like product.

FUMO NERO   Literally "black smoke," *fumo nero* is what Italian cheesemakers call the coating that seals Parmesan in a mixture of lamp black and burnt umber liquefied with wine.

FU-YÜ (soybean)   Most of China knows no dairy products because cattle contribute more to the economy as beasts of burden. Chinese ingenuity, however, created a source of "milk" by transforming the soybean; it was softened and ground and, with water added, converted first to a white liquid "milk," then to curd, and finally to cheese for use in sauces.

FYNBO (COW)   Named for Denmark's largest island, this is a firm yellow cheese with mild and aromatic taste that is sometimes labeled Gouda or Baby Gouda. When marked with a "T" or labeled "Trope," Fynbo has been especially treated to ensure longer life for the tropical market; it is saltier and has a thick rind to withstand high temperatures.

G

GAISKÄSLI (goat)   A small circular cake, this "little goat" cheese is popular among Swiss and German connoisseurs.

GALANTINE (cow)   An imitation Edam, originating in Flanders, and produced in other parts of France. See Broodkaas.

GALLOWAY (cow)   Scottish dairies have given the name of the Lowland peninsula to Cheddar-like blocks now much in demand.

GAMMELOST (cow)   Strong and aromatic, with blue veins, Gammelost is one of Norway's best cheeses. It comes from the dairylands of Sogne and Hardanger, usually is made of sour skim milk, and the curds often are inoculated with three molds.

GAPRON, GAPERON (cow)   Originally made on Auvergne farms of buttermilk (as the name indicates), this is a semihard flattened ball seasoned with salt, pepper, and garlic. It has a natural rind, is tied with a ribbon, and now comes from small factories. Farmers once hung their Gaprons in the kitchen to age, the number of them often serving to measure a man's wealth and thus indicate the marriageability of his daughter.

GARDIAN (sheep)   See Camargue.

GAUCHO (cow)   Firm and buttery in taste, reminding some of a combination of Port Salut and Havarti, this skim-milk cheese bears the export trademark assigned to Argentina's Queso de Postre and is marketed in the U.S. in small wheels with round rims that weigh 28 ounces.

GAUTRIAS (cow)   A cylindrical cheese weighing between 6 and 10 pounds that resembles Port Salut in flavor and texture; manufactured in the French province of Maine.

GAVOT (goat, cow, sheep)   One of the small French goat cheeses in which other milk is sometimes added or substituted.

GBEJNA (cow)   An ancient Maltese cheese. It is now a popular Australian loose-curd product that is soft and white, delicately flavored when plain, but also commonly coated with peppercorns which give it a sharp, tangy taste.

GEBNA, GIBNA (buffalo, cow, goat, sheep)   In the Middle East, this word, spelled variously, refers to unripened cheese. *Gebna beida* (white cheese) is a simple home product that can be ready to eat in 24 hours; it is porcelain-white and, cut into cubes, is served as an appetizer, or perhaps with a meal that includes couscous. In *A Book of Middle Eastern Food,* Claudia Roden says it is delicious when dried for several days, then fried with eggs.

GEHEIMRATH (cow)   The name means privy councilor, but the cheese is a minor version of characteristic Holland cheese, manufactured both in the Netherlands and in southern Germany.

GÉROMÉ (cow)   Like its close relative, Munster, Géromé originated in France's Vosges Mountains, and its name comes from the slurring pronunciation of its chief market town, Gérardmer (see Lorraine). Géromé is now made in small commercial dairies, but it has been said that it can be truly experienced only when eaten in a one-room mountain-side dairy where herdsmen traditionally produced cheeses every day.

GERVAIS (cow)   The Cream Cheese called Petit-Suisse (see below) was first distributed in Paris by Charles Gervais, who then built a dairy business that in the following century made his name synonymous with his product. According to a French gastronome the millions of cream-enriched Gervais cheeses sold in France each year would make a column "a thousand times higher than Everest."

GESUNDHEITKÄSE (cow)   As the German name implies, this is considered a "health" cheese and is based on skim milk.

GIGHA (cow)   A firm cheese from the Scottish island of the same name.

GILMOUR, BARBARA   Fabled "inventor" of Dunlop; see Chapter 2.

GISLEV (cow)   A little-known, hard Danish cheese.

GJETOST (cow, goat)   An ancient product of Norwegian and Swedish farmers, sometimes spelled Gietost (the first syllable means goat, the second cheese), this is now labeled Ekte, meaning the real thing, when it is made of pure goat's milk. More often it has only 10 percent, the remainder coming from cows. Whatever the milk, the end result is utterly different from the usual conception of cheese, having a rather sweet caramel-like flavor and consistency. However, as T. A. Layton has said in his *Cheese and Cheese Cookery,* "Gjetost does not deserve the cruel epithets that have been hurled at it . . . it is an acquired taste, and when acquired, delicious." See Chapter 6.

GLAMORGAN (cow)   This product of the Welsh county washed by the Bristol Channel disappeared long ago, but it was once popular in South Wales, requiring the milk of a now extinct breed of cattle known as Gwent. A mixture of Glamorgan Cheese, onion, herbs, and bread crumbs became a rural classic known as Glamorgan sausage (see Recipes, page 146); it is still popular even though another cheese must be substituted in the recipe.

GLÄRNERKÄSE (cow)   See Sapsago.

GLARUS (cow)   Taking its name from its own canton, Glarus is a whole-milk product a little like Tilsit, but softer and sweeter in flavor.

A Swiss dairyman named Wegmuller is said to have combined the methods of his Glarus neighbors with techniques of East Prussian immigrants who made Tilsit in Switzerland in the nineteenth century.

GLOUCESTER, DOUBLE GLOUCESTER (cow)   Black cows named for their home county of Gloucester, England, once were the source of the rich milk that gave distinction to both Single Gloucester (so called because it requires only half the milk and much less aging than Double Gloucester) and its sibling. But Gloucester cattle are gone now, and so, virtually, is Single Gloucester. In fact, Double Gloucester all but disappeared during World War II, and is now made in factories as the result of work by England's Milk Marketing Board which is fully described by John Ehle in *The Cheeses and Wines of England and France*. Today Double Gloucester is sometimes called "the golden cheese" by English fans because of its rich creamy color and its mellow flavor; sometimes it is compared favorably to well-made Cheddar.

GLUMSE (cow)   This German Cottage Cheese is made by curdling skim milk, and it is usually mixed with sweet milk or cream before it is eaten.

GOLDEN BUCK   A Welsh Rabbit topped by a poached egg.

GOLDEN VALE (cow)   In the southwest of Ireland the dairy region known as the Golden Vale produces a rich, firm cheese using the Cheddar process, and much that bears this name is exported to other countries, including the U.S.

GOLD'N'RICH (cow)   A buttery American semisoft loaf, Gold'n'Rich was developed from the Port Salut formula for the Pure Milk Association and first produced at Elgin, Illinois.

GOMSER (cow)   Cheese made especially for use in making raclette (see below) commonly is called Gomser in Switzerland; it is produced in Val du Bagne.

GORGONZOLA (cow)   Distinguishing one of the half-dozen most famous cheeses, the name of Gorgonzola—borrowed from the village between Milan and Bergamo—became widely known abroad in the fifteenth century when French troops brought back blue-veined rounds after the conquest of Naples. Now made uniformly in numerous factories in northern Italy (and several in America), it is also still produced by a few meticulous Italian farmers. The interior is mottled with blue-green veins produced by introduction of *Penicillium glaucum*. Gorgonzola is slightly fatter in texture than Roquefort, and moister than Stilton. White Gorgonzola (see Pannarone) has no visible veins.

GORNYÏ (cow)   A hard, granular cooking cheese used by Russian house-wives.

GORNYÏ ALTAÏ (cow)   The cheddaring process is used to make this large cheese in Russia's mountain region called Gorno Altayskaya; it is shaped like either wheels or truncated cones.

GOUDA (cow)   Gouda is a small city near Rotterdam to which Dutch farmers took cheeses to market long ago, and the Gouda cheeses still made on farms are incomparably superior to those from factories, no matter how hard technicians try. Good commercial Goudas have mild flavor and are shaped in 6- to 11-pound wheels with very convex rims; sometimes yellow wax is applied. Goudas have more fat content than Edams, as well as firm supple texture well liked by many gastronomes. A well-aged handmade Gouda from a South Holland farm is one of the great experiences. The name is used by foreign factories, including some in Belgium which turn out a flat cylinder coated in paraffin, and in Iceland, where Arctic dairymen copied Dutch Goudas long ago, but now turn out a cheese without rind that has the shape of a rectangular loaf and weighs something less than 5 pounds.

GOUDAMM (cow)   A descriptive name given a smoked cheese made by Bill Wilke of Spruce Farm, Pine Plains, New York; he defines Goudamm as a mixture of Gouda, Edam, and Gruyère formed into rectangular loaves weighing 5 pounds.

GOUDAOST, SVENSK   Pale, mild, semihard Swedish cheese with round holes and fresh, somewhat tangy flavor. Unlike Dutch Gouda, it is shaped as a disk rather than a ball; often in ½-pound weights.

GOUDSCHE KAAS   Dutch term for Gouda.

GOURMANDISE (cow)   A cheese product flavored with cherry extract or, in France (where it is classified as *fromage fondu*), kirsch; nuts are frequently used as embellishment, and the net result is more cake than *le vrai fromage*. However, many people who are enthusiastic about Gourmandise consider it, mistakenly, to be a cheese in its own right.

GOURNAY (cow)   When fresh, Gournay is a typical Normandy un-ripened cheese; when matured about one week it resembles a rustic Camembert. Its flavor is delicate and lactic.

GOUSTER (cow)   Introduced in 1974 by Gerard Paul as a hybrid combining techniques of making factory Gouda and factory Munster
(hence the somewhat outrageous name), Gouster is shaped in flattened balls and covered with pink wax. Annatto is used to marble the
paste in tones of yellow and orange, the texture is semisoft, and the
flavor unlikely to offend those who prefer mild cheese.

GOYA (cow)   A semihard imitation of Asiago is made by Argentinians
in the province of Corrientes.

GOYÈRE (cow)   A cylindrical cheese made in Denain, France, and on
both sides of the French-Belgian border; sometimes spelled goère.

GRADAOST (cow)   Not to be confused with Swedish Gräddost, this is
a Scandinavian Blue Cheese.

GRÄDDOST (cow)   Rich, cream-colored Swedish cylinders exported under various trademarks earn the right to be called Gräddost only
when the fat content is 60 percent or more; most shipments come
from the Småland region. Västerbotten Gräddost, from the province of
that name, is a licensed product produced in limited quantity and
considered one of the prize Swedish cheeses.

GRANA   The literal meaning of this Italian word is "grain" and refers to
the texture of Parmesan and other grating cheeses; it is also used in
slang, just as "bread" is used in America, to indicate money. Grana
Reggiano and Parmigiano-Reggiano are both terms used for hard
grating cheeses made in Reggio Emilio. Italian laws and an agreement at the Convention of Stresa designated Parmigiano-Reggiano
as the accepted term for *grana* cheeses made in the district of Bologna,
Mantua, Podena, Parma, and Reggio. Grana Padano is the official
term for those produced in the regions around Padua. In Lombardy
the general term *grana Lombardo* is used, and *grana Lodigiano*
applies to products of Lodi.

GRANULAR OR STIRRED CURD   This raw-milk process using cow's milk
results in something like Cheddar, except that the curd is not matted
or milled; it is stirred until dry enough to salt, then pressed in hoops.
Colby is the result of a variation in this technique.

GRAPPE, GRAPE, GRAPPA (cow)   A carapace of grape seeds covers this
French factory-made processed cheese.

GRATIN, AU GRATIN   Cooking terms used to describe dishes on which a
top crust is formed by bread crumbs, sometimes mixed with cheese.

GRATZ, GRAZ (cow)   An Austrian farm product named for the market
city not far north of the Yugoslavian border; the mature cheese is
popular locally.

GRAVIERA (cow)   A Greek version of Gruyère made in Crete, Skyros,
and in the northern Sporades in the Aegean Sea, this is rich in cream

and firm enough to slice well; Greeks eat it as an appetizer or as dessert.

GRAVYER (cow)   An imitation Gruyère manufactured in Turkey.

GREEN CHEESE   Immature cheese, the looks of which once caused people to say fancifully that the moon was made of it. The term also is used in reference to Sage Cheese and to Sapsago (see both below).

GRESSONEY (cow)   In the Gressoney Valley, just south of Zermatt and the Swiss-Italian border, dairymen produce a dense, heavy cheese of reddish hue about which it is said by oldsters: "Gressoney has three virtues—it sates hunger, it quenches thirst, and it cleans the teeth."

GREVÉOST (cow)   A high-moisture factory version of Emmenthal originated in Sweden after the invention of Jarlsberg (see below) in 1959.

GRIÈGES (cow)   A blue-veined cheese produced in a factory at Grièges, not far from Lyon, exports of which are labeled also as "Blue de Bresse"; the mold is the result of injections of *Penicillium glaucum,* and the texture is unusually creamy.

GRIS DE LILLE (cow)   One of the most assertive French types, Gris de Lille is similar to Maroilles (see below) but is further matured in a brine for about three months.

GRÖNMÖGELOST (cow)   This is sold abroad as "Swedish Blue" and is perforated with long needles to encourage the growth of *Penicillium roqueforti.*

GROVIERA (cow)   Italian Gruyère, produced in Lombardy and Piedmont.

GRÜNERKÄSE (cow)   See Sapsago.

GRUTH (cow)   A simple Irish cheese made in ancient times. *Grus* is also a vanished Gaelic cheese, said to have been very strong in flavor.

GRUYÈRE (cow)   The name derives from the charming Alpine village of Gruyères and the valley of the Gruyère River in Switzerland, and the famous cheese is produced in several parts of western Switzerland as well as across the border in France. Sometimes confused with Emmenthal as the generic "Swiss" cheese, Gruyère is made in wheels about half the size of Emmenthal and is not distinguished by large holes. It is creamier, and so firm in texture it is almost hard.

GUAJAQUENO (goat)   A Mexican curiosity made of long cheese fibers rolled up like a skein of yarn and appreciated for its flavor, in spite of a rubbery texture.

GUDBRANDSDALSOST (cow, goat)   This takes its name from the so-called "valley of the valleys" in central Norway and is a mixture of two milks.

GUERBIGNY (cow)   A Picardy type that is often heart-shaped and compared to Rollot (see below).

GÜSSING (cow)   Very similar to the American Brick in character, this

Austrian cheese follows the same dairy procedures except that it is produced from skim milk.

H

HABLÉ CRÈME CHANTILLY (cow)   Very white and soft, this Scandinavian cheese with a French name was developed before World War II at the Walla Gard dairy in Stockholm by a Gallic cheese master named Hablé. It is sometimes compared to France's Fromage de Monsieur Fromage, and was saluted on its first arrival in the U.S. by *The New Yorker* as "a historic event." It is very delicate, and export is restricted.

HALOUMI, HALUMI (goat, sheep)   Salty and hard when preserved in whey, this Middle Eastern cheese is often grated for use in various cooked dishes and is cubed for grilling and frying. Sidqui Effendi, in his nineteenth-century Turkish cooking manual, gives the following instructions: "Put a portion of cheese in silver paper. Wrap it up and put it over a fire. When the paper starts to glow the cheese is ready to eat and deliciously creamy. . . . This is good food which enhances sex for married men." In Cyprus, Haloumi is rolled in salt and dried mint on separate plates, then folded and stacked in earthenware jars with whey poured over. It can be eaten at once, or covered and kept for 40 days.

HALSINGE (cow, goat)   White, semihard, this Swedish loaf has a salty aroma, is mild when fresh and rather strong when aged six months or more. Its goat's-milk content is 10 percent, its fat 45 percent. Halsinge is made in factories in several variations and usually in blocks weighing about 10 pounds.

HAND (cow)   So called because it is casually shaped, this is a popular cheese with Germanic people throughout the world; it is unsophisticated and not to the taste of some.

HARDING, JOSEPH   An English dairyman who systematized the production of Cheddar by devising the method now called "cheddaring" (see above); the result was an increase in production that helped to make Cheddar famous as it made it easier for it to be imitated in various parts of the world.

HAREL, MARIE   This much romanticized *fermière* of Normandy is memorialized in both Vimoutiers, France, and Van Wert, Ohio (where Liederkranz as well as Camembert is made), but the cheese which some give her credit for inventing undoubtedly evolved before her time. It may be that Mme. Harel's Camemberts were made by her with greater care than those of her neighbors and that she passed on her "secrets" to her daughter, Mme. Marie Paynel. In any event, it seems likely that new fame came to Camembert when, according to legend, Mme. Harel's daughter presented one to Napoleon III, to the emperor's delight.

HARRACHER (cow)   A strong cheese, not unlike Limburger, made in Hungary.

HARZ, HARZER (cow)   One of Germany's "Hand" Cheeses (see above), this takes its name from the Harz Mountains.

HARZE (cow)   One of the numerous Trappist products is made at the Abbey of Harze in Belgium.

HAUSKÄSE (cow)   So called because it is a homemade product, Hauskäse is of the Limburger type.

HAVARTI (cow)   On her Havarti farm in Denmark, Mrs. Hanne Nielsen developed the recipe for a cheese called Danish Tilsit until its name was changed to Havarti at the Stresa Convention (see below) of European cheesemakers. It has very open texture, tangy flavor, and piquant aftertaste.

HAYONS (cow)   A fresh cheese of Normandy, consumed locally.

HECHO (sheep)   Mountain shepherds of the northern Spain province of Huesca make a rich, savory cheese that has a thin golden crust and a hard white consistency with holes "the size of a bullet."

HERKIMER (cow)   A Cheddar bearing the name of the market town in Herkimer County, New York, had enthusiastic partisans in nineteenth-century America. Today Herkimer is a trademark for factory-made products.

HERRGARDSOST (cow)   Originally made in Swedish farm dairies of the province of Västergötland, Herrgardsost has been compared to various other Swiss-type cheeses and—when it is made with full cream and labeled "Herrgard-Elite"—sometimes rivals Emmenthal. It is now produced in factories throughout Sweden and is the country's most popular cheese. Herrgardsost is sometimes labeled "Manor," which should indicate a farmhouse product.

HERVE (cow)   Named for the Belgian city, Herve is often compared to Limburger or Remoudou because of its strong aroma and flavor. When exported it is subject to stringent government standards.

HOBEL (cow)   In German-speaking cantons of Switzerland the term hobel, meaning a carpenter's plane, is applied to a cheese so hard that a special tool was devised to shave off thin fragments. See Saanen; Sbrinz.

HOCHSTRASSER (cow)   A Hungarian type similar to Limburger and Romadur.

HOFKÄSE (cow) Bavarian farm cheese is now factory produced and exported under this label; it has firm, supple texture and mild flavor suggestive of Tilsit.

HOKKAIDO (cow) A firm cheese somewhat like Cheddar that is Japan's best-known and takes its name from one of the four principal islands, Hokkaido is only one of many imitations of Western dairy products now exported by the Japanese.

HOLANDA (cow) Versions of Dutch cheeses are sold under this label in South America.

HOLSTEINER MAIGERKÄSE (cow) Cylindrical cheeses are made in Schleswig-Holstein from a combination of fat-free milk and butter-milk; the fat content is as little as 15 percent.

HOPFENKÄSE (cow) Also known as Kräuterkäse (a description Swiss apply to herb products like Sapsago), Hopfenkäse means simply "hop cheese," a distinction earned because it is cured between layers of hops. The prepared curd is salted, seasoned with spices such as caraway, and ripened three to four days; then fresh curd is added and the mixture molded into small cylinders.

HRAMSA (cow) The ancient word for a kind of wild garlic has been applied to this very rich and smooth herb-flavored cream cheese produced in Tain, Scotland.

HUSHALLSOST (cow) Cylinder-shaped Swedish cheese of pale color and somewhat open texture.

HUSKER (cow) See Cornhusker.

HYPATA, THESSALY During the second century A.D. in this ancient Greek city the locally made fresh cheeses, according to Lucius Apuleius in *The Golden Ass,* were so exceptional and so famous that traders came from long distances to buy them for resale in the Mediterranean world.

I

IDIAZÁBAL (sheep) Also known as Aralar, Urbasa, or Urbia, Idiazábal is one of Spain's popular mountain cheeses, lightly smoked during initial curing and delicately scented by the wild herbs of the craggy pastureland.

IGNY (cow)   One of France's Trappist products, Igny takes its name from the abbey in the Champagne country.

ILCHESTER (cow)   Mature farmhouse Cheddar blended with beer and herbs, this is a post–World War II innovation named for a village in Somerset.

ÎLE D'ORLÉANS (cow)   A small soft-ripened disk originally made by seventeenth-century farmers in the St. Lawrence valley of Quebec and called Fromage Raffiné, this has its own unique, rather strong flavor; it is made commercially at St. Pierre on the outskirts of Montreal, taking its name from the island on which the city was built.

ILHA (cow)   This hard cheese comes from the islands of the Azores and is sometimes compared with Cheddar or Derby, but is usually somewhat smaller in size.

ILLIEZ (cow)   Like Bagnes and Conches, Illiez is one of the mountain cheeses used by the Swiss for raclette (see below); it is named for the great valley in Valais near the French border.

IMPÉRIAL-FRISCHKÄSE (cow)   A little like Cottage Cheese, this is a popular Austrian product made of skim milk.

INCANESTRATO (cow)   Cheeses thus described in Italian are drained in baskets (see Canestrato).

INCHEVILLE (cow)   A fresh Cream Cheese named for a Norman town.

IRATY (cow, sheep)   Basque shepherds make big flat cylinders of supple cheese that bears the name of a Pyrenees town not far from Roncevaux pass.

ISIGNY (cow)   A fresh Cream Cheese named for a Norman town.

ISLAY (cow)   The southern Scottish island of this name is the home of a popular, firm cheese of the Cheddar type.

ISOLA (cow)   A relative of Gruyère, Isola is made by French dairymen not far from Nice; the wheels are smaller than Gruyère.

ITALICO   As decreed by Mussolini in 1941, this term designates a range of soft cheeses sold under different names; Robiola, Robbiole, and Robbiolini have been included.

J

JACK (cow)   See Monterey; Teleme Jack.

JACKIE (cow)   Danes sometimes use this term for so-called Cream Havarti, or Double Tilsiter.

JARLSBERG (cow)   Originated in Oslo in 1959, this buttery, wide-holed

Norwegian product with a distinctive nutty flavor looks a little like Emmenthal, but on its own merits it has become one of the fastest sellers in many U.S. retail outlets.

JAVORSKI SIR (sheep)   A traditional Serbian cheese still made in Yugoslavia.

JBANE (goat)   The Moroccan name for fresh cheese; it is also applied to cheese that becomes hard after drying on drainage racks made of the African grass called "alfa."

JOCHBERG (cow, goat)   The name comes from the mountain town in Austria's Kitzbuhl where Tyrolian farmers sold their dairy products; the cheese is traditionally about 20 inches in diameter and 4 inches thick.

JONCHÉE (goat, sheep)   This general term for any French fresh cheese sold in woven baskets may include those of Béarn and the Basque country which are made of sheep's milk, those of Brittany infused with laurel, or those made of goat's milk in the region south of Brittany.

JOSEPHINE (cow)   A Silesian soft paste cheese.

JOSSI, JOHN   A Wisconsin cheesemaker of Swiss lineage, Jossi developed the formula for Brick Cheese, accepted as an American original, when he was a producer of Limburger, about 1877; his cheese is now made in several other countries.

JOUX (cow)   See Vacherin.

JUHTÚRÓVAL (cow)   A Hungarian fresh cheese.

K

KAAS   The Dutch word for cheese.

KĂCKAVALJ (sheep)   Kăckavalj is the spelling of the Yugoslavian version of Caciocavallo, the white, hard cheese brought from the East by nomadic tribesmen. Some of the best Kăckavalj takes the name of Pirot, the Serbian border town on the main road from Belgrade to Sophia. It is one of the cheeses cut in cubes (sometimes fried) and served as hors d'oeuvre; when very hard it is grated for cooking.

KAERTHER FLEURIE (cow)   A pliant texture distinguishes this Austrian loaf that has mild flavor but a fresh, pastoral aftertaste; it is often recommended as a cheese to eat with fresh fruit.

KAGGOST (cow)   A Swedish open-textured cylinder, creamy in color and tasting something like Svecia (see below), Kaggost is sometimes seasoned with cumin seeds.

KAJMAK (sheep)   The Turkish word meaning "cream" is applied to a primitive fresh cheese in Yugoslavia where, in the vicinity of Belgrade, it is known as "Serbian butter." Kajmak is also permitted to age, and can develop as much tang and flavor as a good blue cheese in other countries.

KANTER (cow)   A firm, mild-flavored, skim-milk cheese of Holland.

KAREISH (buffalo)   A skim-milk Egyptian product, pickled in salt brine, and resembling Damietta.

KARPAÏTSKI (cow)   Taking its name from the Carpathian region, this is a large, supple Russian cheese that matures in 60 to 70 days.

KARTANO (cow)   A version of Gouda made in Finland.

KÄSE   German word for cheese.

KASER (sheep)   A supple, eastern Turkey ewe's-milk product now made in the same dairy areas as Edirne (see above).

KASHKAVAL, KÁSKAVAL, KATSCHKAVALJ, KATSHKAWLJ (sheep)   Variously spelled, this is a Caciocavallo type produced throughout the Balkans. The ripe curd is heated and becomes plastic, then is molded in wooden or metal frames, cooked in water, and kneaded like bread dough. Kashkaval is shaped in balls, washed in whey, and salted for curing. Balkan Kashkaval, made for export, is pale yellow in color, and—ripened in the Rila, Rhodope, and Balkan Mountains of Bulgaria—has distinctive flavor enhanced by the herbs on which the sheep feed in the high pastures.

KASSERI, KASERI (sheep)   In Greece, and other parts of the Mediterranean, the firm, white, aged Kasseri, mild in flavor and similar to Provolone, is sliced as a table cheese or grilled over charcoal; sometimes it is dipped in flour, fried in very hot oil or butter, then served very hot sprinkled with lemon juice. A U.S. imitation is made of cow's milk.

KAUNAS (cow)   An unsophisticated cheese named for a Lithuanian city and unlikely to be sampled outside the Baltic region.

KAVALJER (cow)   A product of the Swedish province of Värmland and considered a type of Tilsit.

KEBBOCK, KEBBUCK (cow, sheep)   Variously spelled, this ancient Scottish word describes a rustic cheese made of mixtures of cow's and ewe's milks; it is cited by Robert Burns, Walter Scott, and R. L. Stevenson. See Caboc.

KEFALOTYRI (goat, sheep)   This word, spelled a number of ways, is a combination of the Greek for "head" and "cheese," and is descriptive because the shape has made people think of a man's skull or, some say, of his hat. Kefalotyri, similar to Parmesan and Romano, is much used in cooking. It is also found in Syria and has been made by goat farmers in the Ozark Mountains.

KELLE (sheep) One of Turkey's fresh cheeses, sold where it is made.

KENTISH (cow) One of England's legendary farmhouse products that disappeared in what Winston Churchill once called "the mists of time."

KERNHEM (cow) Soft and extremely creamy, Kernhem is a relatively new Dutch dairy product that is dull yellow with a somewhat sticky red-brown crust; its flavor reminds some of a good monastery cheese.

KHACHPURI Small cheese tarts bearing this name are so popular in Russian Georgia that they are sold regularly by street vendors, just as hot dogs are sold in places like New York.

KIBARTAÏ (cow) See Kaunas.

KILMALLOCK (cow) A cheese made in the village of this name in Limerick County, Ireland, was once well known in its homeland.

KING CHRISTIAN IX (cow) See Christian IX.

KIRBY, LYDIA One of the last makers of an American mountain cheese that is semisoft and loose-textured, with edible rind, and similar to English Smallholder (see below). Buttermilk is used as a starter in the Kirby method, the pressed curds are carefully dried for about three days in the sun, then aged in a cool room; texture is moist, somewhat like butter, and the flavor has a mild tang.

KJARSGAARD (cow) Firm, hard, skim-milk cheese made by Danish dairymen.

KLOSTERKÄSE (cow) A German cloister-produced cheese of the Romadur type.

KNAOST (cow) A Norwegian mountain cheese; see Pultost.

KOBIÏSKI (cow, sheep) Cured in brine, Kobiïski comes from the Russian regions of northern Caucasia and Transcaucasia.

KOMET (cow) A semisoft cheese with mild creamy flavor made in Denmark.

KOMINJE KAAS (cow) Dutch name for Leyden; see below.

KÖNIGKÄSE (cow) A German variation of Bel Paese.

KOPANISTI (cow) A soft, creamy, pungent blue-veined cheese, Kopanisti has a peppery butter taste and is good for spreading. One of the best versions is produced on the Greek island of Mikonos in the Aegean Sea. Kopanisti is sometimes canned or bottled.

KOPPEN (goat) See Bauden.

KOSHER CHEESE Because Jewish dietary laws do not permit mixing dairy products with meat, cheeses requiring fermentation of animal rennet are forbidden. Sometimes coagulation occurs through a natural souring process, sometimes through use of vegetable acids.

KOSTROMSKOÏ (cow)   A Russian version of Gouda.

KRASNODARSKI (cow)   Firm and piquant, this Russian cylinder, about 5 inches wide and 10 inches high, is made in the region of Krasnodar on the Black Sea.

KRÄUTERKÄSE (cow)   The German term means "herb cheese"; in Switzerland it is another name for Sapsago.

KREMSTALER (cow)   A strong-smelling Hungarian type.

KRYDDOST (cow)   In Sweden this is an open-textured Svecia type, flavored with cumin or other seeds.

KÜHBACHER (cow)   Made of whole milk and partly skimmed milk, this soft-paste Bavarian product derives its name from a village north of Munich.

KULM (cow)   A Bavarian version of Bel Paese exported in 4-pound wheels, Kulm has mild flavor and full-bodied, creamy texture.

KUMINOST, KUMMINOST (cow)   Various Scandinavian cheeses, seeded with cumin, caraway, or other spices, are known under such names.

KÜMMEL (cow)   The German name for spiced Leyden; see below.

KURT (goat, sheep, yak)   A sun-dried, ball-shaped, extremely hard cheese of Oriental Russian nomads, with the appearance and feel of marble; Kurt's chief virtue is that bits of it can be reconstituted in water, and it has been pointed out that the first makers of Kurt anticipated dry milk by a millennium or two.

KVARG (cow)   Swedish Cottage Cheese; see Quark.

KVARGLI (cow)   An aromatic, fresh cheese made on Hungarian farms.

L

LABEL OF ORIGIN   French laws have been written in the attempt to define the permissible use of various cheese labels and their authentic sources. Thus, "Roquefort" cannot be used for any blue-veined cheese except that produced by members of the Roquefort Society. The word "Camembert," however, had been so misused that a law of definition was considered almost useless. Products that are protected in France must bear the words *appellation d'origine* (see above), and these include Bleu du Haut Jura, which must be made in either Gex or Septmoncel, Gruyère de Comté, Cantal, and St. Nectaire. For other protective regulations regarding European cheeses, see Stresa Convention.

LABNA, LABNEH (goat)   Middle Eastern Cream Cheese; goat's-milk yogurt, from which whey has been drained away, is turned into a very light, soft, creamy white curd cheese, when it is shaped in small balls and rolled in olive oil and paprika. A product of sour milk, it is said to represent a third of the cheese production of Syria.

LAGUIOLE (cow)   Named for a town near France's Aubrac Mountains in the Rouergue region that once produced cheese for the ancient Gauls, today's Laguiole is a natural, brushed-rind cylinder which bears comparison with a good Cantal. It is eaten year round and is much used in cooking—in local rustic soups and in the famous *aligot,* a blending of mashed potatoes and cheese. Traditionally, Soupe au Laguiole, also called Soupe de Mariage, was served the morning after the nuptials in a chamber pot ornamented with an eye emblazoned on its bottom.

LAMIA (goat, sheep)   The market city in central Greece gives its name to a superior cheese made by mountain shepherds of the Roumeli region.

LA-MOTHE-ST.-HÉRAY (goat)   One of the traditional *chèvres* of western France, this takes its name from its market town and looks like a small Camembert wrapped in leaves. Other goat cheeses bearing this name are made in the town's commercial dairy and are shaped variously as logs, pyramids, etc.

LANCASHIRE (cow)   A crumbly, cream-colored cheese with mild flavor that sharpens with age, a well-made Lancashire is considered by Britons to be a splendid accompaniment to biscuits, ideal for toasting, and excellent in many kinds of cooking. It is now almost exclusively produced in factories, but once was made by Lancashire County small landholders who had only a little milk to spare each day, developing as a result a technique of making one large cheese out of three days' milkings. It had the delicate consistency of custard when heated, and could be spread like butter when three months old. Some English cooks preferred farmhouse Lancashire for making Welsh Rabbit (see below).

LANGLOIS (cow)   In the middle of the twentieth century Hans Hanan, in his small dairy in Langlois, Oregon, produced a much admired, veined cheese he called Langlois Blue; he is said to have died without passing on whatever his secret may have been.

LANGRES (cow)   Not unlike Époisses (see above) in character, Langres is made in the shape of a truncated cone; it has delicate, smooth brownish crusts, a strong bouquet, and a pleasantly sharp taste.

LAPLAND (reindeer)   Bearing the name of its homeland, this Arctic product is hard, has large holes, and has been compared to Swiss types of other countries.

LAPPI (cow)   A firm cheese made in Finland factories.

LARRON D'ORS (cow)   One of Belgium's assertive cheeses described as "a sort of Maroilles" (see below); it matures in six to eight weeks.

LARUNS (sheep)   One of the best of Pyrenees wheels, comparable to Oloron (see below). Laruns has a firm texture and a mild nutty flavor when three months old, and it is used for cooking when it has aged and becomes hard.

LATVIÏSKI (cow)   A sharp, sourish, Russian rectangular loaf.

LAUMES (cow)   There are some green pastures in France's Côte d'Or wine country, and one of the results is a brick-shaped cheese that is washed with Burgundy (or sometimes coffee); the aroma of Laumes is penetrating, and the taste is often slightly smoky.

LAVAL (cow)   Near the French city of Laval is the abbey of the same name at which Trappist monks make a creamy disk sometimes labeled "Abbaye de Laval," sometimes "Trappiste de Laval."

LEDER (cow)   Made from skim milk, with buttermilk added, this Schleswig-Holstein product is much like Holsteiner Maigerkäse (see above).

LEICESTER (cow)   In the old days the flagrant orange color that makes this the brightest hued of English cheeses was the result of an addition of carrot juice; today, however, the tint comes from annatto. Before World War II a blue-veined Leicester was one of England's "noble cheeses" and rivaled Stilton. According to Henry Stevens in *Cheddar Gorge,* the color of ordinary red Leicesters, "like the lips of most ladies nowadays, is admittedly not quite natural, but their sweetness (I mean the cheeses') is unimpaired." Leicester is rather crumbly in texture, but its flavor, when farmhouse-made, is mellow.

LE MOINE (cow)   Monks at the Abbey of St. Benoit du Lac, in Brome County, southern Quebec, make three kinds of cheese, including a hearty Port Salut type that bears this name and is sold at the monastery shop as well as at retail Canadian outlets.

LESCIN (sheep)   Russian shepherds devised this cheese by milking directly into skin sacks, adding rennet, and draining the curds in usual ways; after being pressed in a form the cheese is wrapped in leaves and bound with grass ropes, then matured about a fortnight before being set aside for final curing.

LEUTGEB, IGNAZ   Horn player and friend of both Leopold and W. A. Mozart, Leutgeb moonlighted by running a cheesemonger's shop in a Vienna suburb which was described by the elder Mozart as "the size of a snail's house."

LEYDEN, LEIDEN (cow)   Genuine Leyden is one of Holland's classic dairy achievements, bearing the arms of the city of Leiden (two keys crossed), north of Rotterdam. Pressed in circular forms after caraway has been added to the curds, the wheels are usually 14 to 16 inches in diameter, 3 to 4 inches thick, and weigh 1 to 12 pounds. Cloves or cumin or anise or all three may sometimes be added. See Nagelkaas.

LIEDERKRANZ (cow)   A soft-ripened product developed by Emil Frey and considered by many gastronomes to be the best U.S. cheese. See Chapter 7.

LIMBURGER (cow)   The strongest of the bacteria surface-ripened cheeses was first made in the Belgian town for which it is named, near Liège. A good deal is made in Bavaria, and it has been produced by German dairymen for so long that it is often supposed to be German. Americans make good versions in Illinois, New York, and Wisconsin.

LIPSKI (cow)   A Serbian version of Port Salut made in Yugoslavia.

LIPTÓ (sheep)   From Liptó in northern Hungary, this is the prototype of sheep cheeses made in the mountains of Central Europe under such other names as Altsohl, Bryndza (Brynza, Brindza, or Brinsen), Ftinoporino, Landoch, Neusohl, Siebenburger, Zips. Liptó lends its name to the cheese spread called Liptauer, or *Liptauer garniert,* which is seasoned with caraway, onion, and paprika, sometimes with anchovies, capers, and various other flavors. Rich Hungarians, George Lang says in his *The Cuisine of Hungary,* have been known to gild the lily with a topping of Beluga caviar.

LISIEUX (cow)   A small version of Livarot. See just below.

LIVAROT (cow)   Famous as one of Normandy's remarkable cheeses, this takes its name from the market town of a region which produces, according to 1971 statistics, 1,700,000 rectangular cakes every year; they have smooth, glossy, dark-brown rinds and a satisfying assertive flavor.

LOCKERBIE (cow)   In the dairy country north of Solway Firth, the name of a Scottish market town is given to a local Cheddar-like loaf packed in 10- and 40-pound blocks.

LODIGIANO (cow)   Parmesan-type wheels made around the northern Italy city of Lodi, these are dark and slightly oily on the outside, pale yellow inside with largish holes. They are cured as long as four years, and the flavor is piquant but not quite as strong as other *granas.*

LOMBARDO (cow)   Smaller than Lodigiano, Lombardo is a *grana* type made in the same province.

LONGHORN (cow)   Sometimes American Cheddar is sold under this label—a term which refers to size and shape; according to USDA standards Longhorns should be 6 inches in diameter, 13 inches long, and weigh 12 to 13 pounds. See Cheddar.

LOR (sheep)   A provincial Turkish fresh cheese.

LORMES (cow, goat)   In the French village of this name traditional cow's-milk disks look like Camemberts, and goat's milk is shaped in delicate, bluish-rinded truncated cones that are highly esteemed by connoisseurs.

LORRAINE (cow)   A flat cylinder typical of the region that also produces the more famous Géromé and Munster.

LOS BELLOS (goat, sheep)   Known also as Bellusco, Los Bellos cheese is a product of Asturias on Spain's northern coast and is lightly smoked during initial maturation; it has strong flavor, pungent aroma, is nearly white inside and dark yellow outside.

LOS PEDROCHES (sheep)   These small ewe's-milk flattened balls are ancient products of the Valle de los Pedroches, near Cordova, Spain; ready to eat after a month or so, they are usually immersed in olive oil after three months to ensure longer preservation.

LOU PALOU (cow)   One of the black-rinded wheels from Pyrenees mountain pastures, this country cheese is now produced in quantity in cheese factories and has become popular on both sides of the Atlantic. It is supple and has a pleasant, creamy texture and mild tang.

LOUBITELSKI (cow)   This is a Russian version of Camembert.

LOUR (sheep)   Shepherds of Iraq make a fresh whey cheese locally known by this name.

LUCULLUS (cow)   Trade name of a French type containing 75 percent fat.

LUNEBERG (cow)   Milk, colored with saffron, is prepared in the Austrian province of Voralberg by old Swiss methods and transformed into a cheese which has characteristics of both Limburger and Emmenthal.

M

MACQUÉE (cow)   A skim-milk cheese made in Belgium in soft, brick-shaped rectangles.

MACQUELINES (cow)   Sometimes called Brie de Macquelines, this French product is made of partly skimmed milk by Vosges farmers and resembles a Coulommiers or a Camembert but is less rich.

MACZOLA (cow)   An Australian copy of Gorgonzola made at Frederickton, New South Wales; the name combines the first syllable of the nearby Macleay River and the last two of the Italian town.

MAGERER SCHWEIZERKÄSE (cow)   A "lean Swiss cheese," as its name indicates; it is produced from skim milk that is not pressed quite as much as the Swiss classic rounds.

MAGGIAKÄSE (cow) A mountain type produced by dairymen of the Maggia Valley in the canton of Ticino which is sold locally.

MAGNUM (cow) Like Excelsior (see above), Magnum is a triple-cream Normandy type that has 75 percent fat, a very soft paste, and a downy rind; it is 5½ inches in diameter, 1½ inches thick, and weighs usually just over 1 pound.

MAGYARÓVÁR (cow) A Gruyère type produced in the Hungarian city of that name.

MAHÓN (cow, sheep) It takes its name from the port city of Mahón on the island of Minorca, and it has become a favorite among visitors to the Balearics, where it has been produced since prehistoric times. Today Mahón has a cow's-milk base with 4 to 8 percent sheep's milk occasionally mixed in; it is ready to eat after 20 days but can be cured up to a year if coated with olive oil. The 2- to 3-pound squares have rounded corners and a brownish-yellow skin.

MAIGRELET (cow) A skim-milk, semisoft cheese made in Quebec.

MAILE (sheep) In the Crimea Russian dairymen still make a briny cheese by molding curds and keeping them in a salt solution for as long as one year. When rennet is added it is called Maile Pener, meaning fat cheese, and it develops a crumbly, open texture and satisfying taste.

MAINAUER (cow) The island of Mainau, in the German part of Lake Constance, gives its name to a Munster-like cheese cured four to five months. See Radolfzeller.

MAINZER (cow) One of the "Hand" Cheeses (see above) of Germany, taking its name from the Hessian city of Mainz, this is made from sour milk and is sometimes cured in kegs or jars, usually with the addition of cumin.

MAIORCHINO (sheep) A firm sheep's-milk round produced by dairymen around Catania, Sicily.

MALAGA (goat) The milk of Spanish goats that graze on the mountains above Malaga produces a soft but firm round with a flat top and bottom that is cream-colored inside and has a yellow skin.

MALAKOFF (cow) Despite its Russian name, Malakoff is one of the rich white cheeses belonging to the Neufchâtel group (see below).

MAMIROLLE (cow) The French dairy school at Mamirolle, not far from the northern Swiss border, has created a version of Limburger sold under the school's name; it is rectangular, usually weighing a little over 1 pound, and has a delicate reddish rind. Surprisingly, it has no smell to speak of, yet offers hearty flavor.

MANCHEGO (sheep)   Produced in the Don Quixote country of Spain with an annual output of more than 5 million pounds, Manchego is popular throughout the country, and now much exported. Farmers preserve the straw-colored wheels in olive oil, while factories use paraffin; the mature product is flavorful and rich in nourishment.

MANICAMP (cow)   Manicamp, a village in Flanders not far from St. Quentin, gives its name to this very strong type, similar to Maroilles (see below).

MANOORI (goat, sheep)   A soft white cheese from Crete and Macedonia which is eaten with honey by Kretiki islanders and others; when flavored with dill it is known locally as *anthotyro*.

MANTECA, MANTECHE (buffalo, cow)   Made in various shapes in the Italian region of Basilicata, Manteca is a bland cheese with a heart of pure butter. Known also as Buriello, Burrino, Burro, and Butirro, it sometimes has a base of Caciocavallo, Mozzarella, or Provolone, and the shape is often that of an irregular gourd, but it may be rectangular or ball-shaped; sometimes the surface is smoked. The sweet butter inside is preserved by being sealed off from air, which made Manteca popular in hot southern Italy, with its lack of refrigeration.

MANUR (cow, sheep)   Serbian farmers in Yugoslavia produce Manur by heating whole milk and adding it to buttermilk, fresh whey, and rennet, then draining off the curds to be kneaded before salting; it is ready to eat after it has dried.

MARCEOLINUS   In ancient Etruria this was the name given by Etruscans to cheese made annually in the month of March.

MAREDSOUS (cow)   A soft supple loaf made by monks of the abbey of this name in Belgium, Maredsous is often compared to St. Paulin (see below) and is usually exported in rectangular blocks.

MARE'S-MILK CHEESE   Nomads of the Middle Ages are reported to have made a type similar to Caciocavallo (see above), using the milk of horses. For some, this explains why Italians used the term "horse cheese" in the first place.

MARGOTIN (cow)   Trade name of a rich creamy type produced in Périgord. See Chapter 11.

MARIBO (cow)   A mild Danish cheese that becomes firmer and tangier as it is aged as much as a year or two; when caraway seeds are added it is known as the genuine King Christian IX (see Christian IX above) and is considered by many Scandinavians as one of the truly superb cheeses of the world. It is also produced in Iceland, where Maribo Kümen is the term when caraway is added.

MARIENHOFER (cow)   A Tyrolian answer to Limburger made in the Austrian tourist-land of Carinthia, this assertive type takes its name from the village of Marienhofer-Pichler.

MARMORA (cow)   A Danish blue-veined wheel.

MAROILLES, MAROLLES (cow)   A strong-smelling, assertive-in-flavor cheese that has been made in Picardy since its invention by a monk at the Abbey of Maroilles, it was this beloved French cheese for which a pontifical mass was celebrated in the town church on its 1,000th birthday in May 1961. It is said to have been the favorite cheese of Philip Augustus and other French kings, and it roused Curnonsky, the Prince of Gourmets, to proclaim that "its thunderous savor resounds like the voice of the saxophone in the symphony of cheeses!" A traditional Maroilles is about 5 inches square, 2½ inches thick, and weighs about 1¾ pounds, and its production is limited by French law prohibiting the use of the name outside the region.

MAROMME (cow)   Taking its name from a market town near Rouen, Maromme is a variety of Neufchâtel once common in Normandy.

MASCARPONE (cow)   A fresh cheese with a large-curd consistency produced in Lombardy, Tuscany, and southern Switzerland, Mascarpone has a sweet yet slightly acid taste. (In England it has been compared to Devonshire clotted cream.) Sometimes lemon juice is used in the making of Mascarpone, and when finished it is served with fruit or sprinkled with cinnamon. In the Trieste area it is mixed with Gorgonzola, anchovies, caraway, leeks, and mustard to produce something quite like Hungarian Liptó cheese spread.

MATKI SER (cow)   A Polish-style Farmer Cheese (see above) that is sometimes called Mothers Cheese; a caraway-seeded version is produced in Scottville, Michigan.

MATURATION   A cheesemakers' term for the period of chemical change that must be undergone before cheeses are ready to eat.

MECKLENBURG SKIM (cow)   Named for the German province on the Baltic Sea, Mecklenburg is a hard, skim-milk, salt-ripened round, not widely distributed.

MEDYNSKI (cow)   Soft, supple, and formed in rectangular blocks, Medynski is a Russian pasteurized cheese product that reminds one of Limburger.

MEIRA (sheep)   Said to be the largest-selling cheese in Baghdad markets,

Meira is drained under pressure, then salted and matured for six months to a year in sheepskin. See Roos.

MERSEY VALLEY (cow)   An Australian product said to combine the best qualities of Cheddar, Edam, and Gouda, made in Burnie, Tasmania.

MESHANGER (cow)   A soft, cylindrical Dutch cheese that melts easily bears this name; it has a thin yellow crust and a creamy yellow center.

MESITRA (sheep)   A Crimean cheese that is usually eaten fresh in Russia, but is also sometimes salted and pressed slightly. See Mezithra.

MESOST (cow)   Lightly brown in color, with a buttery consistency, Mesost is a soft, unripened Swedish product composed of caramelized lactose, fat, proteins, and minerals from the whey which is its base; the flavor is milky and sweetish, recalling Norway's Gjetost.

METTON (cow)   In the making of Cancoillotte (see above), dairymen in eastern France use Metton as a base; the term applies specifically to the hard, grainy product resulting when skim-milk curds are recooked.

MEZITHRA (goat, sheep)   White and mild, Mezithra is delicious when fresh, and is used in Greece as a grating cheese when aged. It is virtually identical to Mitzithra, a pot cheese made by shepherds in the Athens region from the whey remaining from the production of Feta.

MI-CHÈVRE   French products so labeled must have a minimum of 25 percent goat's milk, which usually provides a little of the flavor of a true *chèvre* (see above) if not the characteristic consistency.

MICH, MISH (cow)   Egyptian farmers make salty (perhaps the world's saltiest), grayish cheese by mixing curds and a little mature Mich and putting it away to age one year; it is served with thin pastry as a rustic "cocktail dip."

MIGNON (cow)   A smaller version of Maroilles.

MIHALIC   Turkish term for fresh cheese.

MILANO (cow)   See Bella Milano.

MILLSEN (cow)   A soft cheese of ancient Ireland.

MIMOLETTE (cow)   A flattened sphere of deeply orange-colored pressed curd, Mimolette originated in the Dutch province of Noordholland and is now made in Flanders, Belgium, and other parts of northern Europe. When mature it develops a sharp, interesting flavor, but is more often sold when mild and semisoft; the name derives from the soft texture of the paste. Some American cheesemongers erroneously identify it with Cheddar.

MINAS (cow)   In the cattle country of the Brazilian province of Minas Gerais farmers make white cheese that is sometimes aged, becoming hard and yellow.

MINNESOTA SLIM (cow)   A moist, loose-textured loaf developed by University of Minnesota dairy experts and given its name by Lund's Market in Minneapolis, through which it gained attention. Annatto gives the paste a bright orange hue, and the soft, resilient consistency lends itself to melting; it has been used to give more piquancy to homemade pizza.

MINTZITRA (sheep)   A soft Macedonian cheese; see Mezithra.

MISCHLING (cow)   A highly pungent product of Austria's western mountains.

MITCHELSTOWN (cow)   One of the versions of Cheddar, it takes its name from an important dairy center in County Cork, Ireland.

MITZITHRA (goat, sheep)   See Mezithra. Greek cooks away from home commonly use Ricotta as a substitute.

MOLBO (cow)   A relative of Samsoe, once called Danish Edam, Molbo is shaped like a ball and painted red; it is made in the region of Mols in the Danish province of Randers.

MOLITERNO (cow, sheep)   A strong, yellowish cheese made in the southern Italy region of Lucania, Moliterno somewhat resembles Caciocavallo (see above) and takes its name from a mountain village; sheep's-milk versions are called Pecorino Moliterno.

MON CARRÉ (cow)   A vanished Normandy fresh cheese.

MONCENISIO (cow)   Made in the highlands west of Torino and much like Gorgonzola; for French version produced across the border see Persillé.

MONDSEER (cow)   A strong-smelling Munster type originally made from whole or partly skimmed milk in the Salzburg region, Mondseer Schachtelkäse is so called because dairymen of the Mond lake area packed their pungent wheels in *schachteln* (boxes). Mondseer Schlosskäse (see Schloss) is richer and creamier.

MONOSTORER (sheep)   A Romanian pressed wheel made in Transylvania; it matures in eight to ten weeks after frequent washings in salt water.

MONSIEUR FROMAGE (cow)   About the turn of the century a Normandy farmer whose surname was Fromage developed a small cylinder with about 60 percent fat which has been perfected since and is established as a classic double-cream type.

MONT D'OR (cow, goat)   Made solely with goat's milk when available and at other times with a mixture of cow's and goat's milk, Mont d'Or once was looked upon as one of the treasures of Lyon, one of France's great gastronomic centers. It is a small flat disk with a bluish skin flecked with red.

MONTAÑA (goat)   One of Spain's fresh, goat types made in the Camerano mountains and ready to eat in 24 hours, Montaña is small and round. Sometimes it is wrapped in cloth to preserve it for about one week.

MONTASIO (cow)   Like Asiago and Bitto (see both above), Montasio may be eaten young as a table cheese or aged for use as a condiment; it originated in the thirteenth century at Moggia Monastery and was probably then a sheep cheese.

MONTAVONER (cow)   A sour-milk Austrian cheese flavored with herbs.

MONT-CENIS, MONTECENISIO (cow, goat)   Respectively, French and Italian names for the blue-veined cheeses made on either side of the Savoy frontier, sometimes referred to as Persillé (see below).

MONTEREY (cow)   Commonly called Monterey Jack, the cheese that originated in Monterey County, California, is considered indigenous to the U.S. It was known as *queso del pais* when first made in the seventeenth-century Spanish missions, but its manufacture was developed by other immigrants, among them a Scot named David Jacks whose surname was coupled with that of the nearest shipping point. Early in the twentieth century the increasing popularity of Monterey Jack brought about mass production of the high-moisture variety (see Chapter 2) in factories using methods similar to those that turn out Colby. Dry Monterey, or Dry Jack, is made from skimmed milk or partly skimmed milk and is cured six months or more.

MONTRACHET (goat)   Creamy log shapes produced in Burgundy wine country have become among the most popular of exported goat cheeses; some are dusted in edible vegetable cinders, some are plain white.

MORBIER (cow)   Distinguished by a dark horizontal line (mistaken sometimes for a vein of blue mold) because the original formula used morning and evening milkings, separating the respective curds with a layer of edible ash; Morbier is a French mountain type from the Jura with somewhat mild flavor but piquant aftertaste.

MORNAY, SAUCE   It is the opinion of the editors of *Guide Gourmand de la France* that the classic cheese sauce "was dedicated without doubt" to a nineteenth-century chef "who carried this name." At any rate, it seems agreed that the addition of grated Parmesan and Gruyère to sauce béchamel was first accomplished by Chef Joseph Voiron, who presided at Paris's Restaurant Durand during the late nineteenth century.

MORÓN (cow, goat, sheep)   Named for the town of Morón de la Frontera, not far from Seville, this flattened ball is made of cow's milk sometimes mixed with a little ewe's milk, or entirely of goat's milk.

The cheeses weigh between 3 and 5 pounds and are ready to be eaten after 24 hours; if they are kept more than a week they are immersed in olive oil and rubbed with paprika before shipment to markets throughout most of Spain.

MORVEN (cow)   Taking its name from the mountain in Caithness, Scotland's most northern mainland county, Morven is sometimes compared to German Butterkäse. Spreadable, it is often seeded with caraway.

MOSKOVSKI (cow)   A Russian pressed cheese of piquant flavor.

MOSSHOLDER (cow)   Mild semisoft cheese made near Appleton, Wisconsin, by Mossholder family; it is said to have originated when methods for making Emmenthal, Brick, and Cheddar were combined. Five-pound rectangular loaves are sold by mail.

MOTAL (cow, sheep)   Farmers in Russia's Caucasus Mountains make a briny cheese under this name, and it is consumed locally.

MOTHAIS (goat)   The term is applied generically to farmhouse products in the La-Mothe-St.-Héray (see above) area.

MOTHERS (cow)   Farmer Cheese of Central Europe, once made in kitchens by women, is sometimes so designated. See Matki Ser.

MOZZARELLA (buffalo, cow)   White and soft, this spun-curd buffalo cheese is appreciated by Italians when it is at its freshest, immediately after making, and it is much used in their traditional cuisine. Now produced mostly from cow's milk, it is a pleasing table cheese with a pungent lactic taste when made by hand, but the name also applies to a rubbery factory-made product intended for pizza and other cooking uses. Mozzarella Affumicata is smoked.

MULCHAN, MULLHAWN (cow)   A cheese made from skim milk once marketed in Waterford, and perhaps other parts of Ireland.

MUNSTER (cow)   Shopping for Munster presents difficulties; it may be spelled Muenster, Münster, even Mynster (see below). The word "munster" is related to "monastery," and in France the use of it is protected by decree, under the "label of origin" law (see above). It must be made on farms in the province of Alsace in the same craftsmanlike way that monks employed as early as the seventh century; true Munster is semisoft and, as the French would say, unctuous. It develops a brick-red skin but not the runny quality of Brie or even Camembert, and it has spicy, tangy flavor and penetrating aroma. In France Munster Laitier is made in commercial dairies. Other factory Munster is made in many countries, including the U.S., where, according to "Standards of Identity" law, "Muenster" is considered a semisoft cheese that has not undergone any surface ripening—the result is bland, not a bit unctuous.

MUNSTER-PLATE   A large piece of strong creamy cheese served in Strasbourg and other European gastronomic havens with a bowl of finely minced raw onion, some caraway seeds, and good, fresh, crusty bread—and beer rather than wine.

MUNTANACCIU (sheep)   One of the rustic shepherd cheeses of Corsica, Muntanacciu comes from the mountains near Venaco; it is made in midsummer and consumed about the time the grapes ripen in October.

MUROL (cow)   A flat disk with a hole in the center, Murol is named for an Auvergne town where Jules Berioux developed the shape as a new form of St. Nectaire (see below).

MUTSCHLI (cow)   Produced of whole milk in the mountains of northern and eastern Switzerland, Mutschli is mild, semisoft in texture, and used in making raclette; it is the smallest of Switzerland's wheel-shaped cheeses, weighing from ½ to 2 pounds.

MYCELLA (cow)   Borrowing its name from *mycelium* (mushroom filaments), which produces green veins, Mycella was called Danish Gorgonzola until the Stresa Convention (see below), at which restrictions for the use of established names were agreed upon. Mycella has the same creamy color of Gorgonzola and is considered by Scandinavians an acceptable substitute for Stilton. It is sometimes packaged in foil-covered wedges.

MYNSTER (cow)   Denmark's version of Munster is a wheel usually weighing between 8 and 10 pounds, about 8 inches in diameter, and 3 inches high. It has a dry, yellowish rind, sometimes waxed, a creamy firm consistency that varies from white to yellow, and mild flavor. See Munster.

MYSINGER (cow)   Packed in plastic jars, Mysinger is a soft, brown, easy-to-spread whey product that is flavored with caramel and has about 15 percent fat content. It is made in Iceland.

MYSOST (cow)   A nationally popular cheese in each of the Scandinavian countries, and also produced in the U.S., Mysost is a caramelized product, not unlike Gjetost; it often contains cinnamon, cloves, cumin, and brown sugar.

MYSUOST (cow)   Icelandic dairymen make this whey product in three ways—hard-pressed varieties containing, respectively, 33 percent and 7 percent fat, and a soft version of varying fat content.

N

NAGELKAAS (cow)   A Dutch skim-milk type, seasoned with cumin and sometimes cloves; a similar loaf is sold in America as Spice Cheese.

NANTAIS (cow)   See Curé.

NATTE RABINALE (cow)   A fresh, creamy type made in Holland just before summer starts and sometimes known as May cheese.

NAUVOO BLUE (cow)   A subtly veined blue admired by many Americans, Nauvoo was developed shortly before World War II by Oscar Rohde through use of caves (abandoned by a brewery) that reached back into cliffs above the Mississippi River at Nauvoo, an Illinois town built by Mormons a century earlier.

NAZARETH BLUE (cow)   A factory product of Israeli cheesemakers.

NEUFCHÂTEL (cow)   The town of Neufchâtel-en-Bray is one of the oldest markets for Normandy cheese, and its name has identified one of the best-known Cream Cheeses for many generations; they are small and vary in shape—sometimes rectangular, sometimes heart-shaped, sometimes cylindrical. American Neufchâtel is smoother, more like U.S. commercial Cream Cheese, but with less butterfat.

NEW YORK (cow)   The term is applied to Cheddar produced in 40-odd plants in New York and is a common designation in the South, particularly for aged American Cheddar.

NEWMARKET (cow)   A firm type taking its name from a market town in County Cork, Ireland.

NIEHEIMER (cow)   West German dairymen make several cheeses from sour cream, one of which is named for Nieheim, a Westphalian town. Like Hopfenkäse (see above), it is cured between layers of hops, then broken up and mixed with caraway seeds, milk, or sometimes beer, before aging.

NIELSEN, HANNE   Heroine of the Danish dairy industry, Mrs. Nielsen canvassed Europe in the nineteenth century in search of new techniques for making various cheese types. She is often given credit for the wide selection now produced in Denmark, and the name of the place from which she started her explorations has been given to the cheese now known as Havarti.

NIOLO (goat, sheep)   Named for a Corsican plateau, Niolo is produced by herdsmen who drain curds in baskets before the cheese is cured in brine for three to four months.

NIVA (cow)   A Czechoslovakian blue cheese.

NIZA (goat, sheep)   One of the rustic mountain cheeses of Portugal, Niza is similar to Serra and is seldom found far from home.

NÖKKELOST (cow)   The Norwegian word for "key" is applied to this product because it is a copy of Leyden, the Dutch cheese that traditionally has been stamped with the hallmark of the city of Leyden; caraway, cloves, and cumin are usually added to skim-milk curds.

NORBO (cow)   A holey cheese, with rosy, fat paste and a yellow rind; a Norway product.

NORMANNA (cow)   A creamy, somewhat piquant soft-ripened cheese to be found in Norway, usually in small portions wrapped in foil.

NOSTRALE (cow)   Loosely, the Italian term means "ours" and is applied to rustic types produced around Cuneo, Italy; they are further distinguished as *formaggini* when fresh and *caciotta* when mature.

NOTRE-DAME (cow)   A name once used for one of Normandy's fresh cheeses.

NOTRE DAME DE BONNE ESPÉRANCE (cow)   A semisoft, tangy wheel of the Echourgnac type (see above), described in Périgord as a product of *"les soeurs."*

NOVO-OUKRAÏNSKI (cow)   A pear-shaped Russian type from Ukraine.

NUWORLD (cow)   A white-mold type developed by dairy scientists at the universities of Minnesota and Wisconsin after World War II.

O

OAXACA, QUESILLO DE (cow)   Soft, braided, slightly acid, "the little cheese of Oaxaca," named for the mountainous state south of Mexico City, is much used in cooking and considered particularly suitable for stuffing chilies and making *quesodillas* (cheese-filled tortillas).

ODALSOST (cow)   Icelandic dairymen describe Odalsost as a variety of the original Emmenthal, although it has no rind and is much smaller, weighing 22 to 24 pounds; it has distinctive flavor and is rather chewy.

ODEN (cow)   A firm, mild-to-sharp Icelandic type.

OELENBERG (cow)   A Trappist type weighing 3 pounds or slightly less, Oelenberg takes its name from an Alsatian monastery; it is mild and supple, with a smooth, pale-yellow rind.

OKA (cow)   When French monks established a monastery at La Trappe, Quebec, in 1881, they brought with them a recipe for making a Port Salut type, and their product has developed its own very pleasing characteristics. Made near the small town of Oka, it is available in Montreal, but supplies elsewhere are undependable because of the demand.

OLD HEIDELBERG (cow)   Somewhat like Liederkranz, Old Heidelberg is a soft-ripened 4-ounce rectangle made by the Kolb family in Lena, Illinois.

OLENDA (cow)   Meaning Hollander, or Dutch, in Italian, Olenda is the name given a copy of sphere-shaped Netherlands products.

OLIVET BLEU (cow)   The same cheese of the Loire Valley that is often sold fresh gets its blue exterior much the way Camembert develops its floury rind; aged on straw mats, the salted curds become filmed with bacteria of reddish hue and a blue cast appears when mature. A drier version of Olivet is given a protective coating of vegetable ash and is known in France as Olivet Cendré.

OLMÜTZER (cow)   A smelly "Hand" Cheese (see above), finished variously, including the addition of seeds, Olmützer takes its name from the city on the Morava River in Central Europe.

OLOMOUC (cow)   The Czechoslovakian name for Olmützer.

OLORON (sheep)   Made in shepherds' huts in the French Pyrenees, Oloron is much like Esbareich (see above). Oloron is named for a Basque market town where the annual cheese fair is held in September.

OPIAS TYROS (goat)   In the fifth century B.C. this cheese was curdled by the juice (*opos*) of fig trees.

ORKNEY (cow)   In the days of Dr. Johnson's travels with Boswell, country people of the Orkney Islands made cheese and let it ripen in oat bins (see Caboc). Today Orkney is a hard white cheese of mild Gaelic character that is sometimes smoked; it is occasionally exported to the U.S., where it has been compared, rather loosely, to Caerphilly.

ORSERA (cow)   The Italian name for the mild, rustic cheese that originated in southern Switzerland.

ORSIÈRES (cow)   Taking its name from a Swiss town near the border with France, Orsière is one of the fine wheels used for making raclette (see below).

ORVAL (cow)   A monastery type produced at a Belgian abbey of this name.

OSSETIN (cow, sheep)   Also called Ossetinski, Touchinski, Tuchinsk, and Kasach, this Caucasian briny cheese is considered best when it is made of ewe's milk, and is softer and milder if left in salt solution no more than two months.

OST   Scandinavian word for cheese.

OSTIEPKY (sheep)   Spelled in a variety of ways—Oscypki, Oschtjepek, Oschtkepka, Ostyepka—this name is applied to mountain cheeses of Central Europe, traditionally produced from sheep's milk. The Slovakian version is comparable to Caciocavallo (see above). A lightly smoked "Ostyepka" is made in the shape of a baby ham and, along with one labeled "Smoked Ostiepky," is imported by Paprikas Weiss of New York.

OUGLITCHSKI (cow)   A nonpressed Russian cheese.

OURDA (cow, sheep)   One of Romania's rustic white cheeses, often flavored with wild herbs.

OUST (cow)   A village in the central Pyrenees gives its name to this Camembert-like cheese.

OUSTED, OUSTET (cow)   A hard-pressed Pyrenees type.

OVCJI SIR (sheep)   A salt-cured hoop type from the Slovenian Alps.

OVELHEIRA (goat, sheep)   From Portugal's central mountains, Ovelheira is sometimes oval-shaped, sometimes small and round.

OVOLI (cow)   Small, egg-shaped Mozzarella (see above).

OXFORDSHIRE (cow)   Almost forgotten, Oxfordshire once turned up in eighteenth-century writings referring mostly to its stalwart aroma.

℘

PAGLIA (cow)   The word means "straw" in Italian, and the cheese is made in Switzerland's Italian-speaking region; it is aged on straw in cool caves and is wheel-shaped, about 8 inches in diameter and 2 inches thick.

PAGLIARINO (cow)   Yellowish, straw-colored, and a purely local Piedmont product, Pagliarino is strong in flavor and eaten with oil and pepper.

PAGO (sheep)   On the island of Pag, off the west coast of Yugoslavia, shepherds make a rustic cheese varying from ½ to 8 pounds in size.

PAILLOR (cow)   Described as a cross between Limburger and Pont l'Évêque, and produced in central France, Paillor is a recent factory product with musty pungency.

PANEDDA (cow)   See Casigliolo.

PANELA (cow)   A fresh Mexican white cheese; see Queso Blanco.

PANNARONE, PANNERONE (cow)   The Italian word panna (cream) is accented in the name of this rich relative of Gorgonzola, sometimes also called Gorgonzola Bianco or Gorgonzola Dolce; it has no visible mold and is found locally in Lombardy.

PANNONIA (cow)   Hungarian dairymen make this yellow cheese that has extremely strong and unusual flavor; it is punctuated by tiny holes and comes in cylinders weighing about 80 pounds.

PARENICA (sheep)   Sometimes spelled Parenitza, the word is used for Caciocavallo types made in Czechoslovakia and Hungary.

PARENYICA (sheep)   Importers like Paprikas Weiss in New York sell a so-called ribbon cheese from Hungary under this name; the curd is fashioned in long narrow strips that are wound in bolts and lightly smoked.

PARMESAN (cow)   The French and English term for Parmigiano, the hard cheese taking its name from Parma, Italy (see Grana). "Italians," T. A. Layton wrote, "take as much care in maturing a good Grana as French peasants take to produce a fine wine." The good cheese from Parma is now known by Italian law as Parmigiano-Reggiano, but the term Parmesan is used commonly in many countries, including the U.S., for grating types that do not have the quality demanded in the original. Genuine Parmesan (which must be indelibly labeled "Parmigiano-Reggiano") is two to three years old, shaped in wheels that weigh a minimum of 53 pounds 13 ounces and a maximum of 88 pounds.

PARMIGIANO (cow)   See Parmesan.

PARTÉ (cow)   A bland, semisoft, factory-made Swedish counterpart of Havarti.

PASIEGO PRENSADO (cow, sheep)   From Valle del Pas and other areas of the Spanish province of Santander, Pasiego Prensado is a pressed round of cow's-milk curds, occasionally mixed with a little ewe's milk, that is ready to eat after ten days; its flavor is subtle, its texture supple and creamy, its color yellowish white. An unpressed fresh version is called Pasiego sin Prensar.

PASKI SIR (cow)   A Yugoslavian imitation of Parmesan.

PASSE L'AN (cow)   During a period when shipments to France of Italian *granas* were cut off, French dairymen experimented with formulas for duplicating Parmesan; the result is Passe l'An, one of several imitations made in several parts of France.

PASSENDALE (cow)   Called *bloc noir* by the monks who produce it at the monastery of St. Bernard de Passendale, Belgium, Passendale has a black rind as the result of a formula treatment that is closely guarded; the interior is somewhat moist and the flavor has been compared to a strong Gouda.

PASTA FILATA   The Italian words meaning "spun paste"—or plastic curd —refer to the cheeses resulting when whey is drained away and the curd immersed immediately in hot water or hot whey, then is kneaded and stretched, and molded while the consistency is plastic. The category includes Caciocavallo, Mozzarella, Provatura, Provolone, Scamorze, and others.

PASTORELLA (cow)   A smaller-size Bel Paese (see above) is made in Lombardy and known under this name; in Australia "Pastorello" is a brand name for a white semihard type suitable for cooking or as a table cheese and produced at Parramatta, New South Wales.

PATAGRAS (cow)   A Latin American type, based on Dutch cheesemaking techniques.

PAVÉ D'AUGE (cow)   Large, flat, rectangular cakes closely related to Pont l'Évêque are marketed under this name. See Pavé de Moyaux.

PAVÉ DE MOYAUX (cow)   Because of the likeness in shape to that of ancient paving stones, several cheeses long made in Moyaux and other parts of Normandy are called *pavés;* they are closely related to Pont l'Évêque (see below), having great pungency. *Pavés* in the form of a truncated cone are also made of goat's milk in Valencay and elsewhere in central France.

PECORINO (sheep)   About 15 percent of all cheese in Italy is made from sheep's milk and classified as *pecorino,* which derives from the word for sheep. In such countries as Australia, Canada, and the U.S. the term is used for imitations produced from cow's milk. Italy's most common sheep cheese is widely known as Pecorino Romano, served both as a pungent table cheese and as the favorite grating type of southern Italians. In Tuscany, for instance, a dozen or more villages give their names to the local Pecorino Toscano, and many Italian connoisseurs consider that called Valdorciano, from the herb-covered slopes along the Orcia River, to be *perfetto.* In nearby Pienza an annual *fiera del cacio,* a cheese fair, has been held for generations; here a poet once described the year's prize-winning Pecorino as having "the savor of a first kiss."

PENA SANTA (sheep)   An imitation Roquefort made in Corsica.

PENETELEU (sheep)   A low-fat version of Balkan Kashkaval, made in Romania.

PENICILLIUM   A genus of acetomycetous fungi identified in the nineteenth century as yeast producers and present in the formation of various mold cheeses; the best-known mold growths are the white *Penicillium camemberti, Penicillium glaucum,* used in making Gorgonzola, and *Penicillium roqueforti.* Penicillin, the antibacterial substance, derives from *Penicillium notatum,* one of the green molds.

PENNSYLVANIA DUTCH (cow)   Trademark of a semisoft, smooth-textured bland cheese made in eastern Pennsylvania.

PEPATO (sheep)   The Italian word meaning "peppery" is the established name for the Romano type seasoned with flecks of cracked peppercorns. It may be that the word can be found as a label for other cheeses dusted with pepper. Versions of the classic Pepato are made in Latin America and Michigan, among other places.

PERMENSIS (goat, sheep)   Ancient cheese of the Cisalpine region referred to by Platinus as Maielem, after the month of May.

PERSILLÉ (goat, cow)   "Parsleyed" cheeses, as the French describe them, have scattered spots of visible mold that reminds their makers of parsley leaves and is caused by *Penicillium glaucum* (see above), an edible fungus that develops in the ripening caves of the Savoy Mountains and elsewhere. They are generally classified as Persillés des Aravis, after the Alpine region; within this group are Persillé du Grand-Bornand and Persillé de Thônes, named for the places of origin. Persillé du Mont-Cenis comes from a neighboring area. Few, if any, are now made entirely of goat's milk, but of a mixture instead that is increasingly dominated by cow's milk.

PESTO   A classic Genoese cheese and olive oil sauce (see Recipes, page 172), with garlic, basil, and nuts. The French version, *pistou,* has tomatoes and no nuts and enhances soups.

PETIT LISIEUX (cow)   Thin, cylindrical, and with a reddish-brown rind, Petit Lisieux is one of the oldest of Norman cheeses, directly related to the ancient Angelot. It is comparable to Livarot in character.

PETIT-SUISSE (cow)   The famous French unripened cheese contains extra fat, either 60 percent or 75 percent, as the result of the addition of cream. A Swiss dairyman who worked for a Norman woman named Héroult in the nineteenth century is said to have devised the process. Gervais (see above) is the oldest manufacturer to describe its product as Petit-Suisse.

PEYNIR (cow, sheep)   A bland white Turkish cheese when fresh, Peynir is very salt-tasting when aged.

PFISTER (cow)   Said to have been originated in Switzerland by a farmer named Pfister Huber, the hooped type called Pfister looks a little like a small Emmenthaler but is differently cured and is ready in about six weeks.

PICKLED   Cheeses variously cured in some form of brine and loosely so described; they are usually soft white products of Mediterranean countries, heavily salted when in curd form or packed in salted milk whey or in water. They include Damietta and Kareish from Egypt, Greek Feta, or Sardinian *fetta,* Bulgarian Teleme, and Romania's Brandza, as well as others.

PICODON (goat)   Various goat's-milk products of France are known familiarly under this name.

PINEAPPLE (cow)   In 1845 when newel posts and other household *objets d'art* were shaped like the then exotic pineapple, Lewis M. Norton, a Litchfield, Connecticut, farmer, devised a net in which to hang his maturing Cheddars; the fruit-shaped cheese was for many years very popular; a tasty, rose-colored, mellow-hard cheese to spoon out down to the rind.

PINZGAUER BERGKÄSE (cow)   An Austrian mountain cheese produced in the region south of Salzburg.

PIORA (cow, goat)   Produced in the Swiss canton of Ticino, Piora is a hard cheese available in three styles: Vero Piora is made with milk of cows grazing on the high pastures of Piora above the Valle Leventina; Tipo Piora can be produced from cow's milk found elsewhere; Uso Piora has a mixture of cow's and goat's milk.

PIPER (cow)   A semifirm Scottish Cream Cheese that is almost spreadable.

PIPO CREM' (cow)   See Bleu de Bresse.

PIROTSKI KATSCHKWALJ (sheep)   A smelly, crude Serbian type taking its name from Pirot, a town on the Yugoslav-Bulgarian border.

PLANINSKI SIR (cow)   Very dry Serbian mountain cheeses.

PLATEAU (cow)   A factory-made Belgian round sometimes compared to St. Paulin (see below).

PLATTEKEES (cow)   A Belgian fresh white cheese, Plattekees is common in Flanders and Brabant.

PLOUGHMAN'S LUNCH   In much of Britain a thick slice of cheese—traditionally Cheddar, but now often including Stilton and others—is arranged with bread or rolls, pickled onions, and a mug of ale or beer as a farm worker's midday fortifier; tourists also find it in pubs and fast-food establishments.

PLYMOUTH (cow)   A granular or stirred-curd type (see above), Plymouth is made in the Vermont town of that name according to an original New England formula; it is constantly mistaken for Cheddar but has looser texture and flavor that is close to Crowley. Proprietor John Coolidge says, "So far as I can determine, we are the only ones making the old traditional Vermont cheese."

POIVRE D'ÂNE (cow, goat, sheep)   "Donkey's pepper," as the French call it, is made in Provence, shaped by hand in small balls rolled in sprigs of rosemary and savory.

PONT L'ÉVÊQUE (cow)   True believers insist this soft-ripened cheese can be successfully made only in the immediate environs of Pont l'Évêque, the market town in Normandy's Pays d'Auge, and this region must be cited on the label to be sure of a Pont l'Évêque worthy of its name. The best is a direct descendant of a medieval cheese called Angelot, and the distinctive characteristics of an authentic Pont l'Évêque are due to a bacteria which thrives in walls of certain old cellars. Small, flat, and square, with a smooth golden-brown skin, Pont l'Évêque has pronounced and attractive tang.

POONA (cow)   A surface-ripened type developed before World War II by Mrs. Kent Leavitt on a farm near Amenia, New York, but no longer produced; often compared to Normandy cheeses, it was round, flat, and creamy, about 4 inches in diameter, 1¾ inches thick, about 1 pound in weight.

POPCORN (cow)   A term for Cottage Cheese, meaning large unpressed curds.

PORT SALUT, PORT DU SALUT (cow)   Both terms spring from the name ("Port of Salvation") given by Trappist monks to their abbey in Brittany after return from years of exile caused by the French Revolution; bringing with them a secret formula, they made and sold their own cheese until the rights to the name were granted to a commercial manufacturer. In either version the name applies to factory-made cheeses of St. Paulin type (see below). Trappist monks in various countries still use the original formula but apply their own names; and those of the Brittany abbey market their product locally as Entrammes (see above). Similar cheeses are produced in several countries, including Iceland, and are labeled "Port Salut" or "Port du Salut."

POT (cow)   Fresh, so-called Cottage Cheese was once commonly made in British and American kitchens; it is still made today, sometimes of sour milk.

POTATO (cow, goat, sheep)   A cheese originating in Thuringia, Germany, in which sieved potatoes and curds combine with salt and sometimes caraway seeds.

PRÄSTOST (cow)   A firm, creamy, open-textured round made in Swedish factories, and to some extent on farms. See Saaland Pfarr.

PRATO (cow)   A Gouda-like round, Prato is named for a place in Minas Gerais province, Brazil, and is similar to Patagras (see above).

PRATTIGAU (cow)   Often compared to Limburger, Prattigau is a large skim-milk cake originating in the Swiss valley from which it takes its name; some is also made in the French Alps.

PRESENT (cow)   A factory-made Dutch product, somewhat like Gouda.

PRESSATO (cow)   A skim-milk Italian product; fairly creamy and open-textured.

PRIMOST (cow, goat)   A Scandinavian whey product, some of which is also made in America.

PROCESSED   The word denotes an artificial product consisting of one or more kinds of cheese which has been heated and mixed with emul-

sifiers, lactic, citric, and/or phosphoric acids, artificial coloring, flavorings, etc. The consistency is usually that required for easy spreading; the flavor equally smooth and lacking in character.

PROVATURA (buffalo, cow)   Most of today's Provatura is made of cow's milk, and like Mozzarella it is best when eaten fresh; it is one of Italy's spun-curd products (see below).

PROVIDENCE (cow)   A variety of St. Paulin made by Trappists at Bricquebec (see above), near Cherbourg.

PROVOLA (buffalo, cow)   A spun-curd type similar to Provatura and Scamorze.

PROVOLONA DI PECORA (sheep)   A mountain cheese made near Sorento, Italy; similar to Scamorze.

PROVOLONE (buffalo, cow)   Produced in several countries as well as its native Italy, Provolone is eaten fresh or hung in nets to dry for as long as six months, sometimes exposed to smoke. It is shaped like sausages, pears, and such amusing forms as piglets.

PULTOST (cow)   A soft sour-milk product of Norwegian mountains, sometimes seasoned with caraway seeds.

PUSZTADOR (cow)   The Puszta, central Hungary's great plains, is the source of a semihard cheese often compared to Limburgers and Romadurs.

PYRENEES (cow, sheep)   Any of several locally named firm round cheeses sold in the U.S. under the generic label referring to France's southwest mountain country; often coated black, with tangy flavor and sourish aftertaste.

Q

QUACHEQ (sheep)   In Macedonia, Yugoslavian herdsmen add sour whey to fresh ewe's milk, allow the mixture to coagulate, then remove the curd and submit it to pressure; it is eaten either fresh or after ripening.

QUARGEL (cow)   Small fresh cheeses curdled naturally and sold encased in red or gold wax by Austrian dairies; the term Sauermilchkäse is sometimes used.

QUARK (cow)   Commercial Cottage Cheese is sold under this label in German-speaking countries.

QUART (cow)   A small version of Maroilles.

QUARTIROLO (cow)   A thick, rectangular Italian cheese compared to

Bel Paese; it takes its name from its pastoral season, called *erba quart-irola,* referring to regrowth of meadow grass at the end of summer. In Argentina, Quartirolo is the name of a local type that is likened to Mozzarella.

QUEIJO   Portuguese word for cheese.

QUEIJO DE MINAS (cow)   A chalky cheese made in the Brazilian state of Minas Gerais.

QUERCINOIS (cow, goat)   The term applies both to a blue-veined cow's-milk round and to small, pure-goat cheeses from the plateaus around Gramat in southwest France.

QUESILLO DE OAXACA (cow)   See Oaxaca.

QUESO   Spanish word for cheese.

QUESO AÑEJO (cow)   Literally "aged cheese" in Spanish, the term in Mexico refers to a national favorite made from skim milk that is salty, crumbly, and used for making various *antojitos* (appetizers) and enchiladas; rounds weighing 11 to 22 pounds are traditionally packed in burlap bags.

QUESO BELLUSCA (goat, sheep)   Produced in the Los Bellos region of Asturias, Spain, Bellusca cheeses are usually about a pound in weight, with firm, pungent consistency, ready to be eaten any time from nine to 30 days; they are made of either goat's or sheep's milk, or a combination of both, and have a dark yellow skin that results from light smoking. See Los Bellos.

QUESO BLANCO (cow)   Latin America's white whey cheese is eaten fresh, without pressing, when it is moist and only a day or two old; it has a resemblance to Mozzarella and reminds some of lightly salted fresh Ricotta. See Queso de Prensa.

QUESO DE CABRA (goat)   Literally "goat cheese," and the common term for products of Chilean herdsmen; Queso de Cabra de Alicante is a fresh cheese common in the Spanish Mediterranean province of the same name.

QUESO DE CABRALES (sheep, goat)   See Cabrales.

QUESO DEL CEBRERO (cow)   Also known in northwest Spain as Queixo d'o Cebriero, the popular cheese of the province of Lugo is semihard but creamy and shaped a little like a mushroom cap.

QUESO DE CHALCO (cow)   A Latin American Cream Cheese taking its name from the suburb of Mexico City.

QUESO CHIHUAHUA (cow)   A porous, spongy paste with creamy flavor that has a slightly acid accent, Queso Chihuahua is made in Mennonite communities near Chihuahua, Mexico; it is much used for stuffing chilies or for Mexican gratiné dishes and other melting purposes.

QUESO ENCHILADO (cow)   White and crumbly, this salty Mexican product is made in blocks dusted in annatto or chili powder; it is the common stuffing for cheese enchiladas.

QUESO FRESCO (goat)   Literally "fresh cheese" and a generic term in Spanish-speaking countries; the fresh goat's cheese that is always consumed before it is a week old in its native province of Logroño, Spain, is sometimes known as Camerano, or Queso Fresco de Montaña. Another fresh goat product, from the Cádiz area, is allowed to mature 15 to 20 days until it is hard and compact and has pronounced flavor and aroma.

QUESO GALLEGO (cow)   Named for the Spanish region north of Portugal and Léon, more familiarly known as Gallicia, Queso Gallego takes its style from various other monastery cheeses generally related to St. Paulin (see below).

QUESO DE GAMONEDO (cow, goat, sheep)   A Spanish Blue, similar to Cabrales (see above), which is produced nearby. The Gamonedo cakes are smoked 10 to 20 days before being wrapped in fern leaves and placed in mountain caves for two months or more; the flavor, although it has a subtle smokiness, can be compared to that of Roquefort when the basic cow's milk has been mixed with a percentage from goats and sheep.

QUESO DE GRAZALEMA (sheep)   Produced by dairymen around Cádiz and named for a mountain town, the Grazalema rounds are ready to eat after 15 to 20 days, considered half-cured after 30 days, or aged two to three months to obtain firmness, flavor, and shape similar to that of Manchego.

QUESO DE HOJA (cow)   Puerto Rico's "leaf cheese," this salt-cured rectangle is made by flattening layers of curds which are then folded and wrapped in cloth; when cut vertically the folds, or leaves, are exposed.

QUESO MONTECOSO (cow)   Known affectionately as *chanco* and considered Chile's finest cheese; it is a copy of Port Salut, made of cream.

QUESO DE PRENSA (cow)   A generic pressed cheese in Spanish-speaking areas, Queso de Prensa is usually a hard white round in Latin America and, having started as Queso Blanco (see above), it is variously aged.

QUESO PRENSADO DE ORDUÑA (sheep)   A pressed flat-bottomed cake from the Spanish province of Álava; similar to Idiazábal (see above).

QUESO DE VACA DE LEÓN (cow)   Flat, round, semihard, and weighing up to about 2 pounds, this cow cheese of the Spanish region of León has strong flavor and is not often found outside its locality.

QUESUCOS (cow, goat, sheep)   One of the rustic smoked cheeses of northern Spain, produced from one or more kinds of milk; it is ready to eat after about six days.

QUITTEBEUF (cow) A vanished Norman farmhouse cheese that was a variation of Camembert.

R

RABACAL (goat, sheep) The flat cylinders of firm cheese made by Portuguese mountain dairymen share their name with a river running through the northern part of the country; Rabacal is produced from one or another milk and has rustic flavor.

RACLETTE (cow) Derivative of the French word for scraping off, the term *raclette* is now used to describe certain cheeses as well as a popular Swiss dish of melted cheese; the cheeses include Anivier, Bagnes, Conches, Gomser, Orsières, etc., and some of them are heavily embossed on their rims with the word "Raclette."

RADENER (cow) Mecklenburg farmers in northern Germany make a hard skim-milk wheel about 16 inches in diameter, 4 inches thick, weighing 30 to 35 pounds; it is made in much the same way as Switzerland cheeses.

RADOLFZELLER (cow) Often compared to Alsatian Munster, Radolfzeller is named for a town on Lake Constance (see Mainauer); it is creamy and ready to eat in two to three days.

RAGNIT (cow) Sometimes used in Australia and Central Europe for Tilsit.

RAGUSANO (cow) Sicilians in the province of Ragusa make bars of cheese that are yellow when just ripe enough to eat and dark brown when aged for grating; some Ragusano is smoked, some preserved in olive oil.

RAHMKÄSE (cow) The German term for Cream Cheese, Rahmkäse applies specifically to an Austrian farm product having 55 to 65 percent fat; as made on mountain farms in the Allgäuer it rarely travels far. That marketed as Imperial-Frischkäse has less fat and salt and is comparable to American Cream Cheese.

RAMEKIN, RAMEQUIN Cheese tarts; the word derives from the German *Rahm* (cream) and *chen* (diminutive), thus "creamlet," and by extension small, creamy morsels of which cheese is a base.

RAMOST (cow) See Pultost.

RANCHERO (cow) A dry, salty Mexican cheese much used in cooking.

RAPÉ The French word for "rasp" or "grate" is used to identify mountain cheeses in provincial markets when they are suitable for grating; they are freshly grated while the customer waits.

RAT CHEESE   Affectionate description of homely types, "good but not fancy," often referring to sound Cheddar; see Store Cheese.

RÄUCHERKÄSE (cow)   A generic term for smoked cheese in German-speaking countries, sometimes applied to a processed blend of two or more types to which "smoke flavor" has been added.

RAVIGIOLO (sheep)   Soft, creamy, and sweet, Ravigiolo is a local product of Tuscany and Umbria, sometimes compared to Crescenza (see above).

RAYON (cow)   Hard, skim-milk grating cheese is made in Fribourg, Switzerland, and in parts of northern Italy, and labeled with the French word for ray of light; much is shipped to Turin for aging in caves and future distribution as a grating cheese.

REBIBES (cow)   A term used for Saanen when it has been shaved with a plane and the shavings curl together in a roll.

REBLÈQUE (cow)   A fresh Cream Cheese, usually eaten with sugar, made by Valle d'Aosta farmers near the French border.

REBLOCHON (cow)   Much Reblochon is now made in French and Swiss factories, but the type was developed hundreds of years ago and is thought by some to have monastery influence; its paste is rich and supple, and it has a thickish brushed rind. The word may come from *reblocher,* a dialect term meaning to milk a second time, or from *re-blasser,* to maraud, referring to tales of hired hands who milked once for their bosses and once for themselves, turning the surreptitious yield into cheese which was spirited away. Reblochon takes on bitterness when old, and is therefore best when it has matured no more than two months.

RÉCOLLET (cow)   Originally produced by monks of the Récollet order in the Vosges Mountains of eastern France, traditional Récollet was similar to Carré de l'Est with some of the pungency of Munster. It is now made in a factory at Tholy.

RECUITE (cow)   French Ricotta.

REGGIANITO (cow)   South American version of Parmesan, much of which is produced in Argentina.

REGGIANO (cow)   Grating cheese from Reggio, Italy; the word is also used loosely for cheeses of this type. See Grana.

REGGINO (cow)   Argentinian term for locally produced grating cheese.

REINDEER (reindeer)   Produced on a very small scale from the milk of domesticated animals in Lapland, Norway, and Sweden, this salt-cured cheese is pressed in rounds and, in Lapland, is used by some to replace cream in coffee.

REINO (cow, goat)   Brazilian mountain type made according to Portuguese formulas; see Serra.

REMOUDOU (cow)   An ancient Belgian cheese made at Battice, near Liège, Remoudou is likened by some to Herve, and its name associates it with the German Romadur (see below). The Belgian name derives from *Rahm,* the German word for cream, and the cheese is very rich, with a powerful smell and assertive flavor, so appreciated in Belgium that its fans have organized (see Confrérie du Remoudou). In Battice visitors may watch local Remoudou makers at work for an admission charge of 65¢ (1975), which includes a taste of the local product.

RENNET   The contents of the stomach of an unweaned calf, or other domestic animal; sometimes the lining membrane of the stomach. In the making of cheese, rennet brings about the curdling of milk, and the resulting separation of curds and whey. The word is an archaic form of the verb "run." Various plants also are still sometimes used as rennet. Rennin is the specific milk-curdling enzyme of rennet.

RÉPARSAC (goat)   A Camembert-like product of goat's milk, adorned with a grape leaf; now made in the cooperative creamery at Réparsac, a village near Cognac, France.

REQUEIJÃO (cow)   A Brazilian product of skim milk in which, although cream and butter are added, there is very little fat content in the finished cheese; Requeijão is traditionally packed in parchment containers.

RESURRECTION (cow)   A nineteenth-century Welsh farmhouse product that was so called because it was pressed by gravestones taken from churches that had fallen into ruins; often the Resurrection rounds were embossed with the names of those memorialized by cemetery markers.

REXOLI-LUNCH (cow)   A soft-ripened, mild, rindless cheese made in Lena, Illinois.

RHUBARBE (sheep)   A paste made of scrapings of *bleu* or Roquefort and local brandy is covered with pepper and cured in pots to be aged in natural caves near Millau, France; it develops very tart flavor, hence the name.

RICHELIEU (cow)   A Canadian variation of Bel Paese developed by Dr. J. M. Rosell at the St. Hyacinthe Dairy School in Quebec; Richelieu is made commercially in several Canadian plants.

RICOTTA (cow)   In its fresh form, as it is best known in the U.S., Ricotta is somewhat like commercial Cottage Cheese; when it is dried and pressed, it is firm enough to slice; in Italy it is allowed to harden sufficiently for grating. It is made from whey or buttermilk, often in a process in which steam is injected to help form curds. The Italian word means "recooked."

RIDDAROST (cow)   An open-textured, mild loaf originally produced in the Swedish province of Västergötland.

RIESENBIRGE (goat)   A mountain cheese developed by Bohemian goat-herds; cured by surface salting and matured about four days in humid caves.

RIGOTTE (cow, goat)   Several small, round, flat cheeses, originally made only of goat's milk, take their name from what may be a corruption of the Italian *ricotta* or the French *recuite*. Traditionally the size of the ancient five-franc piece, they are sold in stacks weighing 1 pound in the Lyon region, where they are known as Rigottes de Condrieu, for their home village. Rigottes de Pelussin come from the Auvergne and are sometimes shaped like a truncated cone. Cow's milk is now frequently mixed with that of goats or is the sole milk used. The Condrieu disks are tinted on the outside by annatto.

RIKSOST (cow)   Semisoft to hard Farmer Cheese with caraway seeds added; produced in Sweden, it has mild, slightly tangy flavor and aftertaste.

RINDLESS LOAF   Where volume rather than traditional quality is the by-word, new techniques have been developed to produce such cheeses as Brick, Cheddar, and "Swiss" in blocks which form no natural rind but are cured in vacuum packaging employing one or another form of plastic. To borrow a phrase from Vivienne Marquis and Patricia Haskell in *The Cheese Book,* the result is to natural cheese "what a Madame Tussaud dummy is to a human being."

RINNEN (cow)   In German *rinnen* means something like "groovy"—this cheese develops after the curds are put in a wooden groove or trough from which the whey drains; afterward the curds are kneaded by hand and caraway seed is added, then the developing paste is pressed into forms and rubbed with salt before being packed in boxes for ripening.

RIOLA (goat, sheep)   An assertive, soft-textured hooped cheese made in the Italian mountains, Riola is about 4 inches in diameter, usually rather thick, and ready to eat in about three months; it resembles Mont d'Or (see above).

ROBIOLA (goat)   Variously spelled, Robiola is produced in Piedmont and Lombardy; it is formed into flat rounds that weigh between 8 ounces and 2 pounds, depending on diameter; Ticino farmers make a Swiss version. The consistency is not unlike Taleggio (see below).

ROCAMADOUR (goat, sheep)   Tiny, flat, rustic cheeses that are prototypes of many goat's-milk disks of southwestern France; named for the pilgrimage city of the Middle Ages, they are often wrapped in leaves.

ROCHEFORT (cow)   A monastery type made in southeastern Belgium at the Abbey of Rochefort.

RODOPA (sheep)   A full-fat product of pasteurized sheep's milk in hexahedral shapes. Like Feta, Rodopa brined cheese is white and slightly crumbly; it has a piquant, sour taste and is now made in recently built factories in the Rhodope Mountains of southern Bulgaria.

ROLLOT (cow)   Heart-shaped, or cylindrical, Rollot is one of the best-known of Picardy products and takes its name from a market village; it is soft-ripened, with reddish skin and full, aromatic flavor. Guerbigny is much like it.

ROMADUR, ROMADOUR (cow)   Germany's rendition of the Limburger-Liederkranz formula is a rectangular cheese developed in Bavaria; it is mildly pungent, if not kept too long.

ROMANELLO (cow)   "Little Romano" is one of Italy's very hard types with sharp flavor now being copied by manufacturers in South America and the U.S.

ROMANO (cow)   Almost as popular in Italy and the U.S. as Parmesan, Romano is hard and sharp in flavor, used as a table cheese when aged a matter of months and as a grating cheese after one year; Italians distinguish the cow's-milk version, Vacchino Romano, from Pecorino Romano (see Pecorino); cow's-milk Romano is also manufactured in Australia, Canada, and several American dairy states. Piccolo Romano is the mark of a small flattened ball produced in Wisconsin. Caprino Romano is made of goat's milk.

RONCAL (cow, sheep)   Produced in the Pyrenees, traditionally from ewe's milk, Roncal is very hard with piquant flavor; the large cylinders weigh about 7 pounds and have a hard brown crust.

RONDELÉ (cow)   Small Cream Cheeses are variously seasoned with herbs or spices in Wisconsin factories and widely distributed under this label; the texture is slightly grainy, a little like white Farmer Cheese (see above).

ROOS (sheep)   A salty ball shape, slightly bigger than an orange, made by shepherds of Iraq.

ROQUEFORT (sheep)   Famous since the first century A.D. when Pliny

the Elder singled it out for high praise, genuine Roquefort, from Roquefort-sur-Soulzon, France, is matured in the caves of Combalou only, is wrapped in foil and stamped with the image of a sheep in red ink; it is considered a prototype of blue-veined products, and the use of the name is protected. Trademarks of 14 legal producers are Agricole, Bee Brand, Bell, Caves, J. Couderc, Gabriel Coulet, Joan of Arc, Franco-Americaine, Marie Grimal, Le Flambeau, Rigal, Société Roquefortoise, Union Fromagère, Vernier Frères. See Chapter 4.

ROSSISKY (cow)   Large wheels of supple but firm pasteurized cheese are produced under this name in Russian factories; they are mature in 2½ months.

ROUERGUE (cow)   A firm, pliant consistency is characteristic of this cheese from France's southwest region; it has been compared by some to St. Paulin, by others to Cantalon.

ROUSSEL, ANTOINE   The "father" of the blue-veined types made in the French region of Auvergne was a farmer who in 1850 started experimenting with methods of making a uniform *bleu* as a means of improving the economy of neighboring dairymen. He sprinkled curds with blue molds he found growing on rye bread and salted the paste at high temperatures to produce a protective crust. The result was the 8-inch wheel known as Bleu de Laqueuille (see above) for his hometown; Laqueuille citizens have erected a bust of Roussel in honor of his work.

ROYAL BRABANT (cow)   A Belgian type, similar to Limburger, named for the next-door province.

ROYALDIEU (cow)   A factory-made French version of St. Paulin (see below), having higher fat content and creamier texture.

S

SAALAND PFARR (cow)   For hundreds of years this Swedish cylinder has been made by mixing the curds with ardent spirits and, when the cheese is formed, brushing the outside repeatedly with spirits. Made in factories today, it has open texture but is reminiscent of Gouda; it is also known as Prästost (see above), which means "priest cheese."

SAANEN (cow)   Taking its name from the valley of the Saane River and from a small town in the Gstaad resort area, this is the hardest of all Swiss cheeses, some having been known to have aged 200 years. In other times a Saanen was set aside on the birth of a child and eaten on special holidays and on birthdays. A cheese plane is used to shave off pieces (see Hobel; Rebibes).

SAGE (cow)   Some English farmhouse cheeses have been flavored with minced fresh sage for at least 300 years. In Derbyshire, Lancashire, Gloucestershire, and Wiltshire the traditional season for making sage cheeses was after the harvest, and for many people Christmas would have seemed incomplete without a green-marbled cheese. Good Sage Derby is available in the U.K., and in Vermont it is sold in many supermarkets.

SAINGORLON (cow)   A copy of Gorgonzola created by French dairymen during World War II when imports were restricted.

ST. ANDRÉ (cow)   A widely exported French Cream Cheese, very rich and very popular among certain cheeselovers. See Triple Crème.

ST. EDI (cow)   An imitation Brie made in County Wexford, Ireland.

ST. FLORENTIN (cow)   Soft, with a washed rind, and compared variously to Coulommiers and Soumaintrain (see below).

ST. GALLER ALPKÄSE (cow)   First made by Benedictine monks at St. Gall, Switzerland, this is a mountain cheese much like Appenzeller (see above), which is made nearby.

ST. GERMAIN (cow)   A French version of Fontina (see above).

ST. MARCELLIN (cow, goat)   Once one of France's *pur chèvres*, St. Marcellin is now frequently made of cow's milk alone and occasionally of a mixture of two milks. It comes from the Dauphiné region and is shaped in small disks, sometimes wrapped in leaves.

ST. MORITZ (cow)   A name for Danish Munster, or Mynster (see above); semisoft, mild, with sweet aroma.

ST. NECTAIRE (cow)   Named for the market town near Clermont-Ferrand, and one of the best semisoft cheeses in all of France; when made on farms it is labeled as such under legal restrictions, is about 8 inches in diameter, 1½ inches thick, and weighs about 3 pounds, having supple texture and mild tang and fragrance.

ST. OTHO (cow)   A Gruyère type for the cholesterol-wary from which 95 percent of the butterfat has been removed.

ST. PAULIN (cow)   This name is used generically for factory-made products deriving from the Port Salut (see above) formula. St. Paulin is produced under various names in many dairy countries, including Austria, from which a version for export is called L'Amour. A good St. Paulin feels supple and tender, has a smooth, thin skin, and cuts easily; it has mild, somewhat poignant flavor and a light smell of lactic fermentation.

ST. SAVIOL (goat)   A pure-goat, surface-ripened type produced for export in western France.

ST. STEPHANO (cow)   A rare version of Bel Paese produced in Germany.

ST. THOMASIO (cow)   Similar to Port Salut, St. Thomasio is produced by Trappist monks in the Austrian Alps.

STE. MAURE (goat)   The name of this French village in Touraine is sometimes used as a common term for certain goat types. It has been reported that two-thirds of a million gallons of goat's milk is annually processed in the immediate vicinity of Ste. Maure.

STE. MAURE FERMIER (goat)   One of France's most loved cheeses, from the highlands of Touraine; formed by hand into a long cylinder through which runs a heavy straw for support, it has a delicate bluish rind dotted with red. Factory-made Ste. Maure is downy-skinned and shaped by machine regularity.

SALAMANA (sheep)   A soft type with very pronounced flavor originating in Greece but common through the Mediterranean.

SALAMAVRA (goat)   A brine-cured white cheese of Turkey.

SALIGNON (goat, sheep)   A variety of Formagelle (see above), this rustic cheese is made in the Italian Alps in spring and fall and is seasoned with minced pimiento or dried flowers from mountain herbs.

SALIGNY (cow)   A 50 percent butterfat product, sometimes labeled "Époisses" (see above), Saligny takes its name from a village south of the Île-de-France.

SALMISTRA (cow)   See Aostin.

SALOIO (cow)   A rustic farmer's product of the dairy region near Lisbon, Saloio is made from skim milk and is very low in butterfat.

SAMSOE (cow)   Once called Danish Swiss Cheese, Samsoe is named for a Danish island; it has round shiny holes and a mild, somewhat sweet flavor.

SAN FANDILA (cow)   One of Mexico's much-used cooking cheeses.

SAN SIMON (cow)   In the shape of an elongated cone usually weighing about 3 pounds, this Spanish type takes its name from San Simon de la Cuesta in the northwest province of Lugo; similar to Tetilla (see below), it is lightly smoked during maturation.

SAPSAGO (cow)   A very hard, green, truncated cone that gets color and aroma from clover (*Melitotus coerulea*), Sapsago has been made for five centuries in Glarus, Switzerland, as a cheese to be grated as a condiment. The name is a corruption of the German word *Schabzieger;* in Europe it also is known variously as Glärnerkäse, Grünerkäse, and Kräuterkäse.

SARDO (sheep)   See Fiore Sardo.

SARRAZIN (cow)   A Swiss version of blue-veined cheese named for

La Sarraz, a town midway between Lake Neuchâtel and Lake Leman.

SAVOIA (cow) A forerunner of factory-made Bel Paese (see above) from mountain farms on the Italy-France border.

SAVOUREUX DE NEIGE (cow) A creamy mountain type made in late summer in Savoy when cows graze on frost-touched grass, hence "tasting of snow"; it is aged through the winter for eating in spring.

SBRINZ (cow) Originating in central Switzerland and known in Roman times, Sbrinz is considered by Swiss dairymen to be the finest of grating cheeses. It has very hard, fine-grained texture, aromatic flavor, and is often packaged in fragile slices cut as thin as paper.

SCAMORZE (buffalo, cow) Like Mozzarella, this spun-curd type is eaten when fresh, but is also aged, often taking the form of a pear.

SCANNO (sheep) An Italian table cheese from the Abruzzi area, this buttery-textured product is named for the mountain village of Scanno and is a very popular accompaniment to fruit.

SCHABZIEGER (cow) See Sapsago.

SCHAMSER (cow) A skim-milk wheel made in the dairy country west of St. Moritz; it is also called Rheinwald.

SCHICHTKÄSE (cow) As the German name indicates, this is a fresh type composed of layers of skimmed-milk curds and full-fat curds, having delicate, supple consistency; its flavor is comparable to that of Cottage Cheese.

SCHLOSS, SCHLOSSKÄSE (cow) "Castle cheese" is made in Austria, Germany, and Petaluma, California, among other places, and is reminiscent of Romadur or mild Limburger. Old Heidelberg, made in Lena, Illinois, belongs to the same family.

SCHMELZKÄSE A kind of cheese made in various German factories especially for melting; one processed version is a combination of Tilsit (see below) and German-made Chester.

SCHMIERKÄSE (cow) A generic term in Germany for white spreadable cheese, sometimes applied to Cream Cheeses mixed with herbs; in Pennsylvania Dutch country it is a word for Cottage Cheese.

SCHNEE KAESE (cow) White mold gives distinctive character to this Illinois product with a soft interior and a downy skin, shaped in rectangular loaves.

SCHÖNLAND (cow) A German variant of Bel Paese.

SCHOTTENZIGER (cow) In Germany whey cheese, not unlike Ricotta, is called either Schottenziger or Ziger; in Switzerland it is called Hudelziger, or Mascarpone (see above) when it is made of goat's milk. On the Alpine frontier a mixture of Ziger and rich cream long ago took the name of Gruau de Montagne (grains of the mountain).

SCHÜTZENKÄSE (cow)   An assertive cheese from Austria. See Chapter 7.

SCHWARZENBERGER (cow)   An assertive cheese from Austria. See Chapter 7.

SCHWEIZEROST (cow)   Swedish-made Swiss-type cheese.

SCOURMONT (cow)   A soft, smooth round not unlike St. Paulin; it is an ancient product of monks at the Abbey of Scourmont, Belgium.

SELLES-SUR-CHER (goat)   Traditionally a very flat truncated cone, but also available in other shapes, sometimes powdered with cinders; one of the best-known of French goat types, Selles-sur-Cher comes from farms south of Orléans.

SERAC   One of the French terms used to identify fresh cheese similar to Ricotta.

SERENA (sheep)   Small, semihard flattened balls from western Spain that are ready to eat in about six weeks; see Los Pedroches.

SERRA (goat, sheep)   These "mountain" cheeses of Portugal have many variations, most often produced from sheep's milk and sometimes from mixtures; the best come from the mountain range called Serra de Estrella and are so labeled.

SEVERNY (cow)   The Ural Mountains town gives its name to a hard Russian cheese usually sold in blocks weighing about 2 pounds.

SILBA (cow)   A Yugoslav imitation of Port Salut made commercially for export.

SIR   A common generic term for cheese in Balkan countries.

SIRAZ (cow)   Small, sun-dried cakes rubbed with salt; a common rustic cheese of Serbia.

SIRENE (sheep)   A Balkan type of brined cheese (see Rodopa) used much in cooking, especially in Bulgaria.

SKANDIA (cow)   Smooth, firm, easy to slice, Skandia is a factory-made Swedish product with mild flavor.

SKYR (cow)   Traditional in all Scandinavian countries, Skyr belongs in a category somewhere between cheese and yogurt. When served, it is often thinned with milk, whipped to a creamy consistency, and sprinkled with sugar.

SKYROS (goat, sheep)   A kind of Kefalotyri (see above) named for the island in the Aegean Sea.

SLIPCOTE, SLIPCOAT (cow)   A form of fresh Cream Cheese, smooth as butter, once commonly made in English homes. Cambridge, Colwick (see above), and York are related types.

SLIVOTCHNY (cow)   A Russian Cream Cheese, made in factories.

SMALLHOLDER (cow)   A simple cheese made on small English farms which hadn't enough milk to make large rounds, Smallholder was a pressed type once very common, and is now made in U.K. kitchens in places like Devonshire. In the Appalachians there are still oldsters using inherited recipes that result in a semisoft, usually loose-textured cheese that has some pungency.

SMJÖR (cow)   An Icelandic Cream Cheese.

SMOKED   Cheese infused with the flavor of smoke may be almost as old as cheese itself. In Rome's heyday it was considered a luxury among the affluent classes, and the smoked cheese from the shopping center at Velabrum, outside the city, was considered excellent. Cheese that is genuinely smoked develops heightened flavor, but those in which the effect has been produced through use of chemical additives may be ignored. See Chapter 11.

SMOLENSKY (cow)   A cylindrical form of soft cheese with piquant flavor produced in the western Russia region of Smolensk.

SOBADO (cow)   Also known as Queso de la Armada, or Queso de Calostro, Sobado is considered unique, the only cheese to be produced from milk of cows immediately after calving for the first time. Compact, semihard, and slightly spicy, its source is the northwest Spanish province of León, in the villages of Lillo, Reyero, and Vegamian, which turn out perhaps 500 cheeses annually.

SODA CHEESE (cow)   Similar to Egg Cheese (see above); a little soda is added to curds made of sour milk, and the result is a popular Mennonite spread.

SORBAIS (cow)   A variant of Maroilles.

SORIA (goat)   A fresh Spanish cheese ready to eat after 24 hours and for about a week thereafter, Soria takes its name from the province in which it is made, north of Madrid.

SOUMAINTRAIN (cow)   A classic soft cheese with a washed crust from Burgundy, Soumaintrain is smooth, shiny, and brown on the outside, formed in a flat disk that weighs about ¾ pound; both taste and aroma have some pungency. See St. Florentin.

SPALEN (cow)   One of Switzerland's very hard cheeses, sometimes equated with Sbrinz (see above), this originated in the canton of Unterwalden; its flavor is sharp and nutty, and it is most often grated for use in cooking.

SPERMYSE   It is said that in the Middle Ages there were four kinds of English cheeses: hard, soft, green, and spermyse—the last a Cream Cheese flavored with the juice of herbs.

SPITZ (cow)   Snappy, biting (as its name translates from German), this little-known farmhouse product is similar to Limburger as made in Germany and Belgium.

SPUN CURD   A technique developed by Italians (who call it *pasta filata*—*filata* means to spin, or run), in which the curd is mixed with hot water, kneaded, stretched repeatedly, then molded while hot and rubbery. The method produces Mozzarella and Caciocavallo, the new so-called Pizza Cheese, Provolone, Scamorze, and others.

STANGEN (cow)   A German variant of Limburger.

STAR VALLEY, WYOMING   A Rocky Mountain area where a Swiss type is made.

STARTER, LACTIC   Buttermilk and yogurt are often used to induce coagulation in simple homemade cheeses. The primary lactic acid organisms used in the making of most cheeses are called *Streptococcus lactis* and *Streptococcus cremoris*.

STEIERMARK (cow)   A firm-textured Austrian table cheese, Steiermark takes its name from the mountainous central province; it has robust flavor, not unlike Appenzeller (see above).

STEINBUSCHER (cow)   A buttery rectangular cheese with a moist surface, originating near Steinbusch, Brandenburg, Germany, about 1860; it is sometimes compared to Romadur.

STEPPE (cow)   Called Stepnoï in Russia, where it was first produced by German colonists, Steppe is a rich, mellow, Tilsit-like wheel, or block, made also in Austria, Germany, Scandinavia—and western Canada, where it is very popular.

STILTON (cow)   Blue-veined and of creamy, firm texture, Stilton is considered by many connoisseurs as the best British cheese and by many Britons as the best of veined cheeses. Its name comes from a Leicestershire market town, but it is produced now in various counties and sold throughout the world, its tall cylindrical shape distinguishing it from others like Gorgonzola and Roquefort.

STIRRED CURD   See Colby, or see granular or stirred curd.

STORE CHEESE   In Canada and northeastern U.S. a common term for regional Cheddars and related cheeses.

STRACCHINO (cow)   *Stracca*, a dialect Italian word for "tired," was applied to a generic type of cheeses made from milk of cows that lagged when driven south from summer pasturage in the mountains. More than likely their milk was affected less by the long walk than by the change of grazing, and the cheeses resulting from rest periods given migrant cattle include some of Italy's best: Gorgonzola, Stracchino di Milano, and others.

STRAVECCHIO   Italian term for three-year-old Parmesan.

STRAVECCHIONE   Italian term for Parmesan aged four years or longer.

STRESA CONVENTION   Representatives of Austria, Denmark, France,

Italy, the Netherlands, Norway, Sweden, and Switzerland, gathering in Rome in 1951, agreed to restrict the use of names of classic cheeses to their original source; for instance, the name of Roquefort cannot be used by makers of blue-veined cheeses who do not belong to the Roquefort Society. Other names thus limited to their original source: Ädelost, Asiago, Brie, Caciocavallo, Camembert, Danablu, Danbo, Edam, Elbo, Emmenthal, Fiore Sardo, Fontina, Friesian, Fynbo, Gouda, Gruyère, Gudbrandsdalsost, Havarti, Herrgard, Leyden, Maribo, Marmora, Nökkelost, Pecorino Romano, Pinzgauer Bergkäse, Provolone, St. Paulin, Samsoe, Sbrinz, Svecia, Tybo.

STRING CHEESE (cow)   Much like Mozzarella, this is tubular in shape and gets its name because it is pulled apart in shreds which, in in Armenia, are arranged in heaps on plates. It is made in the U.S., and in Russian Georgia is packed in brine.

SUFFOLK (cow)   According to an old English saw, "Hunger breaks through anything except Suffolk Cheese." Today Suffolk farmwives make a creamy cheese, often using cake tins as molds, drying the drained curds in summer heat for about three days, then turning them morning and night until a rind develops. Modern Suffolk Cheese is produced almost exclusively for home consumption.

SULUGUNI   A generic term for white, cow's-milk cheese in southern Russia; it is often deep-fried and served in wedges like pieces of pie.

SUPPLI AL TELEFONO   In Italy a ball of rice with a center of melted Provatura is called a "telephone croquette" because, when the balls are hot, the oozing cheese strings out when bitten into. See Recipes, page 126.

SUPRÊME (cow)   One of France's soft-ripened triple-cream types.

SURATI (buffalo)   A sharp-flavored, white Indian product of Gujarat, near Bombay, ready to eat in about 15 days.

SUSSEX (cow)   Though scarcely remembered by the British, Sussex was a firm cheese distinguished enough in the seventeenth century to have been listed among the "luxuries" brought to Virginia in 1636 on the trading ship *Tristan and Jane*.

SVECIA (cow)   An airy, white Swedish product, wheel-shaped and low in fat content; much of it is marketed when mild in flavor, but Svecia at the age of a year or more is considered one of the best made by Scandinavians, with firm, open texture and fresh, strong taste.

SWISS (cow)   A generic term for imitations of Emmenthal (see above); only when the word "Switzerland" is a part of the label is the origin unimpeachable; "Imported Swiss" may come from one or another European source. Instead of being cured six to ten months, much of the "Swiss" made in the U.S. and other countries is three to four months old; it is often a semisoft product with large glistening eyes and mild, sweet flavor. See Chapter 5.

SWISS DESSERT (cow)   A double-cream soft cheese with white-mold crust, described by manufacturers as "fine and downy like a fur"; Swiss Dessert is smaller and thicker than Camembert, which it otherwise resembles.

SWISSCA (cow)   A Tilsit type made in Brome County, Quebec.

SZEKELY (sheep)   A traditional Transylvanian soft type characterized by its packing in sausage casings.

𝒥

TAFFEL (cow)   Table cheese, as the name indicates; made in all the Scandinavian countries, where it originated, and now produced elsewhere. As imported into the U.S., the rindless loaves have close, dense texture and a resilient yellow paste, with pleasing, piquant flavor.

TAFI (cow)   A mountain cheese, somewhat like Cantal, produced in the Tucumán highlands of western Argentina.

TALEGGIO (cow)   Taleggio, a small market town near Bergamo, Lombardy, gave its name to this Stracchino type (see above); it is soft, square, and flat with a tender crust, and the taste is rich and slightly piquant. It is also known as Talfino.

TAMBO (cow)   A mild type, compared to Samsoe (see above), and named for the Tambo River in eastern Australia, where it is produced.

TAMIÉ (cow)   Produced in traditional ways by Trappists at the Abbey of Tamié on Lake Annecy, this Savoy cheese is a little bigger than Reblochon (see above), to which it is often compared.

TANDIL (cow)   A firm, flavorsome Argentinian product named after a provincial city south of Buenos Aires, Tandil is the same type as Cantal.

TANZENBERGER (cow)   A Limburger type (see above) produced in southern Austria.

TARA (cow)   A recently developed Irish type that is firm and bland, having a scattering of holes.

TARTARE (cow)   A Neufchâtel type, Tartare is factory-produced in
Périgord, having 70 percent fat content and a seasoning of *fines
herbes.*

TCHANAKH (cow, sheep)   A salty Russian brine-cured product of the
Caucasus.

TELEME (cow, goat, sheep)   Apparently originating with migrant shepherds of eastern Romania's highlands, Teleme is a brine-cured type,
sometimes known as Bryndza, or Braila Brandza, after the Danube
delta city of Braila. In Romania, Turkey, and nearby regions it is
almost indistinguishable from Feta. However, the name has been
applied to soft, very pliant cow's-milk cheese produced in California;
its somewhat elastic quality is a little like factory Mozzarella.

TELEME JACK (cow)   Not to be confused with Teleme (above), this
California product is labeled variously as "Teleme," "Cream Jack," or
"High Moisture Jack," and is said to have been originated about 1922
by makers of Monterey Jack who had immigrated from Greece and applied the Middle Eastern word to their new cheese. It is now produced
in Pleasanton and Riverbank, outside of San Francisco. A vegetable
rennet is used in its manufacture and rice flour in the curing; it is
marketed when five to ten days old. Very pliant in consistency, Teleme
Jack is considered by many American cooks to be an ideal ingredient in
baked dishes.

TÊTE DE MOINE (cow)   Originally made by monks in the fifteenth-
century Swiss abbey at Bellelay, in the Bernese Jura, this firm, compact cylinder was also produced by nearby tenant farmers as a means
of paying their rents. Called either Bellelay or Tête de Moine, these
"monk's head" cheeses come now from small dairies in the same
area and have a particular tang said to suggest the herbs that grow in
the mountain pastures.

TETILLA (cow)   Creamy, soft, with a slightly salty lactic taste, Tetilla
is a rustic Gallician product, with a suggestive name, that is common
in northwest Spain; it can be eaten within a week or when it has aged
two months or so. When it is pear-shaped it is known as Perilla
de Vaca.

TEXEL (sheep)   One of Holland's rare ewe's-milk cheeses is named for
the island of Texel, where it was first made; it is less rich than other
Dutch types.

THOLSTRUP, HENRIK   Fourth-generation Danish cheesemaker who set
out to develop a luxury Cream Cheese at a modest price, and thus
invented Crema Dania (see above).

TIBET (yak)   Very hard; a type made by Trans-Himalayan herdsmen that is hung out to dry like large beads on a string and is later used for grating.

TILLAMOOK (cow)   An American Cheddar produced in Tillamook County, Oregon. See Chapter 2.

TILSIT (cow)   Originated by Dutch dairymen who had migrated to East Prussia near the city of Tilsit; it is now made in many countries, and production of Swiss Tilsit was begun in the Thurgau village of Felben by a cheesemaker named Wegmuller, who brought the recipe from Germany. There is a wide range of character in the Tilsits of various countries. Good Tilsit is mildly piquant in taste, soft but firm in texture, a really commendable table cheese.

TIPO ARAGON (goat, sheep)   Traditionally a Spanish ewe's-milk type, with some goat's milk occasionally used, this Aragon cheese is sometimes called Tronchon and is occasionally flavored with ground thistle flowers; it is matured about one week, and its rustic, concave shape takes on a yellow cast to the thin crust.

TOGGENBURGER (cow)   Produced in the Toggenburger Mountains of eastern Switzerland, and of Lichtenstein; it matures about nine months, developing a white granular paste and a sticky surface.

TOMA VEJA (cow)   Dense, with reddish skin, Toma Veja is described vividly by natives of the Italian-Swiss frontier: it has three virtues— it satisfies hunger, ends thirst, and cleans the teeth.

TOME, TOMME   In the region of Savoy, particularly, this term in one or the other of its spellings is a dialect word for cheese. It applies to a type of goat cheese in the Dauphiné, and gets both French and Italian spellings in Switzerland (see Toma Veja).

TOME AU MARC (cow)   Produced by Savoy winemakers, these cheeses are similar to Beaufort (see above) and very likely the originals of grape-seed-encrusted products. The natural rind is brushed repeatedly, then coated with marc, the insoluble residue of skins and seeds left in the bottom of wine vats.

TOMINI DEL TALUCCO (goat)   A goat's-milk cheese made at Pinado, in the Italian Piedmont.

TOMME BLANCHE DE CORSE (sheep)   Many wheels of Corsican sheep cheese are aged in the caves at Combalou to become genuine Roquefort, but some are set aside to be sold in France as "white cheese," and are much appreciated by connoisseurs.

TOMME DE FENOUIL (cow)   A fennel-flavored mountain cheese still to be found occasionally between September and June in the French Alps.

TOMME DES NEIGES (cow)   A new, downy-skinned, creamy-centered

French product made in the Dauphiné and somewhat reminiscent of Brie; the 8-inch cylinder, however, is about twice as thick.

TOMME VAUDOISE (cow)   A white-mold soft-ripened type produced either in flat Camembert-like cylinders or in rectangles of about 9 ounces in western Switzerland; there is a version made with cumin seeds added.

TONNELAIT, FROMAGE DE (cow)   Firm, with smooth texture and gray inedible crust, Tonnelait is somewhat barrel-shaped and produced in Brittany, ostensibly from the milk of cows that graze on fields of flowering herbs.

TORTA DEL CASAR (sheep)   Milk from the Sierra de San Pedro near Spain's western boundary is transformed into round flat cheeses with yellowish-brown crusts, weighing about 2 pounds. Maturation takes between 15 and 25 days, and the creamy *tortas* (cakes) are considered perfect when the thin crust splits open and the rich interior oozes out.

TOUAREG (goat)   The Touareg nomads of North Africa often use the leaves of the korourou trees to make a substitute for rennet and produce a soft curd which they dip out on mats in very thin layers; the final maturation takes place in the sun or in the heat given off by an outdoor fire. As Touareg is turned occasionally but is not salted, it becomes very hard and brittle.

TOULOUMISIO (cow)   A Greek type cured in brine that is contained in skin bags, Touloumisio is much like Feta.

TRAPPIST (cow)   Generically this term refers to any cheese made by monks of the Trappist order, founded at La Trappe, Normandy, but scattered throughout the world. See Chapter 8. In addition to the Port Salut or St. Paulin types of Europe, Trappists make cheese near Gethsemane, Kentucky, and produce the famous Oka of Canada. "Trappisten" is used as a trademark by an Austrian monastery.

TRAVNIK (sheep)   Herdsmen of Yugoslavia's central highlands first made this rustic flattened ball in the 1870's. Drained in woolen sacks, the curd is shaped by hand, dried in the open air, then packed in kegs that hold 50 to 130 pounds. Mild, fresh, this white cheese is named for its market town; when aged it becomes hard.

TREBOLGIANO (cow)   In Argentina large wheels with black skins, looking very much like Parmigiano, are produced for grating purposes under this name; Trebolgiano Chico is usually aged 14 months, Trebolgiano Grande about 18 months.

TRECCE, TRECCIA (cow)   An Italian braided cheese made similarly to Caciocavallo.

TRIPLE CRÈME (cow)   Any of a number of soft-ripened products of

French factories which have at least 72 percent fat; the flavor is deliciously mild and very rich.

TRÖNDER (cow)   A large, cylindrical soft-paste cheese made in Norway.

TRÔO (goat)   One of the many fine, small, cinder-dusted cylinders of France's Orléanais country is named for the troglodyte-haunted village of Trôo, on the Loir River, a tributary of the more famous Loire.

TROYES, TROYEN (cow)   Similar to Camembert and produced in Champagne, these cheeses are also sometimes known as Barberey, or Ervy.

TRUCKLES, WILTSHIRE (cow)   An English type, not unlike Gloucestershire, the Truckles of Wiltshire disappeared in the late nineteenth century. But the term, possibly deriving from the word for small wheels, refers to small barrel-shaped cheeses, weighing 7 to 10 pounds, or rectangular loaf shapes, both of which were designed for easy portability; leaf cheese is considered ideal for loading ships carrying exports abroad.

TSCHIL (cow, sheep)   A rustic Armenian type that is matured in pots.

TULUM (goat)   Taking its name from the goatskin in which the curds mature, Tulum is a Turkish product with sharp flavor and a grayish white aspect; when the milk has more butterfat than usual, the cheese turns yellow.

TUMA (cow)   Fresh cheese made by Italians, sometimes called "basket cheese"; several California factories produce it.

TVDR SIR, TWDR SIR (sheep)   A skim-milk farm cheese that bears some resemblance to American Brick (see Brick above); it is traditional in Yugoslavia.

TVOROG, TWOROG (cow)   A fresh cheese made from sour milk that is sometimes pressed in wooden forms, this ancient Russian farm product is the basis for a famous cake called Vatrushki.

TYBO (cow)   A hard Danish loaf, in the Edam family, and also known as Banquet; Tybo is usually recognizable by its red wax exterior and its cream-colored interior in which occasional pea-size holes appear. It is mild and aromatic and sometimes seeded with caraway.

TYROFAGOS   A celebration, called "cheese-eating Sunday," begins a ten-day carnival on Cyprus to mark the Easter season; all meat is forsworn in place of cheese dishes in myriad array.

TYROLEAN (cow)   A German blue-veined type also known as Rastadt.

TYROPHILE   One who loves cheese.

U

ULLOA (cow)   A typical Spanish cheese known also as Gallego (it is produced in the northwest region of Gallicia), Ulloa is eaten fresh or matured five to six months, when it is semihard and somewhat oval in shape, pale yellow outside, creamy and mild within.

URBASA (sheep)   Better known as Idiazábal (see above), and also as Aralar and Urbia; one of Spain's most popular cheeses.

URI (cow)   From the canton of the same name, Uri is one of Switzerland's smaller rounds and little known to outsiders.

URSEREN (cow)   See Orsera.

V

VACHERIN (cow)   Putting aside the fact there are French desserts known under this name, there is room for confusion about the cheeses so called. Vacherin Fribourgeois is a classic Swiss flat cylinder with brushed rind and a firm but creamy consistency, often combined with Gruyère in Swiss fondues. Vacherin Mont d'Or, as the Swiss make it, is usually a small disk with tender rind and an interior the consistency of heavy honey, so creamy it is eaten with a spoon; the French version with the same name is larger and has a firm interior. Other such Vacherins made in France vary somewhat in dimension and take the names of their localities: Abondance, Bauges, Joux, and so on.

VALALOFFEN (cow)   A Swedish variant of Steppe (see above), made in Jämtland.

VALDETEJA (goat)   Occasionally a little cream from cow's milk is added, but characteristically Valdeteja (named for a town in the northwest panhandle of Spain) is a goat cheese matured between 15 and 25 days; when kept a matter of months its light-brown crust is lubricated with olive oil.

VALENCAY (goat)   Shaped like a truncated pyramid, with bluish skin dusted with vegetable ash when it comes from farms; the factory version, exported in large numbers, has white skin without pigmentation. Valencay takes its name from the town in the château country of the Loire, and it is now produced in several French regions.

VALENCIANA (cow, sheep)   Some of these fresh cheeses from the province of Valencia, Spain, are shaped like doughnuts through which the hole has not been completely pushed; others are peaked on top and have a little cow's milk mixed with the basic ewe's milk; they are often recommended as easily digested cheeses.

VÄSTERBOTTEN, VÄSTERGOTA (cow)   Similarly made Swedish cheeses often compared to Svecia (see above).

VENDÔME (cow)   Thick cylinders of soft-ripened type that have a vague likeness to Coulommiers (see above) are traditional products of Orléanais farms in France. The so-called Vendôme Bleu has a delicate pale-blue rind and supple consistency; Vendôme Cendré is aged in the ashes of grape vines, and often compared with Olivet.

VENETO (cow)   Similar to Asiago (see above) with a dark oiled surface and dense, dull-yellow interior, Veneto has sharp flavor that can be bitter. It originated in the area around Venice.

VERDO SARDO (sheep)   A firm, rich Sardinian round with bluish-green veins.

VERMONT (cow)   A Cheddar made in the state of Vermont, some of the best of which comes from Cabot; loosely used, the term is also applied to Crowley and Plymouth (see both above).

VIEUX PANÉ (cow)   A large, flat, square type made in southwest France not far from Villefranche de Rouergue; it is semisoft and has been described as a mild Pont l'Évêque.

VILLALON (sheep)   Also called Pata de Mulo (mule's hoof), Villalon looks like its nickname; it is eaten fresh or allowed to mature up to 12 days, developing a very subtle flavor described as "like drinking fresh ewe's milk."

VILLEDIEU (cow)   A variant of Neufchâtel.

VILLE-ST.-JACQUES (cow)   A small version of Brie named for its market town.

VITMÖGELOST (cow)   Soft-ripened, downy-white, Vitmögelost is a Swedish product classified as a *dessertostar* (dessert cheese) and compared to Brie, Camembert, and Crème Chantilly.

VIZE (sheep)   A Greek grating cheese.

VLASIC (sheep)   Made by Yugoslav farmers in the region of Bosnia, Vlasic is much like Travnik (see above).

VOID (cow)   Reminiscent of Limburger and Pont l'Évêque; produced in the Meuse River town of this name.

VOLOGODSKY (cow)   A Russian smoked cheese from Vologoda province.

VORARLBERG (cow)   A low-fat sour-milk cheese, Vorarlberg is a product of Austrian farmers in the region near the borders of Switzerland and Lichtenstein; its surface is moist, its consistency hard, and it has pronounced flavor and aroma.

W

WALLISER   A term used by German-speaking Swiss for cheeses made in the canton of Wallis (or Valais). See Bergkäse.

WARSAWSKY (cow)   Poland's original is a ewe's-milk product, described as having a "barnyard" flavor, but a cow's-milk version made in the U.S. is almost white and compares favorably to domestic Cheddar.

WASHED CURD (cow)   A semisoft paste made in cylindrical and rectangular-block shapes by a process evolved, perhaps, in New York; as the name implies, the curds are washed before salting, the process otherwise like that for Cheddar, and the result is a moister, more open, and less firm cheese.

WASHED RIND   Certain cheeses (for instance, Livarot, Munster, Pont l'Évêque) require moisture for proper fermentation and are therefore washed on the outside with wine or another liquid; the treatment gives them a smooth, almost shiny appearance.

WEISSLACKER (cow)   Cube-shaped and weighing 3½ pounds, Weisslacker is sometimes called Bierkäse and is the traditional Bavarian counterpart of Limburger.

WELSH RABBIT   Welsh cheese melted as a substitute for meat. See Recipes, page 158.

WENSLEYDALE (cow)   White Wensleydale is a young, white, flaky block, or small sphere, now made in quantity in several English factories; it has a mild, sourish, rather fresh taste and is considered an excellent accompaniment to apple pie. It is named for a Yorkshire valley where it is still aged in some farmhouses and by monks; Wensleydale originated when the Abbey of Jervaulx came to England with the takeover by the Normans. It began as a ewe's-milk cheese and remained so until the eighteenth century. The best of Wensleydale is allowed to develop blue veins and is compared to Stilton.

WERDER (cow)   A Prussian cheese that looks like Gouda, although sizes vary; it has an acidulous but mild flavor, less sharp and with more moisture than Tilsit, to which it has been compared.

WEXFORD (cow)   Firm, orange-colored, and sharp in flavor, Wexford takes its name from the fertile county in southeast Ireland. The fat, crumbly texture invites comparison with Cheshire, but Wexford is accepted as wholly Irish in origin.

WHEY CHEESES   Natural by-products, especially in places where people are poor; cheeses made from the watery milk residue called whey are as ancient as the dairy industry. Scandinavians have maintained their appetite for light-brown, sweetish products that include Flötost,

Mysost, Primost; Gjetost is made by the same Nordic process using goat's milk. Swiss Mascarpone is also made of goat whey (while Italian Mascarpone demands cream). Among other whey cheeses are Recuite, Ricotta, and Schottenziger; nor should the curds and whey of Miss Muffet be forgotten.

WILSTERMARSCH (cow)   Wilster is a town in the Holstein region of Germany which gives its name to a rapidly made version of Tilsit.

WILTSHIRE (cow)   A sweet curd cheese, similar to Derby, now a thing of the past; but much other cheese—including Caerphilly and Cheddar—is made in Wiltshire cheese factories. See Truckles.

WILTSHIRE GREEN (cow)   In the past, sage, parsley, and marigold leaves were bruised and steeped in milk overnight; the resulting green milk and fresh milk were then heated separately, and the two lots of curds were mixed in any proportion chosen by the cheesemaker. The result was much like Derby (see above).

WINDSOR RED (cow)   In Britain this term is a label for a "red-vein cheese," described by its makers as the result of infusing Cheddar with "British red wine from South England." The gaudily marbled product is formed in cylinders of varying size and packaged in wedges or in various containers.

WITHANIA (cow)   Named for the berries of the withania plant, from which a coagulant is made, the cheese called Withania is produced in Southeast Asia.

X

XAINTRAY (goat)   Farmers and small dairies in the goat country of western France produce many cheeses including the one named for Xaintray, a village not far from Parthenay.

Y

YAROSLAVSKY (cow)   A firm Russian cheese made in cylinders weighing between 20 and 25 pounds.

YORK (cow)   See Cambridge.

YOUNG AMERICAN (cow)   An American form of Cheddar which, according to USDA standards, should be 7 inches in diameter, 7 inches thick, and weigh 11 to 12 pounds (see Cheddar); the name describes the mold in which it is shaped, as well as the cheese.

YUNNAN (goat)   A rustic cheese made by herdsmen on the steep slopes and high plateaus of Yunnan province in southwest China.

Z

ZAKOUSSOTCHNYÏ (cow)   A Russian effort to copy Camembert, using pasteurized milk.

ZIEGELKÄSE (cow)   As the name indicates in German, a brick-shaped type about the size of Liederkranz; it is produced in Austria.

ZIEGENKÄSE   *Ziege* is the German word for "goat," and thus Ziegenkäse is the generic term for any cheese made from goat's milk in Austria, Germany, Lichtenstein, and the German-speaking parts of Switzerland. See Appenzeller-Ziegenkäse.

ZIGER (cow)   See Schottenziger.

ZLATIBORSKI SIR (sheep)   A regional Cream Cheese of Yugoslavia.

ZSENDICE (sheep)   An ancient Hungarian type of creamy Cottage Cheese.

For Further Reading

Mail Order Sources

Index

For Further Reading

Cheddar Gorge: A Book of English Cheeses, edited by Sir John Squire, London, 1937.

The Cheese Book, Vivienne Marquis and Patricia Haskell, New York, 1965.

Cheese and Cheese Cookery, T. A. Layton, London, 1967.

Cheese Making at Home, Don Radke, New York, 1974.

The Cheeses and Wines of England and France, John Ehle, New York, 1972.

Cheese Varieties and Descriptions, United States Department of Agriculture Handbook No. 54, Washington, D.C., revised 1969.

The Complete Book of Cheese, Bob Brown, introduction by Clifton Fadiman, New York, 1955.

Dictionnaire des Fromages, Robert Courtine, Paris, 1972.

English Cheeses of the North, Ambrose Heath, London, n.d.

English Cheeses of the South and West, John Arlott, London, n.d.

A Guide to Australian Cheeses, Josef Vondra, Melbourne, 1971.

Guide du Fromage, Pierre Androuët, Paris, 1971. Translated as *The Complete Encyclopedia of French Cheese,* New York, 1973.

Guide Gourmand de la France, Henri Gault and Christian Millau, Paris, 1970.

A Little Book of Cheese, Osbert Burdette, London, 1935.

Le Livre du Fromage, Christian Plume, Paris, 1968.

A Quintet of Cuisines, Michael Field, New York, 1970.

The Roquefort Adventure, Henri Pourat, Roquefort-sur-Soulzon, 1956.

Serve It Forth, M. F. K. Fisher, New York, 1937.

The Story of Cheese-Making in Britain, Val Cheke, 1959.

Mail Order Sources

EAST

The Cheese Shop
44 Mason Street
P.O. Box 661
Greenwich, Connecticut 06830

Nodine's Smokehouse
Route 63
Goshen, Connecticut 06756

Frigo House of Cheese
109 South Main Street
Torrington, Connecticut 06790

Cheese and Wine Cellar
Montgomery Mall
Bethesda, Maryland 20034

Cardullo's Gourmet Shop
6 Brattle Street
Cambridge, Massachusetts 02138

Gourmet Cottage & Cheese Shop
Route 23
South Egremont, Massachusetts
02158

Calef's Country Store
Barrington, New Hampshire 03825

Cheeses of All Nations
153 Chambers Street
New York, New York 10007

Cheese Village Ltd.
3 Greenwich Avenue
New York, New York 10011

Ideal Cheese Shop
1205 Second Avenue
New York, New York 10021

Paprikas Weiss
1546 Second Avenue
New York, New York 10028

Great Valley Mills
Quakertown, Bucks County,
Pennsylvania 18951

Yankee Cheese & Gift House
P.O. Box 47
Ashton, Rhode Island 02864

Cabot Farmer's Cooperative
Cabot, Vermont 05647

Crowley Cheese
Healdville, Vermont 05147

Grafton Village Cheese Company
Box 33
Grafton, Vermont 05146

Owl's Basket Cheese Shop
Village Square
Waitsfield, Vermont 05673

Plymouth Cheese Corporation
Box 1
Plymouth, Vermont 05060

Sugarbush Farm
Route 2
Woodstock, Vermont 05091

Vermont Country Store
Weston, Vermont 05161

Wine & Cheese Shop
1413 Wisconsin Avenue, N.W.
Washington, D.C. 20007

SOUTH

The Cheese Shop
76 Miracle Mile
Coral Gables, Florida 31334

Davison's
180 Peachtree Street, N.W.
Atlanta, Georgia 30303

D. H. Holmes
819 Canal Street
New Orleans, Louisiana 70112

Early's Honey Stand
Route 2, Box 100
Spring Hill, Tennessee 37174

Cheese Market of Houston
12850 Memorial Drive
Houston, Texas 77024

MIDWEST

Kolb-Lena Cheese Company
301 West Railroad Street
Lena, Illinois 62354

Maytag Dairy Farms
Box 806
Newton, Iowa 50208

Nauvoo Blue Cheese
Nauvoo Milk Products, Inc.
Nauvoo, Illinois 62354

Old World Cheese Mart
210 South Woodward
Birmingham, Michigan 48011

The Big Cheese
Skyway Level
IDS Crystal Court
Minneapolis, Minnesota 55402

Lund's
1450 West Lake Street
Minneapolis, Minnesota 55408

Treasure Cave Blue Cheese
Box 247
Faribault, Minnesota 55021

Paul's Cheese Stall
116 Union Market
St. Louis, Missouri 63101

Cornhusker Cheese
116 H. C. Filley Hall
University of Nebraska
Lincoln, Nebraska 68503

Samos Grocery
727 Bolivar Road
Cleveland, Ohio 44115

Mossholder Farm
Route 2
Appleton, Wisconsin 54911

Steve's Cheese
Route 2
Denmark, Wisconsin 54208

WEST

Cheese & Stuff
5042 North Central
Phoenix, Arizona 85012

The Cheese Factory
2 Spain Street
Sonoma, California 95476

The Cheese Shop
Farmer's Market
Los Angeles, California 90036

Marin French Cheese Company
7500 Red Hill Road
Petaluma, California 94952

Cassidy's Delicatessen
2406 East Third Avenue
Denver, Colorado 80223

Coquille Valley Dairy Co-op
Box 515
Bandon, Oregon 97411

Rogue River Blue Cheese
Box 3606
Central Point, Oregon 97501

Tillamook Cheese
Box 313
Tillamook, Oregon 97141

Cache Valley Dairy Association
Smithfield, Utah 84335

Northwest Gourmet Center
1208 Lake Street, Renton
Seattle, Washington 98055

Star Valley Swiss Cheese
Thayne, Wyoming 83127

CANADA
The Cheese Shoppe
611 Maisonneuve West
Montreal, Quebec

The Cheese Shop
258 Laurier Avenue, West
Ottawa 4, Ontario

Continental Cheese Shoppe
Yorkdale Shopping Centre
Toronto, Ontario

Global Cheese Shop
76 Kensington
Toronto, Ontario

FRANCE
Androuët
41, rue d'Amsterdam
Paris 8

Cantin
2, rue de Lourmel
Paris 15

Creplet-Brussol
Place de la Madeleine
Paris 8

Ferme St. Hubert
21, rue Vignon
Paris 8

GREAT BRITAIN
Fortnum & Mason
181 Picadilly
London SW1

Paxton & Whitfield
93 Jermyn Street
London SW1

Wells Stores
A329
Reading-Oxford, U.K.

R. W. Forsyth, Ltd.
30 Princes Street
Edinburgh 2

Scott's Fish Shop
3 Bridge Street
Kirkwall, Orkney, U.K.

ITALY
Casa de Formaggio
Fred Peck
Milan

NETHERLANDS
Fromagerie Crignon
Gravenstraat, 28
Amsterdam

Index

NOTE: The letters RCP before one or more page numbers indicates recipes; LEX indicates a discussion of cheeses in the International Cheese Lexicon, pages 183 to 292. Cheeses mentioned in the Lexicon but not elsewhere in the text are generally not included in this index; therefore, if a particular cheese cannot be found in the index, the reader may wish to look in the alphabetically arranged lexicon.

acid, need for in cheesemaking, 12, 14, 63, 96
  in holey cheeses, 50
  in natural-mold blues, 43
Ädelost, 45; LEX 187, 282
affineur, 4, 33, 105–6
aging of cheese, 9–10, 15, 48, 76, 100, 101, 105; LEX 252; see also curing
Ajoqueso, RCP 127; LEX 187
alcohol, as flavoring, 89; see also wine
aligot, RCP 167; LEX 188
Allgäuer, 63; LEX 188, 194
Alsace-Lorraine, 65, 70
American Cheddar, see Cheddar, American
"American Cheese," 16, 27; LEX 188
  homemade, 100–1
Amfrom, see Anfrom
Amish, the, 49; LEX 188
Anchovy-Mozzarella Crostini, RCP 125
Androuët, Henri, 201, 229
Androuët, Pierre, 210; Guide du Fromage, 106, 189
Androuët family, 106, 189
Anfrom, illus. 71; LEX 188–9; illus. back spread
Angelot, angelot, 32, 33; LEX 189, 265
animals, milk-producing, 9
annatto, 17, 22, 24, 33; LEX 189
aphrodisiacs, 40, 55; LEX 238
Appellation d'origine (label), LEX 189–90, 245
Appenzeller, illus. front spread, 50, illus. 51, 118; LEX 190, 276, 281
appetizers, 111, 123–9
  Ajoqueso, RCP 127
  anchovy Mozzarella crostini, RCP 125–6
  Camembert Amandine, RCP 129
  caraway Cream Cocktail Cheese, RCP 124
  cheese pistachio, RCP 123
  cheese sticks, RCP 128
  chili-flavored cheese log, RCP 125

appetizers (continued)
  filled pastries, RCP 128–9
  garlic Cheddar–Cream Cheese roll, RCP 124–5
  garlic–Monterey Jack spread, RCP 127
  Jeannette Seaver's Boursinoise, RCP 124
  Mozzarella: croquettes, deep-fried, RCP 126
    crostini, with anchovy, RCP 125–6
    Milanese, RCP 126–7
  puffed-up cheese canapés, RCP 127
  Sapsago cocktail spread, RCP 128
  Wensleydale dip, 111; RCP 125
apples and cheese combination, 25
Arlott, John, 44
Arroz verde con chilies rellenos, RCP 154
artichokes: Jerusalem, fried in cheese batter, RCP 160–1
  Romano- and anchovy-stuffed, RCP 160
Asiago, 10, illus. 76, 77, 107, 151; LEX 191, 255, 282, 289
Athens, ancient, 8
Auge Valley, France, 29, 63
Australia, 20, 26, 29, 50, 71, 108
Austria, 29, 60, 62, 63, 65, 71, 73, 116
Austrian "Swiss," 14; LEX 196
Auvergne region, France, 25, 41, 63, 167; LEX 195

Backsteiner, 63; LEX 191
bacon-cheese spaghetti sauce, RCP 172
bacteria, in cheesemaking, 9, 10, 14, 30, 31, 38, 96, 281
Bacterium linens, 63, 200
Bagnes, 52, 119; LEX 191, 216, 270
Baguette Laonnaise, 64; LEX 192
Baguette de Thiérache, 64; LEX 192
Bailey, Nathan, 18
baked corn with chilies and cheese, RCP 163
baked endives with two cheeses, RCP 164

baked okra, tomatoes, corn, and cheese, RCP 166
Balkans, 55
Banon, *illus. 56, 57*; LEX 192
Baronet, 73; LEX 192
Battelmatt, 77; LEX 192, 194
Baulny (cheesemaker), 217
Bavaria, Germany, 62, 63
beans, refried, with cheese, RCP 161
Beard, James, *Delights and Prejudices,* 110
Beaufort, 50, 118; LEX 193, 216, 285
Beaumont, 72; LEX 193
béchamel, 123, 170, 255
Beck, Simone, 111, 123, 149, 159
    Simca's Cuisine, 111, 149, 171
beef: and Mozzarella meat loaf, RCP 133
    Tyrolean roast, with cheese, RCP 134–5
beefsteak au fromage, 53
beer: as cheese accompaniment, 117, 118, 124
    and cheese soup, RCP 131
    use in cheese aging, 105
Beeton, Isabella, 79
beets, cheese-flavored, RCP 161
Bel Paese, 68–9; RCP 126, 133; LEX 193, 211, 244, 245, 262, 277, 278; *illus. back spread*
    in pasta and rice dishes, RCP 152, 153, 168–9
Bel Piano Lombardo, 69; LEX 193
Belgium, 62, 63, 64, 71, 95; LEX 187
Bell Inn, Stilton, England, 42–3
Bella Alpina, 69; LEX 193
Bella Milano, 69; LEX 193
Belloc, Hillaire, 76
Benedictine monks, 46, 70, 71
Benoit, Jehane, 169
Berber tribes, 54
Berioux, Jules, 257
Bidwell, John, 42, 89
Bierkäse, 60; LEX 194–5, 290
biscuits, cheese, RCP 175–6
Bismarck Schlosskäse, 60–1
Bleu de Bresse, 41 and *illus.,* 118; LEX 196, 237
Bleu de Corse, 41; LEX 196
Bleu de Laqueuille, 41; LEX 196, 275
Bleu des Causses, 41; LEX 196
Bleu du Haut Jura, LEX 196, 245
bleus de brebis, 57

Blue Castello, 45, 110; LEX 197
blue cheeses, 10, 38–41 and *illus.,* 42–6, 57, 169, 170; LEX 195–6, 197, 275
    buying tips, 107
    cream filling, for pastry, RCP 129
    Danish (Danablu), *illus. front spread, illus. 41, 45,* 118
    differences between Roquefort, Gorgonzola, Stilton, 42, 43, 107; LEX 234, 281
    of England, 17, 25, 38, 42–4 and *n.;* LEX 197, 281
    of France, 38–41, 63; LEX 195–6, 245
    homemade, 101–2
    of Italy, 42; LEX 234, 281
    labeling, 40; LEX 189, 196, 245, 275, 282
    making of, 39–40, 42, 43; LEX 275
    meatballs, RCP 133–4
    natural-mold kinds, 42, 43, 44
    sauce for fish, RCP 172
    terminology of, LEX 197
    vegetable dishes with, RCP 161, 164–5
    and wine, 115, 117, 118
    see also Gorgonzola; Roquefort; Stilton
Blue Cheshire, 17, 43; LEX 197, 213
blue mold, growing, 101
Blue Vinny, 38, 44 and *n.;* LEX 197
Blue Wensleydale, 25, 44; LEX 197
Blumer, Adam, 49
Boël, Marius, 197, 221
Bondon, 29 *n.;* LEX 198
Bonneville, 29 *n.,* 32; LEX 198
books, booklets:
    Book of Household Management, by Isabella Beeton, 79
    A Book of Middle Eastern Food, by Claudia Roden, 55, 232
    Cheddar Gorge, by Sir John Squire, et al, 247
    The Cheese Book, by V. Marquis and P. Haskell, 273
    Cheese Varieties, USDA publication, 225
    The Cheeses and Wines of England and France, by John Ehle, 95, 234
    Classic Italian Cook Book, by Marcella Hazan, 77
    The Cuisine of Hungary, by George Lang, 202, 228, 248

books, booklets (*continued*)
 Delights and Prejudices, by James
  Beard, 110
 English Food, by Jane Grigson, 146
 Food for Pleasure, by Ruth Lowinsky,
  181
 The Food of Italy, by Waverley Root,
  77
 Good Things, by Jane Grigson, 179
 Guide du Fromage, by Pierre
  Androuët, 106, 189
 Guide Gourmand de la France, by
  H. Gault and C. Millau, 255
 Guide to Cheese and Cheese Cookery,
  by T. A. Layton, 181, 217
 *Jeannette's Secrets of Everyday Good
  Cooking,* by J. Seaver, 124
 From Julia Child's Kitchen, by Julia
  Child, 149
 Larousse Gastronomique, 158
 Lovely Food, by Ruth Lowinsky, 179
 The Physiology of Taste, by Jean
  Anthelme Brillat-Savarin, 51, 156,
  214
 Simca's Cuisine, by Simone Beck, 111,
  149, 171
 Wine and Cheese, the Perfect Partners,
  by Helen Evans Brown, 115
bourekias, sweet, with Cream Cheese,
 RCP 179–80
Boursault, 110, 116; LEX 199; *illus. back
  spread*
Boursin, 88, *illus. 90;* LEX 199; *illus.
  back spread*
Boursinoise, Jeannette Seaver's, RCP 124
braised fennel with two cheeses,
  RCP 163–4
bread mold, and blue cheeses, 38–9, 42,
  101
breads, RCP 174–6
Brick, *illus. front spread,* 10, 27, 59,
  60, 73, 118; RCP 133; LEX 195,
  200, 242
 rindless loaf, LEX 273
Bricquebec, 29 *n.,* 71; LEX 200, 267
Brie, 10, 28, 29, 30 and *illus.,* 31–2, 33–4,
  illus. 34, 35–7, 106, 108; LEX 200–1,
  217, 282; *illus. back spread*
 buying tips, 108
 Coulommiers, 34, *illus., 35,* 118; LEX
  200, 218; *illus. back spread*
 Delico, 35; LEX 201
 de Meaux, 34; LEX 200–1

Brie (*continued*)
 de Melun, 34; LEX 200–1
 fermier, 33; LEX 201
 kinds of, 33–4; LEX 200–1, 289
 leftovers of, in cooking, 123; RCP 143
 making of, 30
 Rouge et Noir, 35; LEX 200, 201
 serving, 110, 111, 112, 116, 118
 shape and size, 28, 33, 108
 stabilization, 31–2
 U.S. domestic, 29–30, 35–6, 108;
  LEX 201
 U.S. imports, 30, 31
Brillat-Savarin, Jean Anthelme, 36,
  156–7, 226
 The Physiology of Taste, 51, 156, 214
Brillat-Savarin (cheese), 29 *n.,* 35;
  LEX 201, 222
Brittany, 50, 71, 81
Broccio, Brocciu, 56; LEX 201–2
Brockway, Maurice, 62
Bronwyn's cheesecake, RCP 177–8
Brown, Helen Evans: corn, chili, and
  cheese bread of, RCP 174–5;
  *Wine and Cheese, the Perfect
  Partners,* 115
Bruneau, Jean-Claude, 206
Bryndza, 55; LEX 201, 202, 248, 284
buffalo, buffalo cheese, 9, 54, 68, 82
Bühlmann, Willi, 13–14, 107
Bulgarian white brined cow's-milk
  cheese, 55
Buquet, Jean-Pierre, 29
Burgundy, cheeses of, 4, 36, 50, 105, 116
Burns, Robert, 243
Butter cheese, 69; LEX 203
butterfat content: double and triple
  creams, 34; Edam vs. Gouda, 67;
  Minnesota Slim, 74; Monterey
  Jack, 26; Parmesan, 76
buttermilk, LEX 203
 as starter, 11, 16, 79, 96, 97, 102, 281
buying cheese, tips on, 103–4, 106–10
Byron, George Gordon, Lord, 47

Cabécou, 57; LEX 204, 205, 210
Cabrales, 57; LEX 204
cacio duro, 76
Caciocavallo, 10, 68, 151; LEX 204, 209,
  242, 282, 286
 making of, LEX 262, 281
caciotta di pecorino, 77; LEX 205

Caerphilly, *illus. front spread,* 18 n.,
    22, *illus. 24,* 110; Lex 205,
    291
  Glamorgan sausages, Rcp 146
  in potato dishes, Rcp 165, 167
Caesar salad, 169
cakes, 51
  Bronwyn's cheesecake, Rcp 177–8
  Cottage Cheese pancake gâteau, Rcp
    178
  Le friadone, 56
California, 25, 30, 35, 62, 82
California Experiment Station, 197
California Jack, 25; *see also* Monterey
    Jack
Cambridge, 81; Lex 206, 279
Camembert, *illus. front spread,* 10,
    28–32, 34–5, 36, 37, 61, 106;
    Lex 206–7, 238–9
  Amandine, Rcp 129
  au Vin, Rcp 129
  Borden, Lex 206
  crêpes fourrées au, Rcp 143
  fermier, Lex 206, 218
  ice cream, Ruth Lowinsky's Rcp 179
  imitations, 29–30, 35; Lex 206–7, 270,
    272, 287, 292
  judging ripeness of, 30, 103–4, 108–9
  labels, 29, *illus. 32;* Lex 218, 245, 282
  leftover or chalky center, in cooking,
    123; Rcp 143, 171
  making of, 11–13, 30
  medical value of, 31
  sauce, Rcp 171
  savouries, Rcp 181–2
  serving, 110, 112, 115, 116, 117, 118
  stabilization, 31
  true, region of, 29
  U.S. domestic, 29–30, 35–6, 108; Lex
    206, 208
  U.S. imports, 30, 31; Lex 207
Camosun, 26; Lex 207
Canada, 46, 69, 70, 108; Cheddar, 20;
    Lex 212
cannelloni stuffing, Rcp 152
Cantal, 25, *illus. 24,* 63, 77, 110;
    Lex 207–8, 283; *illus. back
    spread*
  label, Lex 189, 245
Caprice des Dieux, *illus. front spread,*
    34, 110; Lex 208
Caprino Romano, 77; Lex 208, 274
Cardini, Caesar, 169

Carentan, 29; Lex 208
Carlton Hotel, London, 181
carob, 84
carré, Lex 198, 208
Carré de Bonneville, 32; Lex 208
Carré de l'Est, 35, 36, 114, 118; Lex
    190, 208
  Domremy, Lex 223
Casanova, 40
casein, 96
casseroles, 142
  Arroz verde con chilies rellenos, Rcp
    154
  baked corn with chilies and cheese,
    Rcp 163
  baked okra, tomatoes, corn, and
    cheese, Rcp 166
  braised fennel with two cheeses,
    Rcp 163–4
  cauliflower, tomato, and cheese, Rcp
    162
  Cypriot eggplant and tomatoes baked
    with cheese, Rcp 162–3
  eggplant with meat and cheese, Rcp
    150–1
  endives baked with two cheeses, Rcp
    164
  green rice with Parmesan, Rcp 153–4
  hominy grits with garlic cheese, Rcp
    164
  Moussaka, Rcp 150–1
  pasta with lamb and Kefalotyri,
    Rcp 155–6
  pastitsio, Rcp 155–6
  pork sausage-cheese strata, Rcp 134
  tian of zucchini, rice, and cheese,
    Rcp 168–9
  two-cheese macaroni-vegetable, Rcp
    154
Castelmagno, 42; Lex 209
Castres, France, 25; Lex 213
cauliflower, tomato, and cheese
    casserole, Rcp 162
cendré, 36; Lex 209–10
Céracée, 82; Lex 210
Cevru, 34
Chambarand, 71; Lex 210
Champagne region, France, 33, 36
Chanteclair restaurant, New York, 147
Chantilly, *see* Hablé Crème Chantilly
Chaource, *illus. front spread,* 36, 37;
    Lex 211
Charlemagne, 6–7, 28

Chaumont, 70; LEX 211
Cheddar, 10, 16–27, 28, 76; LEX 212,
    236, 241, 254, 265, 291; *illus.
    back spread*
  aging terms, 22, 107; LEX 212
  American, 27, 111; LEX 188, 198,
    212, 217, 292
    Longhorn label, LEX 248
    New York State, 20, *illus.* 27, 90;
      LEX 212, 258
    Vermont, 20, 21, *illus.* 27, 86, 88,
      110; LEX 212, 289
    Wisconsin, 20, *illus. back
      spread*
  appetizers, 111; RCP 124–5, 127
  buying tips, 104, 106–7
  Canadian, 20; LEX 212
  coloring, 16, 17, 22, 24, 104; LEX
    189, 212
  English, 3, 5, 16–18, 19–23, 24–5, 89;
    LEX 212; *see also* Cheshire
  in fish dishes, RCP 137–8, 140
  French versions, 19, 25; LEX 213
  Glamorgan sausages, RCP 146
  of goat's milk, 59
  handmade vs. factory-produced,
    20–1, 23, 24, 25
  making of, 16, 20–1
  melting propensity, 17, 23, 24
  pasta dishes with, RCP 151, 155
  in pie filling, RCP 156
  quiche fillings, RCP 145, 146
  rindless loaf, LEX 273
  sauce, 165–6; RCP 170
  Scottish, *see* Dunlop
  serving, 110, 111, *illus.* 114, 117
  sharpness, 106–7; LEX 212
  smoked, 86
  soufflé roll, RCP 149–50
  terminology, 18 and *n.*; LEX 212
  vegetable dishes with, RCP 161, 163,
    165–6, 167–8
  Welsh, *see* Caerphilly
Cheddar Roast restaurant, London, 181,
    217
cheddaring, LEX 212–13, 238
cheese and wine tasting parties, 117-18
cheese bread, RCP 174
cheese clubs, 110, 215
cheese foods, 9, 74; LEX 213
  cold pack, 111–12
cheese pistachio, RCP 123
cheese press, 100–1

cheese sticks, RCP 128
cheesecake, 84
  Bronwyn's, RCP 177–8
cheesemakers:
  Baulny, 217; Jules Berioux, 257;
  Marius Boël, 197, 221; Buquet
  family, 29; Daniel Considine,
  58–9; John Coolidge, 87, 265;
  Daniel Courtonne, 11–13, 29,
  105, 218; George Crowley and
  Crowley family, 21, 216, 220;
  Donadia sisters, 42; Emil Frey,
  60–1, 230, 248; Barbara Gilmour,
  23, 224, 233; Jeremie Girod, 193;
  Victor Golay, 36; Ken Grehan,
  191; Hans Hanan, 246; Joseph
  Harding, 20, 72, 238; Marie
  Harel, 9, 28, 61, 238–9; David
  Jacks, 25, 255; John Jossi, 73,
  242; Lydia Kirby, 16, 17, 244;
  Alois Koch, 57, 58; Karl Kolb
  and Kolb family, 35, 201, 206,
  259; William Lawrence, 83; Mrs.
  Kent Leavitt, 265; Mossholder
  family, 27; Hanne Nielsen, 9, 72,
  258; Lewis M. Norton, 264; Vrest
  Orton, 88; Wallace Parrish, 49;
  Gerard Paul, 236; Mme. Marcel
  Pinot, 29, 32; Clayton Raw-
  houser, 59; Jan Reeslev, 87; Oscar
  Rohde, 258; Steinwand family,
  26, 216; Susannah and Reg Stone,
  80, 88, 204; Henrik Tholstrup,
  37, 219, 284; Thompson family,
  35, 201; Wegmuller, 234, 285;
  Bill Wilke, 235
cheesemaking, 95–102
  basic equipment, 96–7
  basic process, 96
  blues, general, LEX 275
  Brie, 30
  Caciocavallo, LEX 263, 281
  Camembert, 11–13, 30
  Cheddar, 16, 20–1
  Colby, 26; LEX 216, 236
  double and triple creams, 34
  Edam, 67
  Emmenthaler, 13–15
  Gorgonzola, 42
  granular-curd process, 26; LEX 216,
    236
  Gruyère, 50

cheesemaking (*continued*)
  homemade:
    American, 100–1; blue, 101–2;
      Cottage Cheese, 97–8; Cream
      Cheese, 98–100
    ingredients, 11, 15; *see also* rennet
    Lancashire, 24
    Liederkranz, 61
    Limburger, 62–3
    Livarot, 33, 64; LEX 290
    Mozzarella, LEX 262, 281
    pasta filata method, 82; LEX 262, 281
    plastic-curd method, 82; LEX 230, 262
    Pont l'Évêque, 32
    Provolone, 68; LEX 262, 281
    rindless loaf, LEX 273
    Roquefort, 39–40; LEX 229
    sage cheeses, 87–8
    spun-curd method, LEX 230, 262, 281
    starters for, 96, 102
    Stilton, 43
    stirred-curd method, 26; LEX 216, 236
    washed-curd process, 26–7; LEX 290
Cheshire, *illus. front spread*, 3, 10,
      16–17 and *illus.*, 18–19, 21, 76;
      RCP 166; LEX 213
    Blue, 17, 43; LEX 197, 213
    terminology, 18 *n.*
Cheshire School of Agriculture, 81
Chester (French Cheshire), 19, 25;
      LEX 213
Chester, England, 17
chèvre, *illus. 59*, 116; LEX 213–14, 253
Chez Androuët, Paris, 106, 189
Chiberta, LEX 214; *illus. back
      spread*
chicken: breasts, stuffed with Lieder-
      kranz and ham, RCP 135–6
    croquettes with Farmer Cheese, RCP
      138–9
    roast, stuffed with Gruyère and
      noodles, RCP 135
Child, Julia, *From Julia Child's Kitchen,*
      149
chili-flavored cheese log, RCP 125
chutney cheese, savoury, RCP 181
Citeaux, 71; LEX 215
clubs, cheese, 110, 215
Coeur à la crème Américaine, 81;
      RCP 178–9; LEX 216
Colby, *illus. front spread,* 26, 74, 100;
      LEX 198, 216, 220, 255

Colby (*continued*)
    Ajoqueso, RCP 127
    of goat's milk, 59
    making, 26; LEX 216, 236
    oysters baked with, RCP 140
    pasta dishes with, RCP 154
    soufflé roll, RCP 149–50
    vegetable dishes with, RCP 163
cold pack, 111–12
Colette, 37
Colwick, 81; LEX 216, 279
Combalou, Caves of, 5, 38, 39–40, 146,
      229
Comté, Gruyère de, 50; LEX 216, 224
    label, LEX 189, 245
Confienza, Pantaleone da, 230
Confrérie des Chevaliers du Taste-
      fromage, 216
Confrérie du Remoudou, 216, 272
Congress of Vienna, 216–17
Considine, Daniel, 58–9
Convention of Stresa, 189, 236, 245,
      257, 281–2
cookies, Lisl's cheese, RCP 180
Coolidge, John, 87, 265
corn, chili, and cheese bread, RCP 174–5
corn with chilies and cheese, baked,
      RCP 163
Cornhusker, 26; LEX 217
Corsica, 56
Cottage Cheese, 10, 11, 80, *illus. 83,*
      91, 123, 141–2, 169; LEX 217–
      18, 228
    appetizer, RCP 124
    Creamed, 80, 98; LEX 218
    crêpe filling, RCP 142
    making of, 97–8
    moisture content, 217–18
    pancake gâteau, RCP 178
    in pie filling, RCP 156
coulant, defined, LEX 218
Coulommiers, 34, *illus. 35,* 118; LEX
      200, 218; *illus. back spread*
Courtine, Robert, 38, 130
Courtonne, Daniel and Simone, 11–13,
      29, 32, 37, 105, 218
crabmeat and shrimp lasagne, RCP 141
Cream Cheese, 10, 79–80, 83–4, 91,
      142; RCP 152–3, 162–3; LEX 218
    appetizers, 111; RCP 123–5
    chili steak sauce, RCP 173
    country or farm style, 80
    crêpe filling, RCP 143

Cream Cheese (*continued*)
  in desserts, RCP 176–9
  dips, 111
  flavor accents for, 100
  goat's-milk, 59; LEX 218
  making of, 98–100
  mixed with other cheeses, 111, 123
  pastry dough, 128, 145; RCP 176–7
  Philadelphia, 83, 111
  vegetable dishes with, RCP 162–3, 168
Creamed Cottage Cheese, 80; LEX 218
  making of, 98
Crema Dania (*or* Danica), 37, 116;
    LEX 219, 284; *illus. back*
    spread
  leftovers in cooking, RCP 143
Crème de Camembert, RCP 129
Crème Royale, 37; LEX 219
Crémet Nantais, 81; LEX 219
Creole, 83; LEX 219
crêpes, RCP 142–3
  fournées au Camembert, RCP 143
  Mozzarella and tomato filling, RCP
    143
  mushroom and creamy cheese filling,
    RCP 143
  Ricotta and herb filling, RCP 142–3
Croque Monsieur, 111; RCP 159; LEX 219
croquettes, 51
  Camembert, RCP 182
  chicken and Farmer Cheese, RCP 138–9
  Mozzarella, deep-fried, RCP 126
  potato with cheese, 167
Crottin, 116
  de Chavignol, *illus. 59;* LEX 212, 219–
    20
Crowdie, 80, 88; LEX 220
Crowley, 21, 111; LEX 216, 220, 265, 289
Crowley, George, 21
Crowley family, 216, 220
curdling, 6, 7–8, 9, 11, 12, 272; *see also*
  milk, coagulation of
curds: cow vs. goat, 58 *n.*
  separation from whey, 7, 11, 12, 14, 67,
    96, 98, 100–1, 272
curing, 9–10, 96
  blue cheeses, 39–40, 42, 43
  firm cheeses, 15
  soft-ripened cheeses, 13, 30–1, 32, 33,
    34, 36–7
  use of wine in, 36, 50, 105
Curnonsky (gourmet), 252
cutting cheese, tips on, 112–14, and *illus.*

Cypriot eggplant and tomatoes baked
    with cheese, RCP 162–3
Czechoslovakia, 45, 71

Dale pudding, 25
Damietta, Domiati, 54; LEX 221, 264
Danablu, Danish Blue, *illus. front*
    spread, illus. 41, 45, 118; LEX
    221, 282
Danbo, 169; LEX 221, 282
David, Elizabeth, 167
Delalp, 119
Delico, Brie, 35; LEX 201
Denmark, 3, 9, 29, 37, 45, 49, 71, 72, 87,
    108, 110, 169
Derby, 22, 24, 25; LEX 222, 291
  Sage, 88; LEX 276, 291
desserts, RCP 176–80; *see also* cakes;
  pies
Diderot, Denis, 208
dips, 111; Wensleydale, 25; RCP 125
domestic cheeses, *see* United States,
    domestic cheeses
Domiati, Damietta, 54; LEX 221, 264
Donadia, Domenica and Caterina, 42
Doret, 73; LEX 223
Dorrius restaurant, Amsterdam, 137
Dorset, 38, 44
  Blue Vinny, 38, 44 and *n.*; LEX 197
Double Bond, 29 *n.*; LEX 198
double creams (*double crèmes*), 10, 34,
    108; LEX 223
Double Gloucester, *see* Gloucester,
    Double
Downey, Henry, 25
Dunlop, 23; LEX 224
Durand restaurant, Paris, 255
Dutch Cheese, 80

Echourgnac, 71; LEX 224
Edam, *illus. front spread,* 49, 66–7
    and *illus.,* 90, 106, 108; LEX
    198, 224–5, 232, 235, 282, 287;
    making of, 67
Effendi, Sidqui, 238
eggplant: baked with meat and
    cheese, RCP 150–1
  Cypriot, with tomatoes, baked with
    cheese, RCP 162–3
  Parmigiana, RCP 163
Ehle, John, *The Cheeses and Wines of*
    England and France, 95, 234

Elbo, 108; LEX 225, 282
Emmental Français, 50; LEX 225
Emmenthaler, *illus. front spread,*
    10, 37, 47–8 and *n., illus. 48,* 49,
    illus. 51, 53; RCP 152–3; LEX
    225–6, 282
  beets, RCP 161–2
  canapés, 111
  imitations, 49–50, 107; LEX 188, 225–
    6, 237, 239
  making of, 13–15
  melting propensity, 53
  serving, 110
  size and weight of, 13; LEX 226
  soup, RCP 130–1
  true, identifying, 53, 107; LEX 226
endives baked with two cheeses, RCP
    164
England, 88, 117
  blue cheeses of, 17, 25, 38, 42–4 and
    n., 107; LEX 197, 281
  Cheddars, 3, 5, 16–18, 19–23, 24–5,
    89; LEX 212
  unripened cheeses, 80, 81
English Country Cheese Council, 228
Entrammes, 71; LEX 226
enzymes, 8, 96, 272
Époisses, 36, 105, 116; LEX 226, 246,
    277; *illus. back spread*
Ermite, 46; LEX 226–7
Ervy-le-Châtel, 36; LEX 227
Esbareich, 57; LEX 227
Escoffier, Auguste, 181
Esrom, 71, 72, 108; LEX 190, 227; *illus.
    back spread*
Excelsior, 29 *n.,* 34; LEX 222, 227
Explorateur, 34, 116; LEX 227; *illus.
    back spread*

Fadiman, Clifton, 74
Farmer Cheese, 123; LEX 228
  appetizer, RCP 124
  chicken croquettes with, RCP 138–9
  crêpe fillings, RCP 142–3
  sauces, RCP 171, 173
  shrimp and green beans with, RCP
    140–1
  in vegetable dishes, RCP 162, 167
"Farmhouse" grade, 20; LEX 228
fennel, braised, with two cheeses, RCP
    163–4

fermentation, 15, 48, 50
fermented soft cheeses, *see* soft-ripened
    cheeses
fermier, defined, LEX 228
Feta, 55, 59 *n.;* LEX 228, 253, 264, 274,
    284; *illus. back spread*
  baked okra, tomatoes, corn and cheese,
    RCP 166
  Greek cheese-spinach pie, RCP 156
  Greek shrimps with, RCP 138
  salads, 169
  and spinach quiche, RCP 145
fettucine al burro, 151
Feuilletée au Roquefort, 128; RCP
    146–8
Field, Michael, 15
fillings (*see also* stuffings):
  for crêpes:
    Mozzarella and tomato, RCP 143
    mushrooms and creamy cheese,
      RCP 143
    Ricotta and herbs, RCP 142–3
    Ricotta and spinach, RCP 143
  for quiches, 145
    Cheddar, onion and bacon, RCP 146
    cheese and ham, RCP 145
    Roquefort, RCP 145
    spinach and Feta, RCP 145
    tomato and Swiss, RCP 145–6
  for pastry, 128
    Blue Cheese Cream, RCP 129
    Swiss and Sapsago, RCP 128–9
  soufflé roll, RCP 149–50
Fin de Siècle, 29 *n.;* LEX 229
Finland, 45
Fior d'Alpe, 69; LEX 228
Fior di Latte, 82; LEX 228
Fiore Sardo, 56; LEX 228–9, 282
firm cheeses, 10, 16–27
fish, 132–3, 137
  Blue Cheese sauce for, RCP 172
  broiled, with cheese, RCP 137–8
  cheese soup, Scandinavian, RCP 132
Fisher, M. F. K., 7, 69
flavorings, 8, 11, 56, 85–91
Fleming, Sir Alexander, 31
Fleur des Alpes, 69; LEX 193, 229
Fol d'Amour, 34; LEX 229
fondu, LEX 229
fondue, 51, 156–7; LEX 229, 230, 288
  cheese, RCP 157–8
  Fribourg style, 37
  wine in, 118–19

fondue and wine party, 118–19
Fonduta, *fonduta,* 107, 119, 157; Lex 229
    piemontese, Lex 230
Fontina, 73, 107, 119; Rcp 139, 152, 163;
    Lex 194, 229, 230, 276, 282; *illus.
    back spread*
Fortingall Hotel, Fortingall, Scotland,
    159
Fougeru, 34; Lex 230
France, 3–4, 5, 6, 105, 108, 110
    blue cheeses, 38–41, 63; Lex 195–6,
        245
    Chester, 19, 25.
    fermier cheeses, 70–2
    goat cheeses, 54, 57, 59, 88, 110, 113,
        116
    herbed cheeses, 88
    monastery cheeses, 70–1
    number of cheeses of, 185
    soft-ripened cheeses, 11–13, 28–35, 36,
        108
    strong-flavored cheeses, 63–5
    Swiss cheese imitations of, 50; Lex
        225
    unripened cheeses, 81, 82
    wine and cheese combinations, 115–17
    see also Île-de-France; Normandy;
        and other regions
Franche-Comté, France, 50, 65
Franklin, Benjamin, 77
freezing fresh and grated cheeses, 114
fresh cheeses, *see* unripened cheeses
Frey, Emil, 60–1, 230, 248
friadone, le, 56
Fribourg Vacherin, 37; Lex 288
Frigo, David, 77
frittata, cheese-vegetable, Rcp 143–4
Fromage à la Crème, 81; Lex 231
Fromage à Raclette, 52
Fromage Blanc, 81; Lex 231
fromager affineur, 4, 33, 105–6
fromages à rebibes, 78
Frühstückkäse, 141; Lex 231
fruit and cheese combinations, 25, 77,
    111, 176
fungi, 38; *see also* Penicillium fungus
Fynbo, 108; Lex 231, 282

Galbani, Egidio, 193
Gammelost, 62; Lex 232
Gapron, Gaperon, *illus. front spread,*
    63; Lex 232

garlic Cheddar–Cream Cheese roll,
    Rcp 124–5
garlic flavoring, 8, 88, 90
garlic–Monterey Jack spread (Ajoqueso),
    Rcp 127
Gault, Henri, 167; *Guide Gourmand de
    la France,* 255
George II, King of England, 42
George III, King of England, 42 *n.*
Germany, 29, 60, 62, 63, 64, 71
Géromé, 70 and *illus.;* Lex 233, 249
Gervais, 82; Lex 222, 233, 264
Gervais, Charles, 233
Gharithes, Rcp 138
Gilmour, Barbara, 23, 224, 233
Girod, Jeremie, 193
Gjetost, 59; Lex 233, 253, 257, 291
Glamorgan, Lex 233
    sausages, Rcp 146; Lex 233
Glärnerkäse, 88; Lex 277; *see also*
        Sapsago
Glarus, 73, 88; Lex 233–4
Gloucester, Lex 234
    Double, *illus. front spread,* 22–3;
        Lex 217, 234
goat, goat's milk, 9, 54, 58 and *n.*
goat cheeses, 36, 54–9, 110, 113, 116,
    118; Lex 213–14
    blues, 41; Lex 197
    demand for, 54, 57–8.
    herbed, 56, 89
    texture of, 58 *n.*
    U.S. domestic, 58–9
goat-and-sheep cheeses, 56
goat-sheep-and-cow cheese, 56–7
Golay, Victor, 36
Golden Buck, 158; Lex 234
Gold'n' Rich, 73; Lex 234
Golding, Dr. N. S., 207
Gomser, 52, 119; Lex 234, 270
Gorgonzola, *illus. front spread,* 10, 38,
    41 and *illus.,* 42, 45, 118; Rcp
        152; Lex 223, 234, 249, 257, 281
    comparisons with Roquefort and
        Stilton, 43, 107; Lex 234, 281
    French versions of, 41; Lex 276
    making of, 42
Gouda, *illus. front spread,* 66, 67, 108;
        Lex 194, 198, 202, 231, 235,
        282
Gourmandise, 89; Lex 235

Gournay, 29 *n.;* LEX 235
Gräddost, LEX 236; *illus. back
    spread*
Grana, *grana,* 75; LEX 236, 262
    Lodigiano, 75; LEX 228, 236, 248
    Lombardo, LEX 236, 248
    Padano, 75; LEX 236; *illus. back
        spread*
    Parmigiano-Reggiano, 75, 77, 107;
        LEX 236, 262
    Reggiano, LEX 236, 271
    stravecchio, 76; LEX 281
    stravecchione, 76; LEX 281
Grand Hotel, Roquefort, France, 39–40
granular-curd process, 26; LEX 216, 236,
    265
Grappe, Grappa, 89, *illus.* 90; LEX 236
gratin, au gratin, gratiné, LEX 236
    broiled fish, RCP 137–8
    mussels and spinach, RCP 139
    of sliced tomatoes, RCP 167–8
grating cheeses, 10, 25, 68, 75, 76–7, 78,
    107, 151; LEX 236, 262, 278; *see
    also* Grana
Greece, 54–5, 169; ancient, 7, 8
Greek shrimps with Feta, RCP 138
green cheeses, 87–8; LEX 237
Grehan, Ken, 191
Grevéost, 50; LEX 221, 237
Grièges, 41; LEX 237
Grigson, Jane: *English Food,* 146; *Good
    Things,* 179
Gris de Lille, 65; LEX 237
Groot, Roy de, 199
Grünerkäse, 88; LEX 237, 277
Gruyère, *illus. front spread,* 10, 36, 47,
    50, *illus. 51,* 53, 89, 141; RCP 153;
    LEX 194, 236–7, 241, 250, 276,
    282
    Beaufort, 50, 118; LEX 193, 216, 285
    beefsteak au fromage, 53
    de Comté, 50; LEX 189, 216, 224, 245
    Doulce, LEX 224
    in fondue, 37
    making of, 50
    marinated, 169
    melting propensity, 53
    natural vs. process, 53
    and noodle stuffing, for chicken, RCP
        135
    origin of, 222
    in soups, 130, RCP 132

Gruyère (*continued*)
    vegetable dishes with, 160, RCP 162,
        164
    weight of, 50
Gudbrandsdalsost, LEX 237, 282
Guérard, Michel, 140
Guerbigny, 65; LEX 237, 274

Hablé Crème Chantilly, 34; LEX 238
Haloumi, 55; LEX 238
ham:
    and cheese quiche, RCP 145
    and Ricotta, manicotti stuffed with,
        RCP 155
Hanan, Hans, 246
Handkäse, 60; LEX 238
hard cheeses, 10, 75–8, 107
Harding, Joseph, 20, 72, 238
Harel, Marie, 9, 28, 61, 238–9
Harracher, 63; LEX 239
Haskell, Patricia (and V. Marquis), *The
    Cheese Book,* 273
Havarti, 9, 72, 73, 111; LEX 239, 259,
    262, 282; *illus. back spread*
Hayons, 29 *n.;* LEX 239
Hazan, Marcella, *Classic Italian Cook
    Book,* 77
Heath, Ambrose, 24, 25, 44
herbs, 8, 56, 85, 87–8, 90
Herkimer Cheddar, 90; LEX 239
Herrgardsost, 50; LEX 221, 239, 282
Herve, 63, 64; LEX 239, 272
Hibben, Sheila, 33 *n.*
Hobelkäse, 78; LEX 239
Hochstrasser, 63; LEX 239
holes in cheese, 15, 47–8, 50, 53
Holland, 29, 66–7, 108
hominy grits with garlic cheese, RCP 164
Hramsa, 88; LEX 195, 240
Huber, Pfister, 264
Hungary, 55, 62, 63, 71
Husker, 26; *see also* Cornhusker
Hutchinson, Geoffrey, 43

ice cream, Camembert, Ruth Lowinsky's,
    RCP 179
Iceland, 29, 45, 50, 71, 257
Île-de-France, 28, 33–4, 88
Illinois, 35, 45, 49, 62, 70, 73
imported cheeses, *see* United States,
    imported cheeses

Incanestrato, 82; LEX 207, 241
Incheville, 29 *n.;* LEX 241
International Wine and Food Society, 181
Iowa, 58
  Swiss Cheese, 49; LEX 221
Iowa State University, 45, 197
Ireland, 29, 108; Irish "Swiss," 50
Isigny, 29 *n.;* LEX 241
Israel, 45, 50
Italy, 3, 5, 68–9, 73, 86, 90, 110
  blue cheeses, 42; *see also* Gorgonzola
  fonduta, 107, 119, 157; LEX 229, 230
  hard and grating cheeses, 75–7, 107; *see also* Grana
  sheep's cheeses, *see* Pecorino
  unripened cheeses, 82

Jack: Cream, LEX 284
  Dry, 25, *illus. 26;* LEX 255; *illus. back spread*
  High-Moisture, 25–6; LEX 255, 284
  Monterey, *see* Monterey Jack
  Teleme, LEX 284
Jacks, David, 25, 255
Jaffry, Chef Jacques, 147
Japan, 29
Jarlsberg, 10, 49–50; LEX 221, 237, 241; *illus. back spread*
  cheese-fish soup, RCP 132
Jefferson, Thomas, 18–19
Jerusalem artichokes fried in cheese batter, RCP 160–1
Johnson, Dr. Samuel, 213, 260
Jossi, John, 73, 242

Kaser, 55; LEX 243
Kashkaval, Kackavalj, Katshkawlj, 55, 68; LEX 204, 242, 243, 263
Kasimir trademark, 63
Kasseri, *illus. front spread,* 55; LEX 243
Kefalotyri, 55; RCP 162–3; LEX 243–4, 279
  Moussaka, RCP 150–1
  pasta with lamb and, RCP 155–6
Kirby, Lydia, 16, 17, 244
Knirim, Dr. Joseph, 31
knives, cheese, 111
Koch, Alois, 57, 58
Kolb, Karl, 201

Kolb family, 35, 206, 259
Königkäse, 69; LEX 244
Kremstaler, 63; LEX 245

labels, 106–7, *illus. 32, 35, 52, 70, 183;* LEX 245
lactic acid, 96, 281
lamb: breast of, cheese, spinach, and rice-stuffed, RCP 137
  and Kefalotyri pasta, RCP 155
Lancashire, 10, 22; LEX 246
  Glamorgan sausages, RCP 146
  making of, 24
Lang, George, *The Cuisine of Hungary,* 202, 228, 248
Larousse Gastronomique, 158
Laruns, 57; LEX 247
lasagne of cheese and seafood, RCP 141
Lawrence, William E., 83
Layton, T. A., 64, 217, 262
  Guide to Cheese and Cheese Cookery, 181, 217
Leavitt, Mrs. Kent, 265
leftovers of cheese, use of, 112, 123, 142, 148
Leicester, *illus. front spread,* 22, 24, *illus. 24;* LEX 247
Leiden, *see* Leyden
"Leigh Toaster," 24
Leland, John, 19
Le Moine, 70; LEX 247
Leutgeb, Ignaz, 247
Leyden, Leiden, *illus. front spread,* 87, *illus. 90;* LEX 244, 245, 247–8, 282
Leyton, Paul, 158
Liederkranz, *illus. front spread,* 10, 60–1, 62, *illus. 64,* 65, 108; LEX 200, 248, 274
  appetizer, RCP 124
  cheese-beer soup, RCP 131
  and ham stuffing, for chicken, RCP 135–6
  leftovers in cooking, 123; RCP 143, 166–7
  making of, 61
  onions stuffed with, RCP 165
  rösti filled with, RCP 166
  serving, 110, 118
Limburger, *illus. front spread,* 10, 60, *illus. 61,* 62–3, *illus. 64,* 65, 118; RCP 166; LEX 200, 248, 261

Limburger (*continued*)
  making of, 62–3
  variants of, 63–5; LEX 195, 239, 250,
    274, 275, 283, 289, 290
Lindy's restaurant, New York, 177
Liptauer, 55–6; LEX 248
Liptó, 55; LEX 248
Lisieux, 29 *n.;* LEX 248
  Petit, 29, 32; LEX 264
Lisl's cheese cookies, RCP 180
Livarot, 29, 32, 33, 60, 63–4; *illus. 64,*
    114; RCP 166; LEX 248, 264
  label, *illus. 32*
  making of, 33, 64; LEX 290
Lockets' restaurant, London, 182
Lockets' savoury, RCP 182
locust bean gum, 84
Lodigiano, 75; LEX 228, 236, 248
Lombardo, grana, LEX 236, 248
Lombardy region, Italy, 42, 68, 75, 82
Long Island oysters baked with cheese,
    RCP 140
Lorraine, 90; LEX 249
Lorraine region, France, 36; *see also*
    Alsace-Lorraine
Loubitelski, 37; LEX 249
Louis XI, King of France, 50
Louis XIV, King of France, 72, 222
Lowinsky, Ruth: Camembert ice cream
    of, RCP 179; *Food for Pleasure,*
    181; *Lovely Food,* 179
Lucullus, 29 *n.;* LEX 249
Lund's Market, Minneapolis, 254

macaroni:
  and cheese, RCP 151–2
  pastitsio, RCP 155–6
  and vegetable casserole, two cheese,
    RCP 154
Mamirolle, 65; LEX 250
manicotti: cheese stuffing for, RCP 152;
    Ricotta and ham stuffing for, RCP
    155
Maredsous, 71; LEX 251
Margotin, 88; LEX 251
Maribo, LEX 251–2, 282
Marmora, LEX 252, 282
Maroilles, Marolles, 60, 64, 105; LEX
    192, 194, 215, 222, 237, 252, 253,
    267, 280
  label, LEX 189
Maromme, 9 *n.;* LEX 252

Marquis, Vivienne (and P. Haskell),
    The Cheese Book, 273
Mascarpone, 82; LEX 228, 252, 278, 291
maturation, 9–10, 13, 15; LEX 252; *see
    also* aging of cheese; curing
meat and cheese dishes, 132–3; *see also*
    beef; chicken; ham; lamb; pork;
    veal
meat loaf, beef-oats-Mozzarella, RCP 133
meatballs, blue cheese, RCP 133–4
medicinal value, of mold-ripened cheeses,
    31, 41
melting propensity, 17, 23, 24, 51–3, 82
Michigan, 77, 90; State University, 221
Middle Ages, 7, 28, 50, 63, 66, 69, 75
Mignon, 65; LEX 253
milk, coagulation of, 7–8, 12; *see also*
    curdling
  kosher products, 244
  temperature, 96
milk-producing animals, 9
Millau, Christian, 167
  Guide Gourmand de la France, 255
Mimolette, *illus. front spread,* 106;
    LEX 253
Miners' Arms, The Priddy, U.K., 158
Minnesota, 36, 45, 59, 74
Minnesota Slim, 74; LEX 253–4
moisture content, 96, 290
mold, blue, growing, 101
mold-ripened cheeses, 13, 30–1, 38–46;
    LEX 263
  medicinal value of, 31, 41
Mon Carré, 29 *n.;* LEX 254
monastery cheeses, 7, 63, 66, 68–73
Moncenisio, 42; LEX 254
Mondseer Schachtelkäse, 65; LEX 254;
    illus. back spread
Monsieur Fromage, 34; LEX 238, 254
Mont d'Or, LEX 254, 273
  Vacherin, 36; LEX 288
Monte-des-cats, 71
Monterey Jack, 25–6 and *illus.;* LEX 198,
    255, 284
  Dry, 25, *illus. 26;* LEX 255; *illus. back
    spread*
  High-Moisture, 25–6; LEX 255, 284
  pasta dishes with, RCP 151, 154
  and spinach quiche, RCP 145
  spread, with garlic, RCP 127
  vegetable dishes with, RCP 161, 163
Montrachet, *illus. front spread, illus. 58,*
    59; LEX 255

Mornay sauce, 160; RCP 170–1; LEX 255
Mossholder, 27; LEX 256
Mossholder family, 27, 256
Moussaka, 142; RCP 150–1
Mozart, Leopold and Wolfgang
     Amadeus, 247
Mozzarella, 68, 82; LEX 256, 261, 268,
     282; *illus. back spread*
   crêpe filling, RCP 143
   croquettes, deep-fried, RCP 126
   crostini, anchovy, RCP 125
   making of, LEX 262, 281
   in meat dishes, RCP 133, 135–6, 137,
     141
   Milanese, RCP 126–7
   pasta dishes with, 151; RCP 152, 154–5
   smoked, 86, 169; LEX 256
   vegetable dishes with, RCP 163
mozzarella di bufalo, 68
Munster, 10, 28, 60, 69–70, 87, 108, 118;
     LEX 249, 250, 256, 257, 270, 276,
     290; *illus. back spread*
   American, 70, 108; LEX 198, 256
   goat's milk, 59
   in meat loaf, RCP 133
   oysters baked with, RCP 140
   Chaumont, 70; LEX 211
   Géromé, 70 and *illus.;* LEX 233, 249
   labeling, 70 and *illus.;* LEX 256
   rösti filled with, RCP 166–7
munster fermier, 70
Murol, 63; LEX 257
mushroom-cheese sauce, RCP 172
mushrooms, broiled cheese-stuffed, RCP
     164–5
mussels and spinach gratin, RCP 139
Mussolini, Benito, 241
Mycella, 45; LEX 257
Mysinger, LEX 257
Mysost, 10; LEX 229, 257, 291

Napoleon Bonaparte, Emperor, 9
Napoleon III, Emperor, 239
natural cheese, 9, 15, 106
Nauvoo, 45; LEX 197, 258
Neufchâtel, 10, 29 *n.*, 81, 82–3; LEX 215,
     218, 223, 250, 252, 258, 283, 289
New York State, 62, 83, 90
   Cheddar, 20, *illus.* 27, 90; LEX 212,
     258
   Liederkranz, 60–1
   washed-curd process, 26–7

New Yorker, The, 33 *n.*, 140, 238
New Zealand, 20, 29
Nielsen, Hanne, 9, 72, 258
Nökkelost, 87; LEX 258, 282
noodles, Italian, with four cheeses, RCP
     152
Normandy, 4, 9, 11–13, 28–33, 34, 61,
     81–2, 88, 117
Norton, Lewis M. 264
Norway, 29, 49, 59, 62, 72, 87
Notre-Dame, 29 *n.;* LEX 260
nuts, as flavoring, 8, 89–90

Ohio, 30, 35, 49, 61, 108, 118
Oka, 70, 118; RCP 168–9; LEX 259, 286
okra, tomatoes, corn, and cheese, baked,
     RCP 166
Old Heidelberg, 62, 118; LEX 259, 278
Oldmeadow, Ernest, 205
omelets, 142; RCP 143–4
onion(s), 8
   and potato scallop, with Caerphilly,
     RCP 165
   stuffed, with Liederkranz, RCP 165
Orton, Vrest, 88
Ostiepky, Ostypka, 86; LEX 260
oyster plant (salsify), in cheese sauce,
     RCP 165–6
oysters baked with cheese, RCP 140

Padano, Grana, 75; LEX 236; *illus. back
     spread*
Paillor, 63; LEX 261
Palets Prinsky au Roquefort, 39
pancake gâteau, Cottage Cheese, RCP
     178
pancakes (*see also* rösti):
   cheese, RCP 144
   Somerset apple-cheese, RCP 180
Paprikas Weiss, New York City, 86, 260,
     261
Parenyica, 86; LEX 261–2
Parmesan, 3, 10, 55, 75–6 and *illus.*, 77,
     78 and *illus.*, 107, 135, 169; LEX
     236, 262, 271; *illus. back
     spread*
   buying tips, 107
   cheese sticks, RCP 128
   green rice with, RCP 153–4
   labeling, 75, 107; LEX 236, 262
   Moussaka, RCP 150–1

Parmesan (*continued*)
  Padano, 75; LEX 236; *illus. back
    spread*
  pasta dishes with, 151; RCP 152–5
  serving, 111, 114
  stravecchio, 76; LEX 281
  stravecchione, 76; LEX 281
  vegetable dishes with, 160; RCP 161,
    162–5, 168
  weight of wheel, 262
Parmigiano-Reggiano, 75, 77, 107; LEX
    236, 262
Parrish, Wallace, 49
pasta, 142, 151
  four-cheese Italian noodles, RCP 152–3
  with lamb and Kefalotyri, RCP 155–6
  macaroni and cheese, RCP 151–2
  sauces, RCP 172–3
  stuffings, 142, 143; RCP 152, 155
  two-cheese macaroni vegetable
    casserole, RCP 154
pasta filata method, 82; LEX 262, 281
pasteurization, 4, 11, 30, 35, 41, 70, 106
pastitsio, RCP 155–6
pastries, 123
  dough for, Cream Cheese, 128; RCP
    176–7
  fillings, RCP 128–9
Pâte Feuilletée au Roquefort, 128; RCP
    146–8
Paul, Gerard, 236
Pavé d'Auge, 32, 33; LEX 263
Pavé de Moyaux, 29 *n.*, 32; LEX 263
Paynel, Marie, 239
Pearce, Donn, 159
Pecorino, 5; LEX 263
  caciotta di, 77; LEX 205
  Romano, 56, 77, 151; LEX 216, 263,
    274, 282; *illus. back spread*
  Toscano, 56, 107; LEX 263
  Valdorciano, LEX 263
Pellegrini, Angelo, 144
penicillium fungus, 31; LEX 195, 263
Penicillium camemberti, 13, 45, 263
Penicillium glaucum, 38, 234, 237, 263,
    264
Penicillium roqueforti, 38, 39, 45, 101,
    197, 237, 263
Penicillium notatum, 263
Pennsylvania, 49, 59, 263
Pepato, 90 and *illus.*; LEX 263
Pepys, Samuel, 76
Périgord region, France, 41, 88

persillés, 57; LEX 195, 263–4
Persillés des Aravis, 41; LEX 264
pesto, RCP 172–3; LEX 264
Petaluma Brie, 35; *see also* Rouge et
    Noir
Petit Lisieux, 29, 32; LEX 264
Petit-Suisse, 82; LEX 264
Peynir, 54; LEX 264
Philadelphia Cream Cheese, 83, 111
Picard, Jean, 52
pickled cheeses, 54, 55; LEX 264
Picodon, 57; LEX 264
Piedmont region, Italy, 75, 107, 119, 157
pies, 51
  fruit, pastry dough for, RCP 177
  Greek cheese-spinach, RCP 156
Pinot, Mme. Marcel, 29, 32
Pinzgauer Bergkäse, LEX 265, 282
Pipo Crem', *illus. front spread*, 41; LEX
    196, 265
Pipo Nain, 41
plant enzymes, 8, 272
plastic-curd method, 82; LEX 230, 262
Pliny the Elder, 274–5
Plymouth, 26, 87; LEX 265, 289
poil de chat, 13
Poivre d'Âne, 57; LEX 265
Pont l'Évêque, 29, 32, 63, 64, 108; LEX
    261, 263, 265, 289, 290; *illus.
    back spread*
popcorn cheese, 80; LEX 266
popovers, cheese, RCP 175
pork sausage–cheese strata, RCP 134
Port (du) Salut, 10, 71 and *illus.*, 72,
    74, 108, 118; RCP 166; LEX 266,
    269, 276, 277, 279, 286; *illus.
    back spread*
  Danish, *see* Esrom
  trademark, 71
Pot Cheese, 10, 80; LEX 266
potatoes: croquettes, 167
  and onion scallop, with Caerphilly,
    RCP 165
  puréed with cheese, RCP 167
  rösti, cheese-filled, RCP 166–7
preservation of cheese, 112, 114; *see also*
    storage of cheese
  by pickling, 54; *see also* pickled
    cheeses
  by smoking, 85; *see also* smoked
    cheeses
preservatives, 15, 84
press, cheese, 100–1

process cheese, 9, 74, 112; LEX 213, 266–7
Promised Land, 50
proprionic acid-former, 14
Provatura, 68; LEX 262, 267
Providence, 29 *n.*; LEX 267
Provola, 68; RCP 126; LEX 267
Provolone, *illus. front spread,* 68, *illus.* 69, 82; RCP 153; LEX 267, 282; *illus. back spread*
affumicato, 86
dolce vs. *piccante,* 68
making of, 68; LEX 262, 281
puffs, cheese, RCP 127
fillings, RCP 128–9
pastry for (Feuilletée), 128; RCP 146–8
Pure Milk Association, 234
Pyramide, *illus. front spread, illus. 59*

Quart, 65; LEX 267
Queso de Cabrales, 57; LEX 204
queso del pais, 25; LEX 255
quiches, 123, 145
Cheddar, onion and bacon, RCP 146
cheese and ham, RCP 145
pastry dough for, RCP 177
Roquefort filling, RCP 145
spinach and Feta, RCP 145
tomato and Swiss, RCP 145–6
Quittebeuf, 29 *n.*; LEX 270

Rabelais, François, 41
Raclette, *illus. front spread,* 52 and *illus.*, 119; LEX 270
raclette (dish), 37, 51–2; LEX 189, 216, 230, 241, 270
making, *illus. 53,* 119–20
Ragnit, 72; LEX 270
Ragusano, 151; LEX 270
ravioli stuffing, RCP 152
Rawhouser, Clayton, 59
Reblochon, 72 and *illus.*, 117, 118; LEX 210, 271
label, LEX 189, 193, 245, 283
Recuite, 82; LEX 271, 291
"Red Cheese," 24
Reeslev, Jan, 87
Reggiano, LEX 236, 271
Reinbold, Dr. George, 45, 53

Remoudou, 95; LEX 216, 239, 272
rennet, 7, 8, 12, 14, 16, 79, 96, 97, 102; LEX 272
rennin, 96, 272
restaurants: Caesar's, Tijuana, 169; Chanteclair, New York, 147; Cheddar Roast, London, 181, 217; Dorrius, Amsterdam, 137; Durand, Paris, 255; Lindy's, New York, 177; Lockets, London, 182; Miners' Arms, Priddy, U.K., 158
Reynière, Grimod de la, 41
ribbon cheese, *illus.*, 86 and *illus.*
rice, 77, 151
Arroz verde con chilies rellenos, RCP 154
green, with Parmesan, RCP 153–4
tian of zucchini and, with cheese, RCP 168–9
Richard, Jean, 216
Ricotta, 10, 82; LEX 272, 291; *illus. back spread*
crêpe fillings, RCP 142–3
pasta dishes with, 151; RCP 152, 155
in vegetable dishes, RCP 162, 167
varieties, 82; LEX 210, 268, 271, 273
Riksost, 87; LEX 273
rind-cured cheese, 49, 118
rindless loaf method, LEX 273
ripening, 4, 10, 96; LEX 252; *see also* aging of cheese; curing
risottos, 77; *see also* rice
roast beef, Tyrolean, with cheese, RCP 134–5
roast chicken stuffed with Gruyère and noodles, RCP 135
robiola, Robiola, 68; LEX 241, 273
robiolina, Robbiolini, 68; LEX 241
Roden, Claudia, *A Book of Middle Eastern Food,* 55, 232
Rohde, Oscar, 258
Rollot, 65; LEX 215, 237, 274
Romadur, 60, 63; LEX 239, 272, 274
Romano, 10, *illus. 76, 77, 107;* LEX 274
Caprino, 77; LEX 208, 274
pasta dishes with, 151; RCP 152
Pecorino, 56, 77, 151; LEX 216, 263, 274, 282; *illus. back spread*
Vacchino, 77; LEX 274
vegetable dishes with, RCP 160
Romans, ancient, 8, 85

Rondelé, 88; Lex 274; *illus. back spread*
Root, Waverley, *The Food of Italy*, 77
Roquefort, *illus. front spread*, 10, 17, 38–41 and *illus.*, 39, 45, 54, 57, 169; Lex 195, 196, 197, 263, 274–5
  beets, Rcp 161
  comparisons with Gorgonzola and Stilton, 43, 107; Lex 234, 281
  Feuilletée au, Rcp 146–8
  label, 40; Lex 189, 245, 275, 282
  making of, 39–40; Lex 229
  mold, how to grow, 101
  quiche filling, Rcp 145
  serving, 111, 115, 117, 118
Roquefort Society, 245, 275, 282
Roquefort-sur-Soulzon, France, 5, 38–40, 275
rösti potatoes, cheese-filled, Rcp 166–7
Rouge et Noir, 35; Lex 200, 201
Roussel, Antoine, 196, 275
Rouzaire, Robert, 33
Russia, 37, 55

Saanen, 78; Lex 239, 271, 275–6
sage cheeses, 87–8, *illus.* 90, 110; Lex 237, 276
Saingorlon, 41; Lex 196, 276
St. André, Lex 276; *illus. back spread*
St. Galler Alpkäse, 50; Lex 276
St. Nectaire, 63, 72, 110; Lex 257, 276; *illus. back spread*
  label, Lex 189, 245
St. Paulin, 71, 72; Lex 193, 198, 211, 266, 267, 269, 275, 276, 282, 286; *illus. back spread*
Ste. Maure, 118; Lex 277
salads, 169
salsify in cheese sauce, Rcp 165–6
salting, 13, 15, 40, 85
Samsoe, 49; Lex 221, 225, 254, 277, 282, 283
Sapsago, 10, *illus. 51,* 88, *illus. 89;* Lex 237, 240, 245, 277; *illus. back spread*
  cocktail spread, Rcp 128
  and Swiss, pastry filling, Rcp 128–9
Sardinia, 8, 56
sauces, 170
  bacon-cheese spaghetti, Rcp 172

sauces (*continued*)
  Blue-Cheese, for fish, Rcp 172
  Camembert, Rcp 171
  Cheddar, 165–6; Rcp 170
  Cream Cheese-chili steak sauce, Rcp 173
  Mornay, 160; Rcp 170–1; Lex 255
  mushroom-cheese, Rcp 172
  pesto, Rcp 172–3; Lex 264
  white cheese, Rcp 171
sausages: Glamorgan, Rcp 146; Lex 233
  pork, strata of cheese and, Rcp 134
savouries, Rcp 181–2
Savoy Hotel, London, 181
Savoy region, France, 41, 50, 116
Sbrinz, 78; Lex 239, 278, 280, 282
scalloped potatoes and onion with Caerphilly, Rcp 165
Scamorze, 82; Lex 262, 267, 278, 281
Scandinavian fish-cheese soup, Rcp 132
Schabzieger, 88; Lex 277, 278
Schachtelkäse, Mondseer, 65; Lex 254
Schlosskäse, 60–2, 118; Lex 254, 278
Schmierkäse, 80; Lex 278
Schönland, 69; Lex 278
School of Country Living, Idaho, 95
Schoonwater, Hubert, 105, 106
Schottenziger, 82; Lex 278, 291
Schützenkäse, 63; Lex 279
Schwarzenberger, 63, Lex 279
Scotch Rabbit, 158
Scotland, 23, 80
Scott, Sir Walter, 243
seafood, *see also* fish; mussels, oysters; shrimp
  lasagne, Rcp 141
seasonings, 8, 11, 56, 85–91
Seaver, Jeannette, Boursinoise of, Rcp 124
seeds, as flavoring, 87, 89
semihard cheeses, 66–8, 118
semisoft cheeses, 10, 108
Serac, 82; Lex 279
serving of cheese, 110–12
sheep, sheep's milk, 9, 54
sheep cheeses, 54–7, 77; *see also* Pecorino
  blues, 40–1, 54
shops, cheese specialty, 65, 103–6; Chez Androuët, Paris, 106, 189; Hubert Schoonwater, Paris, 105, 106; Lund's Market, Minneapolis, 254;

shops, cheese specialty (*continued*)
 Paprikas Weiss, New York City,
  86, 260, 261; Standings, Harrowgate, England, 44 *n.*; Wells
  Stores, Streatley, England, 44 *n.*
shrimp: and crabmeat, lasagne, RCP
  141
 Greek, with Feta, RCP 138
 and green beans, RCP 140–1
 Simon, André, 44
Sirene, 55; LEX 279
skim milk, use of, 67, 73–4, 76, 80; LEX
  191, 192, 194, 210, 211, 227, 228,
  232, 233, 250, 266, 270, 271, 272,
  276, 277
Slipcote, 81; LEX 279
smoked cheeses, 8, 68, 85–7, 271, 280
soft cheeses, 10, 11–13, 28–37
soft-ripened cheeses, 11, 28–37, 118
 butterfat content, 34
 buying tips, 103–4, 108–9
 curing, 13, 30–1, 32, 33, 34, 36–7
 making, 11–13, 30, 32, 33, 34
Sokolov, Raymond, 58 *n.*
Somerset apple-cheese pancakes, RCP
  180
Sopexa (French government agency),
  105
Sorbais, 65; LEX 280
soufflé, 148
 basic, RCP 148–9
 roll, RCP 149–50
soups, 51
 basic cheese soup, RCP 130
 Emmenthaler, RCP 130–1
 Liederkranz-beer, RCP 131
 Scandinavian fish-cheese, RCP 132
 Swiss vegetable-cheese, RCP 132
spaghetti sauce, bacon-cheese, RCP 172
Spain, 56–7
Spalen, 10, 78; LEX 280
Spanakopitta, RCP 156
Spécialité de la Vallée d'Auge (label),
  29
Speed, John, 17
spices, 8, 56, 85, 87, 90
spinach: and cheese pie, Greek, RCP
  156
 and Feta quiche, RCP 145
 soufflé roll, RCP 149–50
spoon-eaten cheeses, 36–7
Sports Illustrated, 147

spreads, cheese, 123
 Liptauer, 55–6; LEX 248
 Monterey Jack, with garlic
  (Ajoqueso), RCP 127
 Sapsago, RCP 128
spun-curd method, LEX 230, 262, 267,
  281
Squire, Sir John, 43
stabilizers, stabilization, 15, 31–2, 106
starter, lactic, 11, 79, 96, 102, 281
Steiermark, 116; LEX 281
Steinwand, Ambrose and J. H., 26
Steinwand family, 216
Stevens, Henry, 24, 247
Stevenson, Robert Louis, 243
Stilton, *illus. front spread,* 9, 38,
  illus. 41, 42–3, 44, 46, 57, 89; LEX
  257, 281, 290
 comparisons with Roquefort and Gorgonzola, 43, 107; LEX 234, 281
 making of, 43
 serving, 110, 111, *illus. 113,* 117, 176
stirred-curd method, 26; LEX 216, 236,
  265
Stockli, Chef Albert, 169
Stone, Susannah and Reg, 80, 88, 204
Stone Age, 7
Stoppani, Antonio, 68–9, 193
storage of cheese, 4, 31–2, 106, 112;
  see also preservation of cheese
store cheese, *illus. 27;* LEX 281
stravecchio, grana, 76; LEX 281
stravecchione, grana, 76; LEX 281
Streptococcus cremoris, 96, 281
Streptococcus lactis, 96, 281
Stresa Convention, 189, 236, 245, 257,
  281–2
stuffings, 123, 135–6; *see also* fillings
 cheese, spinach, and rice, for breast of
  veal or lamb, RCP 137
 Gruyère and noodle, for chicken,
  RCP 135
 Liederkranz and ham, for chicken,
  RCP 135–6
 for pasta, 142, 143; RCP 152, 155
 Swiss and vegetable, for roast beef
  roll, RCP 134
Sumerian frieze, 7, *illus. 8–9*
Suprême, 35; LEX 282
surface-ripened cheese, 10, 30–3, 62–3
Sweden, 29, 34, 50, 73, 87
 Blue Cheese, 45; LEX 237

Swiss Cheese, 10, 13–15, 27, 47–53;
      Lex 282–3
   Austrian "Swiss," 14; Lex 196
   buying tips, 53, 107
   holes in, 15, 47–8, 50, 53
   imitations, 49–50, 107; Lex 221, 277,
      282–3
   "imported," 49, 107; Lex 282
   Mägerer, Lex 249–50
   rindless loaf, Lex 273
   and Sapsago, pastry filling, Rcp
      128–9
   soufflés, Rcp 148–50
   in stuffings, Rcp 134–5, 137
   and tomato quiche, Rcp 145–6
   true Switzerland, 13–15, 47, 53, 107;
      Lex 282; see also Emmenthaler;
      Gruyère
   vegetable dishes with, Rcp 162, 164
Swiss Cheese Union, 13
Swiss Dessert, 37; Lex 283
"Swiss harp," illus. 13, 14
Swiss vegetable-cheese soup, Rcp 132
Swissair, "Wine and Cheese Discovery
      Tours," 116
Swissconsin, 14
Switzerland, 13–15, 47–8, 50–3, 60, 63,
      95, 110, 115–16
   fondue, 37, 51, 119, 156–7
   hard cheeses of, 77–8
   herbed cheese, 88
   monastery cheeses, 72–3
   soft-ripened cheeses, 29, 36–7
   steaks without meat, 51, 53

taleggino, 68
Taleggio, 68, 69, 110, 116; Lex 283;
      illus. back spread
Talleyrand-Perigord, Charles Maurice
      de, 216–17
Tamié, 71; Lex 283
Tartare, 88; Lex 284
tarts, 51
   fruit, pastry dough for, Rcp 177
   Ramekins, Lex 270
Teleme, Lex 264, 284; Teleme Jack,
      Lex 284
Tête de Moine, 73; Lex 284
Tholstrup, Henrik, 37, 219, 284
Thompson, Pierce, 35
Thompson family, 201

Tillamook, 111; Lex 285
Tilsit, 72–3; Lex 285; illus. back
      spread
   adaptations, 72, 77; Lex 233–4, 283,
      285, 291
   Swiss, illus. 51, 72; Lex 234, 285
Toggenburger, 58; Lex 285
Toklas, Alice B., 130, 215
tomatoes: sliced, gratin of, Rcp 167–8
   and Swiss, quiche of, Rcp 145–6
Tomme Vaudoise, 37; Lex 286
Touareg, 54; Lex 286
Trappist monks, 70–1
Trappiste, 29 n., 70–1; Lex 210, 286
triple creams (triple crèmes), 10, 34–5,
      108; Lex 287
Tulum, 54; Lex 287
Tuma, 82
turbot fillet, broiled with cheese, Rcp
      137–8
Turkey, 54, 55
Tybo, Lex 282, 287
Tyrolean roast beef with cheese, Rcp
      134–5
tyrophile, 7, 287

Uni-Bresse, 41
United Kingdom, 88, 117, 176; see also
      England
   grading of cheese, 20, 228
   Milk Marketing Board, 20, 23, 228,
      234
United States, 3, 4, 56, 106
   domestic cheeses, 27; Lex 188
      Bel Paese, 68; Lex 193
      blues, Lex 197
      Brie, 29–30, 35–6, 108; Lex 201
      Camembert, 29–30, 35–6, 108; Lex
         206, 208
      Cheddar-type, 16, 20–1, 25–7, 86, 88,
         90, 111; Lex 198, 212, 217, 292
      goat cheeses, 58–9
      Limburger, 62; Lex 248
      Munster, 59, 70, 108; Lex 198, 256
      Old Heidelberg, 62, 118; Lex 259
      Swiss, 49, 107; Lex 282–3
      see also Brick; Colby; Liederkranz;
         Monterey Jack
   Feta, 55
   fresh cheeses, 80, 82–4
   grading of cheese, 20–1

United States (*continued*)
imported cheeses:
Bel Paise, 68; Lex 193
Brie and Camembert, 30, 31; Lex 207
Cheddar, 212
import statistics, 110
'imported" Swiss, 49, 107; Lex 282
Kasseri, 55
per capita consumption of cheese, 110
Tilsit varieties in, 72–3
U.S. Department of Agriculture, 20–1, 85, 87, 197, 212
Cheese Varieties published by, 225
University of: Minnesota, 52, 74, 197, 253–4; Nebraska, 26, 217; Wisconsin, 197
unripened cheese, 10, 11, 79–84

Vacchino Romano, 77; Lex 274
Vacherin, 36–7, 105; Lex 288
d'Abondance, Lex 187, 288
des Bauges, Lex 192–3, 288
in fondue, 37
Fribourg, 37; Lex 288
Mont d'Or, 36; Lex 288
Valencay, *illus. 113*; Lex 288
Valéry, Paul, 68
V.C.N. (label), 29
veal, breast of, cheese, spinach, and rice-stuffed, Rcp 137
vegetable-cheese soup, Swiss, Rcp 132
vegetables, 159–60, 170
artichokes, Romano- and anchovy-stuffed, Rcp 160
beans, refried, with cheese, Rcp 161
beets, cheese-flavored, Rcp 161–2
cauliflower, tomato, and cheese casserole, Rcp 162
corn, baked, with chilies and cheese, Rcp 163
Cypriot eggplant and tomatoes baked with cheese, Rcp 162–3
endives baked with two cheeses, Rcp 164
fennel, braised, with two cheeses, Rcp 163–4
Jerusalem artichokes fried in cheese batter, Rcp 160–1
and macaroni casserole, two-cheese, Rcp 154

vegetables (*continued*)
mushrooms, broiled, cheese-stuffed, Rcp 164–5
okra, tomatoes, corn, and cheese, baked, Rcp 166
onion-potato scallop with Caerphilly, Rcp 165
onions stuffed with Liederkranz, Rcp 165
salsify in cheese sauce, Rcp 165–6
tian of zucchini, rice, and cheese, Rcp 168–9
tomatoes, sliced, gratin of, Rcp 167–8
zucchini, cheese- and mushroom-stuffed, Rcp 168
Velabrum (Roman market), 8, 85, 86
Vermont, 26, 59
Cheddar, 20, 21, *illus. 27,* 86, 88, 110; Lex 212, 289
Sage, 87–8, *illus. 90,* 110
Vieux Puant, 64
Ville-St.-Jacques, 34; Lex 289
Villedieu, 29 *n.*; Lex 289
Void, 65; Lex 289
Voiron, Chef Joseph, 255

Walliser, 52; Lex 194, 290
washed-curd process, 26–7; Lex 290
washed rind, Lex 290
Washington State University, 218
water buffalo, 68, 82
Wechsberg, Joseph, 106
Wegmuller (cheesemaker), 234, 285
Weiss, Edward, 86
Weisslacker, 63; Lex 290
Welsh Rabbit, 24, 181; Rcp 158; Lex 246, 290
Wensleydale, 24–5, *illus. 24;* Lex 290
blue-veined, 25, 44; Lex 197, 290
dip, 25; Rcp 125
white, 24; Lex 290
whey: cheese products from, 82, 170; Lex 278, 290–1
draining, 7, 11, 12, 14, 67, 96, 98, 100–1, 272
white cheese sauce, Rcp 171
Wilke, Bill, 235
Windsor Red Vein, 89; Lex 291
wine: as cheese flavoring, 8, 11, 89; Rcp 129
and cheese, tips on combinations, 115–20

wine (*continued*)
  in fondue, 118–19
  use in curing of cheese, 36, 50, 105
Wisconsin, 35, 45, 49, 58, 62, 70, 77, 88,
    90, 107
  Brick Cheese, 73
  Cheddar, 20, 26, 27; *illus. back
    spread*
Wood, Dave, 62

Yankee Cheddar Cheese Pie, 145
yeast, in cheese-making, 10, 38, 63
yogurt, as starter, 96, 281

York, 81; Lex 206, 279, 292
Yugoslavia, 71, 116

Zakoussotchnyï, 37; Lex 292
Zanthe, 55
Ziegelkäse, 73; Lex 223, 292
Ziegenkäse, 57; Lex 292
Ziger, 82; Lex 278; *see also* Schot-
    tenziger
zucchini: cheese- and mushroom-
    stuffed, Rcp 168
  tian of, with rice and cheese,
    Rcp 168–9

A Note About the Author

Evan Jones was born and educated in Minnesota. His books and articles—in *Gourmet, Travel and Leisure, Americana, The Reader's Digest, The New York Times,* et cetera—reflect an interest both in the American past and in food. His most recent book, *American Food: The Gastronomic Story,* was published in 1975. Mr. Jones, who lives in New York City, has traveled widely in search of the cheeses of the world.

A Note on the Type

The text of this book was set in Intertype Garamond, a modern rendering of the type first cut by Claude Garamond (1510–1561). Garamond was a pupil of Geoffroy Tory and is believed to have based his letters on the Venetian models, although he introduced a number of important differences, and it is to him we owe the letter which we know as old-style.

The book was designed by Earl Tidwell.

Sapsago

Esrom

Fontina
Val d'Aosta

Boursin
au poivre

Pecorino Romano

Cantal

boursin

Pecorino
Romano

Boursin
aux herbes

(grated)

Provolone

Parmesan Grana Padano

caraway seeds

Parmesan

Époisses

St. André

Munster

Pont l'Évêque

St. Nectaire

Rondelé

Fresh Ricotta

Some cheeses courtesy of:
Foods From France; Mary Lyons;
Mr. Fermo Jaekle, Otto Roth Company;

Cheddar

Feta

Firm Ricotta

Taleggio

Bel Paese

Jarlsberg

Dry
Monterey Jack

Anfrom

Tilsit

Havarti

St. Paulin

Jarlsberg

Port Salut

Wisconsin Cheddar

Gräddost

Explorateur

Crema
Dania

Mondseer

Coulommiers

Brie

Mozzarella

Boursault

Chiberta

Switzerland Cheese Association;
Jarlsberg Cheese, Imported by Gerber
International Foods, Inc.;

Denmark Cheese Association,
570 Taxter Road, Elmsford,
New York 10523;

Holland Cheese Association;
Wisconsin Cheese, Pauly Cheese Company
(Division of Swift & Company).